AN INTRODUCTION TO
HISTORICAL LINGUISTICS

AN INTRODUCTION TO HISTORICAL LINGUISTICS

Terry Crowley

Auckland
OXFORD UNIVERSITY PRESS
Oxford · Melbourne · New York

OXFORD UNIVERSITY PRESS NEW ZEALAND

Oxford New York
Athens Auckland Bangkok Bogotá
Buenos Aires Calcutta Cape Town Chennai
Dar es Salaam Delhi Florence Hong Kong
Istanbul Karachi Kuala Lumpur Madrid
Melbourne Mexico City Mumbai Nairobi
Paris Port Moresby São Paulo Singapore
Taipei Tokyo Toronto Warsaw

and associated companies in
Berlin Ibadan

OXFORD is a trade mark of Oxford University Press

First published 1992
Reprinted 1993, 1994
First published 1997
© Terry Crowley 1992, 1997
© Oxford University Press 1992, 1997
Third edition published 1997
Reprinted 1998

ISBN 0 19 558378 7

Typeset in Times by Egan-Reid Ltd, Auckland
Printed through Bookpac Production Services
Published by Oxford University Press
540 Great South Road, Greenlane,
PO Box 11–149, Auckland, New Zealand

CONTENTS

6

PREFACE

Having taught various linguistics courses at the University of Papua New Guinea (UPNG), and since then at the University of the South Pacific (USP), it has become apparent to me that the English used by writers of nearly all standard textbooks in linguistics was far too difficult for English-as-a-second-language speakers. This seemed to be especially true in books dealing with historical linguistics. Also, foreign words and phrases typically abound in textbooks on comparative linguistics, and beginning students are arrogantly assumed to know what is meant by *Umlaut, Lautverschiebung, spiritus aspirate, un système où tout se tient, sandhi*, and so on. Another problem with standard textbooks for South Pacific students was that the examples chosen to illustrate points and arguments often involved languages that students had never heard of, or had no familiarity with — usually ancient European languages, and sometimes modern North American Indian languages.

Those of us teaching linguistics at UPNG — mainly John Lynch and myself at the time — decided to remedy these faults for our students by producing our own series of textbooks. John produced a series of notes on linguistic analysis, and my contribution was a set of notes on historical linguistics. In these notes we tried to simplify the language and to explain linguistic concepts in a straightforward manner, yet without simplifying the concepts themselves. We also tried to draw examples as far as possible from languages of this part of the world (rather than from the northern hemisphere), as well as from English (this being the language of education with which all tertiary students in the Pacific were familiar).

Contrary to my intentions and expectations, the original UPNG printed notes *Introduction to Historical Linguistics* ended up being used also by students taking comparative linguistics at the Australian National University in Canberra and the University of Auckland in New Zealand. This meant that a set of materials that would have lasted 20 years at UPNG (with our class sizes at the time) was rapidly sold out. This gave me a welcome opportunity to revise the 1981 edition, and a substantially revised second edition appeared under the same title in 1983, in same UPNG printery format as the first. Again I was pleasantly surprised to find that our stocks were rapidly exhausted, so it was decided to produce a third edition, this time in publisher-produced format.

UPNG Press and the Institute of Pacific Studies (at USP) agreed to publish the volume jointly, and I provided a text based largely on the 1983 version, but with some revisions necessitated by the broader audience. This third edition of *An Introduction to Historical Linguistics* appeared in 1987. I would not recommend that anybody try to publish a book in the way that volume was produced, with one publisher in Port Moresby (Papua New Guinea), the

9

other in Suva (Fiji), the typesetter in Auckland (New Zealand), the printer in Suva, and the author by then in Vila (Vanuatu). While the volume received very favourable comment, the results of the geographical dispersal of those involved in the production process are clear to anybody who has used it, as phonetic symbols ended up being cobbled together — some satisfactorily, and some less so. Worse, a considerable number of typesetting errors went uncorrected, or were even compounded before printing. Many people found that it was difficult to get hold of the volume, as the publishers were not well known among mainstream distributors of academic texts in Europe or North America (even in Australia and New Zealand copies were difficult to obtain). Despite these problems, however, the supply from this print-run was also exhausted within a couple of years.

Clearly, in producing this text I had stumbled across a need that was waiting to be met, so I decided to prepare what is effectively a fourth edition of this volume. I have taken the opportunity to correct all typographical, factual, and stylistic errors in the previous edition that have come to my attention. I have also taken into account the experience of my peers who have used the previous edition in substantially revising the text itself. I have broadened the content, added a number of sections, and reorganised the presentation of other sections. However, I have consciously decided to maintain the Pacific bias in exemplification. In doing this, I hope that linguists who are schooled in the Western tradition of the English Great Vowel Shift (which I do not mention) and Grimm's Law (which I mention only in passing) are not disappointed. Rather, I hope that this volume makes it possible to show students that the comparative method has universal applicability.

Of course, this is not to say that the model of language change that is assumed by the comparative method described in this volume is universally accepted by modern linguists. There is a substantial — and growing — coterie of scholars who find many inherent weaknesses in this model. My own work on Pacific pidgins and creoles has left me with many similar doubts. These doubts notwithstanding, I feel that it is probably easiest to show students how languages change by first teaching them the traditional comparative method, just as it is easier to teach classical phonemics than it is to launch straight into underlying phonological representations and morphophonemic rules. Those who are more adventurous or more sceptical can build on the basis provided in this volume to show students how *they* think languages *really* change.

T.C.

Hamilton, New Zealand
October 1991

PREFACE TO THIRD EDITION

The continued use of this book indicates that it is continuing to meet a need, which is gratifying. It has also provided an opportunity to revise the text for a new edition. The order of the material in this edition is identical to that of its predecessor. The main differences between the second and third editions are as follows:

1. Some new material has been added within existing chapters. There are now new subheadings for grammaticalisation and esoterogeny and exoterogeny. There is also new material within existing sections relating to palaeolinguistics, ergative to accusative change, polysynthesis, lexical specialisation, lexicostatistics and glottochronology, and word order change.
2. Discussion on a variety of other points has been expanded or been made more explicit for greater clarity, to take into account more recent developments in the field, or to eliminate confusing or misleading information. Some errors have also been corrected.
3. Additional readings have been added where it is felt that these are appropriate for undergraduate students of historical linguistics.
4. Questions in the exercises have been refined and made more explicit, where appropriate.
5. The index has been made more detailed and more helpful to students seeking information on particular topics.

T.C.

Hamilton, New Zealand
October 1996

ACKNOWLEDGEMENTS

The present form of this volume owes much to a lot of people. First and foremost, I would like to thank my own students of historical linguistics at the University of Papua New Guinea while I was lecturing there between 1979 and 1983. It was largely with their help that I was able to locate areas of inadequacy in exemplification and explanation in earlier versions of this work. In particular, I would like to thank Kalesita Tupou and Sam Uhrle for checking and correcting the Tongan and Samoan data in Chapter 5

Other people have provided a great deal of input. Bill Foley, now at the University of Sydney, helped more than he originally intended in 1979 by providing me with copies of his own comparative linguistics lecture notes and problems, and some of his material has found its way into this book. John Lynch of the University of Papua New Guinea has read and commented on various versions of this work and made specific comments to improve examples and explanations. I would like to thank colleagues in a number of institutions who have used previous editions of this volume as a text in their undergraduate teaching of historical linguistics and others who have made specific suggestions for improvement, in particular Peter Mühlhäusler, Jeff Siegel, Mathew Spriggs, Ray Harlow, Liz Pearce, Lyle Campbell and Julie Auger. I would also like to thank the reviewers of the previous edition of this book, Scott Allan (*Te Reo* 32 (1989): 95–9), Brian Joseph (*Language* 66/3 (1990): 633–4) and Robert Blust (*Oceanic Linguistics* 35/2, (1996): 328–35). Despite the various problems associated with the earliest edition, they provided words of both encouragement and constructive criticism. Thanks are also due to Vagi Bouauka of the University of Papua New Guinea and Frank Bailey of the University of Waikato for assistance in the preparation of maps and diagrams.

Finally, I must also make a formal acknowledgement to Jean Aitchison of the London School of Economics. Her published texts *The Articulate Mammal*, *Teach Yourself Linguistics*, and *Language Change: Progress or Decay?* are, to me, a model of clear and simple expression, and of ideological soundness. She shows it can be done — I just hope I have achieved it.

HOW TO USE THIS BOOK

I would like to think that this book will prove useful to teachers of historical linguistics at all undergraduate levels. I have written it on the assumption that students have already completed at least one basic course in descriptive linguistics, so I have not bothered to define terms such as *phoneme*, *morpheme*, or *suffix*. Some familiarity is also assumed with a distinctive feature analysis of phonology. More specialist linguistic terminology, such as *ergative* or *exclusive pronoun*, however, is introduced at its first appearance in the text in italics and is always explained (and generally also exemplified) for the benefit of students. The linguistic terminology in this volume is used in the same way as in Crowley, Lynch, Siegel and Piau, *The Design of Language: An Introduction to Descriptive Linguistics*. The bold page numbers in the index indicate where definitions are located.

I have attempted to cover the kinds of topics in historical linguistics that are dealt with in most courses on this subject, as well as enough areas of side interest so that lecturers will be able to follow some of the more specialist aspects of this subdiscipline as well. However, it should be kept in mind that *An Introduction to Historical Linguistics* is just that — an introduction. I have deliberately aimed at breadth rather than depth, and students should be encouraged to use other textbooks for wider reading in order to look at different topics, or to look at different interpretations of the same topics. At the end of all chapters, I have included a list of supplementary readings where students can begin this wider reading. I have referred students to readings that are available in fairly well known textbooks, on the assumption that they will be able to find these in university libraries. For more advanced courses, readings in specialist journals or more advanced textbooks may be necessary. I would suggest that if a higher level course is being taught, lecturers compile their own supplementary reading lists.

I have included at the end of each chapter a set of Reading Guide questions. Students may want to test their understanding and retention of the material in a chapter by working through these questions. I have not included answers to these questions — if students do not feel confident about a particular answer, they should refer to the material in the chapter, or ask the lecturer for help.

Each chapter includes exercises based on some of the concepts discussed in that chapter. These can be used in a number of ways. As a lecturer you may want to use this data as illustrative material in lectures. You may want to ask students to work through this material in class, as a way of ensuring that they are able to apply the concepts discussed in that particular chapter. Finally, you may want to use the material as a basis in formulating problems for your students for assessment (for that reason I have not provided answers to the questions that are given). A number of exercises in this volume involve the same set of basic information on particular languages upon which students are asked to perform different sorts of tasks. Rather than repeat this information in each chapter, I have collected the data in a series of Data Sets at the end of the volume. Students should refer to the Data Sets for these forms whenever an exercise requires it.

I have tried to write this volume in a style that is clear in its exposition of sometimes complex concepts, yet at the same time understandable to undergraduate students, so I have aimed to write conversationally rather than ponderously. I have deliberately avoided loading the text with distracting references to my sources for particular pieces of information. Footnotes, endnotes, and the Harvard system of reference have their place in academic publications, but not, I feel, in an introductory textbook. I would not want students to feel that they should not acknowledge sources within the text of their own written work. One's sources of information should always be acknowledged. I have done this in this volume, though in order to maintain readability I have listed my sources in a separate Language Index towards the end.

Many examples in this volume are taken from Austronesian languages, Australian languages, and the non-Austronesian languages of the Papuan area. Since this is a textbook of historical linguistics rather than an introduction to Austronesian linguistics (or those of other areas), I hope that specialist readers will accept the occasional simplification—or other kinds of misrepresentation—of data in the spirit that it is intended, that is, as an introduction to principles of historical linguistics.

Readers of this volume should note that I have used phonetic symbols that correspond to those used in Crowley, Lynch, Siegel and Piau (1995). These are symbols which are widely used by linguists and correspond for the most part to standard IPA symbols. Any deviations from IPA usage have generally been for reasons of typographical convenience. Conventions which are not widely used are explained as they are introduced. Otherwise, I have used the symbols that are set out on the following page. Readers should also note that English words are generally transcribed to reflect the pronunciations that are typical in Australian, New Zealand, and South Pacific English, rather than the pronunciations of North American and British speakers. North American and British readers, however, should experience little difficulty with most transcriptions.

Material is cited in the text in IPA symbols surrounded either by phonetic brackets or phonemic slashes. For examples that are cited without surrounding brackets or slashes, the phonetic vs phonemic status of the forms is not relevant to the particular point being made. Forms cited orthographically appear in italics.

CHART OF PHONETIC SYMBOLS

CONSONANTS

	Bilabial	Labio-dental	Dental	Alveolar	Palato-alveolar	Retroflex	Palatal	Velar	Labio-velar	Uvular	Glottal
Stop	p b		t̪ d̪	t d		ʈ ɖ	c ɟ	k g	kʷ gʷ	q ɢ	ʔ
Nasal	m	ɱ	n̪	n		ɳ	ɲ	ŋ	ŋʷ	N	
Fricative	ɸ β	f v	θ ð				ç	x ɣ	xʷ ɣʷ	χ ʁ	h
Sibilant			s̪ z̪	s z	ʃ ʒ	ʂ ʐ					
Affricate					tʃ dʒ						
Lateral			l̪	ɬ l		ɭ	ʎ	L			
Flap				ɾ		ɽ					
Trill				r						R	
Approx- imant				ɹ							
Glide							j		w		

VOWELS

		Front		Central		Back	
		Spread	Round	Spread	Round	Spread	Round
High	Tense	i	y	ɨ	ʉ	ɯ	u
	Lax	ɪ	ʏ				ʊ
Mid	Tense	e	ø	ə	ɵ	ɤ	o
	Lax	ɛ	œ			ʌ	ɔ
Low		æ		ɐ			
		a				ɑ	ɒ

15

MAPS OF LANGUAGES REFERRED TO IN THE TEXT

In the following maps I have indicated the location of languages that may not be known to the general reader of this volume. I am assuming that readers will be aware of where the better known (or iconically named) world languages (such as French, Bahasa Indonesia, Afrikaans, Icelandic) are spoken. I have indicated the location of lesser known languages that are spoken outside the areas covered by the following maps in the body of the text.

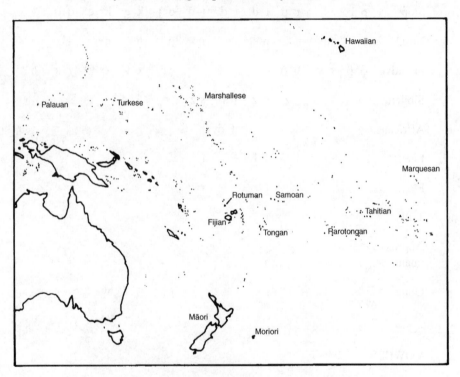

Map 1: Pacific languages referred to in the text

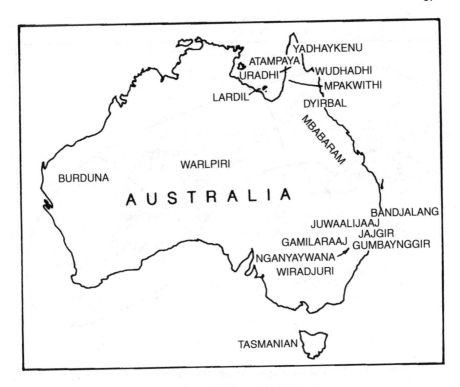

Map 2: Australian languages referred to in the text

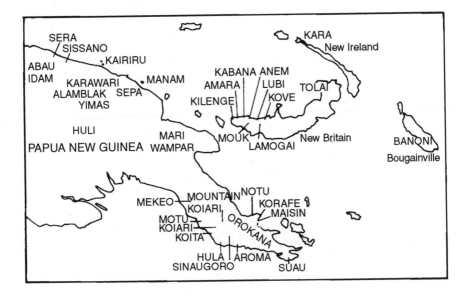

Map 3: Papua New Guinea languages referred to in the text

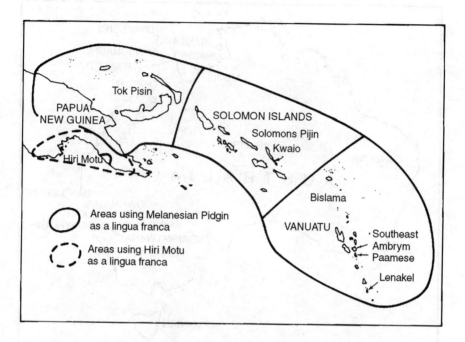

Map 4: Insular Melanesian languages referred to in text, and major
Melanesian lingua francas

CHAPTER ONE

INTRODUCTION

1.1 THE NATURE OF LINGUISTIC RELATIONSHIPS

Many linguists trace the history of modern linguistics back to the publication in 1913 of the book *Course in General Linguistics* by students of the Swiss linguist Ferdinand de Saussure. In this book, the foundation was laid for the scientific study of language. Saussure recognised, as we still do today, that language is made up of a collection of units, all related to each other in very particular ways, on different levels. These different levels are themselves related in various ways to each other. The primary function of language is to express meanings, and to convey these to someone else. To do this, the mental image in a speaker's head has to be transformed into some physical form so that it can be transferred to someone else who can then decode this physical message, and have the same mental image come into his or her head.

One of the points that Saussure stressed was the fact that we need to make a distinction between studying a language from a *diachronic* point of view and from a *synchronic* point of view. Up until the time of Saussure, linguistics had basically involved the diachronic study of languages. This meant that scholars were only interested in describing relationships between various aspects of languages *over periods of time*. Linguistics was until then a purely historical field of study. Languages at a particular point in time were viewed not so much as systems within themselves, but as 'products of history'. Saussure disputed this interpretation and said that all languages could (and *should*) be described synchronically, *without reference to history*. When we describe a language synchronically, we describe what are the basic units that go to make up the language (that is, its phonemes, its morphemes, and so on) and the relationship between these units at that time, and that time only. He therefore proposed a rigid boundary between diachronic and synchronic linguistics, which has been part of linguistics since his time (though lately, many linguists have come to question the need for such a rigidly stated view). This book is intended to introduce you to the concepts and techniques of diachronic linguistics.

Another important concept that Saussure stressed was the fact that the mental image in a speaker's head and the physical form used to transfer this image are completely arbitrary. This accounts for the fact that a certain kind of domestic animal is called a **sisia** in the Motu language of Papua New Guinea, a **huli** in the Paamese language of Vanuatu, a ʃiɛ̃ in French, and a **dɒg** in English. If there were any kind of natural connection between a word and its meaning, we would all use the same word!

Saussure would not have denied that some parts of a language are strongly iconic, or natural. All languages have onomatopoeic words like **rokrok** for 'frog' and **meme** for 'goat' in Tok Pisin in Papua New Guinea, or **kokoroku** for 'chicken' in Motu. However, words such as these are usually very small in number, and not an important consideration in language as a whole.

If we compare two different words used by two different groups of people speaking different languages, and we find that they express a similar (or identical) meaning by using similar (or, again, identical) sounds, then we need to ask ourselves this simple question: *Why?* Maybe it is because there is some natural connection between the meaning and the form that is being used to express it. On the other hand, maybe the similarity says something about some kind of historical connection between the two languages.

Let us go on a diversion for a moment, and look at the topic of stories in different cultures of the world. Probably all societies in the world have some kinds of stories that are passed on from generation to generation, telling of the adventures of people and animals from a long time ago. Often, these stories are told not just for pure interest and enjoyment, but also as a means of preserving the values of the culture of their tellers. The fact that all societies have such stories is not particularly surprising. Even the fact that societies have stories about animals that speak and behave like humans is not particularly surprising, as all humans of whatever culture are able to see similarities between animals and humans.

However, what if we found that two different peoples had a particular story about a person who died, and who was buried, and from whose grave grew a tree that nobody had seen before? This tree, the story goes, bore large green fruit right near its top, but nobody knew what to do with this fruit. A bird then came along and pecked at the fruit to indicate to the people that its thick skin could be broken. When it was broken open, the people found that the fruit contained a sweet and nutritious drink.

This story can be recognised by coastal peoples nearly three thousand kilometres apart, from Vanuatu through to many parts of Papua New Guinea. Surely, if two peoples share stories about the origin of the coconut which contain so many similar details, this cannot be accidental. The fact that the stories are widely dispersed can only be interpreted as meaning that there must be something in common in the history of these different peoples.

So, if we were to come across two (or more) different languages and find that they have similar (or identical) words to express basically the same meanings, we would presumably come to the same kind of conclusion. Look at the following forms that are found in a number of languages that are very widely scattered:

	Bahasa Indonesia	Tolai (PNG)	Paamese (Vanuatu)	Fijian	Māori
'two'	dua	aurua	elu	rua	rua
'three'	tiga	autul	etel	tolu	toru
'four'	əmpat	aivat	ehat	va:	fa:
'five'	lima	ailima	elim	lima	rima
'stone'	batu	vat	ahat	vatu	kofatu

These similarities must be due to more than pure chance. We must presume that there is *some* kind of historical connection between these five widely separated languages (and, we might suspect, some of the intervening languages as well). This connection (and the connection between the stories about the coconut that we looked at earlier) could logically be of two different kinds. First, it could be that four of these five languages simply copied these words from the fifth (or that all five copied from a sixth language somewhere).

Secondly, it could be that these forms all derive from a single set of original forms that has diverged differently in each case. Since these four languages are spoken in widely separate areas, we could guess that the speakers have had little or no opportunity to contact each other until very recent times. Anyway, even if these people were in contact in ancient times, there would seem to be little need for people to copy words for things like basic numbers and the word for 'stone'. These are the sorts of things that people from almost all cultures must have had words for already.

It might be understandable if the words for 'coffee' or 'ice' were similar, as these are certain to be introduced concepts in these areas. Originally, these things would have had no indigenous name. When people first come across things for which they have no name, they very frequently just copy the name from the language of the people who introduced the concept. Since traditionally people in the Pacific did not grow coffee (as this drink was introduced by Europeans, who themselves learned of it from the Middle East), we would expect that the word for 'coffee' in most of the languages of the Pacific would have been copied from the language of early European sailors and traders who first appeared in the Pacific in the last 200 years or so. Thus, the word for 'coffee' in most Pacific languages today is adapted to the sound systems of the various languages of the region, and comes out something like **kofi** or **kopi**. (In areas of the Pacific where the French rather than the British were influential, of course, we find words like **kafe** or **kape** from French *café*.)

Getting back to the words for 'stone' and the numbers 2, 3, 4, and 5 that I showed you earlier, the most likely explanation for their similarity in these widely dispersed languages is that each of these sets of words is derived from a single original form. This brings us to the important concepts of *language relationship* and *protolanguage*. These ideas were first recognised in modern scholarship by Sir William Jones, who was a British judge in colonial India. Jones had studied a wide variety of languages, and in 1786 he delivered a speech about Sanskrit (one of the languages of ancient India) and his words have since become very famous. In this speech he said:

The Sanskrit language, whatever be its antiquity, is of a wonderful structure; more perfect than the Greek, more copious than the Latin, and more exquisitely refined than either, yet bearing to both of them a stronger affinity, both in the roots of verbs and in the forms of grammar, than could possibly have been produced by accident; so strong indeed, that no philologer could examine all three, without believing them to have sprung from some common source, which, perhaps, no longer exists: there is similar reason, though not quite so forcible, for supposing that both the Gothic and Celtic, though blended with a very different idiom, had the same origin with the Sanskrit; and the Old Persian might be added to the same family.

This statement added two significant advances to the understanding of language change at the time. Firstly, Jones spoke of the idea of languages being related. Until then, people had tried to derive one language from another, often with ridiculous results. For instance, people had tried to show that all modern languages of the world ultimately go back to Hebrew, the language of biblical times. Kings of Europe even went to the extreme of separating newborn babies from their parents to see what language they would speak naturally if they were left alone and not taught. The results varied from Dutch to Hebrew (and none of these claims is believable). The similarities between Sanskrit, Latin, and Greek that Jones was talking about were often explained before he delivered his speech by saying that Sanskrit developed *into* Greek, and that Greek then developed *into* Latin:

Sanskrit   →   Greek   →   Latin

Jones, however, introduced the idea of 'parallel' development in languages. The concept that he was introducing was therefore the concept of language relationship. He was saying that if two languages have a common origin, this means that they belong to a single *family* of languages.

Secondly, Jones spoke of the concept of the protolanguage (without actually using the term, as this did not come into general use until modern times). When he said that these three languages, and possibly the others he mentioned (and he was later shown to be correct), were derived from some other language, he meant that there was some ancestral language from which all three were descended by changing in different ways. So, the model of language and relationship that he proposed to replace the earlier model looks like the model that we use today:

The concepts of 'protolanguage' and 'language relationship' both rest on the assumption that languages change. In fact, *all* languages change *all* the time. It is true to say that some languages change more than others, but all languages change nevertheless. But while all languages change, the change need not be in the same direction for all speakers. Let us imagine a situation like this:

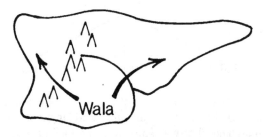

We will assume that there was an area on this island occupied by a group of people who spoke a language called Wala. Perhaps under pressure from population density, perhaps because of disputes, or perhaps out of pure curiosity, some of the Wala people moved out across the river and some across the mountains, and they settled in other areas. As I have said, all languages change, and the Wala language was no exception. However, the changes that took place in the Wala language across the mountains and across the river were not necessarily the same kinds of changes that took place in the original Wala homeland. Eventually, so many changes had taken place in the three areas that people could no longer understand each other. The Wala people in their homeland ended up calling themselves the Walo people, rather than their original name, Wala. Across the river the people came to call themselves the Peke, while the people on the other side of the mountains ended up calling themselves the Puke people. So, what we now have is a situation like this:

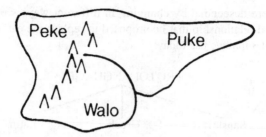

The three languages, Walo, Peke, and Puke, still show some similarities, despite their various differences. What we say, therefore, is that they are all related languages, all derived from a common ancestor, or protolanguage. We could therefore draw a family tree diagram for these three languages which would look like this:

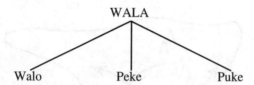

We can say exactly the same kind of thing about Bahasa Indonesia, Tolai, Paamese, Fijian, and Māori. These are all related languages which are derived from a protolanguage that was spoken in the distant past at a time when writing was not yet known. Thus:

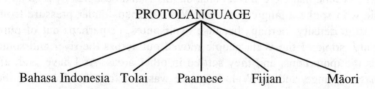

Generally, when a protolanguage evolves to produce a number of different daughter languages, we have no written records of the process. In the case of some of the languages of Europe, however, we have written records going back some thousands of years, and we can actually observe the changes taking place in these records. Latin was the language of most of western Europe at the time of Christ. However, as the centuries passed, Latin gradually changed in its spoken form in different parts of Europe so that it was quite different from the older written records. It is important to note that Latin changed in different ways in what is now Portugal, Spain, France, Italy, and Romania. The eventual result of this was that there are different languages in Europe that are today called Portuguese, Spanish, French, Italian, and Romanian. These languages are all similar to some extent, because they all go back to a common ancestor. In this case, we can draw a family tree to describe this situation, in which the protolanguage actually has a name that was recorded in history:

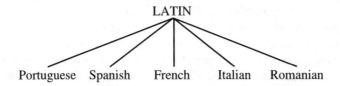

LATIN

Portuguese   Spanish   French   Italian   Romanian

We should ask ourselves this question: did Latin die out? The answer is that Latin did not die out in the same way that some languages have died out. Some languages die out because their speakers die out. The Tasmanian Aborigines, for instance, were badly affected by the diseases introduced by Europeans in the early 1800s, and many died. Many who did not die from disease were shot or poisoned by the Europeans. The last fully-descended Tasmanians died in the 1870s and 1880s, and knowledge of their languages died with them. (Contrary to popular belief the Tasmanians did not become extinct. There are several thousand people in Tasmania today of partly Aboriginal descent who proudly identify themselves as Aboriginal Tasmanians, though their language is English.)

Other languages die out, not because their speakers die out, but because — for whatever reason — they abandon their own language. Sometimes people abandon their own language as a result of having been forced to do so, while at other times people make the choice to switch to another language. In some parts of Australia, for example, Aboriginal people were gathered together and the children were separated from their parents in dormitories and punished by missionaries or government officers if they were caught speaking anything other than English. The result is that many of these languages have disappeared, and the descendants of the original speakers now use only English.

There are parts of Papua New Guinea today, most notably in the area of the Sepik River, where parents are coming more and more to speak to their children in the national lingua franca, Tok Pisin, rather than their local vernacular. Some people have predicted that, within a generation or two, some of these vernaculars could be close to extinction, though in these cases the speakers are not being forced to give up their language. In these cases, there have been no movements of outsiders into these communities. People are making their own subconscious choice to switch from one language to another because Tok Pisin is associated with modernity and development, whereas the vernaculars are associated with tradition and backwardness.

But neither of these situations is true for Latin. Latin is not a dead language in the same sense that Tasmanian Aboriginal languages are dead. A protolanguage can in some ways be compared to a baby. A baby changes over time and becomes a child, then a teenager, and then an adult, and finally an old person. A baby does not die and then become a child, and so on. Similarly, Latin did not die and 'become' French/Latin simply changed gradually so that it came to look like a different language, and today we call that language 'French'. The name 'Latin' was not lost either, as there is a little-known language spoken in Europe that is called 'Ladin'. This is the modern form in that particular language of the old word 'Latin'. One of the four official languages of Switzerland is also known as 'Romansh', which is a modern derivative of 'Roman'. (Even further from Rome is Romania, but the Romanians also speak a language that is derived from Latin and they have retained the original name of the Roman people who spoke Latin as the name of their language today!)

The changes between Latin and French (and Romansh, and Romanian) were gradual. There was no moment when people suddenly realised that they were speaking French instead of Latin, in the same way that there is no single moment when a baby becomes a child, or when a child becomes a teenager. After enough changes had taken place, people who compared the way they spoke with the older written forms of Latin could see that changes had occurred. But this is like looking at a photograph of ourselves taken when we were younger. We may look very different, but the person that we can see is definitely not dead![1]

French and Romanian and Romansh have not stopped changing either. The change continues into the present. French may well turn out to be the ancestor language from which a whole future family of languages is derived. So too may English, Bahasa Indonesia, Tolai, Paamese, Fijian, or Māori.

1.2 ATTITUDES TO LANGUAGE CHANGE

Since we are studying language change in this book, I would like to look at some of the common attitudes that people have towards the ways that languages change. As you saw in the preceding section, all languages are in a perpetual state of change. Sometimes, members of a particular society can observe changes that have taken place. In the case of written languages, people can see the language as it was written a number of generations ago, or even a number of centuries ago. In the case of unwritten languages, we obviously cannot observe how the language was spoken that far back in time, but very often people are able to recognise differences between the way the older people speak and the way the younger people speak.

---

[1] There is one sense in which we *can* say that Latin is a 'dead language'. In medieval and Renaissance Europe, the language of international scholarship and education was Latin, which was based on the written classical varieties of the language that was spoken during the heyday of the Roman empire before the birth of Christ. After the 1600s written Latin became more and more rare as the local vernaculars (i.e. English, French, German, Dutch, Italian, etc.) replaced Latin to the point where Latin is now used only as an official language of the Roman Catholic church for certain religious functions (and there is a continuing trend away from Latin in the church as well). While spoken Latin did not die, we could argue that the situation with regard to the written language is somewhat different.

It seems that in almost all societies, the attitudes that people have to language change are basically the same. People everywhere tend to say that the older form of a language is in some sense 'better' than the form that is being used today. In villages all around the Pacific today, it is not unusual to hear the parents and grandparents of today's generation of children, who have generally been educated in school, saying that their children do not speak the language 'properly' any more. Students at the University of Papua New Guinea or the University of the South Pacific often say that they cannot speak their own language as 'well' as their lesser educated parents speak it. In the early 1980s, Cecil Abel, an elderly European who was born and brought up in the Milne Bay area of Papua New Guinea and grew up speaking both the local Suau language and English, complained on the radio that the Suau spoken by young people today was nothing but 'doggerel'. This seems to be a fairly common attitude.

In most cases, if you ask people what they mean when they say these kinds of things, it turns out that they feel that the younger generation doesn't use some of the words that the older generation uses, or that the younger generation uses words of English origin in its speech. For instance, in Vanuatu the younger people on the island of Paama very often say **ka:ren** for 'garden' and **bu:s** for 'bush', both of which come from English. There are perfectly good Paamese words to express these meanings, i.e. **a:h** 'garden' and **leiai** 'bush'. Although the younger people know these words, they seldom bother to use them. In the Suau example that I just mentioned, Cecil Abel subsequently went on to say that what he meant by 'doggerel' was that some of the expressions used by Suau speakers of his generation are no longer being used by members of the younger generation.

In the preceding section, when I was discussing the ideas of Saussure, I said that forms in language are completely arbitrary. That is, there is no natural connection between a word and its meaning. This means that any sequence of sounds can express any meaning perfectly adequately, as long as members of the particular speech community agree to let those sounds represent that meaning. This means that **ka:ren** and **a:h** are both perfectly efficient ways of expressing the idea of 'garden'; similarly **bu:s** and **leiai** both express the meaning of 'bush' equally clearly. Neither is 'better' than the other. While the younger generations of Suau speakers no doubt use different expressions from those their grandparents used, the young have their own distinct sets of expressions that the elderly do not use. Who are we to judge which expressions are 'better'?

But people still like to insist that the earlier form of a language is 'better' than the later form, and they still like to say that the newer ways of speaking and writing are 'incorrect'. This applies to speakers of English, just as it does to any Pacific language. For instance, the following comments once appeared in the *Post-Courier*, the main daily newspaper in Papua New Guinea:

The English language is murdered daily on the National Broadcasting Corporation and I regret to say particularly in your *Post-Courier* . . . It is true that English is a living and developing language and new words and phrases are introduced from time to time. But the essential grammar must be maintained.

The writer of this letter was complaining not just about new words creeping into English, but also about the 'loss' of grammatical standards. In particular, he complained about people who 'split' their infinitives, by placing adverbs between the word *to* and a verb. He objects when people say things such as:

The minister intended to **speedily** examine the proposal for the introduction of bilingual education.

He says that people should say instead:

The minister intended **speedily** to examine the proposal . . .

You can see in the first sentence that it says *to speedily examine*, while in the second sentence it says *speedily to examine*. People who complain about this practice (and there are many) are ignoring the fact that almost everybody follows the pattern of the first sentence (even they themselves when they are not thinking about it!). The writer of the letter went on to suggest that a good solution to the problem was for children to be physically punished in school when they produce 'incorrect' sentences such as this!

It is doubtful if there was ever a time when English speakers did not split their infinitives like this. This prescriptive rule derives from an assumption that because infinitives in Latin consisted of just a single inflected verb form, the *to* should not be separated from the verb in English. Constructions which contain split and unsplit infinitives are both perfectly adequate ways of getting the meaning across. The choice of construction is purely a stylistic one, but we cannot judge either construction as being inherently 'better' than the other.

Attitudes like those that I have been talking about in this section are probably common to all cultures. Not only this, but these kinds of attitudes also have a long history. Samuel Johnson was the first person to attempt to write a complete dictionary of the English language. His work appeared almost 250 years ago, and he said that its aim was to:

refine our language to grammatical purity, and to clear it from colloquial barbarisms . . .

However, the choice between what is 'barbaric' and what represents 'purity' is completely arbitrary. He always chose to include the 'pure' written forms of the upper classes (of which he was, of course, a member), and labelled the spoken forms of the lower classes as 'barbaric'.

Even among serious scholars of language, we find such attitudes. The words of Sir William Jones which were quoted in the previous section are, of course, laden with such value judgements. It was a common belief among specialist scholars in the nineteenth century that the languages of today were degenerating, and were not as 'pure' in structure as their ancestor languages. For instance, one famous nineteenth century scholar of language, Max Müller, claimed that in the written history of all of the languages of Europe he could observe only a 'gradual process of decay'. The protolanguage from which Latin, Greek, and Sanskrit were derived (that is, the languages that Sir William Jones first mentioned as being related in 1786) was seen as being the most 'pure' form of language that was possible.

The common fault in this line of thinking is that such people regard language change as unnatural, and wish that it would never happen. But all human societies are always changing, and language is just another aspect of human social behaviour. Language change is *natural*, and it is *inevitable*. Even if the language of a Pacific Islander contains more words of English origin than was the case a generation ago, it is still a *Pacific* language. In fact, if this were how we measured how 'real' a language is, then English would be one of the most unreal languages of the world, because about half of the words in the English language originally come from other languages!

1.3 DELIBERATELY CHANGING LANGUAGES

Up till now I have stressed the fact that language change is *natural*. If we, as speakers of our languages, let things take their natural course, our language will inevitably change in one way or another, given sufficient time. Sometimes purists such as Samuel Johnson have tried to reverse changes that have already taken place, but generally even the most ferocious teachers in schools with the most fearsome whips cannot turn time back, as far as language is concerned.

However, there are situations in which the deliberate action of speakers can affect the future of a language. In times of rapid social, cultural, and technological change, speakers of a language need to add new words to their vocabulary in order to talk about new things that come into their daily lives. For speakers of many languages the most natural thing to do in this kind of situation is simply to copy the word from some other language, though at the same time adapting the sound of the word to the sound system of their own language. Typically the source of a new word like this is the language of the people who have introduced a particular new thing or a new belief or activity, as I have already said. That is why we find that in most of the languages of the South Pacific the word for 'coffee' looks something like **kofi** or **kopi**.

As we have already seen, people tend to be linguistic 'purists', and sometimes people regard words derived from another language as some kind of a threat to the integrity of their own language. It sometimes happens that a colonised nation, after gaining its independence, makes a conscious decision to replace the language of the former colonisers with one of their own languages as the official language of the new nation. For example, at the same time that Indonesia declared its independence from the Netherlands just after the Second World War, Bahasa Indonesia was declared to be the national language, in place of Dutch. This meant that Bahasa Indonesia jumped from being a language of relatively lowly social interaction, to being a language that was to be used as a language of the legal system, as well as a language of university education. Suddenly, chemistry lecturers in the universities had to teach their subjects in Bahasa Indonesia. Even though these people were fluent speakers of Bahasa Indonesia, they faced immediate difficulties because until then they had always used Dutch in their teaching, and the only technical vocabulary they knew was in Dutch.

The government of the new Indonesian republic appreciated this difficulty and set up what it called the *Dewan Bahasa dan Pustaka*, or the 'Language and Literature Council'. The task of this council was to develop terminology in areas where Bahasa Indonesia lacked it, and also to translate materials already available in Dutch into the new national language (using, of course, any new terminology that the council had developed). With the establishment of this council, the Indonesian government had become involved in a language planning activity, i.e. the deliberate government-sanctioned intervention in the course of language change.

The council recognised that, in order to develop new terminology, there were three basic choices available to them. Firstly, they could simply 'Indonesianise' Dutch words. Indeed, speakers of Bahasa Indonesia had already been doing this to express new concepts. The Dutch word *bioscoop*, for example, was copied into Bahasa Indonesia as *bioskop* to refer to a picture theatre, and that is the only way that Indonesians have of referring to this concept. Another way to refer to new concepts was to take two words already found in the language, and to join them together according to the patterns of the language to make up a new word. For instance, the word *juru* means 'expert' in Bahasa Indonesia, and this has been joined to a number of verbs to refer to a wide range of new professions:

pustaka	'book'	*juru pustaka*	'librarian'
tulis	'write'	*juru tulis*	'clerk'
terbang	'fly'	*juru terbang*	'pilot'
berita	'news'	*juru berita*	'journalist'

One final way to refer to new concepts is to take an existing word and to extend its meaning to refer to a new thing. Thus, for example, while *surat* originally referred to a letter, the same word has now come to mean a certificate as well.

The examples of change in the vocabulary of Bahasa Indonesia that I have just given are natural, in the sense that they happened spontaneously, without the deliberate intervention of any individuals or any committee. However, the language council that was set up in Indonesia noted these three different ways in which the language had evolved in the past, and decided to follow the same methods in *deliberately* creating new words that had not yet evolved of their own accord.

Rather than take what would probably have been the easiest path, the council chose to use words of Dutch origin only as a last resort. The members of the council felt that it was important that the Indonesian republic should rely as far as possible on its own linguistic resources. Thus, in order to express the linguistic technical term 'voiceless', the council settled upon *takbersuara*. *Tak* is a Bahasa Indonesia word meaning 'not'; *ber-* is a prefix meaning 'having'; and *suara* is the word for 'voice'. An 'exclamation', it was decided, would be a *seruan*, from the verb *seru* 'call' and the suffix *-an*, which makes a verb into a noun, i.e. 'a calling'. However, the council did not reject words of foreign origin altogether. A dictionary of modern Bahasa Indonesia includes large numbers of words copied from Dutch. Most of these are technical terms. Specialist terms that have become fully integrated into the language now include the following: *melokalisir* 'localise', *kampanye* 'campaign', *personalia* 'personnel', *pesimisme* 'pessimism'.

The deliberate creation of new vocabulary in this way can only succeed if a number of conditions are first met. To begin with, those who are responsible for creating the vocabulary must have some way of getting their new words into the community at large. This means that the new words must be incorporated into the education system of the country, and the schoolteachers must be taught to use these words when they are training to be teachers. There must also be some way of ensuring that the editors of books, magazines, and newspapers in the country follow the decisions of the council rather than simply borrow Dutch terms at random. Finally, there must also be a measure of public support for this kind of activity. If ordinary speakers of Bahasa Indonesia felt that it was unimportant to try to keep foreign words out of their language, then the work of the committee would probably be doomed from the outset.

It is the attitude of speakers of a language which is perhaps the most important consideration here. People who do not feel themselves to be under any kind of threat from the bearers of a new culture or a new technology will probably let new words flood into their language. However, when people feel themselves to be under some kind of threat from the new culture, perhaps because they have lost their political independence, or because they have been swamped as a people by an intrusive population, then they are more likely to resent foreign words coming in. When a people perceives itself as being under threat, new concepts are more likely to be expressed by using the indigenous resources of the language rather than simply copying words from some other language.

In New Zealand, the indigenous Māori people make up just over 10 per cent of the total population, with the remainder being predominantly English-speaking Europeans who have dominated in the country for over 100 years. The great majority of Māori today speak English as their first language, and even those whose first language is Māori also speak fluent English. There is a widespread fear that if the situation is not reversed in the immediate future, the language could disappear altogether. The Māori, therefore, are a people who feel very much under threat from the speakers of another language. A language council similar to that which I have already talked about for Indonesia has been set up in New Zealand in order to modernise the vocabulary of Māori. This council is known as *Te Taura Whiri i te Reo Māori*. It has issued a whole set of new vocabulary in Māori for use in the office (and many other domains as well), and includes terms such as the following:

papa pātuhi	'keyboard'	(from *papa* 'board', *pā* 'touch' and *tuhi* 'write')
wai ngārahu	'ink'	(from *wai* 'water' and *ngārahu* 'black')
pae patopato	'typewriter'	(from *pae* 'beam' and *patopato* 'type')

In one sense, probably none of these words are really *needed* in the Māori language, as almost all people who speak Māori are fluently bilingual in Māori and English and probably know and use the English words anyway. Thus it would have been easier for everybody if the English words were simply copied in a Māori form into the language. *Kipoti* 'keyboard' and *tihiketi* 'diskette' would be readily understandable to any speaker of Māori who already knows the corresponding English words. However, *Te Taura Whiri i te Reo Māori* felt that it was important for the Māori language to be 'protected' from the overpowering influence of English, as a way of ensuring the independence of the threatened Māori language, and so there has been a tendency to avoid words of English origin.

While a language still has a fighting chance, it is possible for the purists to succeed in keeping out words of foreign origin. If the tables are not turned for the Māori language and it becomes clear to its remaining speakers in the twenty-first century that the language is doomed, *Te Taura Whiri i te Reo Māori* is likely to find the battle against words of English origin increasingly difficult. You will see in Chapter 12 of this book that Dyirbal is an Australian Aboriginal language that will almost certainly not survive into the next generation. Although the older people still insist on correctness, the younger speakers of this language today make almost no attempt to keep English words (and even whole phrases) out of their speech, much to the annoyance of the older generations who still hope that the old language can be maintained.

READING GUIDE QUESTIONS

1. What statements did Ferdinand de Saussure make that influenced the course of linguistic science from his time on?
2. What is the significance of the discussion of stories told by people of different cultures in this chapter?
3. What possible explanations can we offer if we find that two languages express similar meanings by phonetically similar forms?
4. What do we mean when we say that two or more languages are genetically related?
5. What is a protolanguage?
6. What was the significance of the statement by Sir William Jones in 1786 about the relationship between Sanskrit, Latin, and Greek?
7. Does a protolanguage die out and then get replaced by its daughter languages? What, for example, is the nature of the relationship between Latin and Romanian?
8. How are people's attitudes to language change and ideas of standard and non-standard forms in language interrelated?
9. What is linguistic purism?
10. How is language planning both different from and similar to language change?
11. What are the three ways in which new terminology can develop in a language?
12. What conditions have to be met for language planning to succeed?

EXERCISES

1. What do you think is the importance to historical linguists of the fact that Sanskrit, Latin, and Greek were written languages? Would we have been able to make the same early advances in linguistic reconstruction if they were not?
2. Saussure and the modern linguists who followed him made a great deal of the arbitrary nature of language. How arbitrary is language? Examine the pairs of words below in a number of different languages. One word of the pair for each language means 'big' and the other means 'small'. Say which of each pair of words that you think means 'big' and which means 'small'. Compare the results across the class. Can you offer any explanation for what is going on? What do you think is the importance of such facts to the historical study of languages?

Paamese (Vanuatu)	mari:te	titi:te
Russian	malenkij	bolʃoj
Fijian	levu	lailai
Bahasa Indonesia	kətʃil	bəsar

Tagalog (Philippines)	mali?it	malaki
Kwaio (Solomon Islands)	sika	ba?i
Gumbaynggir (Australia)	barwaj	ɖunuj
Samoan	lapo?a	laiti:ti
Dyirbal (Australia)	midi	bulgan
Lenakel (Vanuatu)	ipwɨr	esua:s

(To find out which of these words mean 'big', refer to the answers at the end of these exercises.)

3. The word *tooth* in English has a long history in English writing, and it goes back to the same source as the German word *Zahn* [**tsaːn**] and the Dutch word *tand* [**tant**], indicating that these three languages are closely related. Latin also has a root for 'tooth' [**dent-**]. This is sufficiently different from the English, German, and Dutch forms to suggest that it is more distantly related to these languages. In written documents in English that are less than a few hundred years old we start finding words such as *dental*, *dentist*, *trident* (a fork with three 'teeth'), and *denture*. What do you think this indicates about the historical relationship between Latin and English?

4. Look at the Lord's Prayer (King James version). Point out the expressions and constructions that would not normally be used in ordinary everyday speech today. Rewrite the prayer as it would be expressed in modern English. Why do you think people prefer to pray in an old-fashioned form of English that is sometimes hard to understand?

5. In his statement in 1786, Sir William Jones said that the various Indo-European languages that he was discussing must have 'sprung from some common source, which perhaps no longer exists'. What did he mean by the comment that the original language perhaps no longer exists? Is he saying that the language became extinct? What sort of wording could you suggest that might more accurately reflect the actual situation?

6. For what sorts of reasons may a society give up its language and replace it with somebody else's? Can you think of any examples from your own general knowledge where such a thing has happened, or where it might happen in future?

7. Comment on Sir William Jones's statement that Sanskrit, which resembles the protolanguage from which Latin and Greek were derived, 'is of a wonderful nature, more perfect than the Greek, more copious than the Latin, and more exquisitely refined than either'.

8. French newspapers contain many English words, like *le football*, *le weekend*, *le camping*, and so on. There are many speakers of French who want to keep the language 'pure', and to prevent the development of what they jokingly call *Franglais* (or *Frenglish*). There is even a government agency called the *Académie Française* (i.e. the 'French Academy'), whose job it is to keep such words from appearing in the dictionary, and to find good French words for all of these things. What comment would you make to members of this council?

9. If you were addressing *Te Taura Whiri i te Reo Māori* who were agonising over whether to accept the word *komopiuta* 'computer' into the Māori language or to encourage the use of the coined word *rorohiko* (from *roro* 'brain' and *hiko* 'electric'), what would you say? What do you think the representatives on that committee might say to somebody who insisted that, as everybody knows the English word *computer* already, they might as well accept *komopiuta* as a new Māori word?

ANSWERS

The following are the words for 'big' from the forms that were given: Paamese **mari:te**, Russian **bolʃoj**, Fijian **levu**, Bahasa Indonesia **bəsar**, Tagalog **malaki**, Kwaio **baʔi**, Gumbaynggir **barwaj**, Samoan **lapoʔa**, Dyirbal **bulgan**, Lenakel **ipwir**.

FURTHER READING

1. Anthony Arlotto *Introduction to Historical Linguistics*, Chapter 1 'The Scope of Comparative and Historical Linguistics', pp. 1–10.
2. Mario Pei *The Story of Language,* Chapter 4 'The Evolution of Language', pp. 35–36.
3. Jean Aitchison *Language Change: Progress or Decay?,* Chapter 1 'The Ever-Whirling Wheel', pp. 15–31.
4. Mary Haas *The Prehistory of Languages,* Chapter 1 'Introduction', pp. 13–30.
5. Theodora Bynon *Historical Linguistics* , 'Relatedness of Languages (genealogical, or genetic relationship)', pp. 63–75.

CHAPTER TWO

TYPES OF SOUND CHANGE

While it may not be particularly surprising to learn that all languages change over time, you may be surprised to learn that different languages tend to change in remarkably similar ways. For instance, if you look at the history of the sound [p] in the Uradhi language of northern Queensland, you will find that it has undergone a change to [w] in the modern language:[1]

Uradhi

*pinta	→	winta	'arm'
*pilu	→	wilu	'hip'
*paṯa	→	waṯa	'bite'

Now, if you look at the history of the same sound [p] in a completely different language, which has no known historical connection with Uradhi, you will find that exactly the same change has taken place. Let us look at the Palauan language of Micronesia. (Ignore all sounds except for those in bold type.)

Palauan

*paqi	→	waʔ	'leg'
*paqit	→	waʔəð	'bitter'
*qatəp	→	ʔaðow	'roof'

It would be easy to find examples in other languages of the world of the sound [p] changing to [w]. But we would also find repeated examples of [p]

---

[1] In the study of the history of languages, the symbol * is used to mark a form that has never actually been heard or written, but which is inferred or reconstructed in a protolanguage on the basis of evidence that is available. We will be looking at how we arrive at such reconstructions in Chapter 5.

changing to other sounds, for instance [f], or [b], or [v]. However, it would be very difficult to find an example of a language in which [p] had changed to [z], [1], or [e].

I will now describe likely sound changes and distinguish these from unlikely sound changes. I will also classify the various kinds of attested sound changes in the languages of the world.

2.1 LENITION AND FORTITION

The first kind of sound change that I will talk about is *lenition*, or weakening. The concept of lenition is not very well defined, and linguists who use the term often seem to rely more on intuition or guesswork than on a detailed understanding of what lenition really is. Linguists sometimes speak of certain sounds as being relatively 'stronger' or 'weaker' than others. Many people would intuitively judge the sounds on the left below to be 'stronger' than those on the right:

Stronger	Weaker
b	p
p	f
f	h
x	h
b	w
v	w
a	ə
i	ɨ
d	l
s	r
k	ʔ

The generalisations that can be made regarding these correspondences are that voiced sounds can be considered 'stronger' than voiceless sounds. Similarly, stops rank higher than continuants in strength; consonants are higher than semi-vowels; oral sounds are higher in rank than glottal sounds; and front and back vowels rank higher than central vowels.

These generalisations about the relative strength and weakness of sounds correspond roughly to the widely discussed sonority hierarchy that is invoked in many discussions of synchronic phonology. This hierarchy is as follows, with the most sonorous sounds to the left and the least sonorous sounds to the right:

a > e > o > i u > rhotics > laterals > nasals > voiced fricatives > voiceless fricatives > voiced stops > voiceless stops

The kinds of changes that I have just presented, therefore, tend to involve a shift from more sonorous to less sonorous sounds. It should be noted, however, that some of the commonly encountered changes listed above are difficult to account for purely in terms of loss of sonority, so the notion of phonetic weakening has to be more complex than I have indicated.

When phonetic change takes place, it is very often in the direction of a strong sound to a weak sound. That is to say, we would be more likely to find a change of [k] to [ʔ], for example, than the other way around, with [ʔ] becoming [k]. Changes of the reverse order are possible, of course, though less likely. These rarer sorts of sound changes could be referred to as strengthening (or *fortition*) to contrast them from lenition. So, for instance, we could say that the final consonant of the English word [naif] underwent fortition when it was copied into Tok Pisin,[2] where the corresponding word is [naip].

I will now give examples of phonetic lenition, or weakening, in different languages. The change of [b] and [p] to [f] in the Kara language of New Ireland (in Papua New Guinea) is one good example of lenition:

		Kara	
*bulan	→	fulan	'moon'
*tapine	→	tefin	'woman'
*punti	→	fut	'banana'
*topu	→	tuf	'sugarcane'

Similarly, the change from [p] to [w] in the Uradhi and Palauan examples given in the introduction to this chapter illustrate lenition. In the Jajgir language of northern New South Wales in Australia, stops are often lenited (or weakened) to semi-vowels at the beginning of a word, as shown by the following examples:

		Jajgir	
*ḍa:laɲ	→	ja:laɲ	'mouth'
*bu:luɲ	→	ju:luɲ	'belly'
*gaɲa:mbil	→	jaɲa:mbil	'tongue'

There is one particular kind of lenition that goes under the name of *rhotacism*. The term *rhotic* is often used to cover all types of *r* sounds (trills, flaps, glides, and so on), as distinct from all types of *l* sounds (which are together referred to as *laterals*). Laterals and rhotics collectively make up the phonetic class of *liquids*. The change known as rhotacism refers to the lenition of [s] or [z] to a rhotic between vowels. This kind of change took place in the history of the Latin language:

---

[2] Tok Pisin is the name given to the dialect of Melanesian Pidgin spoken in Papua New Guinea. The dialect spoken in Solomon Islands is known as Pijin, while the Vanuatu variety of the language is known locally as Bislama.

		Latin	
*ami:kosum	→	ami:korum	'of the friends'
*genesis	→	generis	'of the type'
*hono:sis	→	hono:ris	'of the honour'

There is even evidence in the spelling of modern English that rhotacism has taken place in the history of this language. The plural form of the verb [wɒz] 'was' is [wɜ:] 'were' (though in many dialects it is pronounced as [wəɹ]). Assuming that the spelling of English more closely reflects an earlier pronunciation than the modern pronunciation, it seems that the final *e* of w*ere* represents an earlier plural suffix, and that the root was probably something like [wase] or [wese] and there was later lenition of the [s] to [ɹ], to give [waɹe] or [weɹe]. It is from this form that the modern form [wəɹ] in some dialects is derived. It is also from this form that the pronunciation [wɜ:] has been derived in the case of those dialects of English which have lost syllable-final [ɹ].

A very common kind of sound change that takes place in languages is the loss of one or more sounds. This can be viewed as an extreme case of lenition: the weakest a sound can be is not to exist at all! An example from modern English of a sound being lost altogether would be illustrated by the variable pronunciation of a word such as 'history'. While some people pronounce this as [hɪstəɹi], others people simply say [hɪstɹi], dropping out the schwa vowel [ə]. Some people even say [ɪstɹi], dropping out the initial [h] as well. Another example of sound loss would be the word that is typically written as *long* in all three varieties of Melanesian Pidgin, and which functions as a preposition meaning 'to', 'from', 'in', 'at' (as well as a variety of other meanings). Despite the fact that the word is written as though it is pronounced [loŋ] (reflecting its origin in the English word *along*), people now commonly pronounce it simply as [lo], as in the following sentence:

Mi kam lo   bus
I   come from bush
'I have come from the bush.'

It is very common in languages of the world for sounds at the ends of words to be lost. In many languages of the Pacific, for example, final consonants are regularly dropped, as shown by the following changes that have taken place in the history of Fijian:

		Fijian	
*ɲiur	→	niu	'coconut'
*taŋis	→	taŋi	'cry'
*ikan	→	ika	'fish'
*bulan	→	vula	'moon'
*tansik	→	taði	'sea'

*lajaʀ	→	laða	'sail'
*laŋit	→	laŋi	'sky'

There are some kinds of sound loss that are covered by particular terms. These special terms are described and illustrated below:

(a) Aphaeresis

Initial segments are sometimes dropped. We can refer to this as *aphaeresis*, pronounced [əfɛrəsəs] (or sometimes as *aphesis*). The following examples of aphaeresis come from the Angkamuthi language of Cape York Peninsula in Australia:

		Angkamuthi	
*maji	→	aji	'food'
*nani	→	ani	'ground'
*ŋampu	→	ampu	'tooth'
*ɲukal	→	uka:	'foot'
*ɣantu	→	antu	'canoe'
*wapun	→	apun	'head'

(b) Apocope

Apocope, pronounced [əpɒkəpi], is the name you will come across in textbooks for the loss of word final segments. This is a very common change in languages, and examples are easy to find. For example, look at the following changes that have taken place in the history of the language of Southeast Ambrym in Vanuatu:

		Southeast Ambrym	
*utu	→	ut	'lice'
*aŋo	→	aŋ	'fly'
*asue	→	asu	'rat'
*tohu	→	toh	'sugarcane'
*hisi	→	his	'banana'
*use	→	us	'rain'

(c) Syncope

This term, pronounced [sɪŋkəpi], refers to a very similar process to apocope. Rather than the loss of final segments, *syncope* refers to the loss of segments in the middle of words. It is syncope which often produces consonant clusters in languages that did not formerly have them when medial vowels are lost. The common pronunciation of the word 'policeman' as **[pli:smən]** instead of **[pəli:smən]** is an example of syncope; so too is the pronunciation of 'history' without the schwa that you saw earlier. In some languages, syncope is a very regular change. In Lenakel, which is spoken on the island of Tanna in Vanuatu, we find that this sort of change is very common:

		Lenakel	
*namatana	→	nɨmrɨn	'his/her eye'
*nalimana	→	nelmɨn	'his/her hand'
*masa	→	mha	'low tide'

(You will see in these Lenakel examples that a substantial number of other sound changes have also taken place, such as the lenition of [t] to [r], of [s] to [h], and of [a] to [ɨ], as well as the raising of [a] to [e].)

(d) Cluster reduction

When consonants come together in a word without any vowels between them, we speak of *consonant clusters*. Very often, such clusters are reduced by deleting one (or more) of the consonants. This is one kind of change that has taken place word-finally in English words ending in [mb] and [ŋg], such as *bomb* and *long*, where the spelling reflects the earlier pronunciation, though the modern pronunciations are [bɒm] and [lɒŋ]. This change is still spreading in English, as word-final stops in clusters of [nd] are now being lost. Words such as *hand* are often pronounced as [hæn] rather than [hænd], especially when there is a following consonant. Thus, *handgrip* is frequently pronounced by many people as [hæŋgrɪp] rather than [hændgrɪp].

Cluster reduction has also occurred in the middle of many words in English. Although the word *government* is derived from the root *govern* with the following suffix *-ment*, the resulting cluster [nm] is normally reduced simply to [m]. So, instead of saying [gʌvənmənt], we normally just say [gʌvəmənt]. For many people this is further reduced by syncope to just [gʌvmənt], and consonant cluster reduction sometimes again applies to produce [gʌmənt], or even [gʌmən]!

(e) Haplology

Haplology is a kind of change that is rare and tends to be fairly sporadic in its application. This term refers to the loss of an entire syllable, when that syllable is found next to another identical, or at least very similar, syllable. For some reason, people find it difficult to pronounce sounds when they are near other sounds that are identical or very similar. This is why people so easily make mistakes when they try to say tongue-twisters such as *She sells sea shells by the sea shore* very quickly.

Haplology is the process that is involved when we pronounce the word *library* as [laɪbɹi] instead of [laɪbɹəɹi]. The word *England* [ɪŋglənd] was originally *Anglaland*, meaning the land of the Angles. (The Angles were a group of people who settled in Britain over 1000 years ago, bringing with them the ancestor of the modern English language.) The two *la* syllables in *Anglaland* were reduced by this process of haplology, and now we have only one *l* in the name *England* as a result.

2.2 SOUND ADDITION

While lenition, and particularly the total loss of sounds, is a very common kind of sound change, you will also find that sounds are sometimes added rather than dropped. On the whole, however, sound addition is rather rare. In modern English, you can see evidence of this kind of change taking place when we hear people saying [sʌmpθɪŋk] instead of the more common [sʌmθɪŋ] for 'something'. There are also examples such as [noʊp] 'nope' and [jɛp] 'yep' instead of [noʊ] 'no' and [je:] 'yeah', in which the final [p] seems to be added as a way of emphasising what we are saying by sharply cutting off the flow of air, perhaps symbolising the fact that the speaker's intention is absolutely final.

Sound addition often takes place at the end of words with final consonants, where many languages add a vowel. Many languages tend to have a syllable structure of consonant plus vowel (represented as **CV**), allowing no consonant clusters and having all words ending in vowels. If a language adds a vowel to all words ending in a consonant, then it is moving in the direction of this kind of syllable structure. So, for instance, when words in Māori are borrowed from English, vowels are always added after consonants at the end of the word to make sure that the words follow this kind of pattern:

Māori
ka:fe	'calf'
ko:ti	'court'
korofa	'golf'
kuki	'cook'
mapi	'map'
miraka	'milk'
raiti	'light'

Some kinds of sound addition are known by specific names in the literature of historical linguistics. These terms, with examples of the process that they refer to, are presented below.

(a) Excrescence
Excrescence refers to the process by which a consonant is added between two other consonants in a word. Although this change operates against the general tendency in languages to produce consonant plus vowel syllable structures, in that it creates even longer consonant clusters, it is nevertheless a fairly common kind of change. The insertion of [p] in the middle of the cluster [mθ] in the word *something* that I mentioned earlier is an example of excrescence. Excrescence has also taken place in other words in the history of English, and the added consonant is now even represented in the spelling system, e.g.

		English	
*æmtig	→	ɛmpti	'empty'
*θymle	→	θɪmbl	'thimble'

The excrescent stop that is inserted in these examples has the same point of articulation (or is *homorganic* with) the preceding nasal in all of these examples. The stop is added to close off the velum (which is open during the production of the nasal) before going on to produce the following non-nasal sound (i.e. a stop or a liquid).

(b) Epenthesis or Anaptyxis
The term *epenthesis* (or *anaptyxis*)[3] is used to describe the change by which a vowel is added in the middle of a word to break up two consonants in a cluster. This change therefore produces syllables of the structure **CV** (i.e. consonant plus vowel), again illustrating the common tendency for languages to avoid consonant clusters and final consonants. Speakers of some varieties of English often insert an epenthetic schwa [ə] between the final consonants of the word [fɪlm] 'film', to produce [fɪləm]. Epenthesis has also taken place fairly frequently in the history of Tok Pisin. Compare the English and Tok Pisin forms below and note the occurrence of epenthetic (or anaptyctic) vowels in Tok Pisin:

English		Tok Pisin	
blæk	→	bilak	'black'
blu:	→	bulu	'blue'
nɛkst	→	nekis	'next'
sɪks	→	sikis	'six'
skɪn	→	sikin	'skin'
plɛɪs	→	peles	'village'
fɪlm	→	pilum	'film'

(c) Prothesis
Prothesis is another term used to refer to a particular type of sound addition, i.e. the addition of a sound is at the beginning of a word. In the Motu language of Papua New Guinea, for example, when a word began with an [a], a prothetic [l] was added before it, as shown by the following examples:

		Motu	
*api	→	lahi	'fire'

---

[3] Although anaptyxis and epenthesis are given here as synonymous, you should note that there is some variation in the way that these terms are used in the literature of historical linguistics. Some writers use the term epenthesis as a cover term for excrescence, anaptyxis, and prothesis together, while others prefer epenthesis to anaptyxis when referring specifically to the insertion of a vowel between two consonants occurring in a consonant cluster.

| *asan | → | lada | 'gills of fish' |
| *au | → | lau | 'I, me' |

2.3 METATHESIS

The change known as *metathesis* [mətæθəsəs] is a fairly uncommon kind of change. It does not involve the loss or addition of sounds, or a change in the appearance of a particular sound. Rather, it is simply a change in the order of the sounds. If someone mispronounces the word *relevant* as *revelant*, this is an example of metathesis.

Metathesis has taken place in the history of some English words and the changed form has become accepted as the standard. The English word *bird* [bɜːd] was originally pronounced as [bɹɪd]. This then became [bɪɹd] by metathesis, and this is the form that we still represent in our spelling system. Of course, the sounds [ɪɹ] have undergone further changes in some dialects to become [ɜː] (though in dialects of English such as American, Scottish, and Irish English, the original [ɹ] is still clearly pronounced).

Although metathesis is a rare sort of change, generally occurring in only one or two words in a language, there are still some cases of regular metathesis. In the Ilokano language of the Philippines, for example, there has been fairly consistent switching of word final [s] and initial [t], as shown by the following comparisons with Tagalog, the national language of the Philippines (which reflects the original situation):

Tagalog	Ilokano	
taŋis	sa:ŋit	'cry'
tubus	subut	'redeem'
tigis	si:git	'decant'
tamis	samqit	'sweet'

2.4 FUSION

Phonetic *fusion* is a fairly frequent kind of sound change, in which two originally separate sounds become a single sound. The resulting single sound carries some of the features of *both* of the original sounds.

Before I go on to give examples of fusion, it will be necessary to clarify what is meant by the term *feature*. All sounds can be viewed as being made up of a number of particular features, which determine different aspects of the nature of the sound. The sound [m], for instance, contains the following features (among others):

1. [+ consonantal]
2. [+ voiced]

3. [+ labial]
4. [+ nasal]

The sound [a], on the other hand, contains the following features:

1. [- consonantal]
2. [+ voiced]
3. [+ low]

When two sounds are changed to become one in the process of fusion, some of the features of one sound and some of the features of the other sound are taken and a new sound is produced that is different from both, yet which also shares some features of both of the original sounds. I will take an example of a change of this type from French:

		French	
*œn	→	œ̃	'one'
*bɔn	→	bɔ̃	'good'
*vɛn	→	vɛ̃	'wine'
*blan	→	blã	'white'

(The symbol ˜ is known as a *tilde* and is placed over the vowel to indicate that the vowel is nasalised, with the air coming out through the nasal passage as well as through the mouth.) The generalisation we can make here is that:

Vowel + Nasal → Nasalised Vowel

Expressing this in terms of features, we can say that the [- consonantal] feature of the first sound has been kept, while the [+ nasal] feature of the second sound has been kept, and a single new sound combining both features has been created:

1. [- consonantal]
2. [+ nasal]

A second example of fusion can be quoted from the Attic dialect of Greek. Examine the data below:

		Attic Greek	
*gwous	→	bous	'cow'
*gwatis	→	basis	'going'
*gwasileus	→	basileus	'official'
*leikwɔ:	→	leipɔ:	'I leave'
*jɛ:kwar	→	hɛ:par	'liver'

In the original forms, there was a [g] or a [k] with the feature specification of velar stops. These were followed by a [w], which had the feature specification for a semi-vowel with lip-rounding. In the fused forms of the Attic dialect, we find that the stop feature of the first sound has been taken along with the bilabial feature of the second sound to produce a bilabial stop. Thus, when there was an original voiced stop as in [gw], the fused sound became the voiced bilabial stop [b], and when there was an original voiceless stop as in [kw], the fused sound became the corresponding voiceless bilabial stop, i.e. [p].

A particular type of phonological fusion can be referred to as *compensatory lengthening*. This kind of sound change is illustrated by the following forms from Old Irish:

		Old Irish	
*magl	→	ma:l	'prince'
*kenetl	→	kene:l	'gender'
*etn	→	e:n	'bird'
*datl	→	da:l	'assembly'

What has happened here is that a consonant has been lost and 'in compensation' for this loss, a vowel has been lengthened. If we introduce the idea of *phoneme space* as a feature of a sound, we can treat this kind of change as another type of fusion. If each phoneme carries, among its collection of features, a phoneme space (i.e. the actual space it occupies in a word), then we could say that all features *except* this single feature of phoneme space can be lost, and that only this one feature is fused with the features of the preceding sound. This new sound therefore contains two features of phoneme space. This is reflected in the change in the examples above from a short vowel (i.e. one space) to a long vowel (i.e. two spaces).

2.5 UNPACKING

Unpacking is a phonetic process that is just the opposite of phonetic fusion. From a single original sound, you will find that a sequence of two sounds may develop, each with some of the features of the original sound. We saw earlier that, in French, vowels followed by nasal consonants underwent fusion to become nasalised vowels. It is also possible to find examples of languages in which the reverse kind of change takes place. In Bislama (the variety of Melanesian Pidgin spoken in Vanuatu), words of French origin that contain nasal vowels are incorporated into the language by unpacking the vowel features and the nasal features to produce sequences of plain vowels followed by the nasal consonant [ŋ]:

French			Bislama	
camion	kamiɔ̃	→	kamioŋ	'truck'
accident	aksidɑ̃	→	aksidoŋ	'accident'
carton	kaʁtɔ̃	→	kartoŋ	'cardboard box'
caleçon	kalsɔ̃	→	kalsoŋ	'underpants'

lagon	lagɔ̃	→	lagoŋ	'lagoon'
putain	pytɛ̃	→	piteŋ	'whore'
avance	avãs	→	avoŋ	'advance on wages'
bouchon	buʃɔ̃	→	busoŋ	'cork'

In these examples, the original nasal and vowel features of the final vowels in French are distributed over two sounds, i.e. the oral vowels and the following velar nasal. We therefore have a change that can be expressed as:

Nasal Vowel → Vowel + Nasal Consonant

2.6 VOWEL BREAKING

In the change known as *vowel breaking*, a single vowel changes to become a diphthong, with the original vowel remaining the same, but with a glide of some kind being added either before or after it. When a glide is added before the vowel, we call this an *on-glide*, but if a glide is added after the vowel, we refer to this as an *off-glide*. One of the more noticeable features of some varieties of American English is the 'broken vowels'. What is pronounced in most dialects of English as [**bæd**] 'bad', is pronounced by some Americans as [bæəd], or even as [**bæid**], with an off-glide. One of the distinguishing features of the Barbadian English in the West Indies is the palatal on-glide before the vowel [**æ**]. Instead of pronouncing [**kæt**] 'cat', people from Barbados will say [**kjæt**].

Vowel breaking is fairly common in the languages of the world. A good example of a language apart from American English that has undergone regular vowel breaking is the Kairiru language that is spoken on an island near Wewak in Papua New Guinea:

		Kairiru	
*pale	→	pial	'house'
*manu	→	mian	'bird'
*namu	→	niam	'mosquito'
*ndanu	→	rian	'water'
*lako	→	liak	'go'

(Note that in these examples there is also evidence of apocope, or the loss of the final vowels.)

2.7 ASSIMILATION

Many sound changes can be viewed as being due to the influence of one sound upon another. When one sound causes another sound to change so that the two sounds end up being more similar to each other in some way, we call this *assimilation*. Since assimilation is by far the most common kind of sound change, I will present a fairly detailed discussion of the various sub-types of assimilation along with numerous examples of these.

Before I do that, I will define the concept of *phonetic similarity*. Two sounds can be described as being phonetically more similar to each other after a sound change has taken place if those two sounds have more phonetic features in common than they did before the change took place. If a sound change results in an increase in the number of shared features, then we can say that assimilation has taken place.

As an example I will take a word that contains a consonant cluster of the form [np] in an imaginary language. The two sounds in this cluster each have the following phonetic features:

	[n]	[p]
1.	[+ voiced]	[- voiced]
2.	[+ coronal]	[+ labial]
3.	[+ sonorant]	[- sonorant]

We could assimilate one, or two, or all of the features of one of these two sounds in the direction of the other. For instance, the **[n]** could lose its nasal feature — i.e. [+ sonorant] — and replace it with the stop feature of the **[p]** that is next to it. This change would have the following effect:

*np   →   dp

If, instead of assimilating the nasal feature to the following stop, we were to assimilate the place of articulation of the nasal to that of the following stop, we would have the following change:

*np   →   mp

Finally, if the voiced feature of the nasal were to acquire the voicelessness of the following stop, this change would show up as follows:

*np   →   n̥p

(Note that the **[n̥]** with a circle beneath it represents a voiceless alveolar nasal. Such a sound is rare in the world's languages, and the last change that I referred to would be less likely to occur than the previous two changes.)

The changes that I have just presented all involve the assimilation of only a single feature. It is, of course, possible to assimilate two features at a time, as in the following examples:

*np   →   bp

(keeping only the voicing of the nasal, but assimilating it to the following sound both in its manner of articulation and its place of articulation)

*np   →   tp

(keeping only the alveolar place of articulation of the nasal, but assimilating it to the following [p] both in its voicelessness and in its manner of articulation)

*np   →   m̥p

(keeping only the nasal feature, but assimilating it to the [p] in its voice-lessness as well as in its place of articulation)

All of these changes are examples of *partial assimilation*, because the changed sound always retains at least *one* of the original features by which it is distinguished from the unchanged sound. If *all* of the features are changed to match those of another sound, then the two sounds end up being identical and we produce a *geminate* (or phonetically double) sound. When assimilation produces geminate sounds in this way, we can speak of *total assimilation*. In the case of the cluster [np], an example of total assimilation would be a change of [*np] to [pp].

There is yet another dimension that we should discuss regarding this kind of assimilation. All of the examples that I have just presented are what are called *regressive assimilation*. This means that the 'force' of the change operates 'backwards' in the word, i.e. from right to left. It is the features of the following [p] in all of the examples above that influence the features of the preceding [n], which is why we call this regressive assimilation. This kind of assimilation can be represented in the following way:

A   <   B

(The symbol < indicates the direction of the influence of one sound over the other.)

There is, of course, a second possibility, in which the direction of the change is reversed, and it is the preceding sound that exerts its influence over the sound that follows it. This kind of situation could be represented by the symbol facing forward in the word like this:

A   >   B

Such a situation, in which the features of a following sound are changed to match those of a preceding sound, is called *progressive assimilation*. Of the two types of assimilation, it is regressive assimilation that is by far the more commonly encountered in the world's languages.

If we take the same cluster [np] and this time treat the [n] as the influencing sound rather than the [p] as before, we find that the following changes can all be regarded as examples of partial progressive assimilation:

*np	→	nb	(with assimilation of voicing)
*np	→	nt	(with assimilation of place of articulation)
*np	→	nm	(with assimilation of manner of articulation)
*np	→	nm̥	(keeping only the voiceless feature of the [p])
*np	→	nm̥	(keeping only the bilabial feature of the [p])
*np	→	nd	(keeping only the stop feature of the [p])

Progressive assimilation can be total, as well as partial, so there is also the following final possibility:

| *np | → | nn | (keeping none of the features of [p]) |

With two sounds that have only three different features each, you can see that there are fourteen possible changes that can all be classed as assimilatory. This concept therefore covers a wide range of possible sound changes, and as I said at the beginning of this section, most sound changes that take place in the languages of the world involve assimilation in one way or another.

Rather than continuing to talk about assimilation in the abstract as I have been doing, I will now give concrete examples to show how this process works. To begin with, let us look at the pronunciation of the word [klostu] 'nearby' in the Tok Pisin of some older speakers from the rural areas in Papua New Guinea who have not been to school. Such people may pronounce this as [korottu]. Ignoring for the moment the insertion of an epenthetic [o] and the shift of [l] to [r], the change that is of particular interest to us is the change of the cluster [st] to the geminate stop [tt]. The [s] has totally assimilated in all of its features to the following [t]. This is therefore a case of total regressive assimilation.

As I have already mentioned, progressive assimilation is much less common than regressive assimilation and examples are much harder to find. However, in the history of Icelandic, the following are examples of very regular total progressive assimilation:

		Icelandic	
*findan	→	finna	'find'
*gulθ	→	gull	'gold'
*halθ	→	hall	'inclined'
*munθ	→	munn	'mouth'
*unθan	→	unna	'love'

Examples of partial assimilation are more common than examples of complete assimilation. Partial assimilation can involve a wide range of possibilities, as we have already seen, with the changes involving the place of articulation (including the high, low, front, and back features of vowels, as well as the features referring to the place of articulation of consonants), manner of articulation (whether stop, fricative, nasal, lateral and so on), and voicing (whether voiced or voiceless). Assimilation may also involve any combination of these various features.

Assimilation of place of articulation is a very common change. You can see the results of this change in modern English with the varying forms of the negative prefix [ɪn-] 'in-'. This is normally pronounced with the variant [ɪm-] before bilabial consonants, [ɪŋ-] before velars and [ɪn-] before all other sounds (including vowels), e.g.

ɪn-dəvɪzəbl	'indivisible'
ɪm-bæləns	'imbalance'
ɪŋ-kənsɪdəɹət	'inconsiderate'
ɪn-ədmɪsəbl	'inadmissible'

The [n] has assimilated in its place of articulation to the following consonant, i.e. the alveolar feature has been replaced with the feature for the place of articulation of the following sound when the next sound is bilabial or velar.

The change that is known as *palatalisation* is also an assimilatory change. By this change, a non-palatal sound (i.e. a dental, an alveolar, a velar, and so on) becomes a palatal sound, usually before a front vowel such as [i] or [e], or before the semi-vowel [j]. Sounds that we can class as palatal include the palato-alveolar affricates [tʃ] and [dʒ] and the sibilants [ʃ] and [ʒ] (as well as some other consonants which are less common). This change can be described as assimilatory because the palatal feature of the vowel (i.e. the fact that it is front rather than back) is transferred to the neighbouring consonant.

One good example of palatalisation is the change from [t] to [tʃ] before the vowel [i] in many dialects of Fijian. For example, where Standard Fijian has [tinana] 'his/her mother', many of the local dialects have palatalised the initial consonant to produce [tʃinana]. There are examples of palatalisation having taken place in the history of English too. The velar stops [k] and [g] became palatalised to [tʃ] and [j] respectively when there was a following front vowel, as shown by the following examples:

		English	
*kinn	→	tʃɪn	'chin'
*kɛ:si	→	tʃi:z	'cheese'
*geldan	→	ji:ld	'yield'
*gearn	→	ja:n	'yarn, thread'

(Note that the change of [g] to [j] probably involved palatalisation of [g] to [dʒ] first, and then the [dʒ] underwent lenition to [j].)

Sometimes, a palatal that is produced as a result of this kind of assimilation can undergo lenition to become [s]. For example, in Motu in Papua New Guinea, [t] has shifted to [s] in a similar kind of palatalising environment to that described above for Fijian, even though [s] is a post-alveolar sound rather than a palatal sound. Note the following examples:

		Motu	
*tama	→	tama	'father'
*taŋis	→	tai	'cry'
*tumpu	→	tubu	'grandparent'
*topu	→	tohu	'sugarcane'
*tolu	→	toi	'three'
*tina	→	sina	'mother'
*qate	→	ase	'liver'
*mate	→	mase	'die'

In addition to assimilation involving changes in the place of articulation, changes in the manner of articulation of a sound to make two sounds phonetically more similar to each other are also common. Examine the following changes in the Banoni language of the North Solomons Province of Papua New Guinea:

		Banoni	
*pekas	→	beɣasa	'faeces'
*wakar	→	baɣara	'root'
*pakan	→	vaɣana	'add meat to staple'
*tipi	→	tsivi	'traditional dance'
*makas	→	maɣasa	'dry coconut'

The intervocalic stops in these examples have changed to become voiced fricatives in Banoni at the same place of articulation. This can be viewed as the assimilation of two of the features of the original voiceless stops to the features of the surrounding vowels. The stops have become voiced to match the feature of voicing for the vowels. The change from stop to fricative can also be considered to be assimilatory. Vowels, as well as nasals, fricatives, and laterals, are all continuant sounds in that they can be continued or 'held' as we pronounce them. These sounds contrast with non-continuant sounds, such as stops, affricates, and semi-vowels, as these kinds of sounds cannot be 'held'. The change from a stop to a continuant between two other continuant sounds is a clear case of assimilation in the manner of articulation, as well as of voicing.

Another very common type of change that can also be viewed as a special kind of assimilation is the change called *final devoicing*. Sounds at the end of a word, especially stops and fricatives (but sometimes also other sounds, even vowels) often change from being voiced to voiceless. In German, the devoicing of final stops has been very regular, for example:

		German	
*ba:d	→	ba:t	'bath'
*ta:g	→	ta:k	'day'
*hund	→	hunt	'dog'

| *land | → | lant | 'land' |
| *ga:b | → | ga:p | 'gave' |

In a case like this, the voiced feature of the original sound is changed to voiceless to match the voicelessness of the following silence at the end of the word.

There is a further aspect to assimilation that I have not yet touched on. This is the contrast between what we call *immediate assimilation* and *assimilation at a distance*. In the examples of assimilation that I have presented so far it has always been a case of one sound being influenced by the sound either immediately preceding or following it. These are, therefore, all examples of immediate assimilation.

In the case of assimilation at a distance, however, a sound is influenced by another sound not immediately to the left or the right of it, but further away in the word, perhaps even in another syllable altogether. In the Southern Highlands of Papua New Guinea, when speakers of the Huli language adopt the Tok Pisin word *piksa* 'picture' into their language, it is sometimes pronounced by older people as [kikiɖa] rather than [pikiɖa] as we might expect. What has happened is that the [p] of the first syllable has assimilated (at a distance) in place of articulation to the [k] of the second syllable.

Sometimes assimilation at a distance like this is a very regular feature of a language, and some type of assimilation may even apply over an entire word. When this happens, we call this *harmony*. Many languages have what we call *vowel harmony*, which means, basically, that there is assimilation of one (or more) features of one vowel to some (or all) of the other vowels in the same word. In Bislama, for example, we find a good example of vowel harmony involving the original transitive suffix [-im] on verbs. In Bislama, this suffix has three main variants, as illustrated below:

kuk-um	'cook'	mit-im	'meet'	har-em	'feel'
put-um	'put'	kil-im	'hit'	mek-em	'make'
sut-um	'shoot'	rit-im	'read'	so-em	'show'

Following a syllable with a high back vowel, the [i] of the suffix becomes [u]. This is an example of assimilation at a distance of the feature 'front' in one syllable to the feature 'back' in another. Following a syllable with a mid or a low vowel, the [i] of the suffix is lowered to [e]. This is again assimilation at a distance, this time with the feature 'high' changing to 'mid' under the influence of the vowel of the preceding syllable.

Sometimes you will find harmony involving features other than just vowel features. In the Enggano language (spoken on an island off the coast of southern Sumatra in Indonesia) there has been a change that we refer to as *nasal harmony*. In this language, all voiced stops in a word became homorganic nasals and all plain vowels became the corresponding nasal vowels following *any* nasal sound in a word. So:

		Enggano	
*honabu	→	honãmũ	'your wife'
*ehĕkua	→	ehĕkũã	'seat'
*euʔadaʔa	→	euʔãnãʔã	'food'

There is one special kind of vowel harmony that goes under the name of *umlaut*. This term is most frequently used in Germanic languages to refer to the fronting of a back vowel or the raising of a low vowel under the influence of a front vowel in the following syllable. Very often, the following high front vowel that caused the change to take place in the first place was then dropped in these languages (by apocope), or reduced to schwa. Thus, the new front vowel became the only way of marking the difference between some words. The irregular singular/plural pairs of words such as *foot/feet* in English are the result of such vowel harmony, or umlaut. The original singular form was [foːt], and its plural was [foːt-i]. The [oː] was later fronted to the front rounded vowel [øː] under the influence of the following front vowel [-i] in the plural suffix, so the plural came to have the shape [føːt-i]. Later, the vowel of the suffix was dropped, and the front rounded vowel of the root was unrounded to become [eː]. So, while the singular was [foːt], the plural had become [feːt]. It was this alternation between [foːt] and [feːt] that was the source of the modern irregular pair *foot/feet*. (This kind of umlaut in the history of English is described in more detail in Section 4.3.)

2.8 DISSIMILATION

Now that we have studied at length the concept of assimilation, it should be a relatively simple matter to grasp the concept of *dissimilation*. This process is precisely the opposite to assimilation. Instead of making two sounds more like each other, dissimilation means that one sound changes to become less like some other nearby sound. Dissimilation, therefore, reduces the number of shared phonetic features between two sounds.

I have already mentioned in this chapter the difficulty that we have with tongue-twisters — if you say these fast enough, you will sometimes find yourself dropping out sounds that are very similar to each other when they occur frequently in the same sentence. Another thing that happens when we say tongue-twisters is that we tend to make sounds more distinct from nearby sounds than they are supposed to be. If you say *Peter Piper picked a peck of pickled peppers* frequently, the chances are that you will end up saying *peckers* instead of *peppers*. This would perhaps be partly a case of the [p] in the word *peppers* assimilating at a distance to the [k] in words such as *picked* and *peck*, but at the same time the [p] is probably dissimilating from the other [p] sounds that are found near it in the same word.

I will mention one very famous example of dissimilation here, because it is frequently encountered in textbooks of historical linguistics, where it is often referred to as *Grassmann's Law*. This sound change, first recognised in 1862 by the German scholar Hermann Grassmann, took place both in the ancient Sanskrit language in what is now India, and in the ancient Greek language. In both of these languages, there was a phonemic contrast between aspirated and unaspirated stops. However, when there were two syllables following each other and both contained aspirated stops, the first of these lost its aspiration and became unaspirated. So, in Sanskrit, the earlier form [*bho:dha] 'bid' . became [bo:dha], and in Greek, the form [*phewtho] with the same meaning became [pewtho]. This is clearly a case of dissimilation at a distance.

An example of immediate dissimilation (rather than dissimilation at a distance) can be found in Afrikaans, the language of one of the two major tribes of Europeans in South Africa (the other being English-speakers). Observe the following changes:

		Afrikaans	
*sxo:n	→	sko:n	'clean'
*sxoudər	→	skouər	'shoulder'
*sxœlt	→	skœlt	'debt'

In the original forms, there was a sequence of two fricative sounds, i.e. [s] and [x]. In Afrikaans, the fricative [x] changed to a stop at the same place of articulation, i.e. [k], so that there would no longer be two fricatives next to each other. Thus, the [x] dissimilated in manner of articulation to [k] from the fricative [s].

2.9 ABNORMAL SOUND CHANGES

In this chapter, I have presented a wide range of types of sound changes that you will come across in languages of the world. However, there are numerous examples of sound changes in language that would appear, at first glance, to be abnormal — in the sense that they do not obviously fit into any of the categories that I have set out above. For instance, take the French word *cent* 'hundred', which is pronounced [sã]. This ultimately goes back to a form that can be reconstructed as [km̩tom] (with the first [m] being a syllabic nasal, i.e. a nasal that can be stressed in the same way as a vowel). How can the change from [km̩tom] to [sã] possibly be described in terms of the types of changes that we have been looking at in this chapter?

The answer to this question comes in the observation that, while the changes between these two forms might appear to be immense (and therefore unlikely), we can usually reconstruct various intermediate steps between the two extreme forms that appear to represent quite reasonable sorts of changes. Let us imagine that the change from [km̩tom] to [sã] in fact took place through the following series of steps over a very long period of time:

km̩tom   →   kemtom
(unpacking of features of syllabic and consonant to two separate sounds)

kemtom   →   kentom
(regressive assimilation of [m] to [t] in place of articulation)

kentom   →   kent
(loss of final unstressed syllable)

kent   →   cent
(palatalisation of [k] to [c] before front vowel)

cent   →   sent
(lenition of stop to fricative)

sent   →   sen
(loss of final consonant)

sen   →   sẽ
(fusion of features of vowel and nasal to produce nasal vowel)

sẽ   →   sã
(lowering of vowel)

(Note that while all of these changes in one way or another actually took place in the history of this word, they did not necessarily take place exactly as stated, or in the order given. The exact details of the history of this word are not particularly important for the purposes of the present discussion.)

Sometimes we find that an individual sound has changed in a rather unusual way. Although we should keep in mind the types of sound changes described in this chapter as being somehow more likely to occur than other kinds of sound change, students of languages will always come up against apparently 'odd' changes. For instance, in some languages there have been regular changes of [t] to [w], and in the Mekeo language (spoken in the Central Province of Papua New Guinea), there has been a change of both [d] and [l] to the velar nasal. This latter change is illustrated by the following examples:

		Mekeo	
*dua	→	ŋua	'two'
*dau	→	ŋaŋau	'leaf'

How might we account for such changes? Again, it is possible to suggest a series of more reasonable intermediate stages which have left no trace. The Trukese change of [t] to [w] may have passed through the following stages, for example:

[t]   →   [θ]   →   [f]   →   [v]   →   [w]

Similarly, the Mekeo change of **[d]** and **[l]** to **[ŋ]** may have gone through the following steps:

[d]   →   [l]   →   [n]   →   [ŋ]

Given a sufficient period of time, any sound can change into any other sound by a series of changes such as those we have discussed in this chapter. It is partly for this reason that the reconstruction of the history of languages by the method described in this volume has not really been able to go back further than about 10,000 years. Any changes beyond that time would probably be so great that, even if two languages were descended from a common ancestor, time would have almost completely hidden any trace of similarities that the languages may once have had.

READING GUIDE QUESTIONS

1.   What is lenition?
2.   What is rhotacism?
3.   What is cluster reduction?
4.   What is the difference between apocope and syncope?
5.   What is the difference between haplology and metathesis?
6.   What is the difference between excrescence and epenthesis?
7.   What is the difference between aphaeresis and prothesis?
8.   What is phonetic fusion?
9.   What is meant by compensatory lengthening?
10. What is the difference between phonetic unpacking and vowel breaking?
11. How is assimilation different from dissimilation?
12. What is the difference between partial and complete assimilation?
13. What is the difference between assimilation at a distance and immediate assimilation?
14. What is palatalisation, and how can this be viewed as assimilation?
15. What is final devoicing, and how can we view this as assimilation?
16. What is vowel or consonant harmony?
17. What is meant by the term umlaut?
18. What is Grassmann's Law? What sort of sound change does this involve?

EXERCISES

1.   Some of the phonetic changes described in this chapter can be regarded as belonging to more that one of the named categories of changes. For instance, final devoicing was described in Section 2.7 as a kind of

assimilation, while devoicing in general was described in Section 2.1 as lenition, or weakening. Can you find any other kinds of sound change that can be described under two different headings?

2. What do you think the spelling of the following words indicates about the phonetic history of English: *lamb, sing, night, rough, stone, mate, tune, Christmas.* Describe any changes that might have taken place in terms of the kinds of sound changes described in this chapter.

3. Many place names in England have spellings that do not reflect their actual pronunciations. From the following list, suggest the kinds of phonetic changes that may have taken place as suggested by the original spellings:

Cirencester   [sɪstə]
Salisbury   [sɒlzbɹi]
Barnoldswick   [baːlɪk]
Leicester   [lɛstə]
Chiswick   [ʧɪzɪk]
Cholmondely   [ʧʌmli]
Gloucester   [glɒstə]

4. Speakers of English for whom English is their first language pronounce the following words as shown:

society   [səsaɪəti]
social   [souʃəl]
taxation   [tækseɪʃən]
decision   [dəsɪʒən]

Papua New Guineans speaking English frequently pronounce these words as **[səsaɪəti]**, **[ʃouʃəl]**, **[tækʃeɪʃən]**, and **[dəʃɪʒən]** respectively. What kind of phonetic changes do these pronunciations involve?

5. A change of **[mp]** to **[b]** has taken place in the Banoni language of the North Solomons in Papua New Guinea, as illustrated by the word initial changes in the following words:

*mpaɣa   →   bara   'fence'
*mpunso   →   busa   'fill'
*mpua   →   buɣava   'betel nut'

This change can be described as a kind of fusion. Why?

6. The following changes have taken place in Romanian. Should we describe these changes as phonetic unpacking or as vowel breaking? Why?

*pɔti   →   pwate   'he is able'
*pɔrta   →   pwartə   'door'
*nɔkti   →   nwapte   'night'

*flori	→	flwarə	'flower'
*ora	→	warə	'hour'
*eska	→	jaskə	'bait'
*ɛrba	→	jarbə	'grass'

7. The following changes took place in some dialects of Old English. Should we describe these as phonetic unpacking or as vowel breaking?

*kald	→	keald	'cold'
*erða	→	eorða	'earth'
*lirnjan	→	liornjan	'learn'
*melkan	→	meolkan	'milk'

8. In the following data from the northern dialect of Paamese (Vanuatu), why do we say that assimilation has taken place? What particular kind of assimilation is involved?

*kail	→	keil	'they'
*aim	→	eim	'house'
*haih	→	heih	'pandanus'
*auh	→	ouh	'yam'
*sautin	→	soutin	'distant'
*haulu	→	houlu	'many'

9. In the following data from Toba Batak (Sumatra), what kind of assimilation has taken place?

*hentak	→	ottak	'knock'
*kimpal	→	hippal	'lump of earth'
*cintak	→	sittak	'draw sword'
*ciŋkəp	→	sikkop	'enough'
*pintu	→	pittu	'door'

10. In the following Italian data, what kind of assimilation has taken place?

*noktem	→	notte	'night'
*faktum	→	fatto	'done'
*ruptum	→	rotto	'broken'
*septem	→	sette	'seven'
*aptum	→	atto	'apt'
*somnus	→	sonno	'sleep'

11. In the following Banoni forms, there is evidence of more than one pattern of assimilation having taken place. What are these patterns?

*manuk	→	manuɣa	'bird'
*kulit	→	ɣuritsi	'skin sugarcane'
*nɟalan	→	sanana	'road'
*taŋis	→	taŋisi	'cry'
*pekas	→	beɣasa	'faeces'
*poɣok	→	boroɣo	'pig'

12. Old English had a causative suffix of the form **[-j]**, and an infinitive suffix of the form **[-an]**, both of which have been lost in Modern English, and their original functions are now expressed in different ways. Examine the pair of words below from Old English:

    drink-an   'to drink'
    drink-j-an   'to cause (someone) to drink'

    The modern words *drink* and *drench* respectively evolved from these two words. What sort of change has been involved to derive the final consonant of *drench*?

13. In the Marshallese language of Micronesia, the following changes have taken place:

    | *mataɲa | → | medan | 'his/her eye' |
    | *damaɲa | → | dem^wan | 'his/her forehead' |
    | *masakit | → | metak | 'pain' |
    | *masala | → | metal | 'smooth' |
    | *nsakaɣu | → | tekaj | 'reef' |
    | *madama | → | meram | 'light' |

    How would you characterise the changes that have affected the vowels in Marshallese?

14. In Data Set 1, a series of sound changes in Palauan is presented. Try to classify these changes according to the types of sound change discussed in this chapter.

15. Examine the forms in Nganyaywana in Data Set 2. The original forms are given on the left. Try to classify the changes that have taken place.

16. Refer to the forms in Mbabaram in Data Set 3. Try to describe the kinds of changes that have taken place.

17. From the data in Yimas and Karawari given in Data Set 4, what kinds of changes would you say had taken place in each of these two languages?

18. Assume that in some language, the following sound changes took place. These changes all appear to be quite abnormal in that there is no simple change of features from one stage to the other. Can you suggest a

succession of more reasonable sounding intermediate steps to account for
these unusual results?

b	→	h
e	→	l
k	→	r
k	→	s
p	→	w
l	→	i
k	→	h
ɣ	→	ʔ
s	→	ʔ
s	→	r
t	→	f
b	→	l

19. Can we argue that there is some kind of 'conspiracy' in languages to
    produce **CV** syllable structures? What kinds of sound changes produce
    this kind of syllable structure? What kinds of sound changes *destroy* this
    kind of syllable structure?
20. In the Rotuman language (spoken near Fiji) words appearing in citation
    (i.e. when the word is being quoted rather than being used in a sentence)
    differ in shape from words that occur in a natural context. Some of these
    different forms are presented below. Assuming that the contextual forms
    are historically derived from the citation forms, what sort of change
    would you say has taken place?

Citation Form	Contextual Form	
laje	laej	'coral'
kami	kaim	'dog'
rako	raok	'learn'
maho	maoh	'get cold'
tepi	teip	'slow'
hefu	heuf	'star'
lima	liam	'five'
tiko	tiok	'flesh'
hosa	hoas	'flower'
mose	moes	'sleep'
pure	puer	'rule'

21. In Bislama (Vanuatu), the word for 'rubbish tin' is generally pronounced
    as **[pubel]**. Some speakers pronounce this in Bislama as **[kubel]**. What
    sort of change is involved here?
22. Compare the forms in Standard French and the French that is spoken in
    rural Québec in Data Set 12. Assuming that the Standard French forms

represent the original situation, what kinds of changes have taken place in the French that is spoken in Québec?

FURTHER READING

1. Leonard Bloomfield *Language*, Chapter 21 'Types of Phonetic Change', pp. 369–91.
2. Anthony Arlotto *Introduction to Historical Linguistics,* Chapter 6 'Types of Sound Change', pp. 77–89.
3. Robert J. Jeffers and Ilse Lehiste *Principles and Methods for Historical Linguistics,* Chapter 1 'Phonetic Change', pp. 1–16.
4. Mary Haas *The Prehistory of Languages*, 'Phonological loss and addition', pp. 39–44.
5. Hans Henrich Hock *Principles of Historical Linguistics*, Chapters 5–7 'Sound Change', pp. 61–147.

CHAPTER THREE

EXPRESSING SOUND CHANGES

3.1 WRITING RULES

When reading the literature of the history of sound changes in languages, you are almost certain to come across various formal rules written by linguists to express these changes. You will therefore need to know how to write and interpret such rules. This short section of the chapter aims to provide you with this knowledge.

When a sound undergoes a particular change wherever that sound occurs in a language, we refer to this as an *unconditioned sound change*. Comparatively few sound changes are completely unconditioned, as generally there are at least some environments (however restricted) in which the change does not take place, or in which perhaps some other changes occur. One example of a completely unconditioned sound is that found in the Motu language of Papua New Guinea, where there has been an unconditioned loss of earlier [ŋ], as shown by the following forms:

		Motu	
*asaŋ	→	lada	'gills of fish'
*taŋi	→	tai	'cry'
*laŋi	→	lai	'wind'
*taliŋa	→	taia	'ear'

Similarly, in Hawaiian there was an unconditioned change of [t] to [k], and another of [ŋ] to [n], as shown by the forms presented below:

63

		Hawaiian	
*tapu	→	kapu	'forbidden'
*taŋi	→	kani	'cry'
*taŋata	→	kanaka	'man'
*ŋutu	→	nuku	'mouth'
*tolu	→	kolu	'three'

Unconditioned sound changes such as these are the simplest historical changes to express in terms of formal rules. The earlier form is given on the left, and the later form on the right, with the two being linked by an arrow. So, the Hawaiian changes just described can be expressed simply as:

t	→	k
ŋ	→	n

The Motu change involving the loss of the velar nasal can be expressed as:

ŋ	→	ø

(The symbol ø represents the absence of any sound.)

A great many sound changes only take place in certain phonetic environments, rather than in all environments in which the sound occurs. Such changes are referred to as *conditioned sound changes*, or sometimes as *combinatory sound changes*. Most of the sound changes that you saw in chapter 2 were conditioned sound changes. A sound change can be conditioned by a great range of different types of environments. Factors to consider include the position of the sound in a word (whether it is initial, final or medial), the nature of the preceding and following sounds, the position of stress, whether or not the syllable is open, or perhaps some combination of such conditioning environments.

If a change takes place only in a specific phonetic environment, this environment is written following a single slash (/). The location of the changing sound with respect to the conditioning environment is indicated by a line (____). If a change takes place before some other sound, then the line is placed before the sound that conditions the change; if a change takes place after some other sound, then the line follows the conditioning sound. Some examples of rules expressing conditioned changes that we have looked at, with their expressions in words, are given below:

t → s / ____ front   [t] became [s] before front vowels (in Motu)
            V

x → k / s ____   [x] became [k] after [s] (in Afrikaans)

p → v / V____V   [p] became [v] between vowels (in Banoni)

(Note that the symbol **V** is the standard symbol to express any unspecified vowel. Similarly, any unspecified consonant is expressed by the symbol **C**.)

To express the fact that a change takes place word finally or word initially, we use the symbol # to represent the beginning or end of a word, as follows:

$$p \rightarrow w \,/\, \# \underline{\quad}$$

(Initial [**p**] became [**w**] (in Uradhi).)

$$\text{voiced} \rightarrow \text{voiceless} \,/\, \underline{\quad} \#$$
$$\quad C \qquad\qquad C$$

(Final voiced consonants became voiceless (in German).)

$$V \rightarrow \emptyset \,/\, \underline{\quad} \#$$

(Word final vowels were deleted (in Southeast Ambrym).)

Elements that are optional (i.e. whose presence or absence does not affect the application of the rule) are placed in round brackets. Thus:

$$V \rightarrow /\, V \;\; (C) \underline{\quad}$$
$$\quad\;\; [nas]$$

(Vowels were nasalised after nasal vowels, whether or not there is an intervening consonant (in Enggano).)

When there are two different sets of sounds involved in a change, this can be represented by placing the sounds one above the other in curly brackets. The Enggano nasal harmony rule described in Section 2.7 earlier can actually be described more fully in the following way:

$$
\left\{ \begin{matrix} V \\ \text{voiced stop} \end{matrix} \right\}
\rightarrow
\left\{ \begin{matrix} V & / & V \\ [nas] & & [nas] \\ \text{nasal} & & \text{nasal} \end{matrix} \right\}
\;\; (C) \;\; \underline{\quad}
$$

(A vowel or voiced stop became a nasalised vowel or a nasal consonant respectively when there is a preceding nasal vowel or nasal consonant.)

Also, the change in Motu involving palatalisation (and subsequent lenition) that I described earlier can be alternatively expressed as:

$$t \rightarrow s \,/\; \underline{\quad} \;\; \left\{ \begin{matrix} i \\ e \end{matrix} \right\} \qquad \text{[t] became [s] before [i] or [e]}$$

(Note that although this is an alternative formulation for the change in Motu, it is considered to be a less 'elegant' statement because it misses the generalisation that the conditioning environment is the class of front vowels.)

Rules should always be stated in as general a way as possible, without being *too* general. They are meant to be interpreted literally, so they should not point to changes that did not actually take place. So, while it is true to say that both [i] and [e] are unrounded vowels, we cannot represent this change in Motu as follows:

$$\text{V}$$
$$t \rightarrow s / \underline{} \quad \text{unrounded}$$

This would be incorrect because [a] is also an unrounded vowel and the change of [t] to [s] did *not* take place before [a].

3.2 ORDERING OF CHANGES

When a language undergoes a whole series of sound changes, it is sometimes possible to reconstruct not only the changes themselves, but also the order in which the changes took place. Let us examine the following data from Hawaiian:

		Hawaiian	
*taŋi	→	kani	'cry'
*kaso	→	ʔaho	'thatch'
*takele	→	kaʔele	'back of canoe'
*aka	→	aʔa	'root'
*pito	→	piko	'navel'
*paki	→	paʔi	'slap'
*tapu	→	kapu	'forbidden'
*taŋata	→	kanaka	'man'
*isu	→	ihu	'nose'
*sika	→	hiʔa	'firemaking'

This set of data reveals that the following unconditioned changes have taken place:

t	→	k
k	→	ʔ
ŋ	→	n
s	→	h

Of these four changes, we can say something about the order in which they applied. To begin with, let us check the first two sound changes to see if we can decide whether [t] shifted to [k] first, or whether [k] first shifted to [ʔ]. If we were to assume that the [t] first shifted to [k], and that the other shift of [k] to [ʔ] took place after this, then changes like the following would have taken place:

*takele	→	kakele	'back of canoe'
*pito	→	piko	'navel'
*tapu	→	kapu	'forbidden'

If [k] then shifted to [ʔ], these words would also have changed as follows, along with all of the other words that contained [k]:

*kakele	→	ʔaʔele	'back of canoe'
*piko	→	piʔo	'navel'
*kapu	→	ʔapu	'forbidden'

The forms [ʔaʔele], [piʔo] and [ʔapu], however, are not the correct forms in Hawaiian, as these words should contain the [k] sound rather than glottal stops. So we must conclude that at the time that [k] shifted to [ʔ] in Hawaiian, there must still have been a distinction between [k] and [t], otherwise all original [k] and [t] would have ended up as [ʔ]. If we were to assume that these two changes applied in the opposite order, then we would get the correct results:

Protolanguage	Stage 1 k → ʔ	Stage 2 t → k	Modern Hawaiian	
*takele	taʔele	kaʔele	kaʔele	'back of canoe'
*aka	aʔa		aʔa	'root'
*pito		piko	piko	'navel'
*paki	paʔi		paʔi	'slap'
*tapu		kapu	kapu	'forbidden'

We can represent this by placing one rule over another and linking the two in the following way:

$$\left\{ \begin{array}{l} k \to ʔ \\ t \to k \end{array} \right.$$

But what about the other changes that have taken place? Can we say anything about whether these changes took place before or after (or between) the two changes that we have just looked at? In fact, we can only come to conclusions about the ordering of sound changes when the changed sound, or the sounds involved in the conditioning of a change, actually *overlap* in some way. In the shift of [t] to [k] and the shift of [k] to [ʔ], we were able to say something about the ordering of the two rules because the symbol [k] appears somewhere in the statement of *both* of these changes. In the Hawaiian data that I presented above, there were also two other changes involved:

ŋ → n
s → h

None of the symbols in these two rules appear in the statements for either of the changes that I have just been describing. As there is no overlap between the symbols involved in the statement of any of these rules, we cannot come to any conclusion about the ordering of these rules. It does not make any difference whether we apply these two rules first, last, or between the other rules — the end results will not be affected in any way. Historically, of course, these two changes must have applied at some period, either before the change of [k] to [ʔ], or after it, or perhaps at the same time as that change. However, on the evidence that we have, there is no way that we can find out when these other changes took place.

In listing the full set of changes for this set of data in Hawaiian, we can indicate the fact that there is no evidence that a particular change is ordered either before or after any other change simply by not linking them as we did above. So, the ordering of these four changes could be equally represented in any of the following ways:

k → ʔ	k → ʔ	ŋ → n
t → k	s → h	s → h
ŋ → n	t → k	k → ʔ
s → h	ŋ → n	t → k

In fact, it does not matter in what order you write the rules for these changes, as the only changes that are linked in time are those that are marked with the special symbol that is used for indicating the ordering of sound changes. The placement of any other changes among a set of changes is purely a matter of convenience.

Let us now look at a more complicated example, in which conditioned sound changes are involved. The data comes from the Banoni language of the North Solomons Province of Papua New Guinea.

		Banoni	
*koti	→	kotsi	'cut'
*tina	→	tsina	'mother'
*puti	→	putsi	'pull out'
*mata	→	mata	'eye'
*mate	→	mate	'die'
*matua	→	matsua	'rise'
*makas	→	maɣasa	'dry coconut'
*pakan	→	vaɣana	'add meat to staple'
*kulit	→	ɣuritsi	'skin sugarcane'

The sound changes that I will look at are the following:

$$
t \;\rightarrow\; ts \;/\; \underline{\quad} \; \text{high V}
$$

$$
\emptyset \;\rightarrow\; \left\{\begin{array}{c} i \\ e \\ a \\ o \\ u \end{array}\right\} \;/\; \left\{\begin{array}{c} i \\ e \\ a \\ o \\ u \end{array}\right\} \; C \underline{\quad} \#
$$

The first rule changes [t] to [ts] before the high vowels [i] or [u]. The second rule involves the addition of a harmonising vowel after a consonant at the end of a word. (There are some other changes indicated in this data, but these will be ignored at this point.)

The question that you should ask yourself is: can these two changes be ordered with respect to each other? According to what I said earlier, if two changes involve some common sound either in the changing sounds or in the conditioning sounds, then we can test to see which applied first. Since these two rules both involve the symbol V referring to vowels, we can test them for ordering.

If we were to assume that the change of [t] to [ts] took place first, we could correctly predict the application of this change in all cases but one — the Banoni form of the original word [*kulit] 'skin sugarcane'. Because this form has no following vowel in the protolanguage, it does not meet all of the conditions for the application of the rule that changes [t] to [ts]. However, if the vowel addition rule were to apply only after the change of [t] to [ts], we would end up with [ɣuriti] for this word (assuming that we apply the other incidental consonant changes as well). The fact that the actual form is [ɣuritsi] rather than [ɣuriti] means that there must already have been a high vowel after the [t] when the rule affecting the [t] applied. This shows that the rule adding a final harmonising vowel must have applied before the rule changing the [t] to [ts]. So, we can state the ordering of these two changes as follows:

$$
\left(\begin{array}{l} \text{Harmonising Vowel Addition} \\ [t] \rightarrow [ts] \end{array}\right.
$$

READING GUIDE QUESTIONS

1. What is meant by saying that rules should be written to be as general as possible but not *too* general?
2. What is meant by speaking of ordered rules?
3. How do we decide on the ordering of rules and how do we show the relative ordering of rules?

EXERCISES

1. Express the following changes formally:
   (a) intervocalic [s] undergoes rhotacism while [s] before consonants is deleted
   (b) word initial consonants undergo weakening to [j]
   (c) intervocalic [h] changes to glottal stop
   (d) the second member of all consonant clusters is deleted
   (e) an epenthetic [o] is added between the two members of a word final consonant cluster
   (f) word final high vowels are deleted while interconsonantal high vowels become schwa
   (g) a prothetic [h] is added before [e] and [o]
2. Examine the Nganyaywana forms in Data Set 2.
   (a) Under what conditions are the vowels of initial syllables retained, and when are they lost?
   (b) Long vowels are shortened. Did this change take place before or after the loss of vowels dealt with in the previous question? Why?
3. Examine the Mbabaram forms in Data Set 3.
   (a) Some word-final [a] became [e], some became [o], and some remained unchanged. What are the conditioning factors?
   (b) Initial syllables were lost. Did this change take place before or after the changes affecting final [a]? Why?
4. Examine the Yimas and Karawari forms in Data Set 4.
   (a) Formulate explicit rules for the changes that have taken place in each of the two languages.
   (b) Can you find any evidence concerning the ordering of any of these changes either in Yimas or Karawari?
   (c) Given the following original forms, what would you expect the modern Yimas and Karawari words to be?

*simari	'sun'
*simasim	'sago'
*naŋgun	'mosquito'

5. Examine the Lakalai forms in Data Set 5.

(a) Write formal rules to account for all of the changes that have taken place.

(b) Do any of these changes need to be ordered with respect to each other? Why?

6. Examine the changes in Motu in Data Set 9.

(a) What are the rules that express the various changes that have taken place here?

(b) What is the ordering of these rules?

7. Examine the Burduna forms in Data Set 11.

(a) Write rules that express the changes that have taken place.

(b) Is there any evidence that any of these changes must have taken place before any others? If so, say what they are.

8. Examine the following data from the Mpakwithi language of Cape York Peninsula in northern Queensland (Australia):

*maɹa	→	ʔa	'hand'
*kuta	→	ʔwa	'dog'
*pakaj	→	kaɹa	'down'
*pama	→	ma	'person'
*puŋku	→	gu	'knee'
*ɲipima	→	pimi	'one'
*muŋka	→	gwa	'eat'
*ʈuma	→	mwa	'fire'
*ɲaŋku	→	gaw	'that'
*japi	→	paj	'forehead'
*ŋampu	→	baw	'tooth'

(a) Describe in words the changes that have taken place in this language. (There is not enough data here for you to be able to write fully explicit rules.)

(b) Can you suggest anything about the order in which these changes have taken place?

9. Examine the standard French and rural Québec French forms in Data Set 12. Assuming that the standard French forms represent the original pronunciation, except that [ʁ] was originally pronounced as [r], write rules expressing the changes that have taken place in rural Québec French.

CHAPTER FOUR

PHONETIC VS PHONEMIC CHANGE

When a linguist describes the synchronic sound system of a language, she or he must be aware of the fact that there is a difference between a phonetic description of a language and a phonemic description of the language. A phonetic description of a language simply describes the physical facts of the sounds of the language. A phonemic description, however, describes not the physical facts, but the way that these sounds are related to each other for speakers of that particular language. It is possible for two languages to have the same physical sounds, yet to have very different phonemic systems. The phonemic description therefore tells us what are the basic sound units for a particular language that enable its speakers to differentiate meanings.

Just as it is possible to describe a language synchronically both in phonetic and phonemic terms, it is possible to make a distinction between a diachronic phonetic study and a diachronic phonemic study of a language. It is possible, therefore, for some sound changes to take place without altering the phonemic structure of a language, though many sound changes *do* alter the phonemic structure of a language. However, it is also possible for a phonemic change to take place in a language without there being a phonetic change.

4.1 PHONETIC CHANGE WITHOUT PHONEMIC CHANGE

Many phonetic changes take place in languages without in any way altering phoneme inventory or the relations between phonemes. Such change is therefore purely *allophonic* or *sub-phonemic*. All that happens is that a phoneme develops a new allophone (or changes its phonetic form slightly), or the distribution of existing allophones of a phoneme is changed.

One example of a sub-phonemic change in the history of English involves the phoneme /r/. This phoneme has always been spelt *r*, suggesting that speakers of English have not perceived any change in this sound. However, we do know that earlier, the phoneme /r/ was pronounced phonetically as a flap or as a trill (as is still the case in Scots English), rather than as the frictionless continuant [ɹ] that most speakers of English pronounce today. However, although this sound has changed phonetically, it has not caused any reanalysis of the phonological system to take place. The same words that used to be distinguished in meaning from other words by a flap or a trill are now distinguished instead by [ɹ]. This change could be represented as:

/r/: [ɾ] ~ [r] → /r/: [ɹ]

Another example of phonetic change without phonemic change from the history of English involves the short high front vowel phoneme. In most dialects of English this is pronounced as [ɪ]. In the New Zealand dialect of English, however, this has been centralised in the direction of [ɨ]. The change from [ɪ] to [ɨ] has again not caused any new meaning contrasts to develop. The same words are distinguished in New Zealand English as in other varieties of English, only by a slightly different phonetic form. Again, this purely allophonic change can be represented as:

/ɪ/: [ɪ] → /ɪ/: [ɨ]

The final example that I will give of sub-phonemic change comes from the Motu language of Papua New Guinea. The previous two examples from English involve a change in the phonetic form of the phoneme wherever it occurs, i.e. they are examples of unconditioned allophonic change. However, in the case of a conditioned sub-phonemic change, a new allophone is created in a particular phonetic environment, though the sound remains unchanged in other environments. No new phonemes are created, only a new allophone of an existing phoneme.

You should remember from Chapter 2 that, in Motu, [t] has shifted to [s] before front vowels, while remaining unchanged in other environments. This change is the only source of the sound [s] in Motu, as no other sound changes have produced any [s], and there was no [s] sound at all in the protolanguage. This means that the shift of [t] to [s] did not in any way affect the phonemic structure of the language. All instances of the sound [s] in Motu today are in complementary distribution with [t]. The sound [s] only ever occurs before front vowels, while [t] never occurs before front vowels. The [s] that developed was simply a new allophone of the phoneme /t/.[1] This change can therefore be stated as:

---

[1] Note that although the Motu spelling system distinguishes *s* from *t*, this is only because the European missionaries who devised the spelling system were not familiar with the concept of the phoneme, and simply assumed that because [s] and [t] need to be distinguished in English, they should also be distinguished in Motu.

$$/t/ : [t] \rightarrow /t/ : \begin{cases} [s] \text{ before front vowels} \\ [t] \text{ elsewhere} \end{cases}$$

4.2 PHONETIC CHANGE WITH PHONEMIC CHANGE

You saw in the preceding section that a phonetic change need not necessarily lead to a change in the phonemic system of a language. Very often, however, phonetic change *does* lead to some kind of phonemic change. Generally speaking, we can say that phonetic change is a 'tool' of phonemic change in the sense that most instances of phonemic change are the result of a phonetic change in that particular sound. Phonemic changes can be subcategorised into three different types: *phonemic loss, phonemic addition,* and *rephonemicisation.*

(a) Phonemic loss
The term *phonemic loss* is self-explanatory. Phoneme loss takes place when a phoneme disappears altogether between different stages of a language. All cases of unconditioned sound loss at the phonetic level necessarily imply complete phonemic loss. An example of such a loss is the disappearance of the velar nasal from the phoneme inventory of Motu, which you saw in the previous chapter.

Phoneme loss often involves a conditioned sound change, occurring in some environments and not in others. While the loss of the velar nasal in Motu is an unconditioned sound change, you will frequently find that only *some* occurrences of a phoneme are lost, while others are retained. This situation can be referred to as *partial loss*, in contrast to *complete loss*. For an example of partial loss in Fijian, refer to the earlier discussion of the loss of final consonants. This change can be represented as:

$$C \rightarrow \emptyset / \underline{\quad} \#$$

In the Angkamuthi example that immediately followed the Fijian example in Chapter 2, you can see that there has been partial consonantal loss again, this time in word initial position (which I referred to then as aphaeresis), according to the following rule:

$$C \rightarrow \emptyset / \# \underline{\quad}$$

(b) Phonemic addition
This term is also self-explanatory. *Phoneme addition* takes place when a phoneme is inserted in a word, in a position in which that phoneme did not originally occur. For example, in Motu again, a prothetic /l/ was added before

the vowel /a/, creating a new set of words distinguished by this sound, as you saw in Chapter 2.

Note, however, that simple phonetic addition does not necessarily lead to phonemic addition. It is possible for a sound to be added without actually affecting the phonemic form of a word. In the Mpakwithi language of northern Queensland (in Australia), for example, words beginning with fricatives and the rhotic flap have added an optional prothetic schwa, for example:

/βaði/ : [βaði] ~ [əβaði]   'intestines'
/ðaj/ : [ðaj] ~ [əðaj]   'mother'
/ra/ : [ra] ~ [əra]   'stomach'

There is no separate schwa phoneme in this language. The sound [ə] occurs only in forms such as those just given, and it is competely predictable in its occurrence. Since it is completely predictable, it has no phonemic status. It can, in a sense, be considered to be a word-initial allophone of /ø/, which could be described as follows:

$$/ø/ : [ø] \sim [ə] / \# \_\_\_ \begin{Bmatrix} \text{fricative} \\ r \end{Bmatrix}$$

While the following phonetic change has taken place (i.e. a schwa is added before fricatives and /r/ at the beginning of a word), the actual *phonemic* form of such words has not changed:

$$ø \rightarrow ə / \# \_\_\_ \begin{Bmatrix} \text{fricative} \\ r \end{Bmatrix}$$

This has therefore been an example of phonetic addition *without* phonemic addition.

(c) Rephonemicisation

The most common kind of phonemic change to result from phonetic change is *rephonemicisation*. What this involves is the creation of a new pattern of oppositions in a language by simply changing around some of the existing phonemes, or by changing some of the existing phonemes into completely new phonemes. Whereas phoneme addition means adding a new phoneme in a word where there was no phoneme originally, and phoneme loss means deleting a phoneme from a word where there originally was one, re-phonemicisation involves changing around the phonemes that are already there in the word. There are a number of different kinds of rephonemicisation: *shift*, *merger*, and *split*. I will describe each of these below.

The first kind of rephonemicisation that we will consider goes under the name of *shift*. When phonemic shift has taken place, two words that were distinguished in the protolanguage by means of a particular pair of sounds are still distinguished in the daughter language, but the distinction between the two words is marked by a different pair of sounds. That is to say, a minimal pair in the protolanguage will still be different in the daughter language, but the difference will not be marked by the original sounds. For instance, in the Banoni language of Papua New Guinea, you saw in Section 2.7 that voiceless stops between vowels became voiced fricatives (along with a number of other changes). It is quite possible to imagine a minimal pair in the protolanguage in which meanings are distinguished by the presence or absence of a voiceless stop between vowels. In the modern language, however, the same difference in meaning will be marked instead by the presence or absence of a voiced fricative in the same position.

A thoughtful reader should have noticed that this description of phonemic shift does not seem to be very different from what I said earlier about purely phonetic change. When allophonic change takes place, there is also a change in the actual sounds that are used to distinguish meanings. The important difference between the two situations is that, with phonemic shift, the original sound and the new sound must actually belong to separate phonemes. In Banoni today, there are pairs to show that voiceless stops and voiced fricatives are phonemically distinct, for example:

> [kasiː]   'my brother'
> [ɣasi]   'open'

This shows that when the voiceless stops changed to voiced fricatives, there was an actual shifting around of phonemes in the language, and not just a shifting around of the allophones within a phoneme.

The second kind of rephonemicisation that I will describe is phonemic *merger*. This is the process by which two separate phonemes end up as a single phoneme. Words that used to be distinguished by some difference in sound cease to be distinguished, and what were originally minimal pairs become *homophones* (or *homonyms*) i.e. words with the same form but different meanings. For instance, the Motu word /**lada**/ is a homophone, referring both to 'gills of fish' and 'name'. In the protolanguage from which Motu was derived, there were originally two different words, distinguished by different phonemes:

> *aɟan   'name'
> *asaŋ   'gills of fish'

There has been a phonemic merger of /ɟ/ and /s/ as /d/ (as well as a loss of final consonants and the addition of a prothetic /l/), producing the modern homophone.

There are also numerous examples of phonemic merger between English and Tok Pisin. For instance, in some cases, the English vowels [ɒ], [aː] and [æ] have all merged in Tok Pisin as [a]. Many speakers of Tok Pisin do not distinguish a three-way set of minimal pairs in English such as the following:

/hɒt/	'hot'
/haːt/	'heart'
/hæt/	'hat'

The result of this merger in Tok Pisin is the homophone **/hat/** 'hot, heart, hat'.
   Phonemic merger can be represented as:

$$\left.\begin{array}{c} X \\ \\ Y \end{array}\right\} \quad \rightarrow \quad Z$$

(although merger can involve more than just two sounds).
   When phonemes merge in this way, there are two possible forms for the phoneme that is symbolised above as Z. Firstly, Z could be identical to one of the original phonemes. Secondly, it could be different from either of the original phonemes (i.e. a completely new phoneme). An example of phonemic merger where the resulting phoneme is phonetically the same as one of the original phonemes is Uradhi, an Australian language of northern Queensland:

		Uradhi	
*paṯa	→	waṯa	'bite'
*pinta	→	winta	'arm'
*pupu	→	wupu	'buttocks'
*wapun	→	wapun	'head'
*wujpu	→	wujpu	'old man'

The original /p/ and /w/ have merged as /w/ (though only in word-initial position):

$$\left.\begin{array}{c} p \\ \\ w \end{array}\right\} \quad \rightarrow \quad w\ /\ \#\ \underline{\quad}$$

An example of the second possibility is the following change in Fijian:

		Fijian	
*tuba	→	tuva	'fish poison'
*batu	→	vatu	'stone'
*ubi	→	uvi	'yam'
*pitu	→	vitu	'seven'
*pəɲu	→	vonu	'turtle'

The original phonemic distinction between /b/ and /p/ is lost, and the descendant of the merged phoneme is different from either of the original phonemes, i.e. /v/:

$$\left.\begin{array}{c} b \\ \\ p \end{array}\right\} \quad \rightarrow \quad v$$

I have been talking about *merger*, but I have not pointed out that there is a distinction to be made between *partial merger* and *complete merger*. Complete merger means that the sound change that produces the merger is unconditioned, i.e. the change affects that particular sound in all environments in which it occurs. Partial merger, on the other hand, means that the sound change is a conditioned one, i.e. the particular phonemes merge only in certain environments, and are kept distinct in others. The example that I gave above of Uradhi as an example of the merger of /p/ and /w/ is actually an example of partial rather than complete merger, as it was necessary to indicate the environment in which the change took place. The merger takes place only word-initially, while in word-medial position the original distinction between /p/ and /w/ is maintained.

Phonemic *split* is the category of rephonemicisation that I will now describe. This kind of change has precisely the opposite effect to that of phonemic merger, in that words which originally contained the same phoneme end up having different phonemes. Phonemic split can arise when a single sound changes in different ways in different phonological environments. We can represent this kind of change in the following way:

$$X \; \rightarrow \; \left\{ \begin{array}{l} Y \, / \, A \\ \\ Z \, / \, B \end{array} \right.$$

However, if there is a conditioned sound change of this type, and the *only* source for the new sound is this change, then we cannot speak of phonemic split. What we have is a case of sub-phonemic change, as we have only produced a new allophone of an existing phoneme in a specific environment. This is exactly what we saw happening in Motu, where the original [t] has changed to [s] in some environments, and remained as [t] in others. This cannot be considered as phonemic split, because no new phonemes are involved.

But if two or more sound changes operate at once to produce the same sound, then we can speak of phonemic split. In the Angkamuthi language of Cape York in Queensland (Australia), the following change took place:

$$l \; \rightarrow \; \left\{ \begin{array}{l} j \, / \, \# \, \underline{\quad} \, a, \, i \\ \\ l \, / \, \# \, \underline{\quad} \, u \end{array} \right.$$

If there were no other changes word-initially (and if there was not already a phoneme /j/ in the language) we could say that this change simply produces a new allophone of /l/ word initially before /a/ and /i/. If there was not an original /j/ phoneme and the following change were to take place, we could also speak of genuine phonemic split taking place:

l   →   j

With this change, /j/ and /l/ could no longer be in complementary distribution, so a phonemic split would have resulted.

4.3 PHONEMIC CHANGE WITHOUT PHONETIC CHANGE

In this section, we will look at a series of situations in which the phonemic status of a sound changes without any actual phonetic change taking place in the sound that has changed phonemically (though there may be phonetic changes elsewhere in the word).

(a) Loss of conditioning environment
Originally, in English, there was no velar nasal phoneme /ŋ/, though this sound did occur as an allophone of the phoneme /n/ before velar sounds. This can be represented by the allophonic statement below:

/n/ :
  [ŋ] before velars

  [n] elsewhere

A word like *singer*, which we now write phonemically as /sɪŋə/, was originally phonemically /sɪngə/, but phonetically the medial nasal had the same pronunciation as it has today. This word was therefore pronounced as [sɪŋgə]. This is therefore an example of a phonemic change (i.e. /n/ shifting to /ŋ/) that does not involve any phonetic change. How did this come about?

The separate status of the phoneme /ŋ/ came about as the result of *another* change that caused the loss of the sound that conditioned the choice between the alveolar and the velar allophones of /n/. Look at the following earlier forms and the changes that they underwent. (These forms are given first phonemically; the second form in square brackets gives the actual phonetic form.)

Earlier English		Modern English	
*/sɪn/ : [sɪn]	→	/sɪn/ : [sɪn]	'sin'
*/sɪng/ : [sɪŋg]	→	/sɪŋ/ : [sɪŋ]	'sing'
*/læmb/ : [læmb]	→	/læm/ : [læm]	'lamb'

Word-finally after nasals in English, the voiced stops /b/ and /g/ (but not /d/) were lost by a rule of the form:

$$\left.\begin{array}{c} b \\ \\ g \end{array}\right\} \rightarrow \text{ø / nasal \_\_\_ \#}$$

This explains the presence of the so-called 'silent *b*' in words such as *climb*, *lamb*, and so on. Now, you will remember that it was the presence of a velar phoneme earlier in English that conditioned the choice of a velar allophone of the phoneme /n/ rather than an alveolar allophone. So, phonemic /sɪng/ was phonetically [sɪŋg] (as it still is in some northern dialects in England). However, once the final /g/ was lost, the [ŋ] now came to be in contrastive distribution with [n], whereas before the two were in complementary distribution. As evidence of this, we find the minimal pair /sɪŋ/ 'sing' and /sɪn/ 'sin'. Here you can see that although the velar nasal itself did not change *phonetically* in English, its *phonemic* status has changed because its original conditioning environment has been lost.

Another well known example of this kind of change is the development of umlaut in Germanic languages. Umlaut is the changing of a vowel of a root to become either more front or more high in certain morphological categories. As we saw in Chapter 2, the irregular plural in English of *foot/feet*, as well as other forms such as *tooth/teeth*, derive from an earlier plural suffix /-i/, which was added to the singular roots /fo:t/ and /to:θ/ respectively. Then a purely allophonic change took place, by which all back rounded vowels became front rounded vowels when the following syllable contained a front vowel. So although there was no phonemic change in the plural, there was a change in the phonetic form of the plural of these two words under the influence of the following plural suffix:

| /fo:ti/ : [fo:ti] | → | /fo:ti/ : [fø:ti] | 'feet' |
| /to:θi/ : [to:θi] | → | /to:θi/ : [tø:θi] | 'teeth' |

The next change involves a change in the phonemic status of the front rounded vowels. Although these vowels themselves did not then change phonetically in any way, there was a general rule of apocope at this stage in the history of English which deleted the final /-i/ marking the plural. Thus:

| /fo:ti/ : [fø:ti] | → | /fø:t/ : [fø:t] | 'feet' |
| /to:θi/ : [tø:θi] | → | /tø:θ/ : [tø:θ] | 'teeth' |

This loss of the conditioning vowel resulted in the existence of minimal pairs between back and front rounded vowels, with the back rounded form occurring in the singular and the front rounded form occurring in the plural. It is from these two forms that the modern irregular plurals are directly derived.

I mentioned in the preceding section that although Motu has undergone a change by which /t/ developed a new allophone of the form [s] before a front vowel, this did not introduce any new phonemic contrasts into the language. Now, there is a tendency among younger Motu speakers to drop word final vowels. So we find alternative pronunciations such as the following:

/tinagu/ : [sinagu ~ sinag]	'mother'	
/oiemu/ : [oiemu ~ oiem]	'your'	
/namo/ : [namo ~ nam]	'good'	
/mate/ : [mase ~ mas]	'die'	

Let's imagine that in two generations' time this change might have become general, and that all word-final vowels following consonants were lost by a rule that we could write as follows:

$$V \rightarrow \emptyset \ / \ C \ \underline{\quad} \ \#$$

Let us examine what would happen to minimal pairs such as **/lati/** 'no' and **/lata/** 'long'. These forms are currently pronounced as follows:

/lati/ : [lasi ~ las]	'no'	
/lata/ : [lata ~ lat]	'long'	

If the rule of optional word-final vowel loss were to become general, this pair, which is now distinguished phonemically by the nature of the final vowel, would come to be distinguished solely by the nature of what were originally intervocalic consonants, as follows:

/las/	'no'
/lat/	'long'

Thus, what was originally just a phonetic difference between [t] and [s] would become a phonemic contrast between /t/ and /s/.

(b) Words copied from foreign languages

When words from one language are copied into another, they are normally phonetically reinterpreted so that they fit the patterns of the language they are being adopted into. For instance, English words that are copied into Motu are normally made to fit the Motu **CV** syllable structure by deleting consonants and adding vowels to avoid the consonant clusters and syllable-final consonants of English, for example:

English	Motu	
gʌvəmənt	gavamani	'government'
bɒtl̩	botolo	'bottle'

When the influence of the foreign language becomes strong enough, there is often less pressure for words to conform to the phonological structures of the receiving language, and the words are likely to be pronounced much closer to the pronunciation of the source language. If there are sufficient numbers of such copied words, and speakers of the language no longer feel them to be 'foreign' words, this can influence the phonemic interpretation of existing sounds.

Let us look at the overall impact of words of English origin on the phonemic system of Motu. Many words have been copied into Motu to express a wide range of new cultural and technological concepts. In the early days, these were generally fully incorporated into the Motu phonological system. As Motu has no contrast between [t] and [s], words in English containing these sounds were simply treated as allophones of the same sound, and the distribution of these allomorphs followed the rules of the language as I have already described them. So, older speakers of Motu pronounce the following words of English origin as indicated below:

/teti/ : [sesi]		'shirt'
/maketi/ : [makesi]		'market'
/tini/ : [sini]		'tin'
/tupu/ : [tupu]		'soup'
/topu/ : [topu]		'soap'

The words /**teti**/ 'shirt' and /**maketi**/ 'market' are sometimes heard with the alternative pronunciations [**sedi**] and [**makedi**] respectively. There is a separate phoneme /d/ in Motu, so when these words are pronounced in this way, they are still being fully incorporated into the phonological system of the language. The reason that older people are likely to substitute the /d/ in these words is that they are somehow aware that these words of English origin are a 'problem' of some kind for their phonology, and they are trying in two different ways both to preserve what they know of the English pronunciation, and to maintain the integrity of the phonological system of their own language.

In the younger generations, whose English is better, we are more likely to find pronunciations such as the following for the same set of words:

[seti]	'shirt'
[maketi]	'market'
[tini]	'tin'
[supu]	'soup'
[sopu]	'soap'

In these forms, there is phonetic [t] followed by front vowels, and there is phonetic [s] followed by non-front vowels. This is in direct violation of the allophonic rules of Motu as I have described them. Younger speakers of the language have, therefore, introduced a contrast between the sounds [s] and [t]. So, although the [s] and the [t] have themselves not changed in any way phonetically in indigenous Motu words, their phonemic status is being changed from being in complementary distribution to being in contrastive distribution as a result of the introduction of words copied from English.

(c) Change of structural pressure

A final possible explanation for the change in status of a sound from being an allophone of a phoneme to being a completely independent phoneme is a change in the overall structure of the phoneme inventory.

Phonetic sequences of more than one sound can sometimes be treated as a single phoneme, depending on the syllable structure of the language. For instance, in Fijian phonetic sequences of [mb] are treated phonemically as /b/. The reasons for this are that:

(i)   [b] occurs only in this environment and nowhere else in the phonology of the language
(ii) the only consonant clusters in the language are those of the type represented as [mb], so we would complicate the statement of the syllable structure of the language if we were to allow phonemic consonant clusters.

The /b/ phoneme in Fijian derives from earlier phonemic consonant clusters of the form /mb/ and /mp/, as the following examples show:

		Fijian	
*tumbu	→	tubu	'grow'
*ləmbut	→	lobo-lobo	'soft'
*ləmpit	→	lobi	'fold'
*kampit	→	kabi	'fasten'

However, although there has been a phonemic change of /mb/ to /b/, there has been no phonetic change in these segments at all. How, then, has this phonemic change taken place? The answer is that in the original language there was a different distribution of sounds, and this distribution has been changed in Fijian. Firstly, in the past there *was* a sound [b] occurring independently of [m], unlike in modern Fijian. This independent [b] changed to [v] between vowels and word initially in modern Fijian, leaving [b] only occurring after [m]. Thus:

		Fijian	
*batu	→	vatu	'stone'
*bulan	→	vula	'moon'

Secondly, there *were* consonant clusters in the language other than those of the type represented by [mb]. There were, for instance, contrasting [mp] clusters, as shown in the examples given above. In this original language, therefore, /b/ had to be distinguished phonemically from /mb/, unlike in modern Fijian. So, while [mb] sequences have not changed phonetically in Fijian, their phonemic status has changed from /mb/ to /b/ because changes which took place elsewhere in the phonological system altered the structural pressure and brought about a phonemic reanalysis.

READING GUIDE QUESTIONS

1. What is allophonic change?
2. What is phonemic loss?
3. What is the difference between partial and complete loss?
4. What is rephonemicisation?
5. What is phonemic shift? How does this differ form allophonic change?
6. What is phonemic merger?
7. What is the difference between complete and partial phoneme merger?
8. What is phonemic split?
9. Explain in what ways a sound can change phonemically without changing phonetically.

EXERCISES

1. There are some phonemic differences between the Motu vernacular and the pidgin form of the language (known as Hiri Motu) that is used as a lingua franca in many parts of the southern area of Papua New Guinea. These differences can be represented by the following examples:

Motu	Hiri Motu	
gado	gado	'language'
hui	hui	'hair'
kehoa	keoa	'open'
ɣau	gau	'thing'
hahine	haine	'woman'
haginia	haginia	'build it'
boga	boga	'belly'
maɣani	magani	'wallaby'
tohu	tou	'sugarcane'
ɣatoi	gatoi	'egg'
heau	heau	'run'
sinagu	sinagu	'my mother'

Assume that the vernacular Motu forms represent the original forms, and that the Hiri Motu forms are derived from these. What kinds of phonemic changes would you say had taken place in terms of what we have been talking about in this chapter?

2. Examine the following forms in Tongan and Māori. Assume that the vowels of Tongan reflect the vowels of the original language and that Māori has innovated. Both Tongan and Māori today have five short vowel phonemes. Would you classify the changes to the vowels in Māori as phonetic change, phonemic shift, phonemic merger, or phonemic split?

Tongan	Māori	
ŋutu	ŋutu	'mouth'
au	au	'I'
hoa	hoa	'friend'
fulufulu	huruhuru	'feather'
ihu	ihu	'nose'
inu	inu	'drink'
hiŋoa	iŋoa	'name'
mala'e	marae	'open ground'
mata	mata	'face'
mate	mate	'dead'
moana	moana	'sea'
mutu	mutu	'finish'
nifo	niho	'tooth'
lau	rau	'leaf'
nima	rima	'five'
tolu	toru	'three'
tapu	tapu	'forbidden'

3. Less educated speakers of some regional dialects of Tok Pisin in Papua New Guinea change some of the sounds used by speakers of the standard dialect. Imagine somebody speaking the following extremely non-standard regional dialect. Standard Tok Pisin has no [f] while the non-standard dialect described here has no [p]. There is no [s] or [l] in the non-standard dialect. Describe the changes they have made to the phonemic system of the standard language in terms of the kinds of changes that we have been looking at in this chapter.

Standard Tok Pisin	Non-standard Tok Pisin	
ples	feret	'village'
poret	foret	'frightened'
mipla	mifara	'we'
larim	rarim	'leave'
kisim	kitim	'take'
lotu	rotu	'church'
sarip	tarif	'grass knife'
popaia	fofaia	'miss'
sori	tori	'concerned'

belo	bero	'bell'
sapos	tafot	'if'
kirap	kiraf	'get up'
gutpla	gutfara	'good'

4. Examine the Mbabaram forms in Data Set 3. In the original language, there were only three vowel phonemes: /i/, /u/ and /a/. Describe how the changes that have taken place have affected the phonemic system.
5. In the Lakalai forms in Data Set 5, describe the various changes that have taken place as merger, loss, or shift.
6. How would you characterise the various changes that have taken place in Burduna in Data Set 11, in terms of their effect on the phonemic system?

FURTHER READING

1. Winfred P. Lehmann *Historical Linguistics: An Introduction,* Chapter 10 'Change in Phonological Systems', pp. 147–76.
2. Raimo Anttila *An Introduction to Historical and Comparative Linguistics,* Chapter 4 'Sound Change', pp. 57–87.
3. Robert J. Jeffers and Ilse Lehiste *Principles and Methods for Historical Linguistics,* Chapter 5 'Phonological Change', pp. 74–87.
4. Hans Henrich Hock *Principles of Historical Linguistics.* Chapter 4 'Sound Change and Phonological Contrast', pp. 52–60.

CHAPTER FIVE

THE COMPARATIVE METHOD

Up to now, I have been giving examples of changes in languages from an earlier form (marked with the asterisk *) to a later form, but I have not said how these earlier forms have actually been worked out. So far, this has all simply been done on trust! The use of the asterisk is intended to mark the words as unrecorded, never actually seen or heard by anbody who is around now. Do linguists just guess at these forms and hope they are more or less right, or is there some special method by which we can deduce what these forms were like? How can we 'undo' the changes that have taken place in languages to find out what the original forms were? While I would have to admit that there is a certain amount of guesswork involved in working out these forms, I can also say that it is not blind guesswork, but intelligent guesswork. How, then, do we go about finding out about earlier forms of languages that have never been recorded?

5.1 SOUND CORRESPONDENCES
AND RECONSTRUCTION

I have already discussed the idea of languages being genetically related in families, all of which are descended from a single ancestor, which we call the protolanguage. This model of language evolution looks like this:

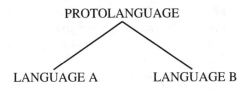

Even if we have no written records of the protolanguage, it is often possible to reconstruct some of the aspects of the original language from the *reflexes* in the daughter languages by using the *comparative method*. When I use the term *reconstruct*, I mean that we make some kind of estimation about what a protolanguage might have been like. We are in a sense 'undoing' the changes that have taken place between the protolanguage and its various descendant languages. To do this, you have to examine what we call *reflexes* of forms in the original language, in these daughter languages. By this, I mean that you have to look for forms in the various related languages which appear to be derived from a common original form. Two such forms are *cognate* with each other, and both are *reflexes* of the same form in the protolanguage.

In carrying out linguistic reconstruction in this way, we use the *comparative method*. This means that we compare cognate forms in two (or preferably more) related languages in order to work out some original form from which these cognates could reasonably be derived. In doing this, we have to keep in mind what is already known about the kinds of sound changes that are likely, and the kinds of changes that are unlikely. (Thus it is necessary to keep in mind the survey of types of sound change that are described in Chapter 2 of this book, when doing reconstruction of this kind.)

Now that we have learnt some of the basic terminology that is necessary for reconstructing languages, let us now go on to look at an actual linguistic situation, and see what we can make of it. We will look at some data from four Polynesian languages: Tongan, Samoan, Rarotongan (spoken in the Cook Islands, near Tahiti), and Hawaiian.

	Tongan	Samoan	Rarotongan	Hawaiian	
1.	tapu	tapu	tapu	kapu	'forbidden'
2.	pito	pute	pito	piko	'navel'
3.	puhi	feula	puʔi	puhi	'blow'
4.	tafaʔaki	tafa	taʔa	kaha	'side'
5.	taʔe	tae	tae	kae	'faeces'
6.	taŋata	taŋata	taŋata	kanaka	'man'
7.	tahi	tai	tai	kai	'sea'
8.	malohi	malosi	kaʔa	ʔaha	'strong'
9.	kalo	ʔalo	karo	ʔalo	'dodge'
10.	aka	aʔa	aka	aʔa	'root'
11.	ʔahu	au	au	au	'gall'
12.	ʔulu	ulu	uru	poʔo	'head'
13.	ʔufi	ufi	uʔi	uhi	'yam'
14.	afi	afi	aʔi	ahi	'fire'
15.	faa	faa	ʔaa	haa	'four'
16.	feke	feʔe	ʔeke	heʔe	'octopus'
17.	ika	iʔa	ika	iʔa	'fish'
18.	ihu	isu	putaŋio	ihu	'nose'
19.	hau	sau	ʔau	hau	'dew'
20.	tafuafi	siʔa	ʔika	hiʔa	'firemaking'

21.	hiku	si?u	?iku	hi?u	'tail'
22.	hake	a?e	ake	a?e	'up'
23.	huu	ulu	uru	komo	'enter'
24.	maŋa	maŋa	maŋa	mana	'branch'
25.	ma?u	mau	mau	mau	'constant'
26.	maa	mala	mara	mala	'fermented'
27.	na?a	fa?aŋa	maninia	naa	'quieten'
28.	nofo	nofo	no?o	noho	'sit'
29.	ŋalu	ŋalu	ŋaru	nalu	'wave'
30.	ŋutu	ŋutu	ŋutu	nuku	'mouth'
31.	vaka	va?a	vaka	wa?a	'canoe'
32.	va?e	vae	vae	wae	'leg'
33.	laho	laso	ra?o	laho	'scrotum'
34.	lohu	lou	rou	lou	'fruit picking pole'
35.	oŋo	loŋo	roŋo	lono	'hear'
36.	ua	lua	rua	lua	'two'

Assuming that there was once a language that we can now call Proto Polynesian, what do we have to do in order to reconstruct this language out of this body of data in its modern descendant languages?

There are a number of steps that you must follow. The first step is to sort out those forms which appear to be cognate from those which do not. If two words are not cognate, it means that they are derived from different original forms, and are not reflexes of the same original form as the others. In deciding whether two forms are cognate or not, you need to consider how similar they are both in form and meaning. If they are similar enough that it could be assumed that they are derived from a single original form with a single original meaning, then we say that they are cognate.

You can begin by excluding from the list above a word such as /tafuafi/ 'firemaking' in Tongan (20). The words to express the same meaning in the other three languages are /si?a/ in Samoan, /?ika/ in Rarotongan, and /hi?a/ in Hawaiian. These last three forms are all quite similar phonetically as well as being identical in meaning, and it is easy to imagine that they might be reflexes of a single original word in Proto Polynesian. The Tongan word /tafuafi/, although it has the same meaning, is so different in its shape that you can assume that it has a totally different source altogether.

The fact that the Tongan word /tafuafi/ contains the final element /-afi/, along with the fact that the Tongan word for 'fire' is /afi/ (14), suggest that this word may be a combination of some unknown element /tafu-/ and the word for 'fire'. Example 4 presents us with a similar case:

	Tongan	Samoan	Rarotongan	Hawaiian	
4.	tafa?aki	tafa	ta?a	kaha	'side'

It seems clear that the first two syllables of the longer Tongan word are cognate with the words in the remaining Polynesian languages. The second two syllables of the Tongan form, however, do not have any cognate forms in the other languages. We can therefore assume that in Tongan, at some stage in its history, an extra morpheme was added. What was originally regarded as being a morphologically complex word then came to be regarded by speakers as morphologically simple. That is to say, some other morpheme came to be *reanalysed* as part of the root. In carrying out comparative reconstruction, you must also exclude examples such as these which involve reanalysis, and consider *only* those parts of words which are actually cognate. We can therefore set out the cognate forms in these four languages in this case as follows, with the non-cognate part of the Tongan word removed, and a hyphen being used to indicate that something has been left off:

	Tongan	Samoan	Rarotongan	Hawaiian	
4.	tafa-	tafa	ta?a	kaha	'side'

From the data in the list given above, there are several other forms expressing the same meaning which we would want to exclude as not being cognate, because they are phonologically so different from the forms in the other languages. In the Samoan data, you should probably exclude the following: (2) /pute/ 'navel', (3) /feula/ 'blow', and (27) /fa?aŋa/ 'quieten'. In Rarotongan, you must exclude the following forms which are apparently not cognate with words in other languages expressing the same meaning: (18) /putaŋio/ 'nose', and (27) /maninia/ 'quieten'. Finally, in Hawaiian, you will need to exclude the following: (12) /po?o/ 'head', and (23) /komo/ 'enter'. (While we are discussing which words we should consider to be cognate, I will also make the very obvious point that, although the Samoan word /i?a/ 'fish' (17) and the Hawaiian word /hi?a/ 'firemaking' (20) are very similar in shape, they are *not* considered to be cognates because their meanings are totally different.)

Having completed the first step, you are now ready to move on to step two. The second step is to set out the complete set of *sound correspondences*. When I talk about a sound correspondence, I mean that we try to find each set of sounds that appears to be descended from the same original sound. So, if you take the first word in the list that I have given, you will find the following correspondences between the sounds:

Tongan	t	a	p	u
Samoan	t	a	p	u
Rarotongan	t	a	p	u
Hawaiian	k	a	p	u

You can see that there is an initial correspondence of /t/ in Tongan to /t/ in Samoan, to /t/ in Rarotongan, and to /k/ in Hawaiian. The /a/ in Tongan corresponds to an /a/ in all of the remaining three languages. Similarly, there is a correspondence of /p/ in all four languages, and finally, there is a correspondence of /u/ in all four languages. These correspondences can be set out like this:

Tongan	Samoan	Rarotongan	Hawaiian
t	t	t	k
a	a	a	a
p	p	p	p
u	u	u	u

What you have to do is list *all* such sound correspondences that are present in the whole of the data.

Actually, a quick examination of the vowel correspondences reveals that the vowels are identical in all four languages in all words. (Don't let this make you think that for other languages the vowels will be as straightforward as this! Sometimes it will be the vowels rather than the consonants which have the most complicated sets of sound correspondences. With other languages, both consonants *and* vowels will exhibit variations in their correspondence sets.) In order to be completely thorough, I will set out the vowel correspondences for you, even though there are no differences between the four languages:

Tongan	Samoan	Rarotongan	Hawaiian
a	a	a	a
e	e	e	e
i	i	i	i
o	o	o	o
u	u	u	u

Let us now concentrate on the consonant correspondences, which is where the differences are to be found between these languages. The correspondence sets for consonants work out to be as follows:

Tongan	Samoan	Rarotongan	Hawaiian
p	p	p	p
f	f	ʔ	h
t	t	t	k
k	ʔ	k	ʔ
h	s	ʔ	h
m	m	m	m
n	n	n	n
ŋ	ŋ	ŋ	n
v	v	v	w
l	l	r	l
ø	l	r	l

There is one brief point that I should make before continuing, and this concerns the use of the zero symbol ø. This symbol is used to express correspondences such as the following in the word for 'faeces' (5):

Tongan	t	a	ʔ	e
Samoan	t	a		e
Rarotongan	t	a		e
Hawaiian	k	a		e

In these forms, the /ʔ/ in Tongan corresponds to the absence of any sound in the other three languages. Thus, you will need to set this correspondence out as follows:

Tongan	Samoan	Rarotongan	Hawaiian
ʔ	ø	ø	ø

Similarly, in the word for 'gall' (11), you will see that there are two sounds in Tongan corresponding to nothing in the other languages:

Tongan	ʔ	a	h	u
Samoan		a		u
Rarotongan		a		u
Hawaiian		a		u

The word-initial correspondence of ʔ = ø = ø = ø is the same correspondence I have just set out for the medial consonant in the word for 'faeces'. (Note that I have just used a slightly different way of expressing sound correspondences, using the = symbol. From now on, I will use both methods interchangeably.) The word-medial correspondence is a different one, which we can set out as h = ø = ø = ø.

One problem that you might face in drawing up your set of sound correspondences is that, in cases where you have had to exclude a form in one or more languages because it is not cognate, you might have some correspondences that appear to be incomplete. For instance, go back to cognate set 20 in the list. If we are to exclude the Tongan word /tafuafi/ because it is not cognate with Samoan /siʔa/, Rarotongan /ʔika/, and Hawaiian /hiʔa/, then we could be faced with gaps in the Tongan data for some sounds. In this case, however, it is not too difficult to fill in the gaps as there are plenty of other words in Tongan that contain sounds which are cognate with words in the other languages in which the same correspondences occur. Where Samoan has /s/, Rarotongan has /ʔ/, and Hawaiian has /h/, other cognate sets (such as 18, 19, and 21) indicate that Tongan has /h/. For the intervocalic consonant, the cognate sets numbered 9, 10, 16, 17, 21, 22, and 31 all indicate that Tongan has /k/. You already know that the vowels in all four languages are identical in all words. So, while the Tongan word for 'firemaking' is /**tafuafi**/, if Tongan *had* retained the original word, we can predict that its shape would have been /**hika**/. Of course, we must not add this word into our data (though we might find somewhere else in the vocabulary of Tongan that /**hika**/ is found, but that it has shifted in its meaning so that it was not originally spotted as a possible cognate). If we did not have all of these other sets of cognate forms which indicate what sound corresponds in a particular language to the sounds in the other languages in a family, then it might be necessary simply to leave the slot for that sound in that language blank.

Having set out all of the sound correspondences that you can find in the data, you can now move on to the third step, which is to work out what original sound in the protolanguage might have produced that particular range of sounds in the various daughter languages. Your basic assumption should be that each separate set of sound correspondences goes back to a distinct original phoneme. In reconstructing the shapes of these original phonemes, you should always be guided by a number of general principles:

(i) *Any reconstruction should involve sound changes that are plausible.*

(You should be guided by the kinds of things that you learned in Chapter 2 in this respect.)

(ii) *Any reconstruction should involve as few changes as possible between the protolanguage and the daughter languages.*

It is perhaps easiest to reconstruct back from those sound correspondences in which the reflexes of the original phoneme (or protophoneme) are identical in all daughter languages. By principle (ii), you should normally assume that such correspondences go back to the same protophoneme as you find in the daughter languages, and that there have been no sound changes of any kind. Thus, you should assume that the vowels of Proto Polynesian are exactly the same as you find in the four daughter languages that we are looking at. So, for the correspondence **a** = **a** = **a** = **a** you should reconstruct an original /***a**/, for **e** = **e** = **e** = **e** you should reconstruct /***e**/, and so on.

Turning our attention now to the consonant correspondences, it will also be easiest to deal with those correspondences in which the daughter languages all have the same reflex. Such correspondences include the following:

Tongan	Samoan	Rarotongan	Hawaiian
p	p	p	p
m	m	m	m
n	n	n	n

Again, you need to ask yourself the question: what protophoneme could reasonably be expected to have produced a /p/ in all of the daughter languages? The obvious answer is again /***p**/. Applying the same reasoning, you can also reconstruct /*m/ and /*n/ for the other two correspondences that I have just listed.

The next thing that you should do is look at sound correspondence sets that only have slight differences between the various daughter languages, and try to reconstruct original phonemes from the evidence that these provide. So, from the correspondence sets that I listed earlier, we will now go on to look at the following:

Tongan	Samoan	Rarotongan	Hawaiian
t	t	t	k
ŋ	ŋ	ŋ	n

In these two cases, only one language, Hawaiian, differs from the other three languages. Logically, in the first case, you could reconstruct either a /*t/ or a /*k/. Which would be the best solution? It would obviously be better to reconstruct /*t/ as the original form and to argue that this changed to /k/ in Hawaiian. To suggest /*k/ as the original form, you would need to say that this changed to /t/ in three separate languages. So, in keeping with guiding principle number (ii) above, you should normally reconstruct as the original form the sound that has the widest distribution in the daughter languages. Using the same argument, you should reconstruct /*ŋ/ for the second correspondence set presented above.

You should now go on to deal with those correspondences which have a greater amount of variation in the reflexes of the original phoneme. Where there is greater variation, it is going to require greater consideration on your part in doing the reconstruction. Let us take the correspondence below:

Tongan	Samoan	Rarotongan	Hawaiian
k	ʔ	k	ʔ

Here there are two instances of /k/ in the daughter languages, and two of /ʔ/, so the second guiding principle will no longer help us as there is no single reflex with a wider distribution than other reflexes among the daughter languages. We are therefore torn between reconstructing /*k/ and /*ʔ/.

However, you should also remember that you are to be guided by principle (i) that I mentioned earlier. This guiding principle requires that you should prefer a solution that involves 'natural' sound change over an 'unnatural' one. If you were to propose an original /*k/ rather than /*ʔ/, you would need to say that the following change took place in Samoan and Hawaiian:

k → ʔ

This is a well known sound change that goes under the general heading of weakening or lenition. However, if you were to reconstruct, instead, /*ʔ/ for this correspondence, you would need to say that in Tongan and Rarotongan, the following change took place:

$$? \rightarrow k$$

While this is not an impossible change, it is certainly a rarer kind of change than the change of /k/ to /?/. Thus, according to guiding principle (i), you should probably reconstruct /*k/ in this case.

At this point, I will add a third guiding principle:

(iii) *Reconstructions should fill gaps in phonological systems rather than create unbalanced systems.*

Although there will always be exceptions among the world's languages, there is a strong tendency for languages to have 'balanced' phonological systems. By this I mean that where there is a set of sounds distinguished by a particular feature, this feature is also likely to be used to distinguish a different series of sounds in the language. For example, if a language has two back rounded vowels (i.e. /u/ and /o/), we would expect it also to have two front unrounded vowels (i.e. /i/ and /e/). Thus, the following represent balanced phoneme inventories, and these kinds of inventories tend to recur in the world's languages:

	Front	Back
High	i	u
Low	a	

	Front	Back
High	i	u
Mid	e	o
Low	a	

		Front Spread	Back Round
High	i	y	u
Mid	e	ø	o
Low		a	

The following, however, are 'unbalanced' systems and are less likely to occur than systems such as those I have just given, as they contain gaps (which are indicated by dashes):

	Front	Back
High	i	-
Mid	e	o
Low	a	

		Front Spread	Front Round	Back Round
High	i	-		u
Mid	e	ø		
Low			a	

You can also use guiding principle (iii) to help in reconstructing the original phoneme from which the k = ? = k = ? correspondence is derived. The correspondences that you have already looked at provide evidence for the reconstruction of the following original consonant phonemes in Proto Polynesian:

	Bilabial	Alveolar	Velar
Stop	*p	*t	
Nasal	*m	*n	*ŋ

If you assume that languages operate in terms of balanced phonological systems, you would not expect to find a gap at the velar stop position (i.e. /k/) in the protolanguage, since you already have evidence for the existence of a velar nasal. As you are, in a sense, 'looking for' a /*k/, you can use this fact as evidence in support of your reconstruction of /*k/ rather than /*ʔ/ for this particular sound correspondence.

Let us now take the next problematic correspondence:

Tongan	Samoan	Rarotongan	Hawaiian
f	f	ʔ	h

This correspondence is in fact less problematic than the one you just looked at. Because there are a greater number of /f/ reflexes of this original phoneme than other sounds, by our second guiding principle again, you should reconstruct an /*f/ wherever this correspondence occurs.

Now let us consider the correspondences involving the liquids:

Tongan	Samoan	Rarotongan	Hawaiian
l	l	r	l
ø	l	r	l

We appear to face real problems here. We have to reconstruct two different phonemes in order to account for the two different sets of correspondences, but there is very little difference between the reflexes of these two proto-phonemes in the daughter languages. Three of the four languages are identical in their reflexes of these sounds, and in both sets of correspondences, /l/ is the most common reflex. Since we have to reconstruct two phonemes, we will presumably have to choose /*l/ for one and /*r/ for the other. But which will we assign to which correspondence set? The choice is fairly arbitrary. However, we could argue that loss of /*r/ is possibly slightly more likely to occur than a change of /*r/ to /*l/, so we could suggest that /*l/ is the source of the first correspondence set, and /*r/ is the source for the second correspondence set. If this is correct, we would need to say that Rarotongan underwent a change of /*l/ to /r/, while Samoan and Hawaiian underwent a change of /*r/ to /l/, and Tongan simply lost the original /*r/ phoneme.

With this pair of reconstructions, we really are on shaky ground, and we are operating with little more than guesswork. One way of checking the accuracy of our reconstruction would be to broaden the data upon which the reconstruction is based by introducing forms from a wider range of related languages. If it turns out that by considering a larger number of Polynesian languages, we find greater numbers of lateral reflexes of our suggested /*l/

reconstruction and a greater number of rhotic reflexes of our suggested /*r/ reconstruction, this would be evidence in support of our conclusion.

We have reconstructed the following consonant inventory for Proto Polynesian so far:

```
*p   *t   *k
*m   *n   *ŋ
*f
     *l
     *r
```

Now we will turn to the correspondences involving the glottal sounds:

Tongan	Samoan	Rarotongan	Hawaiian
ʔ	ø	ø	ø
h	ø	ø	ø

When we set the correspondences out like this, it is clear that Tongan is the only language to have any reflexes of these two phonemes. All of the other languages have lost them altogether. It is not too difficult to argue, therefore, that we should reconstruct /*ʔ/ and /*h/ respectively wherever we find these correspondences, especially since /ʔ/ and /h/ are sounds that are very commonly lost in languages.

We have yet to consider the following correspondence, however:

Tongan	Samoan	Rarotongan	Hawaiian
h	s	ʔ	h

Here, all of the languages except Samoan reflect a glottal sound, and /h/ is the most common reflex. However, we have already reconstructed /*h/ for the correspondence **h** = ø = ø = ø that I just presented. Similarly, /*ʔ/ is not a possible reconstruction, because we have already reconstructed this to account for the ʔ = ø = ø = ø correspondence set. The only possibility left seems to be to reconstruct this correspondence as deriving from /*s/. This is actually quite reasonable. Changes of the following type are quite common in languages of the world:

s → h → ʔ

It is also relatively uncommon for languages to have no /s/ phoneme, so this is a sound that we would normally expect to find evidence for in any protolanguage.

Both the change of /s/ to /h/ and the change of /h/ to /ʔ/ can be regarded as weakening, or lenition. Furthermore, if you did not reconstruct an /*s/ in

Proto Polynesian, you would end up with a gap in the phoneme inventory. By reconstructing an /*s/, you would be filling the voiceless alveolar fricative slot, so that you have an inventory that looks like this:

```
*p  *t  *k   *ʔ
*m  *n  *ŋ
*f  *s       *h
    *l
    *r
```

(Note that a glottal nasal is a physical impossibility, and it is probably more common for languages to have the phoneme /h/ than /x/, so the lack of a sound in the velar fricative slot is not a real problem either.)

It could perhaps be argued instead that the two correspondences involving /h/ discussed earlier need to be completely re-examined:

Tongan	Samoan	Rarotongan	Hawaiian
h	ø	ø	ø
h	s	ʔ	h

According to guiding principle (ii) that I mentioned earlier, you should reconstruct as the phoneme in the protolanguage the form that has the widest distribution in the daughter languages. You might, therefore, want to reconstruct the phoneme /*h/ instead of /*s/ for the second of these correspondence sets. This would be phonetically quite reasonable according to guiding principle (i), but doing this would create problems for your handling of the first correspondence for which you have already reconstructed /*h/.

This problem could be overcome by suggesting a separate original phoneme to account for this correspondence, perhaps the voiceless velar fricative /*x/. Although this would be phonetically reasonable as well, I would argue against this solution on the grounds that it would violate a fourth guiding principle that can be set out as follows:

(iv) *A phoneme should not be reconstructed in a protolanguage unless it is shown to be absolutely necessary from the evidence of the daughter languages.*

None of the daughter languages anywhere has an /x/, so you should be automatically suspicious of a solution that suggests an /x/ in the protolanguage. Keeping this in mind, then, you should reject the revised solution and stick with the original solution.

Finally, we have the correspondence below:

Tongan	Samoan	Rarotongan	Hawaiian
v	v	v	w

While we would predict /*v/ as the most likely original form for this correspondence on the basis of the distribution of its reflexes, by doing so we would create an uneven phonemic inventory. As it stands, there is no voiced/voiceless contrast in the stop or fricative series of Proto Polynesian (all are voiceless), and to introduce a single voiced sound here would seem rather odd. Another odd thing about the phoneme inventory so far reconstructed for Proto Polynesian is the lack of semi-vowels. We would therefore probably be more justified in reconstructing /*w/ than /*v/ in this case. The complete original phoneme inventory that we have reconstructed for Proto Polynesian now looks something like this:

*p	*t	*k	*ʔ
*m	*n	*ŋ	
*f	*s		*h
	*l		
	*r		
*w			

*i	*u
*e	*o
*a	

Having arrived at the phoneme inventory of Proto Polynesian by comparing the daughter languages, you can now move on to the comparatively simple task of reconstructing the forms of the individual words. To do this, you need to list the sound correspondences and set out the original phoneme that each of these goes back to.

	Tongan	Samoan	Rarotongan	Hawaiian
Vowels				
*a	a	a	a	a
*e	e	e	e	e
*i	i	i	i	i
*o	o	o	o	o
*u	u	u	u	u
Consonants				
*p	p	p	p	p
*f	f	f	ʔ	h
*t	t	t	t	k
*k	k	ʔ	k	ʔ
*s	h	s	ʔ	h
*ʔ	ʔ	ø	ø	ø
*h	h	ø	ø	ø
*m	m	m	m	m
*n	n	n	n	n
*ŋ	ŋ	ŋ	ŋ	n

*w	v	v	v	w
*l	l	l	r	l
*r	ø	l	r	l

Using the information that is set out in this list, let us try to reconstruct the word for 'four', which is item 15 in the original list of cognates. The reflexes in the daughter languages of the original word that you are trying to reconstruct are set out below:

Tongan	f	a	a
Samoan	f	a	a
Rarotongan	ʔ	a	a
Hawaiian	h	a	a

As you have a word containing three sound correspondences, this indicates that the original word must have had three original phonemes. What were those original phonemes? The **f** = **f** = **ʔ** = **h** correspondence, if you check from the list that I have just given, goes back to an original /*f/. The two **a** = **a** = **a** = **a** correspondences point to an original /*a/. So the Proto Polynesian word for 'four' can be reconstructed as /*faa/.

Now take item 9 in the list of cognates, which gives the various words for 'dodge'. This involves the following correspondences between the four languages:

Tongan	k	a	l	o
Samoan	ʔ	a	l	o
Rarotongan	k	a	r	o
Hawaiian	ʔ	a	l	o

Again, referring to your list of correspondences above, you will find that the **k** = **ʔ** = **k** = **ʔ** correspondence points to an original /*k/. The **a** = **a** = **a** = **a** correspondence, of course, goes back to /*a/. The list above reveals that **l** = **l** = **r** = **l** goes back to /*l/, and finally **o** = **o** = **o** = **o** goes back to /*o/. So, you can reconstruct the original word for 'dodge' in Proto Polynesian as /*kalo/.

Although reconstruction of the vocabulary is relatively simple and straightforward, there are some situations where you cannot be sure of the original form. If you consider the following example from the original list of cognates, it should be clear why this is so:

	Tongan	Samoan	Rarotongan	Hawaiian	
8.	malohi	malosi	kaʔa	ʔaha	'strong'

Here you have *two* clear cognate sets, and both could equally well be reconstructed back to the protolanguage. On the basis of the Tongan and Samoan forms you would be tempted to reconstruct an original word of the form

/*malosi/, while on the basis of the Rarotongan and Hawaiian data, you would need to reconstruct either /*kasa/ or /*kafa/. All you can do in such cases is reconstruct *both* forms and indicate that one of them probably meant something different, but similar, in meaning ('hard', for instance). But which of the two was the original word for 'strong' is impossible to say, on the basis of the evidence that you have. The only way to solve this problem would be to look at the word for 'strong' in a larger number of Polynesian languages.

Another problem that you will sometimes face in reconstructing vocabulary comes when you have incomplete sound correspondences that you are unable to fill from other correspondence sets in the languages that you are examining. For instance, imagine that you had only the forms below:

	Tongan	Samoan	Rarotongan	Hawaiian	
9.	-	ʔalo	karo	ʔalo	'dodge'

If you did not have a cognate in Tongan (either because the meaning 'dodge' is expressed by a completely different form, or because the data itself may be lacking the appropriate form), then you would not be able to reconstruct a single original form to express this meaning. This is because the correspondence of Samoan /l/ to Rarotongan /r/ and Hawaiian /l/ could point equally well to the reconstruction of both /*l/ and /*r/. In order to be able to decide whether the form should be reconstructed as having /*r/ or /*l/, a Tongan cognate is essential, as this is the only daughter language that still makes a distinction between the two original phonemes. If we are faced with a genuine ambiguity in our reconstructions, we can indicate this by reconstructing both phonemes, and separating them by a comma, or by surrounding them by round brackets. So, we could give /*kal,ro/ or /*ka(lr)o/, which would be alternative ways of saying that the evidence points to either /*kalo/ or /*karo/, and there is no way of making a choice between the two. Similarly, on the basis of the forms /kaʔa/ 'strong' in Rarotongan and /ʔaha/ in Hawaiian, all we can do is reconstruct /*kas,fa/ or /*ka(sf)a/.

Of course, if you refer back to item 9 in the original list of cognate sets, the Tongan form actually is cognate, and the Tongan word for this meaning is /kalo/. This indicates that the reconstructed form is unambiguously /*kalo/ rather than /*karo/.

5.2 RECONSTRUCTION OF CONDITIONED SOUND CHANGES

When you write the rules for the changes from Proto Polynesian into the various daughter languages, you will find that all of the changes that have taken place are unconditioned sound changes. That is to say that an original /*s/ always becomes /ʔ/ in Rarotongan, or an original /*r/ always becomes /l/ in Hawaiian. There are no conditioned changes which have taken place only in certain environments and not in others. How does it affect our technique of reconstruction if there are conditioned sound changes involved as well as unconditioned sound changes?

Let us look at some additional data from Tongan and Samoan:

	Tongan	Samoan	
37.	fefine	fafine	'woman'
38.	fiefia	fiafia	'happy'
39.	moʔuŋa	mauŋa	'mountain'
40.	tuoŋaʔane	tuaŋane	'(woman's) brother'
41.	tuofefine	tuafafine	'(man's) sister'

The vowel correspondences that we noted before were completely uniform through all of the languages that we looked at. Thus, on the basis of the correspondence **a = a** we reconstructed /*a/, while **e = e** points to /*e/, and **o = o** points to /*o/. However, these new examples point to two new sets of vowel correspondences:

Tongan	Samoan
e	a
o	a

Must you therefore reconstruct two separate phonemes for these two correspondence sets? If you do, they will certainly need to be phonetically similar to the vowels /e/, /o/, and /a/, yet at the same time they would need to be different to these three vowels. If you retain these three vowels, then you could cater for these additional correspondence sets by reconstructing something like /ɛ/ for the **e = a** correspondence, and /ɔ/ for the **o = a** correspondence. Your reconstructions for these additional words would end up looking like this:

37.	*fɛfine	'woman'
38.	*fiɛfia	'happy'
39.	*mɔʔuŋa	'mountain'
40.	*tuɔŋa(ʔa)ne	'(woman's) brother'
41.	*tuofɛfine	'(man's) sister'

However, one problem with this reconstruction is that you will have violated the general principle that we should not normally reconstruct a phoneme if that phoneme does not occur in any of the descendant languages. Since none of the Polynesian languages that we have been looking at has a contrast between /e/ and /ɛ/, or between /o/ and /ɔ/, we should be suspicious of a reconstruction that suggests such a distinction in the protolanguage.

If you examine the distribution of the suggested reconstructed sounds /*ɛ/ and /*ɔ/ with respect to /*a/, you will find that there is, in fact, complementary distribution. The reconstructed sound /*ɛ/ only ever occurs in the third syllable from the end of a word when the following syllable contains the high front vowel /i/, while /*ɔ/ only occurs in the third syllable from the end of a word when the following syllable contains the high front vowel /u/. The vowel /*a/, however, appears in all other environments. To see this, compare the forms that you have just examined with the following:

	Tongan	Samoan	
1.	tapu	tapu	'forbidden'
5.	taʔe	tae	'faeces'
6.	taŋata	taŋata	'man'
7.	tahi	tai	'sea'
8.	malohi	malosi	'strong'
9.	kalo	ʔalo	'dodge'
10.	aka	aʔa	'root'
11.	ʔahu	au	'gall'
14.	afi	afi	'fire'

This list does not include all of the examples from the original set of cognates between the two languages, but if you carefully go through the entire list, you will find that there are no examples in Samoan which end in either /-aCuCV/ or /-aCiCV/.

What you must do is look for evidence of complementary distribution between phonetically similar correspondence sets before you do your final reconstruction. The correspondence set **e = a** occurs only in the third syllable from the end of a word when the following vowel correspondence involves the high front vowel /i/, while the correspondence **o = a** occurs only in the third syllable from the end of a word when the following vowel correspondence involves /u/. The correspondence set **a = a**, on the other hand, appears in all other environments. You therefore need to reconstruct only a *single* phoneme for these *three* correspondence sets. You will not need to modify your reconstruction of /*a/, and there is certainly no need to reconstruct /*ɛ/ or /*ɔ/, as Tongan has undergone a conditioned change of the following form:

$$a \rightarrow \begin{cases} o/\underline{\quad}CuCV \\ e/\underline{\quad}CiCV \end{cases}$$

Therefore, after you have set out your sound correspondences between the daughter languages, you must also do the following, as the fifth and sixth steps in applying the comparative method:

(v) *You must look for sound correspondences that involve phonetically similar sounds;* and

(vi) *For each of these phonetically 'suspicious' pairs of sound corres-pondences, you should try to see whether or not they are in complementary or contrastive distribution.*

This is very similar to what we do in a synchronic analysis of the phonemes of a language, except that here we are trying to analyse the phonemes of the protolanguage by using the sound correspondences as the 'phonetic' raw data. We then have to decide which sound correspondences are phonemically distinctive in the original language, and which are just positional variants (or 'allo-correspondences' of 'correspondence-emes').

Let us look at another very simple situation that we are already familiar with in order to see how to proceed when it comes to reconstructing conditioned sound changes. We have already seen that in the Motu language of Papua New Guinea, there has been change of *t to s before the front vowels, while in all other environments it remained as t. We wrote this rule formally as follows:

t → s / ___ front V

Rather than working from the protolanguage to the modern language, let us instead work back from Motu and one of its sister languages, applying the comparative method that we have been discussing in this chapter. The sister language that we will look at is Sinaugoro, and the data from these two languages that we will consider is set out below:

Sinaugoro	Motu	
tama	tama	'father'
tina	sina	'mother'
taŋi	tai	'cry'
tui	tui	'elbow, knee'
ɣita	ita	'see'
ɣate	ase	'liver'
mate	mase	'die'
natu	natu	'child'
toi	toi	'three'

Let us apply the technique that I have just shown you. Firstly, remember that you have to sort out the cognate forms from the non-cognate forms. In this case, I have already done this, and all of the forms that are given are cognate. The second step, then, is to set out the sound correspondences. Since you are only interested at this stage in the history of [t] and [s], you should restrict yourself only to correspondences involving these two sounds. (There are many other correspondences in the two languages where the two sounds are identical, of course, and there is also a correspondence of Sinaugoro /ɣ/ and /ŋ/ to Motu /ø/.) The correspondences that we can find are:

Sinaugoro	Motu
t	t
t	s

There are therefore two sound correspondences here. Does this mean that you should reconstruct two separate phonemes in the original language? If you did, these would presumably be /*t/ for the first correspondence, and /*s/ for the second correspondence.

However, since the t = t and the t = s correspondences both involve very similar sets of sounds, you should first of all look for any evidence that there might be complementary distribution involved. If you cannot find any evidence of complementary distribution, then you should also look for direct evidence of contrastive distribution. What you will find when you examine the data is that the t = s correspondence occurs only when there is a following correspondence of front vowels (i.e. i = i or e = e), whereas the t = t correspondence occurs before all other vowel correspondences. If two (or more) correspondence sets are in complementary distribution in this way, then you should reconstruct only a single original phoneme for both correspondences, and we again say that a conditioned sound change must have taken place.

In this case you would want to reconstruct a *t, using the principle that you should normally reconstruct the form that has the widest distribution in the daughter languages. You then need to say that a conditioned sound change took place in Motu whereby *t became s before front vowels, as you saw earlier. The protoforms from which the Sinaugoro and Motu forms were derived can therefore be reconstructed as follows (with the ŋ = ø correspondence presumably coming from /*ŋ/ and the ɣ = ø correspondence coming from *ɣ):

*tama	'father'
*tina	'mother'
*taŋi	'cry'
*tui	'elbow, knee'
*ɣita	'see'
*ɣate	'liver'
*mate	'die'
*natu	'child'
*toi	'three'

(With these reconstructed forms, it is obvious that Sinaugoro directly reflects the original forms without change, with Motu being the only innovating language.)

Now that you know that you must check phonetically similar sets of sound correspondences for complementary or contrastive distribution, you should go

back and check your Polynesian correspondences as well. Which correspondences should you check for complementary distribution because of their
phonetic similarity? The first obvious pair of correspondences that you should
test are those involving the liquids, for which our earlier reconstructions were
as follows:

	Tongan	Samoan	Rarotongan	Hawaiian
*l	l	l	r	l
*r	ø	l	r	l

Has there been a conditioned sound change in Tongan in which a single
original phoneme was lost in some environments and retained in others? Or
were there indeed two separate protophonemes which have merged in
Samoan, Rarotongan, and Hawaiian?

In order to test these two possibilities, I will list the full cognate sets in
which these forms occur:

	Tongan	Samoan	Rarotongan	Hawaiian	
	l	l	r	l	
9.	kalo	?alo	karo	?alo	'dodge'
12.	?ulu	ulu	uru	-	'head'
29.	ŋalu	ŋalu	ŋaru	nalu	'wave'
33.	laho	laso	ra?o	laho	'scrotum'
34.	lohu	lou	rou	lou	'fruit picking pole'
	ø	l	r	l	
23.	huu	ulu	uru	-	'enter'
26.	maa	mala	mara	mala	'fermented'
35.	oŋo	loŋo	roŋo	lono	'hear'
36.	ua	lua	rua	lua	'two'

You will need to test all possible conditioning environments. You should
remember from your study of phonology that when you are looking for
possible conditioning factors for allophones of phonemes, you need to
consider the following:

    (a) the nature of the sound (or sounds) which follow
    (b) the nature of the sound (or sounds) which precede
    (c) the nature of the syllable (i.e. whether open or closed)
    (d) the position in the word (i.e. whether initial, medial or final)
    (e) any possible combination of such conditiong factors

Let us consider these possible conditioning factors to see if these two sets of
correspondences are in complementary distribution or in contrastive
distribution.

Firstly, let us look at the nature of the following sound. Immediately following the first set of correspondences (i.e. l = l = r = l), you will find the following correspondence sets:

    u = u = u = u
    a = a = a = a
    o = o = o = o

After the second set of correspondences (i.e. ø = l = r = l) you will find the following vowel correspondences:

    u = u = u = u
    a = a = a = a
    o = o = o = o

In fact, you have exactly the same sets of sound correspondences occurring after both liquid correspondences. In order to demonstrate the fact that there is no complementary distribution, you only need overlap in the two sets of environments with respect to a *single* correspondence, and here you have all three sets of following environments being the same.

Of course you also have to check all other possible conditioning factors now that you have checked the following sound, so let us now try to find out if it is the nature of the preceding correspondence which acts as a conditioning factor. Before the l = l = r = l correspondence, you will find the following vowel correspondence sets:

    u = u = u = u
    a = a = a = a

Before the second correspondence, you will find the following:

    u = u = u = u
    a = a = a = a

Again, exactly the same two sets of vowel correspondences appear before the two correspondence sets that you are checking, so there is no complementary distribution with respect to this environment either. The third possibility (i.e. whether the syllable is open or closed) is of little use to you here, because all of the syllables in these languages are open. You should check the position in the word. When you do this you will find that *both* sets of correspondences occur both initially and medially. Finally, you should consider the possibility of there being some more complex conditioning factors. However, none is apparent.

This evidence means that you are forced to conclude that the two correspondence sets involving liquids are in contrastive distribution, and that you were correct in the first place in reconstructing two separate phonemes. In fact, you can even find a sub-minimal pair of words from the data that I have presented in order to back up this conclusion. (No complete minimal pairs are available, but perhaps if more data were available we would be able to find one.) Compare the forms for 'head' and 'enter':

	Tongan	Samoan	Rarotongan	Hawaiian	
12.	ʔulu	ulu	uru	-	'head'
23.	huu	ulu	uru	-	'enter'

Between the correspondences in which all of the languages have /u/, we find that *both* correspondence sets occur. Thus, Tongan has the sequence /ulu/ contrasting with /uøu/. So, you can conclude that there was a phonemic distinction in the original language that goes back to an original sub-minimal pair, i.e. /*ʔulu/ 'head' vs. /*huru/ 'enter'. Although Samoan, Rarotongan, and Hawaiian have all unconditionally merged the original distinction between /*l/ and /*r/, the original opposition is still reflected in Tongan, which has retained the /*l/ and unconditionally lost the /*r/.

In conclusion, I have described a means of reconstructing the phonological system of a protolanguage, and also its lexicon. We call this method of reconstruction the comparative method. The comparative method involves carefully carrying out all of the following steps:

1. Sort out those forms which appear to be cognate and ignore the non-cognate forms.
2. Write out the full set of correspondences between the languages you are looking at (including correspondences where the sounds are identical all the way through). Be careful to note correspondences where a sound in one language corresponds to ø (or the absence of a sound) in another language.
3. Group together all correspondences that have reflexes that are phonetically similar.
4. Look for evidence of complementary and contrastive distribution between these suspicious pairs of correspondences.
5. For each correspondence set that is not in complementary distribution with another correspondence set, assume that it goes back to a separate original phoneme.
6. Make an estimation about the original form of the phoneme using the following criteria:
   (i) The proposed original phoneme must be plausible, meaning that the changes from it to the reflexes in the descendant languages must fit our knowledge about what kinds of sound changes are common in the world's languages.
   (ii) The sound that has the widest distribution in the daughter languages is most likely to be the original phoneme.
   (iii) A sound corresponding to a gap in the reconstructed phoneme inventory of the protolanguage is also likely to be a possible reconstruction for one of the correspondence sets.
   (iv) A sound that does not occur in any of the daughter languages should not be reconstructed unless there are very good reasons for doing so.

7. For each group of correspondence sets that are in complementary distribution, assume that they all go back to a single protophoneme, and use the same criteria given in (6) to reconstruct its shape.

5.3 THE REALITY OF PROTOLANGUAGES

At the beginning of this chapter on the comparative method, I said that the method involved a certain amount of guesswork, but that this guesswork was intelligent rather than blind guesswork. But what do our reconstructions actually represent? Do they represent a real language as it was actually spoken at some earlier time, or do our reconstructions only give an approximation of some earlier language?

One point of view is that we are not actually trying to reconstruct the facts of a language as it was actually spoken when we are applying the comparative method — nor should we even try to do this. Some linguists argue that we should not try to suggest any phonetic form of reconstructed original phonemes deduced from the evidence of sound correspondences between daughter languages. Rather, what we should do is simply to deduce that in a particular word, there *was* a phoneme that was distinct from all other sounds, but that we do not know what its phonetic form was. According to this point of view, a 'protolanguage' as it is reconstructed is not a 'language' in the same sense as any of its descendant languages, or as the 'real' protolanguage itself. It is merely an abstract statement of correspondences.

It would be logical, then, to devise totally arbitrary symbols to express the original phonemes in the protolanguage for each of the sets of correspondences in the descendant languages. So, for instance, we could say that the Polynesian correspondence of t = t = t = k should be reconstructed as *\$, the a = a = a = a correspondence should be reconstructed as *@, the p = p = p = p correspondence as *% and the u = u = u = u correspondence as *&. So the original form that produced the following reflexes would be reconstructed as *\$@%&:

	Tongan	Samoan	Rarotongan	Hawaiian	
1.	tapu	tapu	tapu	kapu	'forbidden'

The representation *\$@%& says nothing about the phonetic form of the original word. All it says is that there was a word containing four different phonemes which behaved in four different ways in the daughter languages of Proto Polynesian.

Other linguists, while not going as far as this, have stated that, while languages that are related through common descent are derived from a single ancestor language, we should not necessarily assume that this language really existed as such. The assumption of the comparative method is that we should arrive at an entirely uniform protolanguage and this is likely to give us a distorted or false view of the protolanguage. In some cases, the comparative method may even allow us to reconstruct a protolanguage that never existed historically.

For instance, by applying the comparative method we can reconstruct various protolanguages between Latin and the modern languages Spanish, French, Portuguese, Italian, and Romanian (i.e. Proto Spanish, Proto French, and so on), from which all of the modern dialects of these languages are supposed to have descended. Historically, however, we know that these protolanguages never existed. Innovation from Latin took place in local areas from the time that Latin was spoken in these areas from the beginning. There was no period of uniform change from Latin to Proto French in the area of modern France, with a subsequent split into the multitude of modern French dialects that we find today. We must therefore be careful about assuming that protolanguages ever existed, and that there was ever a speech community to go along with that protolanguage.

As far as the phonological reality of the protolanguages that we are reconstructing is concerned, most linguists do try to make their reconstructions with a view to estimating something about the phonetic form of the language they are reconstructing. We all realise that there are times when we simply cannot be sure what the original phonetic forms were. A good case is the difference between the Polynesian $1 = 1 = r = 1$ and $ø = 1 = r = 1$ correspondences that we looked at earlier. We reconstructed /*l/ for the first of these correspondences and /*r/ for the second. However, it is quite possible that we are wrong. In such cases as these, it would be wiser to regard /*l/ and /*r/ not so much as reliable phonetic indications of the original forms, but simply as indications that there *was* a phonemic distinction of some sort (probably involving liquids).

Sometimes linguists prefer to avoid making a commitment to a particular phonetic shape for a protophoneme, but at the same time want to avoid assigning totally arbitrary symbols to account for a set of sound correspondences in the daughter languages. One frequently employed device in these sorts of situations is to distinguish the protophonemes by which two phonetically similar correspondence sets are derived by using lower and upper case forms of the same symbol. In the case of the example that I have just given, for instance, you could avoid making a detailed claim about the phonetic form of the protolanguage by arbitrarily reconstructing the correspondence $1 = 1 = r = 1$ as going back to /*l/, while suggesting /*L/ as the source for the correspondence $ø = 1 = r = 1$. By using the capital letter here, you are saying that this was probably some kind of liquid, but you are not sure exactly what it was. Another option in these kinds of situations is to use subscript or superscript numerals, e.g. /*l^1/ and /*l^2/.

It is sometimes possible to check on the accuracy of our guesses about the phonetics of a protolanguage. One possibility is to use older written records where these go back as far as the age of the protolanguage itself. In Chapter 1 I described the development of Latin into modern Spanish, French, Italian, and Romanian. We can check on the validity of the comparative method in this case by trying to reconstruct back from the modern languages to see if what we end up with coincides with the actual written Latin records. There are, in fact, many things that the comparative method cannot tell us about Latin. For instance, look at the following forms in these languages:

Spanish	French	Italian	Romanian	
naso	ne	naso	nas	'nose'
kabo	ʃɛf	kapo	kap	'head'
kabra	ʃɛːvʁ	kapra	kaprə	'goat'
aba	fɛːv	fava	faw	'bean'

(Although the French forms are phonetically quite different from the other languages, they are still cognate.) Because of this wide variation in the shape of these words and the small number of examples that I have given, we cannot really attempt to apply the comparative method seriously and come up with valid reconstructions here. We could, however, guess that the original word for 'nose' might have been something like /*naso/, the word for 'head' might have been /*kapo/, the word for 'goat' /*kapra/, and the word for 'bean' /*faba/.

Since we have written records of Latin, we can check the accuracy of our reconstructions. The written records give us the following forms:

nasum	'nose'
caput	'head'
capram	'goat'
fabam	'bean'

We know that the symbol *c* in the Latin alphabet represented the phoneme /k/. However, the written records do *not* provide us with the same forms that the comparative method leads us to reconstruct. We can only reconstruct a feature in the protolanguage when some traces of an original form have been retained in at least *one* of the descendant languages. When *all* of the daughter languages have lost a feature, we are no longer in a position to reconstruct that feature as it has been lost forever. In the examples that we have just looked at, the final consonant has been lost in all of the daughter languages, and the preceding /*u/ has been dropped or changed to /*o/ in all of the daughter languages as well, so *neither* of these features can be reconstructed.

A second possibility for checking on the validity of our reconstruction is to look at words that have been copied from other languages in the past. It is sometimes possible to find that a word was copied from a protolanguage into some other language, and that it has been retained in that language up till the present time with most of the original features of its pronunciation at the time that it was copied. The form in which such words are copied can tell us something about the pronunciation of the word in the language at the time that they were copied.

For example, we can tell something about the pronunciation in the past of the sound that is spelt *ch* in French. Nowadays this is pronounced as [ʃ], though earlier we know that it must have been pronounced as the affricate [tʃ]. We can say this because there are words in English that were borrowed from French in earlier times which have an affricate pronunciation instead of a fricative. In fact, there are even examples where English has 'reborrowed' the same word from French at different periods in history with different pronunciations and slightly different meanings. Take, for example, the words *chief* and *chef*. The word was originally borrowed as *chief* from French at a time when it was pronounced with an initial affricate, and it was borrowed as *chef* at a time much closer to the present, by which time the initial sound in French had already changed from an affricate to a fricative.

READING GUIDE QUESTIONS

1.   What do we mean when we say that one form is a reflex of another form?
2.   What are cognate forms?
3.   What is the comparative method?
4.   What is linguistic reconstruction?
5.   What do we mean by 'sound correspondences' when applying the comparative method?
6.   What kinds of factors must we consider when reconstructing the phonemes of a protolanguage from the sound correspondences in the daughter languages.
7.   How can we reconstruct a phoneme if a conditioned sound change has taken place?
8.   In what situations is the comparative method unable to reconstruct a protolanguage correctly?
9.   How can we check on the accuracy of our historical reconstructions?

EXERCISES

1.   Write formal rules expressing the changes that have taken place in Tongan, Samoan, Rarotongan, and Hawaiian. Also state, for each of these changes, whether it is a conditioned or an unconditioned change, and say whether it is an example of phonemic loss, addition, shift, split, or merger.
2.   Look at the Yimas and Karawari forms in Data Set 4. How do you think the original forms given on the left for the protolanguage were arrived at? Do you think they are reasonable reconstructions to make on the basis of the evidence that you have?

3. Look at the Suena and Zia forms in Data Set 6. Did the ancestral language have contrastive nasals? Why?

4. Look again at the Suena and Zia forms in Data Set 6. There are some correspondences between Suena /a/ and Zia /o/. Do these correspondences require us to reconstruct and additional vowel phoneme? Why?

5. Look at the information in Data Set 7 from the Korafe, Notu, and Binandere languages and reconstruct the original forms.

6. Examine the data from the Northern and Southern dialects of Paamese in Data Set 8 and reconstruct the original language. (It will help if you look at the rules described in Section 6 of Chapter 11 in conjunction with this exercise.)

7. Examine the forms in Data Set 10 from the Sepa, Manam, Kairiru, and Sera languages. Take the language pair Sepa and Manam and say which sets of forms you think are cognate, and which you think are not cognate. Now do the same for the pair Sepa and Kairiru.

8. Check all of the phonetically similar sets of correspondences in the Polynesian data that we have been looking at in this chapter to see if they are in complementary or contrastive distribution. Were the reconstructions that we made in Section 5.1 valid or not?

9. Examine the following pairs of cognate forms in Abau and Idam, which are both spoken in the West Sepik Province of Papua New Guinea. Make an attempt to reconstruct the form in the protolanguage from which these forms are descended, and state what changes have taken place.

Abau	Idam	
anan	anan	'centipede'
am	am	'place'
ak	ak	'talk'
sak	sak	'snake'
hauk	ɸauk	'lake'
sauk	sauk	'sago jelly'
kwal	kwal	'bangle'
nanak	nanak	'get'
naukan	naukan	'branch'
hau	ɸau	'taro'
auk	auk	'string bag'
nausam	nausam	'dry tree'

10. Try to reconstruct the original forms from which the Ndao and the Sawu forms (from eastern Indonesia) are derived, and state what changes have taken place in both languages.

Ndao	Sawu	
haha	wawa	'pig'
silu	hilu	'wear cloth around waist'

ceo	heo	'nine'
əci	əhi	'one'
heʔo	weʔo	'tongue'
saʔu	haʔu	'breast'
caʔe	haʔe	'climb'
həru	wəru	'moon'
dəsi	dəhi	'sea'
hei	wei	'give'
səmi	həmi	'receive'
hela	wela	'axe'

11. Examine the list of cognate forms below from the Aroma, Hula, and Sinaugoro languages of the Central Province of Papua New Guinea. Use the comparative method to reconstruct what you think to be the forms for all of these words in the protolanguage. Do not forget to look for complementary distribution among phonetically similar sets of correspondences, to avoid reconstructing too many protophonemes. (Note that the data has been slightly regularised to make the problem more workable.) Are there any words for which you are unable to reconstruct the original form? Why can you not do this?

Aroma	Hula	Sinaugoro	
pune	-	pune	'pigeon'
opi	kopi	kopi	'skin'
vau	vau	vatu-	'stone'
-	pai	bati	'chop'
ama	ama	tama	'father'
ina	ina	tina	'mother'
aɣi-	aɣi	taɣi	'cry'
uli	uli	tuli	'sew'
inaɣe	inaɣe	tinaɣe	'bowels'
ui	ui	tui	'knee'
upu	upu	tubu	'grandparent'
ia	ɣia	ɣita	'see'
uu	ɣuu	ɣutu	'louse'
ɣae	ae	ɣate	'liver'
ulia	ɣulia	ɣulita	'octopus'
laa	laa	lata	'milk'
mae	-	mate	'die'
nau	nau	natu	'child'
ɣaoi	aoi	ɣatoi	'egg'
upa	kupa	-	'short'
-	kavu	kaɣu	'ashes'
auli	kauli	kauli	'left hand'
-	kopa	koba	'chest'

one	-	kone	'sand'
wau	kwau	-	'tie'
-	kwari	kwari	'hit'
wareɣa	kwarea	-	'die'
-	kwamo	kwamo	'cough'
pipiɣa	pipiɣa	bibiɣa	'lip'
poɣi	poɣi	boɣi	'night'
-	poka	boga	'belly'
-	para	bara	'big'
-	kupa	guba	'sky'
ripa	ripa	diba	'right hand'
repa	repa	deba	'head'
lapia	lapia	labia	'sago'
riri	-	didi	'finger'
roɣe	-	doɣe	'back'
karo	karo	garo	'voice'
kovu	-	goɣu	'smoke'
ima	ɣima	ɣima	'hand'
mauli	maɣuli	maɣuli	'alive'
manu	manu	manu	'bird'
mona	mona	mona	'fat'
mina	mina	mina	'brain'
maa	-	mata	'eye'
maða	maa	maa	'tongue'
-	melo	melo	'boy'
numa	numa	numa	'house'
nivi	nivi	nivi	'dream'
niu	niu	niu	'coconut'
nemo	nemo	nemo	'mosquito'
leɣi	leɣi	leɣi	'long grass'
ðaɣi	aɣi	aɣi	'wind'
waɣi	waɣi	waɣi	'wallaby'
meɣi	meɣi	meɣi	'urinate'
arawa	ɣarawa	ɣarawa	'wife'
vane	vane	vane	'wing'
vui	vui	ɣui	'hair'
vira	vira	vira	'how many?'
vue	vue	ɣue	'moon'
vavine	vavine	vavine	'woman'
vua	vua	ɣua-	'fruit'
vonu	vonu	ɣonu	'full'
valivu	-	valiɣu	'new'
lovo	lovo	loɣo	'fly'
varo	-	varo	'plant'
vaivai	vaivai	-	'flour'

ðara	ara	ara	'name'
ðavala	avala	avala	'wet season wind'
unu	ɣunu	ɣunu	'breadfruit'
ulo	ɣulo	ɣulo	'pot'
uria	ɣuria	ɣuria	'betel nut'
ɣaniɣani	aniani	ɣaniɣani	'eat'
-	oro	ɣoro	'mountain'
mari	mari	mari	'sing'
milo	milo	milo	'dirty'
rawa	rawa	rawa	'sea'
laɹa	laa	laja	'sail'
walo	walo	walo	'vine'
wai	wai	wai	'water'
wapu	-	wabu	'widow'

12. Examine the following original forms in the Gamilaraaj and Juwaalijaaj
languages of New South Wales (in Australia). Assume that the original
language had /*ɹ/. Under what circumstances and in what ways did this
change in Juwaalijaaj?

Gamilaraaj	Juwaalijaaj		
biɹu:	biju:	'hole'
buɹa	buja	'bone'
ḏuɹa:j	ḏuja:j	'flame'
guɹa:r	guja:r	'tall'
jiɹa	jija	'tooth'
muɹa:j	muja:j	'cockatoo'
biɹi	bi:	'chest'
maɹa	ma:	'hand'
jaɹaj	ja:j	'sun'
gaɹaj	ga:j	'language'
ŋuɹu	ŋu:	'(s)he'
juɹu	ju:	'dust'
ḏigaɹa:	ḏigaja:	'bird'
waɹaba	wajaba	'turtle'
waɹaga:l	wajaga:l	'left hand'
waɹawaɹa	wajawaja	'crooked'

13. Examine the following original forms in the Gamilaraaj and Wiradjuri
languages of New South Wales (in Australia). Reconstruct the original
forms of these words and write rules that account for the changes:

Wiradjuri	Gamilaraaj		
ḏalaɲ	ḏalaj	'tongue'
guwaɲ	guwaj	'blood'

julaɲ	julaj	'skin'
muɹaɲ	muɹaj	'cockatoo'
ḍuliɲ	ḍuli	'goanna'
ḍiɲ	ḍi:	'meat'
wiɲ	wi:	'fire'
giɲ	gi:	'heart'
ḍinaŋ	ḍina	'foot'
guja	guja	'fish'
ḍuraŋ	ḍura	'bark'
ganaŋ	gana	'liver'
guwaŋ	guwa	'fog'
miɲaŋ	miɲa	'what'
ŋamuŋ	ŋamu	'breast'
jiliŋ	jili	'lip'
ŋuruŋ	ŋuru	'night'
jiɹaŋ	jiɹa	'tooth'
galiŋ	gali	'water'

14. Modern French has the words *écoute* [ekut] 'listen to', *étranger* [etʁãʒe] 'foreign', and *état* [eta] 'state', which were copied into English in the past as *scout* (i.e. one who listens), *strange* (i.e. something which is foreign), and *state*. At a later stage, English recopied the last two words as *estrange* (as in *estranged wife*), and *estate*. From the form of these lexical copies in English, what can you suggest about the history of the three French words given above?

15. Linguists sometimes use the evidence provided in rhyming poetry to justify their conclusions about the pronunciations of words in the past. The following nursery rhymes contain non-rhyming words. What do you think they can tell us about the history of English?

Ride a cock-horse
To Banbury Cross
To see a fine lady
Upon a white horse
Rings on her fingers
And bells on her toes
She shall have music
Wherever she goes

Jack and Jill
Went up the hill
To fetch a pail of water
Jack fell down
And broke his crown
And Jill came tumbling after

Old Mother Hubbard
Went to the cupboard
To get her poor doggie a bone
But when she got there
The cupboard was bare
So the poor doggie had none

Hickory dickory dock
The mouse ran up the clock
The clock struck one
The mouse ran down
Hickory dickory dock

FURTHER READING

1. Ronald W. Langacker *Language and its Structure*, Chapter 8 'Genetic Relationships', pp. 207–19.
2. Raimo Anttila *An Introduction to Historical and Comparative Linguistics*, Chapter 11 'The Comparative Method', pp. 229–65.
3. Leonard Bloomfield *Language*, Chapter 18 'The Comparative Method', pp. 297–321.
4. Winfred P. Lehmann *Historical Linguistics: An Introduction*, Chapter 5 'The Comparative Method', pp. 83–89.
5. Robert J. Jeffers and Ilse Lehiste *Principles and Methods for Historical Linguistic*, Chapter 2 'Comparative Reconstruction', pp. 17–36.
6. Theodora Bynon *Historical Linguistics*, 'Phonological Reconstruction (the comparative method)', pp. 45–57.
7. Mary Haas *The Prehistory of Languages*, 'Reconstruction and Reality', pp. 44–51.
8. Hans Henrich Hock *Principles of Historical Linguistics*, Chapter 18 'Comparative Method: Establishing Linguistic Relationship', pp. 556–80; Chapter 19 'Comparative Reconstruction', pp. 581–627.

CHAPTER SIX

INTERNAL RECONSTRUCTION

In the previous chapter you learned how to apply the comparative method to reconstruct an earlier form of an unrecorded language by comparing the forms in the various daughter languages that are descended from it. However, the comparative method is not the only method which you can use to reconstruct linguistic history. There is a second method of reconstruction that is known as *internal reconstruction*, which allows you to make guesses about the history of a language as well. The basic difference between the two methods is that in the case of internal reconstruction, you reconstruct only on the basis of evidence from within a *single* language, whereas in the comparative method you reconstruct on the basis of evidence from several different languages (or dialects). With the comparative method you arrive at a protolanguage from which two or more languages (or dialects) are derived, while with the internal method of reconstruction, you simply end up with an earlier stage of a language. We can call this stage of a language that you have reached by internal reconstruction a *prelanguage*.

6.1 SYNCHRONIC ALTERNATIONS

The Dutch linguist van der Tuuk once said: 'All languages are something of a ruin'. What he meant was that as a result of changes having taken place, some 'residual' forms are often left to suggest what the original state of affairs might have been. Applying the method of internal reconstruction is in some sense similar to the science of archaeology. In archaeology we use the evidence of the present (i.e. the covered remains of earlier times) to reconstruct something of the past. Archaeology does not enable us to reconstruct *everything* about the past — only those facts that are suggested by the present-day 'ruins' from the past.

Let us now look at an example of a linguistic change that has taken place in a language, and see what sorts of 'ruins' it leaves in the modern language. The language that we will look at is Samoan. This is a language that has verbs which appear in both intransitive and transitive forms. The intransitive form is used when there is no following object noun phrase, and verbs in this construction involve the bare root with no suffixes of any kind. In the case of transitive verbs (which are used when there is a following object noun phrase) there is a special suffix that is added to the verb. In Samoan, different transitive verbs take different suffixes, as shown by the following examples:

Intransitive		Transitive	
inu	'drink'	inu-mia	'drink (something)'
ŋau	'break'	ŋau-sia	'break (something)'
mata?u	'afraid'	mata?u-tia	'fear (something)'
taŋi	'weep'	taŋi-sia	'weep for'
alofa	'love'	alofa-ŋia	'love (somebody)'
fua	'weigh'	fua-tia	'weigh (something)'
ole	'cheat'	ole-ŋia	'cheat at'
sila	'look'	sila-fia	'see'

Samoan has a variety of suffixes to mark exactly the same function, including the following: /**-mia**/, /**-sia**/, /**-tia**/, /**-ŋia**/ and /**-fia**/. This variety in the transitive suffixes is the result of a sound change that took place at some time before the emergence of modern Samoan.

From comparative evidence, we know that the verb roots of the language that Samoan is descended from originally ended in both vowels and consonants. For instance, compare the following forms in Samoan and the distantly related language Bahasa Indonesia:

Bahasa Indonesia	Samoan	
minum	inu	'drink'
takut	mata?u	'afraid'
taŋis	taŋi	'weep'

There is also comparative evidence to suggest that transitive verbs were once marked by adding the special suffix /**-ia**/ to the verb. Then there was a general change in the history of Samoan by which final consonants were lost. When the final consonants were lost, they disappeared in the intransitive forms of the verb, but were retained in the transitive forms because when the suffix /**-ia**/ was added the consonants were no longer at the end of the word, but in the middle.

Now that, in Samoan, there were no longer any consonants at the ends of words, the consonants that were retained in the transitive forms of the verb came to be reanalysed as part of the following suffix instead of being part of the root. So, what was originally a suffix with a single form has now developed a wide range of different forms, or *allomorphs*, as a result of a single sound change having taken place. These allomorphs are morphologically conditioned, which means that each verb must be learnt with its particular transitive suffix, and there is nothing in the phonological shape of the verb which gives any clue as to which form of the suffix the verb will take. These changes are set out below:

Pre Samoan		Samoan		
Intransitive	Transitive	Intransitive	Transitive	
*inum	*inum-ia	inu	inu-mia	'drink'
*ŋaus	*ŋaus-ia	ŋau	ŋau-sia	'break'
*mataʔut	*mataʔut-ia	mataʔu	mataʔu-tia	'fear'
*taŋis	*taŋis-ia	taŋi	taŋi-sia	'weep'
*alofaŋ	*alofaŋ-ia	alofa	alofa-ŋia	'love'
*fuat	*fuat-ia	fua	fua-tia	'weigh'
*oleŋ	*oleŋ-ia	ole	ole-ŋia	'cheat'
*silaf	*silaf-ia	sila	sila-fia	'see'

In talking about this problem, I have used the knowledge that I already have about the history of Samoan from comparative evidence to help you to understand what has happened in the development of the transitive suffixes in the language. However, it would have been possible to make the same reconstruction on purely internal evidence. What you do when you apply the internal method of reconstruction is to look at cases of morphological alternation (or *allomorphs* of morphemes) and you work on the assumption that unusual or complex distributions of allomorphs may well go back to a simpler state of affairs than you find in the modern language.

The distribution of the different forms of the transitive suffix is complex, in that each verb has to be learned along with its transitive counterpart, and there are no general rules that can be learned to help a speaker of the language. It is relatively unusual for languages to leave so much for the learner to have to remember, so you could assume that in Pre Samoan the language was somehow more 'learnable', and that this earlier, simpler system has broken down because of some sound change having taken place. The unpredictability in the Samoan data does not lie in the vowels as these are consistently -**ia**. What needs explanation is the existence of the preceding consonants. If you assume that the consonants were originally part of the root, and that there was a later loss of word final consonants, then this gives a very simple picture of pre-Samoan morphology, and it involves a very natural sound change (i.e. the loss of final consonants).

Let us look at some data from a different language — German. The change that we will be dealing with is the devoicing of stops word finally that we looked at in Chapter 2. In modern German, the plural of certain nouns is formed by adding the plural suffix /-ə/, while in other nouns, the plural is formed by adding the suffix /-ə/ and at the same time changing the final voiceless consonant to the corresponding voiced consonant. So, compare the following singular and plural nouns in German:

Singular	Plural	
laut	lautə	'sound'
bo:t	bo:tə	'boat'
ta:k	ta:gə	'day'
hunt	hundə	'dog'

Here again, you can see that there is complexity in the morphological alternations of the language, and you should ask yourself if this complexity could reasonably be derived from an earlier, more simple way of forming the plural. The suffix /-ə/ is common to all forms, so you can assume this to be original. You should note, however, that some plurals have preceding voiced consonants and some have preceding voiceless consonants, whereas the singular forms all have final voiceless consonants. If you assume that the plural roots represent the original forms of the roots, then you can say that the singular forms have undergone a change of final devoicing according to the following rule:

voiced C → voiceless C / ___ #

Clearly, the consonants in the plural would have been 'protected' from this rule by the presence of the following plural suffix, and this is why they did not undergo devoicing.

It should be pointed out that not *all* cases of morphological alternation can be reconstructed as going back to a single original form that 'split' as a result of sound change taking place. The important point to keep in mind is that the modern alternations must be derivable from an original form by means of reasonable kinds of sound changes. So, while you might want to reconstruct the /-s/, /-z/, and /-əz/ markers of the plural of English nouns as going back to something simpler in the past because of their phonetic similarity, you would be unlikely to reconstruct irregular plurals such as the following as being derived from the same source (however we might want to reconstruct it):

Singular	Plural
foot	*feet*
goose	*geese*
man	*men*
woman	*women*
child	*children*
louse	*lice*

Forms that are as divergent as this must clearly go back to irregular forms even in Pre English.

6.2 LIMITATIONS OF INTERNAL RECONSTRUCTION

The internal method of reconstruction has a number of inherent limitations, and it is for this reason that it is not used nearly as much as the comparative method in reconstructing the history of languages. For one thing, it clearly does not take us back as far in time as does the comparative method. For this reason, you would normally consider using the internal method only in the following circumstances:

(a) Sometimes, the language that you are investigating might be a linguistic *isolate*, i.e. it may not be related to any other language (and is therefore in a family of its own). In such a case, there is no possibility of applying the comparative method as there is nothing to compare this language with. Internal reconstruction is therefore the only possibility that is available.

(b) A very similar situation to this would be one in which the language you are studying is so distantly related to its sister languages that the comparative method is unable to reveal very much about its history. This would be because there are so few cognate words between the language that you are working on and its sister languages that it would be difficult to set out the systematic sound correspondences.

(c) You may want to know something about changes that have taken place *between* a reconstructed protolanguage and its descendant languages.

(d) Finally, you may want to try to reconstruct further back still from a protolanguage that you have arrived at by means of the comparative method. The earliest language from which a number of languages is derived is, of course, itself a linguistic isolate in the sense that we are unable to show that any other languages are descended from it. There is no reason why you cannot apply the internal method of reconstruction to a protolanguage, just as you could with any other linguistic isolate, if you wanted to go back still further in time.

Apart from the fact that the internal method is restricted in how far back in time it can take us, there are some other limitations that are inherent to the method. As I showed you in the previous section, this method can only be used when a sound change has resulted in some kind of morphological alternation in a language. Morphological alternations that arise as a result of sound change always involve conditioned sound changes. If an unconditioned sound change has taken place in a language, there will be no synchronic residue of the original situation in the form of morphological alternations, so the internal method will be completely unable to produce any results in these kinds of situations.

Another kind of situation in which the internal method may be inapplicable — or worse, where it may even lead to false reconstructions — is when intermediate changes are affected by other later changes, with the first changes leaving no traces in the modern language. For example, in modern French, there are morphological alternations of the following kinds:

Noun		Verb	
nɔ̃	'name'	nɔme	'to name'
fɛ̃	'end'	finiʁ	'to finish'
œ̃	'one (masculine)'	ynə	'one (feminine)'

On the basis of these alternations, you would be justified in reconstructing the Pre French of the forms of the words in the left-hand column as having had the following original shapes:

*nɔm   'name'
*fin   'end'
*yn   'one'

In order to account for the forms of the modern nouns in French, you would need to reconstruct a number of sound changes. (Although I have not given a large number of examples here, you can assume that these changes will account for a large number of other forms in the language which undergo the same kinds of alternations.) The first change would be that vowels preceding word final nasal consonants underwent assimilatory nasalisation. Following this would be a change whereby word final nasal consonants were lost. Finally, you would need to reconstruct a rule which lowered nasalised vowels from high to mid. Thus, we could reconstruct the following sequence of events in the history of French:

Pre French	*nɔm	*fin	*yn
Vowel nasalisation	nɔ̃m	fĩn	ỹn
Nasal deletion	nɔ̃	fĩ	ỹ
High vowel lowering		fɛ̃	œ̃
Modern French	nɔ̃	fɛ̃	œ̃

While these changes all seem to be perfectly plausible, they are in fact not supported by the written evidence that we have for the development of the French language. Written evidence indicates that the changes that actually took place were somewhat more complicated than this. Firstly, the vowel nasalisation rule did not apply as I have just suggested. What actually happened was that first of all the following change took place, i.e. word final [m] shifted to [n]:

m → n / ___ #

It was only then that the vowel nasalisation change took place. However, this did not apply before [n] just in word final position, as vowels before non-final [n] also nasalised. By a yet later series of changes, nasalised vowels in the middles of words lost their nasalisation, while word final [n] was deleted, resulting in the present forms. You can see that there is considerable detail on which the internal method of reconstruction has proved to be inaccurate in this case. It failed to reconstruct the change of final [m] to [n], and it also got the details wrong as to how the vowels came to be nasalised.

Apart from this kind of problem, there are other problems involved in interpreting the results of internal reconstruction. By this method, we may be tempted to reconstruct an earlier stage of Samoan (which I referred to above as Pre Samoan) in which there are final consonants on verbs. However, the method does not give any indication of how much earlier than modern Samoan it was that verbs actually had these final consonants. It is often assumed that a reconstructed prelanguage arrived at in this way represents a form of the language that was spoken somewhere between the present and the time that it split off from its nearest ancestor. However, it would be quite incorrect to equate Pre Samoan with a stage of the language somewhere between modern Samoan and the time that this split off from its closest Polynesian relatives, as these languages also exhibit similar kinds of variations. What we came up with in the exercise above involved a mixture of root final consonants belonging to a protolanguage that goes back considerably earlier than Proto Polynesian, and the shapes of the remainder of the words belonging to modern Samoan. Although we do not have written evidence in this case to show that this reconstruction is in error, we are fortunate in having comparative data on related languages. In the case of a genuine language isolate, we would not be so lucky, and our reconstruction would therefore be that much less reliable.

READING GUIDE QUESTIONS

1. The comparative method and the method of internal reconstruction appear to be quite different. Can you find any *similarities* between them?
2. When might you want to use internal reconstruction instead of the comparative method?
3. What is a language isolate?
4. What sort of data do we take as the basis for applying the method of internal reconstruction?
5. What assumptions do we operate under when we apply the internal method of reconstruction?
6. Can all cases of morphological alternation be reconstructed as resulting from sound changes having taken place?
7. What are some of the problems in using the internal method of reconstruction?

EXERCISES

1. Examine the following forms in southern Paamese (spoken in Vanuatu)
and use the method of internal reconstruction to recreate the original root
forms of the words below, and state what changes have taken place.

aim	'house'	aimok	'this house'	aimos	'only the house'
ahat	'stone'	ahatuk	'this stone'	ahatus	'only the stone'
ahin	'woman'	ahinek	'this woman'	ahines	'only the woman'
atin	'cabbage'	atinuk	'this cabbage'	atinus	'only the cabbage'
atas	'sea'	atasik	'this sea'	atasis	'only the sea'
metas	'spear'	metasok	'this spear'	metasos	'only the spear'
ahis	'banana'	ahisik	'this banana'	ahisis	'only the banana'
ahis	'rifle'	ahisuk	'this rifle'	ahisus	'only the rifle'

2. Examine the data below from Bislama (spoken in Vanuatu) in which the
roots and the transitive verbs derived from these are presented. State what
you think the original form of the transitive suffix might have been and
state what changes have taken place.

Root		Transitive Verb	
rit	'read'	ritim	'read'
bon	'burnt'	bonem	'burn'
smok	'smoke'	smokem	'smoke'
skras	'itch'	skrasem	'scratch'
slak	'loose'	slakem	'loosen'
stil	'steal'	stilim	'steal'
rus	'barbecue'	rusum	'barbecue'
tait	'tight'	taitem	'tighten'
boil	'boil'	boilem	'boil'
draun	'sink'	draunem	'push underwater'
cikı	'cheeky'	cikim	'give cheek to'
pe	'payment'	pem	'pay for'
rere	'ready'	rerem	'prepare'
drai	'dry'	draim	'dry'
melek	'milk'	melekem	'squeeze liquid out of'
level	'level'	levelem	'level out'

3. Examine the following Huli (Southern Highlands, Papua New Guinea)
numerals, which are given in their basic forms used in counting, as well as
their ordinal forms (i.e. first, second, third, etc). Reconstruct the original
ordinal suffix and state what changes have taken place.

Counting	Ordinal	
tebo	tebone	'three'
ma	mane	'four'
dau	dauni	'five'
waraga	waragane	'six'
ka	kane	'seven'
hali	halini	'eight'
di	dini	'nine'
pi	pini	'ten'
hombe	hombene	'eleven'

4. Examine the following forms, again from Huli. Reconstruct the original verb roots and the original pronominal suffixes, and state what changes have taken place.

ebero	'I am coming'
ebere	'you are coming'
ibira	'(s)he is coming'
ibiru	'I came'
ibiri	'you came'
ibija	'(s)he came'
ibidaba	'come everyone!'
laro	'I am speaking'
lare	'you are speaking'
lara	'(s)he is speaking'
laru	'I spoke'
lari	'you spoke'
laja	'(s)he spoke'
ladaba	'speak everyone!'
wero	'I am putting'
were	'you are putting'
wira	'(s)he is putting'
wiru	'I put'
wija	'(s)he put'
widaba	'put everyone!'
homaro	'I am dying'
homare	'you are dying'
homara	'(s)he is dying'
homaru	'I died'
homari	'you died'
homaja	'(s)he died'
homadaba	'everyone die!'
biraro	'I am sitting'
birare	'you are sitting'
birara	'(s)he is sitting'

biraru   'I sat'
birari   'you sat'
biraja   '(s)he sat'
biradaba   'sit everyone!'

5. Use the internal method of reconstruction to suggest what the original roots and the active and passive prefixes might have been from the following data in Bahasa Indonesia.

Active	Passive	
məmbuka	dibuka	'open'
məndapat	didapat	'get'
məɲɉəlaskan	diɉəlaskan	'explain'
məŋgosok	digosok	'rub'
məmərlukan	dipərlukan	'need'
mənanam	ditanam	'plant'
məɲərahkan	disərahkan	'surrender'
məŋaraŋ	dikaraŋ	'compose'
məŋurus	diurus	'arrange'
məɲeɉa	dieɉa	'spell'
məŋambil	diambil	'take'
məɲikat	diikat	'tie'
məŋərikan	diŋərikan	'give a fright'
məŋhapuskan	dihapuskan	'wipe'

FURTHER READING

1. Robert J. Jeffers and Ilse Lehiste *Principles and Methods for Historical Linguistics*, Chapter 3 'Internal Reconstruction', pp. 37–53.
2. Raimo Anttila *An Introduction to Historical and Comparative Linguistics*, Chapter 12 'Internal Reconstruction', pp. 264–73.
3. Winfred Lehmann *Historical Linguistics: An Introduction*, Chapter 6 'The Method of Internal Reconstruction', pp. 99–106.
4. Hans Henrich Hock *Principles of Historical Linguistics*, Chapter 17 'Internal Reconstruction', pp. 532–55.

CHAPTER SEVEN

GRAMMATICAL, SEMANTIC, AND LEXICAL CHANGE

So far in this textbook, I have been talking almost entirely about questions to do with sound change. There is more to language than sounds, however. We also have to consider the grammar of a language, i.e. the ways in which units of meaning are put together to make up larger units of meaning. Grammar is traditionally divided into morphology (the ways in which words are made up of smaller grammatical elements, i.e. morphemes) and syntax (the way that words are combined with other words to form larger elements, i.e. sentences). The grammatical rules of a language are what link sounds to meanings. In talking about a language, we must also talk about the kinds of meanings that are expressed, i.e. the semantic system. Just as languages change in their sound systems, they can also change in their grammatical systems and in the meanings of their words. It is the purpose of this chapter to introduce the kinds of changes that take place in morphology, syntax, and semantics.

I have concentrated so far on the study of sound change, with comparatively little emphasis on grammar and semantics. This is no accident. The study of sound change has a long history, going back over 150 years. Scholars have therefore had lots of time to gather all kinds of information on sound change. Not only this, but it is probably inherently easier to study the changes to the sound system of a language than it is to study its grammatical and semantic systems. The number of individual phonemes of a language ranges from around a dozen or so in some languages, to 140 or so at the very most in other languages. The range of possible variations and changes in phonology is therefore much more restricted than in the grammatical system of a language, where there may be dozens (or even hundreds) of grammatical categories; not only that, we also have to consider the existence of thousands of particular grammatical constructions for any language. Also, when considering the semantic system of a language, the number of semantic relations that hold between different items in the lexicon would be so huge that they would be almost uncountable. So it is not really surprising that we know more about phonological change than we know about grammatical and semantic change.

7.1 TYPOLOGY AND GRAMMATICAL CHANGE

Languages of the world can be classified according to their grammatical *typology*. A typological classification of languages is one that looks for certain features of a language, and groups that language with another language that shares the same features. A typological classification differs fundamentally from a genetic classification of languages. While two languages may be grouped together typologically, this does not mean that they are genetically related, though of course it may turn out that this is the case. Similarly, it is possible for two languages that are genetically related to be typologically quite different. English and the Tolai language of Papua New Guinea, for example, belong to the same typological grouping if we consider the fact that they both share the same basic word order: **SUBJECT + VERB + OBJECT**. Tolai and Motu (also of Papua New Guinea) are both genetically related in the Austronesian language family, yet they belong to different typological groups if we consider their basic word orders. The basic word order in Motu is **SUBJECT + OBJECT + VERB**.

While it is possible for a language to belong to only one genetic classification, we can group languages into as many typological groups as we want, depending on which particular linguistic feature we want to classify them by. If we were to classify languages according to the way in which they express inalienable possession in noun phrases, we would find that Tolai and Motu both belong to the same typological group, while English behaves quite differently. In both Tolai and Motu, there are pronominal suffixes which are added to nouns, whereas in English, there is a separate possessive pronoun which precedes the noun to express the same meaning. Examine the following examples:

Tolai	Motu
bilau-gu	idu-gu
nose-my	nose-my
'my nose'	'my nose'

(In this particular case, Tolai and Motu are typologically similar because they have both inherited a feature that was present in the protolanguage through which they are genetically related.)

Typological classifications of languages can be based on whatever features we might find it useful to base them on. Some shared features are of little general interest, while other features are of much greater interest. In the study of grammatical change, linguists are interested in looking at how languages evolve from one grammatical type to another. I will now describe some of the major grammatical typologies, and you will see how languages that belong in each of these typological groups may have come to be like that, or how they might change typologically in future.

It can be observed that diverse languages tend to change independently in similar sorts of ways. For instance, certain types of lexical items — especially verbs or locational items — often change to become prepositions or post-positions (which can be collectively referred to as *adpositions*). Adpositions can then become attracted to nouns to become affixes. Affixes can then be lost, which means that other grammatical strategies must be developed in order to express the functions originally expressed by the now lost forms.

It should be pointed out, however, that typological changes such as I have just described are not always unidirectional. By this I mean that it is possible for a variety of different sorts of changes to follow from a single starting point, as it is also possible for some of these changes to operate in the reverse direction. If language change were unidirectional, then human language — in all the typological diversity that we find today — would be inexorably moving towards a single type of language. What we find, in fact, is that the typological mix of the world's languages has been constantly changing in a variety of directions at once, resulting in the typological mix that we find today.

(a) Morphological Type

Languages can be grouped according to their *morphological type*, i.e. the way in which the main features of the grammar are expressed morphologically.

The first type of language that I will talk about is the *isolating* type of language. Such a language is one in which there tends to be only one morpheme per word, i.e. there are many free morphemes with very few bound morphemes. A language of this type would be the Hiri Motu language of Papua New Guinea. If you examine the sentence below, you will see that each word expresses only a single meaning:

Lauegu	sinana	gwarume	ta	ia	hoia	Koki	dekenai.
My	mother	fish	one	she	bought	Koki	at

'My mother bought a fish at Koki.'

A second type of language is what we call the *agglutinating* type. An agglutinating language is one in which a word may contain many separate morphemes — both free morphemes and bound morphemes. However, the boundaries between morphemes in an agglutinating language are clear and easy to recognise, and it is as if the bits of the language were simply 'glued' together to make up larger words. In such language, each morpheme will typically express a single meaning, while words will typically consist of several — perhaps even many — morphemes combined together. A language

such as Sye (spoken on the island of Erromango in Vanuatu), has agglutinating constructions in sentences of the following type:

ov-nevyarep   ɣu-tw-ampy-oɣh-or   u-ntoɣ
plural-boy   they-will-not-want-to-see-them   in-sea
'The boys will not want to see them in the sea.'

The single word /ɣu-tw-ampy-oɣh-or/ 'they will not want to see them', for
example, expresses several meanings, some expressed by prefixes, i.e. ɣu-
'they', tw- 'will not', ampy- 'want to', one by the suffix -or 'them', and one
by the root oɣh 'see'.

   A third type of language that we can consider is the *inflectional* type.
Inflectional languages are those in which there are many morphemes included
within a single word, but the boundaries between one morpheme and another
are not clear. So, in inflectional languages, there are many meanings per
word, but there is not a clear 'gluing' together of the morphemes as is the case
with agglutinating languages. An example of an inflecting language is Latin.
Examine the following sentence:

   Marcellus amat Sophiam.
   'Marcus loves Sophie.'

Each of these words contains a number of different meanings. In the first
word, we can recognise the root *Marcell-*, but the single suffix *-us* expresses a
number of different meanings. For one thing, it indicates that *Marcell-* is the
subject of the verb (rather than the object), and it also indicates that *Marcell-*
is both masculine in gender and singular in number. In the case of *Sophiam*,
the root is *Sophia-*, and the suffix *-m* indicates that she is the object (rather
than the subject), that she is feminine, and that she also is singular. Finally,
the word *amat* includes the meaning of 'love', as well as indicating that this
particular activity takes place in the present tense, that the one performing the
activity is in the third person, as well as being singular.

   If any one of these items of meaning in any of these words were to be
changed, then a different form of the word would have to be used. As Latin is
an inflectional language, you should also note that although we can recognise
a suffix of the form *-us* on the root *Marcell-*, and a suffix *-m* on the noun
Sophia-, we cannot further subdivide either of these suffixes corresponding to
the various meanings that these both express. That is, there is no single morpheme that expresses the meaning of 'singular', for example, or 'feminine', or
'subject'. The fact that a singular masculine subject is indicated by means of
the single suffix *-us* is a typical characteristic of an inflectional language.

   There is a tendency for languages to change typologically according to a
kind of cycle. Isolating languages tend to move towards agglutinating
structures. Agglutinating languages tend to move towards the inflectional
type, and finally, inflecting languages tend to become less inflectional over

time and more isolating. This cycle can be represented by the following diagram:

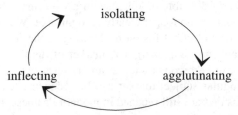

Isolating languages become agglutinating in structure by a process of *phonological reduction*. By this I mean that free form grammatical markers may become phonologically reduced to unstressed bound form markers (i.e. suffixes or prefixes). If we look at modern Melanesian Pidgin, for example, (at least as it is spoken, rather than written) we can see that a number of grammatical changes appear to be taking place. Firstly, the prepositions that are written as if they are pronounced /loŋ/ 'on, at, in' and /bloŋ/ 'of, for' tend to be pronounced nowadays as prefixes to the following noun phrases. The forms of these evolving prefixes are:

lɔ-/blo-   before consonants
l-/bl-   before vowels

So we find that changes such as the following seem to be taking place:

aus   bloŋ mi   →   aus   blo-mi
house   of   me   house   of-me
'my house'   'my house'

loŋ aus   →   l-aus
at home   at-home
'at home'   'at home'

Not only are these two prepositions being phonologically reduced in this way, but so too are some of the preverbal tense and mood markers. For instance, the future marker /bai/ is now sometimes reduced to the prefix /b-/ when the following word begins with a vowel rather than a consonant. Compare the following:

bai   yu go
future you go
'you will go'

b-em   i   go
future-(s)he predicate go
'(s)he will go'

As I have said, languages which are of the agglutinating type tend to change towards the inflectional type. By the process of *morphological fusion*, two originally clearly divisible morphemes in a word may change in such a way that the boundary is no longer clearly recognisable. We could exemplify this process of morphological fusion by looking at the following example from Paamese (spoken in Vanuatu). The marker of the first person singular subject on verbs can be reconstructed at an earlier stage as /*na-/, and the second person singular subject marker can be reconstructed as /*ko-/, and these are the forms that are still retained in modern Paamese, for example:

> na-lesi-ø
> I-see-it
> 'I see it'
>
> ko-lesi-nau
> you-see-me
> 'you see me'

Other tenses, as well as the negative, are expressed by adding other prefixes and suffixes in sequence, for example:

> ko-va-ro-lesi-nau-tei
> you-immediate future-not-see-me-not
> 'you are not going to see me'

The distant future tense was also originally marked in the same way, by a prefix of the form /*i-/ which appeared after the subject marker, in the same position as is occupied in the example that I just gave you by the prefix /va-/. However, the future tense marker /*i-/ fused morphologically with the preceding subject prefix. So, what was originally /*na-/ followed by /*i-/ became /ni-/, and what was originally /*ko-/ followed by /*i-/ became /ki-/:

> *na-i-lesi-ø   →   ni-lesi-ø
> I-future-see-it   I+future-see-it
> 'I will see it'   'I will see it'
>
> *ko-i-lesi-nau   →   ki-lesi-nau
> you-future-see-me   you+future-see-me
> 'you will see me'   'you will see me'

In modern Paamese, we can no longer divide the /ni-/ and /ki-/ prefixes into a subject marker and a future tense marker, as /n-/ and /k-/ do not occur anywhere else in the language as recognisable morphemes, and there is no longer any clearly recognisable /i-/ morpheme as a future marker. We must therefore regard these two prefixes in modern Paamese as expressing two meanings at once. Such morphemes are called *portmanteau morphemes*. This situation has arisen as a result of the fusion of two originally separate morphemes into one form. When this kind of fusion affects the grammar of a language in a major way, then the language can be said to have changed from an agglutinating type to an inflectional type.

Finally, languages of the inflectional type tend to change to the isolating type; this process is called *morphological reduction*. It is very common for inflectional morphemes to become more and more reduced, until sometimes they disappear altogether. The forms that are left, after the complete disappearance of inflectional morphemes, consist of single morphemes. The functions that were originally expressed by the inflectional suffixes then come to be expressed by word order or by free form morphemes. As I indicated earlier, Latin was an inflectional language. So many ideas were expressed in a single word that there was no need in Latin for word order to be rigidly fixed. Words could occur in any order because the one who was performing an action and the one who was on the receiving end of an action were always marked in the suffixes that were attached to the noun phrases themselves. So, the meaning of the sentence that you saw earlier could be equally well expressed in Latin in any of the following ways:

Marcellus amat Sophiam.
Sophiam amat Marcellus.
Sophiam Marcellus amat.
Amat Sophiam Marcellus.
'Marcus loves Sophie.'

To indicate that the roles are reversed in this situation (i.e. that it is Sophie who is keen on Marcus), we would need to change the marking on the nouns, but the word order could be just as variable. We could indicate that it is Sophie who loves Marcus by the following sentence:

Sophia-ø   amat Marcell-um.
Sophie-subject loves Marcus-object
'Sophie loves Marcus.'

However, any of the following would do just as well to express the same meaning in this inflectional language:

Marcellum amat Sophia.
Sophia Marcellum amat.
Amat Sophia Marcellum.

Latin evolved into modern Italian, and in the process lost a lot of its original inflections, thereby moving towards the isolating type. Nouns in Italian are no longer marked by suffixes to indicate whether they are the subject or the object, and they do not change in form as they did in Latin. In modern Italian, the only way to express the fact that Marcus loves Sophie is the following:

Marcello ama Sophia.
Marcus   loves Sophie
'Marcus loves Sophie.'

Whereas, in Latin, we would be free to change the order of these words without changing the meaning, this is no longer possible in Italian, as the nouns have lost their suffixes which indicate subject and object. If we were to change the Italian sentence that I just gave you into the following sentence, we would change the meaning as well:

Sophia ama   Marcello.
Sophie loves Marcus
'Sophie loves Marcus.'

In modern Italian, it is now word order alone which marks the difference between the subject and the object of a verb, whereas before it was the presence or absence of an inflectional suffix on the noun.

This typological cycle, and the processes involved in the transformation from one type to another, can be summarised in the following diagram:

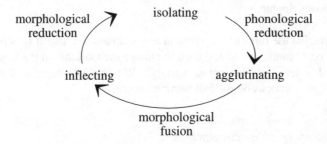

There is, in fact, a fourth type of language: those having *polysynthetic* morphology. Such languages represent extreme forms of agglutinating languages in which single words correspond to what in other kinds of languages are expressed as whole clauses. Thus, a single word may include nominal subjects and objects, and possibly also adverbial information, and even non-core nominal arguments in the clause such as direct objects and spatial noun phrases. The following example from the Yimas language of Papua New Guinea illustrates a polysynthetic structure:

na-ŋa-mpa-na-ŋkan-mpan-ra   amtra
plural-give-now-imperative-few-them   food
'You few give them food now!'

Polysynthetic languages can develop out of more *analytic* (i.e. non-polysynthetic) languages by a process of *argument incorporation*. In English, we find some evidence of this kind of construction in the form of incorporated objects, such as the following:

Professor Hawne took up pipe smoking to make himself look pompous.

In the example, a generic object such as *pipe* can be preposed to a transitive verb such as *smoke*, instead of its usual position after the verb. In fact, we can even incorporate spatial noun phrases in the same sort of way, as in the following:

He just sat there star gazing.

Since *gaze* is an intransitive verb, this sentence can only be derived from the following, in which the incorporated noun *stars* appears in a prepositional phrase:

He just sat there and gazed at the stars.

It is possible for such patterns to become established as the normal pattern in a language, and for these to completely replace earlier patterns in which there are free form nominal arguments and other kind of arguments in a clause.

(b) Accusative and ergative languages

Languages of the world can also be grouped typologically according to the way in which they mark the subject and object noun phrases in a sentence. In a language like English, we speak of the *subject* of a verb, and its *object*. The subject is the noun that comes before the verb and which causes the verb to choose the suffix **-s** if it is singular and **-ø** if it is plural, when the verb is in the present tense. The object is the noun phrase that comes after the verb in English. So we have sentences like the following in English:

The Vice-Chancellor is praising   the students.
SUBJECT (singular) VERB (singular) OBJECT

The Vice-Chancellors are praising   the students.
SUBJECT (plural)   VERB (plural) OBJECT

There are other languages which differ from English in the way that the subject and the object noun phrases are marked. Look at the following sentences in the Bandjalang language of northern New South Wales (in Australia):

Mali-ju bajgal-u mala ḍa:ḍam buma-ni.
the   man   the   child   hit-past
'The man hit the child.'

Mala bajgal gaware-:la.
the   man   run-present
'The man is running.'

Mali-ju ḍa:ḍam-bu mala bajgal ɲa:-ni.
the   child   the   man   see-past
'The child saw the man.'

You will notice that the noun /bajgal/ 'man' appears in two separate forms, either /bajgalu/ (with the suffix /-u/) or just /bajgal/ (with no suffix). The word that precedes it also varies in its shape. When the word for 'man' appears with the suffix /-u/, this word has the form /mali-ju/, but when the word for 'man' appears without any suffix, the preceding word has the shape /mala/. If you examine the sentences carefully, you will find that the noun phrase appears as /maliju bajgalu/ when it is the subject of the transitive verb /buma-/ 'hit', but when it is the subject of the intransitive verb /gaware-/ 'run', it appears without any suffixes, as /mala bajgal/. You will also see that when the same noun phrase appears as the object of the transitive verb /ɲa:-/ 'see', it also has the unsuffixed form /mala bajgal/. The noun phrase referring to 'the child' behaves in exactly the same way. When the child is the object of the verb /buma-/ 'hit', the object appears without any suffix as /mala ḍa:ḍam/ 'the child', but when the child functions as the subject of the transitive verb /ɲa:-/ 'see', it appears with suffixes, i.e. /maliju ḍa:ḍambu/. (The forms of the suffix on the word /bajgal/ 'man' and /ḍa:ḍam/ 'child' are different, but these are phonologically determined allomorphs of the same morpheme.)

If you compare the structure of English and Bandjalang sentences, you will see that there are three basic grammatical functions that are being expressed in the two languages, but in different ways in both cases. In English, we have:

Intransitive subject
Transitive subject

being marked in the same way, and being distinguished from:

Transitive object

In Bandjalang, however, we have:

Intransitive subject
Transitive object

being marked in the same way, while these two functions are distinguished from:

Transitive subject

In a language like English, the transitive and intransitive subject functions are referred to collectively as the *nominative* noun phrases, while the transitive object is said to be the *accusative* noun phrase. In a language like Bandjalang, the transitive subject is referred to as the *ergative* noun phrase, while the intransitive subject and the transitive object noun phrases are referred to collectively as the *absolutive* noun phrases.

Languages in the world fall into one of these two basic typological groupings, though the type represented by English is much more widely distributed than the type represented by Bandjalang. (It is also possible for languages to be structurally intermediate between the two patterns.) With such different types of languages, we cannot really use the term *subject* for all languages of the world because it will have to mean different things depending on which of these two types of languages we are looking at. In order to make it clear which type of system we are talking about, we need to distinguish between two basic types of languages: *nominative-accusative* languages (such as English), and *ergative-absolutive* languages (such as Bandjalang). Sometimes these labels can be shortened, so English can also be called an *accusative* language, and Bandjalang can be called an *ergative* language.

Just as it is possible for a language to change its basic morphological type over time, it is also possible for an accusative language to evolve into an ergative language, and for an ergative language to become an accusative language. Most Australian languages behave like Bandjalang, i.e. they are ergative rather than accusative. Some linguists have argued that they were originally accusative and that they changed to become ergative. The original language might have had constructions like these (in which the roots and affixes are largely hypothetical, as indicated by the double asterisks):

```
**wati-ø        ɲina-ŋu
man-nominative sit-past
'The man was sitting.'
```

```
**wati-ø            jipi-ku           paka-ŋu       juku-ŋku
  man-nominative    woman-accusative  cover-past    blanket-with
'The man covered the woman with a blanket.'
```

These sentences are clearly accusative in type. Just as English has a passive construction, so too, it is argued, did this hypothetical language. The passive could have been marked by the suffix **/-li/** on the verb. In the passive construction, what was originally the accusative noun phrase became the nominative noun phrase, and what was originally the nominative noun phrase was marked by the instrumental suffix, which translates as the *by* phrase of a passive sentence in English:

```
**jipi-ø     wati-ŋku          paka-li-ŋu        juku-ŋku
  woman      man-instrumental  hit-passive-past  blanket-instrumental
'The woman was covered by the man with a blanket.'
```

If you compare this hypothetical passive sentence with the sentence above in which a blanket is referred to as an instrument, you will see that the instrumental suffix and the ergative suffix are the same, with the shape **/-ŋku/**. It is then argued that the passive eventually 'took over' from the active sentences, and the active sentences completely ceased to be a part of the grammar of the language. The last example would then have become the normal way of saying 'The man covered the woman'. So, the performer of the action (i.e. the transitive subject) would always have been marked differently from the intransitive subject and the transitive object. (Note that this hypothesis is not widely accepted for the history of Australian languages, and there are few linguists who would take it seriously now. However, this example does show one way in which a language might change from an accusative type to an ergative type.)

Of course, ergative languages can also change to become accusative languages. Just as accusative languages often have passive constructions, ergative languages often have what are referred to as *antipassive* constructions. In an antipassive sentence, a transitive verb with an ergative subject is structurally marked and detransitivised, with the original subject receiving absolutive marking. The original absolutive object is then marked in some other way. If the original antipassive function of the marker on the verb were to have this function obscured over time — perhaps by phonological reduction or loss, or the acquisition of new functions — then we would be left with a system of accusative marking.

We could take the same original forms that were presented above and start out instead with an original ergative pattern of marking, as illustrated by the following:

> *wati-ŋku   jipi-ø   paka-ŋu
>   man-ergative   woman-absolutive   cover-past
> 'The man covered the woman.'

Let us now imagine an original antipassive verbal suffix of the form **/*-li/**, and an originally dative suffix of the shape **/*-ku/**, which then comes to also mark the object of a transitive verb when it has been antipassivised. We would then end up with sentences like the following:

> *wati-ø   jipi-ku   paka-li-ŋu
>   man-absolutive   woman-dative   cover-antipassive-past
> 'The man covered the woman.'

If the **/*-li/** suffix then became reanalysed in some way as part of the verb — perhaps as a generalised marker of any intransitive verb — then we would have a genuinely accusative pattern, as follows:

```
*wati-ø              jipi-ku              paka-li-ŋu
man-nominative    woman-accusative    cover-intransitive-past
'The man covered the woman.'
```

```
*wati-ø              ɲina-li-ŋu
man-nominative    sit-intransitive-past
'The man sat.'
```

(c) Basic constituent order

When I talk about *basic constituent order*, I am referring to the relative order in the sentence of the three major components, i.e. the verb and the noun phrases that are centrally associated with it, these being the subject and object noun phrases. Languages of the world can be grouped typologically according to the way that these three major constituents in the sentence are ordered. Most languages have the order **SUBJECT + VERB + OBJECT (SVO)** — English is a language of this type. The next most frequently found order is **SUBJECT + OBJECT + VERB (SOV)**. The only other commonly found order is **VERB + SUBJECT + OBJECT (VSO)**. (There are three other logical possibilities for the order of constituents in a sentence, i.e. **OVS, OSV, VOS**. However, these orders are much rarer among languages of the world.)

Many of the Austronesian languages of the Pacific — along with English as I have already said — are **SVO** languages. The Tolai language of New Britain in Papua New Guinea is a language of this type, as shown by the following example:

```
A   pap  i   gire    tikana  tutana.
the dog  it  see     one     man
SUBJECT    VERB  OBJECT
'The dog saw a man.'
```

The Austronesian languages of Central and Milne Bay Provinces of Papua New Guinea, however, are generally of the **SOV** type. For example, the same sentence in Motu would be expressed as:

```
Sisia ese    tau  ta   e-ita-ia.
dog   subject man  one  it-see-him
SUBJECT     OBJECT     VERB
'The dog saw a man.'
```

The Austronesian languages of Central and Milne Bay Provinces appear to have changed their word order from the earlier order of **SVO** to the **SOV** order that they now have. Some scholars have argued that this change took place when the ancestor language from which Motu and its closer relatives are descended came into contact with the non-Austronesian languages of the area, as all of these non-Austronesian languages are **SOV** languages. For instance, in the non-Austronesian Koita language, which is spoken by the neighbouring group to the Motu, the sentence that I have just given for Tolai and Motu would be expressed as follows:

Tora   ata   be   eraya-nu.
dog   man one   saw-him
SUBJECT   OBJECT VERB
'The dog saw a man.'

Language contact is not the only possible explanation for a change in basic word order, as languages clearly do undergo these sorts of changes without any evidence that language contact is involved. Many languages that have one particular basic constituent order often allow competing patterns in certain structural contexts. German, for example is an **SVO** language in main clauses, as shown by the following:

Der   Mann   sah   den   Hund.
the   man   saw   the   dog
'The man saw the dog.'

In subordinate clauses, however, German has **SOV** order, as shown by the following:

Ich   glaube   dass   der   Mann   den   Hund   sah.
I   believe that   the   man   the   dog   saw
'I believe that the man saw the dog.'

When there are competing structures of this type, it is possible for one of the two patterns to be generalised to other contexts and for the typology of the language to change. (Note, however, that I am not trying to say here that German is moving from **SVO** to **SOV** constituent order.)

Other languages allow alternative word orders as a way of expressing purely stylistic contrasts in particular contextual environments. For instance, in an **SVO** language, it may be possible to focus attention on the object by moving that noun phrase to the beginning of the sentence, or by moving the subject to the end of the sentence. Even though English is an **SVO** language, we sometimes find **OSV** orders in sentences such as the following:

I quite like Harry, but John I can't stand.

Similarly, although French is an **SVO** language, we also find constructions such as the following in the colloquial language which appear to have a **VOS** order:

Il   aime   bien   sa   petite   fille   le   vieux   mec.
he   love   much   his   little   daughter   the   old   guy
'The old guy really loves his little daughter.'

Again, if constructions such as these originally purely stylistic variants were to take over from the dominant patterns, then a change of constituent order typology would have taken place.

(d) Verb chains

While there are many grammatical facts that we could consider when setting up language typologies, the final example of typological change that I want to look at in this chapter is the development of what is called in some languages *verb chains* or *serial verbs*. In some languages, we find that whole series of verbs can be strung together, sometimes in a single phonological word, with just a single subject and a single object. For instance, in the non-Austronesian Alamblak language of the East Sepik in Papua New Guinea, we find sentences such as these:

Wifёrt fïr   gёŋgïmё-t-a.
wind   blow   cold-past-it-me
'The wind blew me and I got cold (i.e. 'the wind blew me cold').'

Another example comes this time from the Paamese language of Vanuatu (which is an Austronesian language):

Keik   ko-ro: vul   a:i.
you   you-sat   break   plank
'You sat on the plank, breaking it.'

Verb-serialising languages sometimes even allow three (or more) verbs to be chained together in single constructions of this type. For instance, in the Yimas language, which is a close neighbour of the Alamblak language, we find complex examples of clause chaining such as the following:

Na-bu-wul-cay-pra-kiak.
him-they-afraid-try-come-past
'They tried to frighten him as he came.'

Such constructions are not possible at all in English. Thus, we do not use equivalent constructions such as the following:

*The wind blew-colded me.
*You sat-broke the plank.
*They tried-frighten-he-came him.

Serial verb constructions of this type are quite common in the languages of eastern and southeastern Asia and in western Africa, as well as in the non-Austronesian languages of Melanesia. There is also evidence of serial verb constructions in some of the Oceanic languages, as well as Australian languages.

In languages that have these kinds of constructions, it is often possible to show that these chains of verbs originate from much simpler constructions in which each verb had its own set of subject and object noun phrases. For instance, the complex Alamblak structure that you have just seen could be derived from the Alamblak equivalents of the following:

'The wind blew me.'
'I got cold.'

Languages which develop serial verbs of this type are generally (but not always) **SOV** languages. This is not surprising, as this order allows speakers simply to state the subject and the object once at the beginning and then string the verbs together one after the other following these two noun phrases. It is then a relatively small step for these chained verbs to be 'collapsed' into a single grammatical unit, or even a single word.

7.2 GRAMMATICALISATION

Words in languages can be grouped into two basic categories: *lexical* words and *grammatical* words. Lexical words are those which have definable meanings of their own when they appear independently of any linguistic context: *elephant, trumpet, large.* Grammatical words, on the other hand, only have meanings when they occur in the company of other words, and they relate those other words together to form a grammatical sentence. Such words in English include *the, these, on, my.* Grammatical words constitute the mortar in a wall, while lexical words are more like the bricks.

If a particular meaning is expressed by a grammatical rather than a lexical word, the form is obligatorily present. For instance, in the sentence:

I will come later.

the meaning of 'future tense' is expressed twice — firstly in the auxiliary *will*, and secondly in the adverb *later*. Of these, *will* is a grammatical word and *later* is not, because we cannot omit the future marker *will*, whereas we can omit the future marker *later*:

*I come later.
I will come.

Words in languages can often change from being lexical words to grammatical words. This process is referred to as *grammaticalisation*. We can see evidence of grammaticalisation in progress in English with the following sentences:

I'm going to cut a piece of chocolate cake.
I'm going to the supermarket.

Although these two sentences both contain the sequence *going to*, these two words do not have the same status in both cases, in that it is only in the first sentence that we can contract *going to* to give *gonna*. Thus:

I'm gonna cut a piece of chocolate cake.
*I'm gonna the supermarket.

In the first example, it is clear that the meaning of *going to/gonna* is different to the meaning of *going to* in the second example. Rather than expressing the purely lexical meaning of the intransitive verb *go*, this sequence in the first sentence expresses a kind of intentional future tense. In this case, then, we say that *going to* has been grammaticalised, and that English has acquired a new kind of auxiliary, along with other auxiliaries such as *can*, *will* and *might*, and other more recently grammaticalised auxiliary-like constituents such as *oughta*, *wanna* and *hafta*.

Grammaticalisation can affect lexical words in a variety of ways, though there is a tendency for forms to become increasingly closely linked to some lexical form in a sentence as the process continues. The change from lexical word to grammatical word is only the first step in the process of grammaticalisation, with the next step being *morphologisation*, i.e. the development of a bound form out of what was originally a free form.

In fact, morphologisation can also involve degrees of bonding between bound forms and other forms as it is possible to distinguish between *clitics* and *affixes*. A clitic is a bound form which is analysed as being attached to a whole phrase rather than to just a single word. An affix, however, is attached as either a prefix or a suffix directly to a word.

In the Sye language of Erromango in Vanuatu, the free form /im/ 'and' is currently developing into a clitic with the shape /m-/, and this attaches to the beginning of whatever happens to be the second element of two coordinated noun phrases. It is possible to say either of the following in this language, in which /im/ appears as a free form:

netor	im	nevyarep		netor	m-nevyarep
Netor	and	boy		Netor	and-boy
'Netor and the boy'				'Netor and the boy'	

However, when some other constituent intervenes between the coordinator and the second noun, the coordinator can be attached to whatever happens to be the first constituent of the second noun phrase.

netor	im	ovon	nevyarep	netor	m-ovon	nevyarep
Netor	and	plural	boy	Netor	and-plural	boy
'Netor and the boys'				'Netor and the boys'		

Morphologisation can proceed one step further, with lexical forms (or clitics) becoming genuine word-level affixes. There are many languages in which locative affixes on nouns began as free postpositions or prepositions, while before this they were ordinary lexical items with some kind of locational meaning. In this discussion of morphologisation, it is impossible not to refer back to the earlier discussion of morphological change in languages, where I demonstrated that isolating languages tend to move towards agglutinating structures, while agglutinating structures tend to move towards inflecting structures. These kinds of changes clearly involve increasingly grammaticalised (and correspondingly delexicalised) patterns.

Lexical items can obviously grammaticalise to varying extents and in differing ways in languages. Despite the varying possible end results, the process is a strongly unidirectional one in that lexical items generally become grammaticalised, while grammatical items generally do not become lexical items. As an example of how grammaticalisation can develop along a continuum from a fully lexical item to a fully morphologised affix, let us consider some developments affecting some verbs in Oceanic languages.

In the Paamese language of Vanuatu, there are two verbs of the shape /kur/ 'take' and /vul/ 'break':

inau	na-kur	a:i		inau	na-vul	a:i
I	I-took	stick		I	I-broke	stick
'I took the stick.'				'I broke the stick.'		

In Paamese, the verb /vul/ 'break' can also enter into a serial verb construction in which both verbs retain their lexical status, as follows. Thus:

inau	na-kur	vul	a:i
I	I-took	broke	stick
'I took the stick, thereby breaking it.'			

However, in languages to which Paamese is related, the form that originally occupied the second slot in this kind of serial verb construction no longer occurs as an independent verb. There is typically a restricted set of forms in such languages that can behave in this way, so what was originally a lexical verb has been grammaticalised to become a kind of post-verbal modifier of some kind. Examine the following example from the Numbami language of Papua New Guinea:

i-tala	ai	tomu
he-chopped	tree	broke
'He chopped the tree, thereby breaking it.'		

In this case, the form /tomu/ 'break' cannot be used as a verb in its own right. Thus, it is not possible to say:

    *i-tomu   ai
    he-broke   tree
    'He broke the tree.'

Other languages may then undergo further grammaticalisation in which forms behaving like /tomu/ in Numbami end up as verbal affixes that express meanings that are still clearly related to the meanings of the verbs from which they were originally derived. In some cases, a pre-verbal grammaticalised item may become a kind of classificatory verbal prefix that is attached to a general semantic category of verbs. For instance, all verbs that involve some kind of finger action, such as pinching, picking, plucking, flicking and so on, might be marked by a prefix that derives from a verb that perhaps originally meant something like 'pinch'. In the Manam language of Papua New Guinea such a development has taken place, so we find the verb /sere?/ 'break', along with the prefixed form /?in-sere?/ 'break with the fingers'. The verb /sere?/ 'break' is then free to appear with other classificatory prefixes, such as /tara-/ 'do by chopping', which therefore gives /tara- sere?/ 'break by chopping'.

Given that grammaticalisation is a diachronic process, it is possible for synchronic descriptions of languages to represent situations that are still only partly grammaticalised. In such cases, the distinction that I made at the beginning of this section between lexical and grammatical items will seem somewhat arbitrary. Instead of a clear-cut distinction between these two categories of words, there will appear to be a continuum between two extremes.

For instance, the Paamese serial verb construction that I described earlier is already moving along the way towards grammaticalisation with some verbs. For one thing, the great majority of verbs in Paamese cannot appear in the second structural slot in such constructions. While there are some verbs which can appear in either the first or second slot, there are other forms which can never appear as independent verbs. Such forms have therefore already undergone functional restriction to post-verbal modifiers. Thus, the form /vini:/ 'kill' — which derives from an earlier genuine verb with the same meaning — can now only ever occur as a serialised verb, and never as an independent verb. Thus:

    inau na-sal   vini: vuas   *inau na-vini: vuas
    I   I-speared killed pig   I   I-killed pig
    'I speared the pig to death.'   'I killed the pig.'

Grammaticalisation tends to be a unidirectional process, with forms moving along a continuum of increasingly grammaticalised status:

    lexical word → grammatical word → clitic → agglutinated
    affix → portmanteau affix

While grammaticalisation is quite a common process, the reverse — *degrammaticalisation* (or *lexicalisation*) — is attested, though it is much rarer. There are some examples that can be given of this kind of change, however. For instance, a grammatical item such as the suffix *-burger* in words such as *hamburger*, *cheeseburger* and *fishburger*, has become a genuine noun in English, and it is possible nowadays to ask for just a *burger*. The forms *pro-* and *anti-* were originally just prefixes in English in words such as *pro-democratic* or *anti-Castro*. However, these days, they can also be used as lexical adjectives:

> *Are you pro or anti?*
> *She is more anti than I am.*

7.3 MECHANISMS OF GRAMMATICAL CHANGE

In all of the grammatical changes that I have just discussed, there are three general factors that seem to be involved in one way or another in grammatical change whenever it occurs. These factors are *reanalysis*, *analogy,* and *diffusion*. I will discuss each of these mechanisms in this section.

(a) Reanalysis
Reanalysis in grammatical change refers to the process by which a form comes to be treated in a different way grammatically from the way in which it was treated by speakers of the protolanguage. What often happens in the history of languages is that a particular form may be structurally ambiguous between two interpretations in some of the contexts in which it occurs, i.e. it may be analysed grammatically in more than one way. What can then happen is that one of these analyses 'takes over' from the original analysis in the minds of speakers of the language. This new analysis may then become the basic form for a whole new paradigm of forms or constructions.

For instance, the original word for the first person singular pronoun has been reconstructed for many Australian languages as /*ŋaj/. When this pronoun was used as the subject of a transitive verb, it added the ergative suffix, and after the final glide the form of this suffix was /*-ḍu/. Thus, the pronoun that was used as the subject to an intransitive verb was /*ŋaj/, while the form that appeared when the verb was transitive was /*ŋaj-ḍu/ (and this form was later phonologically reduced to /*ŋaḍu/). The transitive subject form then in some cases 'took over' from the intransitive /*ŋaj/ form. Some languages later reanalysed this new /*ŋaḍu/ form, which was used with both transitive and intransitive verbs, as being basically an intransitive form, then added a new ergative suffix to it when it was used before transitive verbs. There are now Australian languages such as Warlpiri which have the intransitive subject form /*ŋaḍu/ and the transitive subject form /*ŋaḍu-lu/

(in which /-lu/ is the allomorph of the ergative suffix that is found on stems that end in vowels)!

Some Austronesian languages of the Pacific area have also undergone grammatical reanalysis of what were originally noun markers. In languages such as Tolai (spoken in Papua New Guinea), common noun phrases must be preceded by a marker of the form /a/, which simply has the function of indicating that what follows is a noun. So, we find forms in Tolai such as the following:

Tolai
a vat   'stone'
a vavina   'woman'
a pal   'house'

This /a/ is, in fact, inherited from the protolanguage where it apparently had a very similar function. However, in the Paamese language of Vanuatu, this original /*a/ has been reanalysed as part of the root of some (but not all) nouns, and the two cannot be separated, for example:

		Paamese	
*batu	→	ahat	'stone'
*tansik	→	atas	'sea'
*niu	→	ani	'coconut'

The original noun marker has lost its noun marking function, and has become an integral part of the following noun root.

A final example of grammatical reanalysis comes in the morpheme *-burger* that is creeping into the English language in words such as *hamburger*, *cheeseburger*, *eggburger*, *fishburger*, and now even *Kiwiburger* (which refers to a hamburger marketed in New Zealand by McDonalds, and which contains not kiwi meat, but a fried egg and pickled beetroot). The word *hamburger* was originally the only one of these four words to be used in English. Its derivation was from the name of the city *Hamburg*, with the suffix *-er* (on the same pattern as the noun *Berliner* derived from *Berlin*). However, speakers of English perceived an ambiguity between this explanation of the word's origin and the interpretation of *hamburger* as *ham* (because of the meat filling in the bun) plus *burger*. The second analysis seems to be winning out, and a new morpheme *-burger* has come into the English language. The meaning of this new morpheme appears to be something like 'toasted (or, nowadays, perhaps microwaved) bread roll with a certain kind of filling and salad'. This suffix then came to be attached to other nouns that referred to the possible range of fillings around which the *hamburger* could be constructed.

In fact, the suffix *-burger* even seems to be undergoing further reanalysis as a noun root rather than just as a suffix — it is now possible to ask for just a *burger*, instead of what used to be called a *plain hamburger*. This is an example that runs counter to the generally unidirectional tendency for lexical items to become bound morphemes, and not the other way round.

There is another kind of grammatical reanalysis that we can talk about, and that is *back formation*. An example of this process is involved in the development of the English word *cherry*. This word was originally borrowed from the French word *cerise*. In its pronunciation in French, the word is identical in both the singular and the plural, i.e. /səʁiz/. When *cerise* was copied into English, people analysed the word as being plural (as cherries are small fruit that are generally seen in large numbers anyway!). The final /-z/ of the word in French was thought to be the plural suffix, so when English speakers wanted to speak of a single *cerise*, they simply dropped off this /-z/ and came up with the previously non-existent word *cherry*. If those earlier English speakers had not reanalysed this root, we would today be speaking of *one cherries* and *two cherrieses*! (Of course, English copied the French word *cerise* again at a later point in its history to refer to a deep purplish colour, which is pronounced in English exactly as we would predict on the basis of its pronunciation in French, i.e. /səʁiːz/.)

(b) Analogy

Another powerful force in grammatical change in addition to reanalysis is *analogy*. Grammatical systems operate in terms of general patterns. Patterns, however, tend to have exceptions (or special 'sub-patterns') that are used in only a small and unpredictable set of situations. For instance, to form the plural of nouns in English, we regularly add a morpheme which has the following variants or allomorphs: /-əz/ after sibilants, /-s/ after voiceless non-sibilants, and /-z/ after voiced non-sibilants. There are, however, a few irregular plural forms that all speakers of English simply have to learn, including the following:

Singular	Plural
man	*men*
woman	*women*
child	*children*
mouse	*mice*
foot	*feet*
ox	*oxen*

Anybody who makes a mistake and says (as a child might) *mans* for *men*, or *foots* instead of *feet*, would be operating under the influence of analogy. While such forms are clearly regarded by English speakers as mistakes, there are some forms that started out as mistakes but which have become fully standardised as part of the language. For instance, the word *shoe* originally had an irregular plural *shoen*, but this has of course now become completely regularised to *shoes*. The word *book* now has its plural as *books*, but if the word had continued on from its earlier irregular plural we would now be reading *beech* instead of *books*! Finally, what we now call *nuts* would have been *nit* if we had not regularised the earlier irregular plural under the influence of analogy.

Analogy can also operate in the opposite direction. Instead of creating more regularity, it can cause regular forms to become irregular on the basis of partial patterns that already exist in the language. For instance, in most dialects of English, the verb *dive* is quite regular in its past tense, and people simply say *dived*. In American English, however, it is quite normal to say *dove* (even though this sounds as odd to non-Americans as it would if somebody said *squoze* as the past tense of *squeeze*!). The reason for this change in American English is presumably analogy on the basis of the already existing irregular pair *drive/drove*.

(c) Diffusion

Another factor that can influence the direction of grammatical change is *diffusion*. You have already seen that languages can influence each other in their vocabulary, as words are frequently copied from one language to another. Languages do not copy just words, as they can also copy grammatical constructions, and sometimes even the morphemes that are used to construct sentences in a language. This happens when there are enough people who speak two languages, and they start speaking one language using constructions that derive from the other language. In the first section of this chapter, you saw that it has been suggested that an original **SVO** word order in Austronesian languages switched in the languages of the Central and Milne Bay Provinces to **SOV** under the influence of the neighbouring non-Austronesian languages. This means that the **SOV** word order in this case has *diffused* to the Austronesian languages. (In Chapter 12, I look in more detail at how languages can change grammatically as a result of diffusion.)

7.4 SEMANTIC CHANGE

I mentioned at the beginning of this chapter that phonological change has been fairly intensively studied in the world's languages. Grammatical change is less well studied, but it is an area that is receiving a lot of attention from linguists at the present. Semantic change, however, seems to be the area of diachronic linguistics that is least well understood, perhaps because semantics has for a long time been the weak point in synchronic language study. However, there are some observations that we can make as to the kinds of semantic changes that occur in languages, and the forces that are involved in bringing these changes about. Changes in meaning can be divided into four basic types: *broadening*, *narrowing*, *bifurcation*, and *shift*. In the following sections I will discuss each of these in turn.

(a) Broadening

The term *broadening* is used to refer to a change in meaning that results in a word acquiring additional meanings to those that it originally had, while still retaining those original meanings as part of the new meaning. Quite a number of words have undergone semantic broadening in the history of English. The modern English word *dog*, for example, derives from the earlier form *dogge*, which was originally a particularly powerful breed of dog that originated in England. The word *bird* derives from the earlier word *bridde*, which originally referred only to young birds while still in the nest, but it has now been semantically broadened to refer to any birds at all.

(b) Narrowing

Semantic *narrowing* is the exact opposite of the previous kind of change. We say that narrowing takes place when a word comes to refer to only part of the original meaning. The history of the word *hound* in English neatly illustrates this process. This word was originally pronounced *hund* in English, and it was the generic word for any kind of dog at all. This original meaning is retained, for example, in German, where the word *Hund* simply means 'dog'. Over the centuries, however, the meaning of *hund* in English has become restricted to just those dogs which are used to chase game in the hunt, such as beagles. The word *meat* in English has also been semantically narrowed. It originally referred to any kind of food at all (and this original meaning is still reflected in the word *sweetmeats*), though now it only refers to food that derives from the flesh of slaughtered animals.

(c) Bifurcation

A third type of semantic change can be called *semantic split* or *bifurcation*. These terms describe the change by which a word acquires another meaning that relates in some way to the original meaning. For instance, if you take the phrase *pitch black* in English, you will find that some people do not realise that the word *pitch* comes from the name of the very black substance like tar. These speakers of English might simply regard *pitch* in this example as meaning 'very' or 'completely'. If you were ever to hear anybody saying *pitch blue* or *pitch yellow*, then you would know that, for these people, the original meaning of *pitch* has split into two quite different meanings.

(d) Shift

The final kind of semantic change that I will talk about is *semantic shift*, where a word completely loses its original meaning and acquires a new meaning. In all of the examples of semantic shift that you have just learned about, at least something of the original meaning is retained, but this is not the case with semantic shift. The history of the word *silly* in English illustrates this process. This word is cognate with the German word *selig* 'blessed', and it is derived from *Seele* 'soul'. The meaning of the German word represents the original meaning of the word, so there has clearly been a major semantic shift to get from the meaning 'blessed' to the meaning in modern English of 'stupid' or 'reckless'.

Words obviously do not jump randomly from one meaning to another when they undergo semantic shift of this kind. They may shift in smaller steps that go under some of the headings that I have already presented, but as some original meanings are lost, the points of connection between intermediate semantic stages may also be lost. The German word *selig* has also acquired the meaning 'blissful' from its original meaning of 'blessed'. This represents an understandable semantic broadening, as somebody who is blessed is likely to feel blissful at the prospect of getting into heaven. From 'blissful', the more general meaning of 'happy' was acquired in German. Perhaps somebody who is happy ends up skipping around and being silly, giving us the modern English meaning of the word.

When talking about semantic change, we can recognise a number of different forces which operate to influence the directions which these changes take, including *metaphor*, *euphemism*, *hyperbole*, and *interference*. I will discuss each of these in turn.

(a) Metaphor

A *metaphor* is an expression in which something is referred to by some other term because of a partial similarity between the two things. For example, if you say, Kali is a pig, you do not mean literally that he is a pig, but that there are certain things about his appearance or his behaviour that remind you of a pig. Perhaps he eats a lot, or he eats sloppily, or he is an extremely dirty or untidy person. Sometimes the metaphoric use of a word can cause the original meaning to change in some way. The word 'insult' in English originally meant 'to jump on'. Presumably, if you insulted someone, it was as though you had metaphorically jumped on them. However the metaphoric use of the word then completely took over the original word and a semantic shift had taken place.

(b) Euphemism

A *euphemism* is a term that we use to avoid some other term which has some kind of unpleasant associations about it, or a term which is completely taboo in some contexts. For instance, in colonial Papua New Guinea, Europeans often referred to Melanesian people as *natives*. As Papua New Guineans became more aware of the connotations of the word 'native' (as it implies a certain backwardness), people had to find a new word to talk about Papua New Guineans that was not offensive. This is how the expression 'a national' became the accepted expression to replace *native*. The term *national* has therefore undergone a semantic broadening in Papua New Guinea English under the pressure of euphemism. In Vanuatu, the word *native* was also felt to have offensive connotations, and a new term was also created there, but in this case out of local lexical resources, and the word *ni-Vanuatu* (literally: of + Vanuatu) was created. This word has become accepted, but those Europeans who still insist on putting Melanesian people down (but who dare not use the word *native*) have re-created their own insulting word from this new word, and refer to *ni-Vanuatu* as *ni-Vans*.

(c) Hyperbole

Some words in languages are felt to express meanings in a much stronger way than other words referring to the same thing. For instance, the two words *good* and *fantastic* can be used to refer to more or less the same things, but it is the second word which has the greater impact. Stronger words can often change to become more neutral if used often enough. This force in semantic change is referred to as *hyperbole* — this means that an originally strong connotation of a word is lost because of constant use. An example of this kind of development involves the change of earlier French *extonāre*, which originally meant 'strike with thunder'. This form has developed into modern French *étonner*, which simply means to 'surprise'.

(d) Interference

A final force that operates in semantic change is *interference*. Sometimes one of a pair of similar words, or a pair of homonyms (i.e. words with the same form but totally different meanings) can undergo semantic change of one kind or another to avoid the possibility of confusion between the two meanings. The word *gay* in English is undergoing semantic shift at the moment as a result of interference. Until thirty years ago, in mainstream society, this simply meant 'happy' or 'cheerful'. Then the word *gay* underwent a semantic split, and acquired the second meaning of 'defiant and proud homosexual'. When the heterosexual majority of the English-speaking population became aware of this new meaning of the word *gay*, they tended to avoid the word altogether when they wanted to express the fact that they were happy. People are now unlikely to say *I am gay* unless they want to declare that they are homosexual.

Another example of semantic interference involves the Bislama word **melek**. When the English word *milk* was originally copied into Bislama, this was the form that it took. The word **melek** then acquired a second meaning, that of 'semen'. The association of the word **melek** with the taboo connotations of the meaning 'semen' has recently become so strong that younger speakers of Bislama tend to avoid using the word **melek** to refer to plain milk, and have reborrowed the English word *milk* in the shape **milk**.

7.5 LEXICAL CHANGE

If you study the history of particular words in themselves rather than the changes in their actual pronunciations, you are engaging in a study of *lexical change* (which is sometimes known as *etymology*). While some lexical items can be traced back all the way to a reconstructible protolanguage, there are almost certainly going to be some words in the lexicon of any given language that represent innovations since the break-up of the protolanguage.

Innovations in the lexicon can come from a number of different sources. One of the most common sources of new words in a language is words from a different language. Traditionally, linguists refer to this process as *borrowing*. While using this term, many linguists express their unease about it, as a language which 'borrows' a word from another language does not give it back, nor is the first language denied the use of a word that it has 'lent' to another language. It is more accurate to speak of one language *copying* words from another language, because this is precisely what happens. In this book, therefore, I have generally used the term *copying* rather than *borrowing* to refer to this process, though it should be kept in mind that both terms can be used to refer to the same process.

When a language copies a lexical item, it takes the form of a word in one language and it generally reshapes that word to fit its own phonological structure. This means that non-occurring phonemes may be replaced with phonemes that are present in the system of the language that is taking in the new word, and words may be made to fit the phonological pattern of a language by eliminating sounds that occur in unfamiliar positions, or inserting sounds to make words fit its patterns. For instance, Tongan does not allow consonant clusters at all, nor does it allow word final consonants. Tongan has no distinction between [l] and [r] either, so when Tongan speakers want to talk about an ice-cream, they use a word that has been copied from English into Tongan, with the shape /aisikilimi/.

Languages are more likely to copy words from other languages in the area of *cultural vocabulary*, rather than *core vocabulary*. Core vocabulary is basically vocabulary that we can expect to find in all human languages. It is difficult to imagine any language that does not have some convenient way of expressing meanings like the following: *cry, walk, sleep, eat, water, stone, sky, wind, father,* and *die*. Cultural vocabulary, on the other hand, refers to meanings that are *culture-specific*, or which people learn through the experience of their own culture. Culture-specific meanings are obviously not core vocabulary, as only some languages have words to express these meanings: *tepee* and *peace-pipe* (in North America), *frost* and *snow* (in non-tropical climates), *kava* and *tapa cloth* (in the South Pacific), *dreamtime* and *rainbow serpent* (in Aboriginal Australia), *earthquake* and *lahar* (in geologically unstable areas), *television* (in western technological societies), *holy war* and *muezzin* (in Muslim societies), and *trinity* and *resurrection* (in Christian societies).

There is some other terminology which is culture-specific, but this fact may not be obvious at first glance. *Thank you* is one good example of such an expression. Western children are constantly reminded to say *thank you* at every appropriate opportunity, but the verbal expression of thanks is a very Western habit. Many languages in the South Pacific, for example, do not have words to express this meaning, and it is not considered necessary in these cultures to express thanks in words (though thanks can still be expressed in other ways, of course). Even such apparently basic words as the numbers one to ten are not found in all languages. Very few Australian Aboriginal languages, for example, have separate words for numbers above two or three. Anything more than three is simply expressed by the word for *many*, or an awkward compound of the existing numbers could be used. In the Bandjalang language of northern New South Wales in Australia, for example, there are the numbers /**jabur**/ 'one' and /**bula:bu**/ 'two', and if you needed to express *seven*, you would say /**bula:bu-bula:bu-bula:bu-jabur**/. Given that this is awkward once the numbers get any larger, it is clear that counting is something that was not done very often. The obvious explanation for this is that counting was not a major part of the non-acquisitive cultures of the Australian Aborigines.

No culture is constant, and often cultural changes are brought about as the result of contact with culturally or technologically different people. As European technology and beliefs have spread into the Pacific, many words of English origin have been copied into the languages of this region. Speakers of Motu in Papua New Guinea use the word /**botolo**/ for 'bottle', the Māori use the word /**hikareti**/ for 'cigarette', the Tongans refer to a 'car' as /**motuka**/ and the Paamese in Vanuatu refer to a 'letter' as a /**ve:va**/ (from the English word 'paper'). The expression *thank you* has now also been copied into Paamese, where it has been reshaped into the single word /**tagio**/. (In Paamese, sequences of [iu] are not possible, so the final vowel has been changed.) It is not just English words that have been copied into Pacific language; colonial powers have been introducing cultural changes to this part of the world for the last century and half. The French, for example, have contributed the word /**lalene**/ 'queen' into the languages of Wallis and Futuna (from *la reine*), and the Germans have contributed words like /**beten**/ 'pray' into some of the languages of New Guinea.

Lexical copying is not the only source of lexical changes as a way of expressing cultural changes. Speakers of languages also make use of their own linguistic resources in creating new words. If they take an existing word and extend its area of reference to express a new meaning, this becomes an example of semantic change which has been used to fill a lexical gap in the language. For instance, when the Paamese people in Vanuatu saw their first aeroplane, it must have looked to them like a large bird. The word for 'bird' in Paamese is /**aman**/, and this word is now also used as the Paamese word for 'aeroplane'. People also fill lexical gaps by generating new words and joining existing words together in new compounds, according to the existing rules of the language, in order to express new meanings. When the Fijians first saw planes, they called them instead /**waga-vuka**/, which is derived from the words /**waga**/ 'canoe' and /**vuka**/ 'fly'. An airport in Paamese is an /**out ten aman**/, which literally means 'place of birds (i.e. aeroplanes)'.

While the non-core component of the lexicon is highly susceptible to change in a language because of the need to express technological and cultural change, lexical copying is not restricted just to the expression of new meanings. In Chapter 1, I mentioned that the younger generations of Paamese speakers frequently use the English-derived words /bu:s/ 'bush' and /ka:ren/ 'garden', instead of the indigenous words /leiai/ and /a:h/ (respectively) that their parents and grandparents use. There is no *need* for this, as the Paamese language already had perfectly good words to express these meanings. These are not the only 'unnecessary' words that Paamese has copied. For instance, we also find words like /sta:t/ 'start', /ma:s/ 'must', and /ale/ 'OK then' (from French *allez*). Although there are perfectly adequate ways of expressing these meanings using indigenous Paamese words, few people use these words (and younger people would even have trouble saying what the Paamese word for 'start' actually is). Paamese has an efficient counting system, yet few younger speakers of the language can count in their language beyond five, preferring instead to use the English derived terms /wan/, /tu/, /tiri/, /vo:/, /vaiv/, and so on.

Why do people do this? It is quite difficult to find a good explanation. However, if a speaker of English uses the French-derived expression *coup de grâce* instead of 'final blow', many people would suspect that the speaker is trying to demonstrate his or her level of education. In the same way, when speakers of Pacific languages use words that are copied from English, they may simply be trying to say that they consider themselves to be much more of the modern world than the old-fashioned world of their grandparents.

English, French, and German are obviously not the only sources from which the languages of the Pacific can copy vocabulary. Although lexical copying is frequently associated with dominant economic and political powers, *any* kind of cultural contact can bring about lexical copying between languages. There had been long-term contact between Tongans and Fijians from well before the first European arrived in the Pacific, and there has been much copying of vocabulary between these two languages. Similarly, there are many words of Kiribati origin in the lexicon of the Tuvaluan language.

The Rotuman language of Fiji shows evidence of having copied words from Polynesian languages at different periods in history. Sometimes we find the same original form being regularly inherited with one meaning, and later copies with a slightly different meaning. For instance, the form /*toka/ 'come ashore' has been directly inherited as /foʔa/ with the same meaning. However, the word was later copied from another language, where it had not changed its shape, so we now find the word /toka/ meaning 'settle down' in Rotuman. Cases such as this are referred to as *doublets*, i.e. historically related pairs of words in which one is directly inherited, while the other is a later copy from a related language. Obviously, however, if a Pacific language has copied a word from a language to which it is not genetically related, it is going to be very easy to spot the word as being a relatively new part of the lexicon. When a language copies words from another language to which it is fairly closely related, it is often much more difficult to recognise it as a later lexical innovation.

Obviously, if a Pacific language has copied a word from a language with which it is not related genetically, it is going to be very easy to identify the word as being a relatively new addition to the lexicon. When a language copies words from a language with which it is fairly closely related, it is often much more difficult to recognise it as a later lexical innovation.

There are other reasons why languages undergo lexical change. In many cultures in the Pacific and Australia, for instance, there is a strong tendency to name people after some particularly noticeable occurrence in the environment at the time of the child's birth. For instance, a child born during a violent thunderstorm might be called Lightning. One child born out of wedlock in Vanuatu in the 1980s was called Disco because it was after a night of dancing that he was conceived. In some societies, there are powerful social restrictions against mentioning people's names in certain situations. In Australian Aboriginal societies, for example, it is forbidden to mention somebody's name when they have died. In modern times, this restriction carries over to a prohibition against hearing their voice on tape, or seeing their face in a photograph or on video. If somebody is named after some common thing and that person dies, then speakers of that language cannot use the name of that thing either. In situations like this, the easiest way of avoiding the problem is to copy a word meaning the same thing from a nearby language. Australian Aborigines traditionally spoke more than one language anyway, so this was often very easy to do.

In the Kabana language (spoken in the West New Britain province of Papua New Guinea), people typically have personal names that also refer to everyday objects. In this society, as in many other Melanesian societies, there is a strong restriction against saying the names of one's in-laws. This is true even if you want to refer to the actual thing that your in-law is named after, and you are not using the word as a personal name at all. In cases such as these, the language has a set of special words that are held 'in reserve'. These special, reserved items are either words in the Kabana language itself (but have a different meaning), or words copied from neighbouring languages and which have the same meaning. For example, the word in Kabana for a particular kind of fish is /urae/. If your in-law is called Urae, this fish must be referred to instead as /moi/, which is usually the word for 'taro'. The word for 'crocodile' in Kabana is /puaea/, but this word cannot be used if your in-law is called Puaea, and the crocodile must be referred to instead as /bagele/. This form /bagele/ is apparently copied from a nearby language, where the word for 'crocodile' is actually /vavele/.

A similar kind of cultural practice is found in Polynesia, though here the restriction against the use of words is associated with chiefly status. There is a custom in Tahiti, for example, that is known as /pii/, and this custom states that the name of a chief (or even a part of the name of a chief) cannot be used by ordinary people. So, for instance, during the time that the very powerful chief called Pomare was in power, the very common words /poo/ 'night' and /mare/ 'cough' became taboo simply because they sounded like parts of the chief's name. The word /**poo**/ was replaced by the word /**ruʔi**/ and the word /**mare**/ was replaced by the word /**hota**/.

Another kind of restriction among the Wampar speakers of Morobe province in Papua New Guinea involves place-name taboo. Certain places are regarded as sacred, perhaps because the people's ancestors' blood had been spilt there, or because their ancestors are buried there. If Wampar people today use the names of these places, it is believed that the ancestral spirits will punish the people by causing disasters, sickness, or the failure of the crops upon which they depend for food. The people of this area also have a similar kind of restriction to the Kabana practice of not saying the names of in-laws. People have a range of options available that allow them to talk about things and at the same time avoid breaking these taboos. Some languages have two or three synonymous terms to refer to the same thing, especially for very common words. Another possibility is for people to substitute a word that is semantically related to the taboo word in some way. For example, in the Mari language of this area, if the word /**zah**/ 'fire' is restricted, the word /**pakap**/ 'ashes' can be used to talk about fire instead.

Words can be lost in a language and new words can be created for reasons that are not at all obvious. Sometimes when a new word appears in a language, we have no idea where it came from. The English word *man*, for example, has a very long history. It has cognates in other Germanic languages such as the German *Mann*, and it can be traced all the way back to Proto Indo-European through the Sanskrit word *manu*. The English word *boy*, however, is something of a mystery, as it appears in the historical record only after English became a separate language, and it has no known cognates in any other Indo-European languages. There are several possible explanations for this. One explanation is that the word from which *boy* was derived was in fact present earlier, but that it was lost at the same time in all other languages related to English. Another possibility is that *boy* was borrowed from some other language. However, we have no idea what language that might have been.

A final possibility is that *boy* represents a genuine lexical innovation in English. It is hardly ever the case that words genuinely spring out of nowhere. Occasionally a word like *googol* is invented (in this case by a mathematician's child, to refer to the figure 1 followed by 100 zeroes), but generally words have some basis in pre-existing forms. Presumably what happened in the case of *boy* is that some other existing word took on this new meaning and the old meaning was lost altogether. However, we have no evidence that this is what actually happened, so what we are left with is a word that *looks* as though it suddenly sprang into the lexicon out of nowhere.

There is a special category of lexical innovations that I will refer to at this point. These involve *compression* (or *clipping*). This typically applies only to a few words in a language, and is not general. Compression is the process of dropping off one or more syllables from the end or middle of a word, for example:

administration	→	admin
university	→	uni, varsity
Shepparton	→	Shepp
Wangaratta	→	Wang

In fact, in Australian and New Zealand English there is often an additional syllable added to the compressed forms in order to express a kind of diminutive meaning:

football	→	footie
biscuit	→	bikkie
Christmas	→	Chrissie
present	→	prezzie
hot water bottle	→	hottie
truck driver	→	truckie
wharf labourer	→	wharfie
Salvation Army	→	Salvo, Sallie
journalist	→	journo
politician	→	pollie
conscientious objector	→	conshie
Brisbane	→	Brizzie

A particular kind of compression involves the use of initials. Examples of this kind of lexical change using only initials include the following:

Canadian Broadcasting Corporation	→	C.BC
television	→	TV
World Health Organisation	→	WHO
Ministry of Foreign Affairs and Trade	→	MFAT

It is sometimes possible for initials completely to lose their association with the forms from which they are derived and to be reanalysed as a new lexical item. For instance in Bislama (in Vanuatu), there is a word /kao/ meaning 'flat out, fast asleep, completely used up'. This derives from the French pronunciation of the first letters of the English abbreviation *K.O.*, which stands for 'knock-out' (in boxing). However, very few speakers of Bislama would be aware of the source of this item as an abbreviation for *K.O.*, and a genuinely new word has entered the lexicon in this way.

Another possible source for new lexical items is *word mixes* or *blends*. By this, I mean new words that are created by taking parts of two different words and adding them together to make up a completely new word. For instance, the following word mixes are frequently used in Papua New Guinea:

Administrative College	→	Adcol
Electricity Commission	→	Elcom
University of Technology	→	Unitech

This kind of change seems to be particularly common in government departments and in relation to administration generally. In fact, in Indonesia, there has developed a special register of Bahasa Indonesia that is commonly used in the newspapers where there are many word mixes of this kind (as well as many abbreviations). People in Indonesia sometimes find it difficult to read some parts of the newspaper because so many word mixes and abbreviations are used as totally new lexical items. New lexical items of this type also seem to be entering the English vocabulary in advertisements. For instance, forgettable kettles which switch themselves off when the water has boiled are called *forgettles*, and folding, environmentally friendly bottles are referred to as *fottles*.

READING GUIDE QUESTIONS

1. What is the difference between a genetic grouping and a typological grouping of languages?
2. What is an isolating language?
3. What is an agglutinating language?
4. What is an inflectional language?
5. How can phonological reduction cause a language to change its grammatical typology?
6. What is morphological fusion? What sort of typological change can result from this kind of change?
7. What is morphological reduction? What kind of grammatical type results from this kind of change?
8. What is meant by the terms ergativity and accusativity with respect to language typology? How can a language change its type from one to the other?
9. How can languages change their basic word order?
10. What are verb chains? How can these develop in languages?
11. What is meant by the term grammatical reanalysis?
12. What is back formation?
13. How can analogy cause grammatical change?
14. What is semantic broadening?
15. What is semantic narrowing?
16. What does the term bifurcation mean with respect to semantic change?
17. What is semantic shift, and how does this kind of change differ from the other kinds of semantic change mentioned in this chapter?
18. How can metaphor influence the direction of a semantic change?
19. What is euphemism? How can it influence semantic change?
20. What is meant by hyperbole, and how is this involved in semantic change?
21. What is meant by interference when speaking of change of meaning?
22. What is lexical borrowing, or copying?

23. What is the difference between cultural and core vocabulary?
24. What possible ways are there for a language to fill lexical gaps?
25. What problems can lexical copying cause in reconstructing the phonological history of a language?
26. What is the possible effect of lexical taboo in vocabulary change?
27. What do we mean by lexical innovation?
28. What is lexical compression?
29. What are word mixes?

EXERCISES

1. In Bislama (Vanuatu) it is possible to express contrast by shifting a noun phrase to the front of a sentence, for example:

   Mi no   stap   slip long haos ya.
   I   negative habitual live at   house that
   'I do not live in that house.'

   Haos ya mi no   stap   slip long hem.
   house that I   negative habitual live at   it
   'It is not *that* house that I live in.'

   The basic word order of Bislama is **SVO**. How might the existence of the following sorts of variations affect the basic word order of the language in the future?

   Saki i   bonem   haos ya.
   Saki predicate burn down house that
   'Saki burnt down that house.'

   Haos ya Saki i   bonem.
   house that Saki predicate burn down
   'It was *that* house that Saki burnt down.'

2. Many speakers of Tok Pisin (Papua New Guinea) express a relative clause by simply putting the relative clause inside the main clause without any special marking at all except that a repeated noun phrase is expressed by means of a pronominal copy, for example:

   Dispela man ol paitim em asde   i   dai pinis.
   that   man they beat up him yesterday predicate die completive
   'That man who they beat up yesterday has died.'

   Mi no   stap long ples ol   paitim em long-en.
   I   negative be at   place they beat up him at it
   'I wasn't there where they beat him up.'

Some speakers of Tok Pisin (especially, but not exclusively people from the Highlands area), are coming to mark relative clauses by adding *longen* at the end of the relative clause, for example:

Em i   bin draiv long bris   i   bruk   longen.
He predicate past drive over bridge predicate broken relative clause
'He drove over the bridge that was broken.'

Mi paitem em   long diwai mi holim longen.
I   beat   him with stick I   hold relative clause
'I beat him with the stick which I was holding.'

How has this new function of *longen* evolved in Tok Pisin?

3. Tok Pisin has an interrogative *husat* 'who', which occurs in sentences such as the following:

Husat i   kukim   dispela haus?
who   predicate burn down this   house
'Who burnt down this house?'

Some speakers of Tok Pisin are coming to mark relative clauses by placing *husat* in front of the relative clause (at least in written forms of the language). Here is an example of such a construction that was taken from a student's essay in Tok Pisin for a course in linguistics at the University of Papua New Guinea:

*Bai mi toktok long ol asua **husat** bai i kamap sapos Tok Pisin i kamap nambawan tokples bilong Papua Niugini.*
'I will discuss the problems *that* would arise if Tok Pisin were to become the national language of Papua New Guinea.'

How has this construction arisen?

4. Transitive verbs in Tok Pisin carry an obligatory suffix of the form *-im* (which is illustrated in the forms *paitim* 'beat up', *kukim* 'burn down', and *holim* 'hold' in the previous exercises). There are a small number of transitive verbs in Tok Pisin which are exceptions in that they do not take any transitive suffix, including *save* 'know', *kaikai* 'eat', and *dring* 'drink'. However, while most speakers of Tok Pisin would say the following:

Yu laik dring sampela bia?
you want drink some   beer
'Would you like to drink some beer?'

there are others who prefer to say the following to express the same meaning:

Yu laik dringim sampela bia?

What factor would you say is responsible for bringing about the change from *dring* to *dringim* in this example?

5. Some people might say *He drank two gins and tonic* while others might say *He drank two gin and tonics*. What is happening here?

6. A thesaurus is a book that lists words by meaning, and which makes it possible to find out the synonyms of a word. Look up some synonyms for the following words in a thesaurus: *popular, fantastic, native, juvenile*. Then find a dictionary that goes back a couple of hundred years, if possible (for instance Samuel Johnson's), and see how these words have changed semantically.

7. Compare the meanings of the following forms in English and Tok Pisin (with the meanings in Tok Pisin given on the right). How would you describe the nature of the changes that have taken place?

English	Tok Pisin	Meaning in Tok Pisin
arse	*as*	'buttocks, basis, foundation, tree trunk, stem of plant'
bed	*bet*	'bed, shelf'
box	*bokis*	'box, crate, cardboard carton, vagina'
garden	*garen*	'plot of ground planted out to food crops for a single season'
grass	*gras*	'grass, hair, whiskers'
hand	*han*	'hand, arm, wrist, branch of tree'
cargo	*kago*	'material possessions'
copper	*kapa*	'roofing iron'
cry	*krai*	'cry, weep, wail, moan'
straight	*stret*	'straight, correct'
take away	*tekewe*	'peel (of skin)'

7. What is the plural of *Walkman*? If you use more than one *mouse* with your computer, what do you say? If you say *Walkmans* and *mouses* rather than *Walkmen* and *mice*, why might this be?

FURTHER READING

1. Robert J. Jeffers and Ilse Lehiste *Principles and Methods for Historical Linguistics*, Chapter 4 'Morphological Systems and Linguistic Change', pp. 55–73; Chapter 7 'Syntactic Change', pp. 107–25; Chapter 8 'Lexical Change', pp. 126–37.
2. Mary Haas *The Prehistory of Languages*, 'Problems of morphological reconstruction', pp. 51–58.
3. Theodora Bynon *Historical Linguistics*, 'Morphological and syntactic reconstruction', pp. 57–61; 'Lexical reconstruction', pp. 61–63.

4. Edward Sapir *Language: An Introduction to the Study of Speech*, Chapter 6 'Types of Linguistic Structure', pp. 120–46.
5. Anthony Arlotto *Introduction to Historical Linguistics*, Chapter 10 'Semantic Change', pp. 165–83.
6. Leonard Bloomfield *Language*, Chapter 24 'Semantic Change', pp. 425–43.
7. Dwight Bolinger *Aspects of Language*, Chapter 7 'The Evolution of Language', pp. 100–24.
8. Hans Henrich Hock *Principles of Historical Linguistics*, Chapter 9 'Analogy: General Discussion and Typology', pp. 167–209; Chapter 10 'Analogy: Tendencies of Analogical Change', pp. 210–37; Chapter 11 'Analogy and Generative Grammar', pp. 238–37; Chapter 12 'Semantic Change', pp. 280–308; Chapter 13 'Syntactic Change', pp. 309–79; Chapter 14 'Linguistic Contact: Lexical Borrowing', pp. 380–425.
9. R.M.W. Dixon *Ergativity*, Chapter 7, 'Language Change', pp. 182–206.

CHAPTER EIGHT

SUBGROUPING

By using the comparative method, not only can we reconstruct a proto-language, but we can use the results that it provides to determine which languages are more closely related to other languages in a family. Compare the following words in six Indo-European languages:

English	Dutch	German	French	Italian	Russian
wʌn	eːn	ains	œ̃	uno	adʲin
tuː	tweː	tsvai	dø	due	dva
θɹiː	driː	dʁai	tʁwa	tre	trʲi
fɔː	fiːr	fiːʁ	katʁ	kwatro	tʃetirʲe
faɪv	fɛif	fynf	sɛ̃k	tʃiŋkwe	pʲatʲ

There are enough similarities even here, in the words for 'two' and 'three', for example, to suggest that we could justify putting these six languages into a single language family. However, there are other similarities that seem to suggest that English, Dutch, and German are closer to each other than they are to the other three languages. Similarly, French and Italian seem to be fairly closely related to each other, while being less closely related to the others. Finally, Russian seems to stand out on its own. What we can say here is that we have three *subgroups* of the one language family — one containing the first three languages, one containing the next two, and a final subgroup with only a single member.

We can represent subgrouping in a family tree by a series of branches coming from a single point. The family tree for the six languages described above would look something like this:

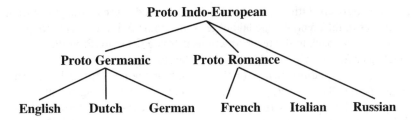

This diagram can be interpreted as meaning that English, Dutch and German are all derived from a common protolanguage (which we can call Proto Germanic) that is itself descended from the protolanguage that is ancestral to all of the other languages (which we can call Proto Indo-European). We can therefore offer a tentative definition of a subgroup by saying that it comprises a number of languages that are all descended from a common protolanguage that is intermediate between the ultimate (or highest level) protolanguage and the modern language, and which are as a result more similar to each other than to other languages in the family.

8.1 SHARED INNOVATION AND SHARED RETENTION

Clearly, languages that belong to the same subgroup must share some similarities that distinguish them from other languages in the family that do not belong to this subgroup. However, the simple fact that there are similarities does not *necessarily* mean that two languages belong in the same subgroup. If we say that two languages belong in the same subgroup, we imply that they have gone through a *period of common descent*, and that they did not diverge until a later stage in their development.

Similarities between languages can be explained as being due to either *shared retention* from the protolanguage, or *shared innovations* since the time of the protolanguage. If two languages are similar because they share some feature that has been retained from the protolanguage, you cannot use this similarity as evidence that they have gone through a period of common descent. The retention of a particular feature in this way is not significant, because you should expect a large number of features to be retained anyway.

However, if two languages are similar because they have both undergone the same innovation or change, then you can say that this is evidence that they have had a period of common descent and that they therefore do belong to the same subgroup. You can say that a shared innovation in two languages is evidence that those two languages belong in the same subgroup, because exactly the same change is unlikely to take place independently in two separate languages. By suggesting that the languages have undergone a period of common descent, you are saying that the particular change took place only once between the higher level protolanguage and the intermediate protolanguage which is between this and the various modern languages that belong in the subgroup. Other changes then took place later in the individual languages to differentiate one language from another within the subgroup.

If you look back to the reconstructions that you made for Proto Polynesian in Chapter 5, you will see that Samoan, Rarotongan, and Hawaiian have all undergone unconditional loss of the original phonemes /*h/ and /*ʔ/. This suggests that Samoan, Rarotongan, and Hawaiian all belong together in a subgroup of Polynesian from which Tongan is excluded. Between Proto Polynesian and the intermediate ancestor language from which these three languages are derived (but not Tongan), there was an intermediate proto-language which we can call Proto Nuclear Polynesian:

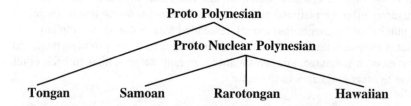

While it is shared innovations that we use as evidence for establishing subgroups, certain kinds of innovations are likely to be stronger evidence for subgrouping than other kinds. As I have just said, subgrouping rests on the assumption that shared similarities are unlikely to be due to *chance*. However, some kinds of similarities between languages are in fact due to chance, i.e. the same changes *do* sometimes take place quite independently in different languages. This kind of situation is often referred to as *parallel development* or *drift*. One good example of drift is in the Oceanic subgroup of the Austronesian family of languages (which includes all of the Polynesian languages, as well as Fijian, and the Austronesian languages of Fiji, Vanuatu, New Caledonia, Solomon Islands, and Papua New Guinea). In Proto Oceanic, word final consonants were apparently retained from Proto Austronesian. However, many present-day Oceanic languages have since apparently lost word final consonants by a general rule of the form:

C → ø / ___ #

The fact that many Oceanic languages share this innovation is not sufficient evidence to establish subgroups. Loss of final consonants is a very common sort of sound change that could easily be due to chance, and the same sound change occurs in Oceanic as well as in some languages that we would not otherwise want to call Oceanic languages. In the Enggano language, spoken on an island off the coast of southern Sumatra, final consonants were also lost, but we would not necessarily want to say that this language belongs in the Oceanic subgroup as this language shares no other features of Oceanic languages.

In classifying languages into subgroups, you therefore need to avoid the possibility that innovations in two languages might be due to drift or parallel development. You can do this by looking for the following in linguistic changes:

(i)   Changes that are particularly unusual.

(ii) Sets of several phonological changes, especially unusual changes which would not ordinarily be expected to have taken place together.

(iii) Phonological changes which correspond to unconnected grammatical or semantic changes.

For example, if Samoan, Rarotongan, and Hawaiian only shared the single change whereby /*h/ was lost, it might be possible to argue that this is purely coincidental, especially as the loss of /h/ is a fairly common sort of change anyway. However, as these three languages also share the change:

$$? \rightarrow \emptyset $$

we can argue that coincidence is less likely to be the explanation and that these three languages are indeed members of a single subgroup.

If two languages share a common sporadic or irregular phonological change, this provides even better evidence for subgrouping those two languages together, as the same irregular change is unlikely to take place twice independently. One piece of evidence that can be quoted for the grouping of Oceanic languages into a single subgroup of Austronesian is the irregular loss of /*ʀ/ that has taken place in the Proto Austronesian word *maʀi 'come'. On the basis of evidence from the present-day Oceanic languages, we can reconstruct the form /*mai/ 'come' in Proto Oceanic. On the basis of the reconstructed Proto Austronesian form /*maʀi/, however, we would have expected the Proto Oceanic form to be /*mari/ instead of /*mai/. Proto Oceanic appears to have lost this sound in just this single word to produce an irregular reflex of /*maʀi/. It is highly unlikely that every single Oceanic language would have independently shifted /*maʀi/ to /*mai/, so we conclude instead that this irregular change happened just once, between Proto Austronesian and Proto Oceanic, and that the modern Oceanic languages reflect this irregularity as a retention from Proto Oceanic.

The Oceanic subgroup of the Austronesian family has not been established on the basis of just this single innovation, even though it is an irregular one. There are several other regular phonological changes that have also taken place at the same time. These include the following:

$$ \partial \rightarrow o $$
$$ b \rightarrow p $$
$$ g \rightarrow k $$

These involve a change of schwa to /o/, as well as the devoicing of stops, so parallel development is unlikely to be the explanation. We can therefore conclude that any Austronesian language that shares all of these innovations is a member of the Oceanic subgroup.

The pair of shared innovations that I gave above in Samoan, Rarotongan, and Hawaiian are also better evidence for subgrouping than just a single change. For instance, both Tongan and Hawaiian have undergone a shift of /*s/ to /h/. It would contradict the conclusion that I just reached to say that Tongan and Hawaiian belong to a single subgroup on the basis of this shared innovation. Where there is information that is consistent with competing subgrouping interpretations, we should evaluate this and see which solution is the most reasonable one. The fact that the first conclusion was reached on the basis of a pair of shared innovations, whereas the second conclusion would have to be based on just a single innovation, makes the first conclusion a more reliable one. We must simply conclude that both Tongan and Hawaiian independently changed /*s/ to /h/ at separate times in history after the two had diverged.

Finally, if we can match phonological innovations with shared grammatical or semantic innovations, then we can argue that we have good evidence for putting the languages that share these features into the same subgroup. Although the grammatical reconstruction of Proto Austronesian is much less well developed than its phonological reconstruction, there are some linguists who argue that there are many aspects of the basic clause structure of Oceanic languages that are different from that of Proto Austronesian. If this turns out to be confirmed, then this would be further evidence for the existence of an Oceanic subgroup.

When we speak of subgroups of languages, it is possible to speak of *higher level subgroups* and *lower level subgroups*. As you have seen, languages that belong to a subgroup within a single language family have experienced a period of common descent. However, it is possible for languages within a single subgroup of a larger language family also to be subgrouped together on the basis of shared innovations. This means that we can speak of subgroups *within* subgroups. For instance, there are strong arguments for saying that the Polynesian languages represent a separate subgroup within the Oceanic subgroup, on the basis of their shared phonological, lexical, and grammatical innovations. In this kind of situation, we can speak of Oceanic being a higher-level subgroup, while the Polynesian languages constitute a lower-level subgroup. Languages that belong together in higher-level subgroups therefore diverged relatively early, while lower-level subgroups involve later developments. Of course, the Polynesian languages can be further subgrouped into even lower-level subgroups again, and I have already indicated that we can justify a subgroup consisting of Samoan, Rarotongan, and Hawaiian, as well as a Western Polynesian subgroup, of which Tongan is a member. We could represent the different levels of subgrouping as follows:

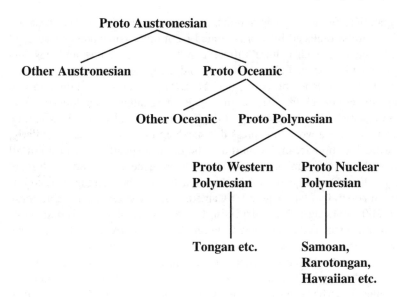

8.2 LEXICOSTATISTICS AND GLOTTOCHRONOLOGY

There is a another rather different technique for subgrouping languages that is often used with languages for which there are relatively limited amounts of data available, and that is *lexicostatistics*. Since Melanesia and Australia are areas of great linguistic diversity, and because comparatively few of these languages are well known to linguists, this is a technique that has to date been used very frequently in trying to determine the nature of interrelationships in that part of the world (though this technique is not frequently used when comparing better known languages). We therefore need to have a good understanding of how linguists have applied this technique, as well as the strengths and weaknesses of the technique as it has been applied.

Lexicostatistics is a technique that allows us to determine the degree of relationship between two languages, simply by comparing the vocabularies of the languages and determining the degree of similarity between them. This method operates under two basic assumptions. The first of these is that there are some parts of the vocabulary of a language that are much less subject to lexical change than other parts, i.e. there are certain parts of the lexicon in which words are less likely to be completely replaced by non-cognate forms. The area of the lexicon that is assumed to be more resistant to lexical change is referred to as *core vocabulary* (or as *basic vocabulary*).

There is a second aspect to this first general assumption underlying the lexicostatistical method, and that is the fact that this core of relatively change-resistant vocabulary is the same for all languages. The universal core vocabulary includes items such as pronouns, numerals, body parts, geographical features, basic actions, and basic states. Items like these are unlikely to be replaced by words copied from other languages, because all people, whatever their cultural differences, have eyes, mouths, and legs, and know about the sky and clouds, the sun, and the moon, stones, and trees, and so on. Other concepts, however, may be *culture-specific*, or known only to people of certain cultures. The word 'canoe', for example, is culture-specific, because somebody who grew up in the desert of central Australia would be unlikely to have a word to express this meaning in their language. Similarly, the word for 'boomerang' would also be culture-specific, because not all cultures have such implements. Such words are generally found much more likely to have been copied. In fact, the English word 'boomerang' was copied from an Australian language after Captain Cook first reported seeing these over 200 years ago. Not surprisingly, he recorded the original word /**bumaraŋ**/ incorrectly, and it is Captain Cook's incorrect spelling that we follow when we pronounce the word 'boomerang' in English today.

The contrast between the amount of lexical change that takes place in the core vocabulary as against the *peripheral vocabulary* (or the general vocabulary) can be seen by looking at the vocabulary of English. If you take the dictionary of English as a whole, you will find that about 50 per cent of the words have been copied from other languages. Most of these have been copied directly from French, as there has been massive lexical influence from French on English over the last 900 years. Many other words have been copied from forms that were found in ancient Latin and Greek. French has also taken many words from the same languages, which makes the lexicons of English and French appear even more similar, even with words that were not directly copied from French into English. However, if we restrict ourselves just to the core vocabularies of French and English, we find that there is much less sharing of cognate forms, and the figure for words copied from French into English in this area of the lexicon drops to as low as 6 per cent.

The second assumption that underlies the lexicostatistical method is that the actual *rate* of lexical replacement in the core vocabulary is more or less stable, and is therefore about the same for all languages over time. In peripheral vocabulary, of course, the rate of lexical replacement is not stable at all, and may be relatively fast or slow, depending on the nature of cultural contact between speakers of different languages. This second assumption has been tested in 13 languages for which there are written records going back over long periods of time. It has been found that there has been an average vocabulary retention of 80.5 per cent every 1000 years. That is to say, after 1000 years a language will have lost about a fifth of its original basic vocabulary and replaced it with new forms.

If these assumptions are correct, then it should be possible to work out the degree of relationship between two languages by calculating the degree of similarity between their core vocabularies. If the core vocabularies of two languages are relatively similar, then we can assume that they have diverged quite recently, and that they therefore belong to a lower level subgroup. If, on the other hand, their core vocabularies are relatively dissimilar, then we can assume that they must have diverged at a much earlier time, and that they therefore belong to a much higher level of subgrouping.

Different levels of subgrouping have been given specific names by lexicostatisticians, as follows:

Level of subgrouping	Shared cognate percentage in core vocabulary
dialects of a language	81–100
languages of a family	36–81
families of a stock	12–36
stocks of a microphylum	4–12
microphyla of a mesophylum	1–4
mesophyla of a macrophylum	0–1

You should note immediately that lexicostatisticians are using the term *family* in a completely different way from the way we have been using it in this textbook. I (and most other historical linguists) take the term *family* to refer to *all* languages that are descended from a common ancestor language, no matter how closely or distantly related they are to each other within that family. According to a lexicostatistical classification, however, a *family* is simply a particular level of subgrouping in which the members of that subgroup share more than 36 per cent of their core vocabularies. Languages that are in lesser degrees of relationship (but still presumably descended from a common ancestor) are not considered to be in the same family, but in the same *stock* or *phylum*.

Having outlined the assumptions behind lexicostatistics and the theory behind its application, I will now go on to show how lexicostatisticians have followed this method. The first problem is to distinguish the so-called core vocabulary from the peripheral vocabulary. I gave some indication earlier about the kinds of words that would need to go into such a list. But how long should it be? Some have argued that we should use a 1000-word list, others a 200-word list, and others a 100-word list. (Notice how the lengths of these lists all involve numbers that can easily divided by 100 to produce a percentage. One suspects that these lists are not being drawn up according to any firm linguistic criterion about what can be shown to be 'basic' as against 'peripheral' vocabulary, but merely to make the lexicostatisticians' task of calculation easier.) It would be awkward to insist on a 1000-word list for the languages of Australia and Melanesia where many languages are only very sketchily recorded and linguists do not have access to word lists of this length. Many people think that a 100-word list is too short and the risk of error is too great, so most lexicostatisticians tend to operate with 200-word lists. The most popular list of this length is known as the *Swadesh list*, which is named after the linguist Morris Swadesh who drew it up in the early 1960s. This list comprises the following items:

all	*dull*	*heart*	*neck*	*skin*	*turn*
and	*dust*	*heavy*	*new*	*sky*	*twenty*
animal		*here*	*night*	*sleep*	*two*
ashes	*ear*	*hit*	*nose*	*small*	
at	*earth*	*hold/take*	*not*	*smell*	*vomit*
	eat	*horn*		*smoke*	
back	*egg*	*how*	*old*	*smooth*	*walk*
bad	*eight*	*hundred*	*one*	*snake*	*warm*
bark	*eye*	*hunt*	*other*	*snow*	*wash*
because		*husband*		*some*	*water*
belly	*fall*		*person*	*spear*	*we*
big	*far*	*I*	*play*	*spit*	*wet*
bird	*fat*	*ice*	*pull*	*split*	*what*
bite	*father*	*if*	*push*	*squeeze*	*when*
black	*fear*	*in*		*stab/pierce*	*where*
blood	*feather*		*rain*	*stand*	*white*
blow	*few*	*kill*	*red*	*star*	*who*
bone	*fight*	*knee*	*right/correct*	*stick*	*wide*
breast	*fire*	*know*	*right side*	*stone*	*wife*
breathe	*five*		*river*	*straight*	*wind*
brother	*float*	*lake*	*road*	*suck*	*wing*
burn	*flow*	*laugh*	*root*	*sun*	*wipe*
	flower	*leaf*	*rope*	*swell*	*with*
child	*fog*	*left side*	*rotten*	*swim*	*woman*
claw	*foot*	*leg*	*rub*		*woods*
clothing	*four*	*live*		*tail*	*work*
cloud	*freeze*	*liver*	*salt*	*ten*	*worm*
cold	*fruit*	*long*	*sand*	*that*	
come	*full*	*louse*	*say*	*there*	*ye*
cook			*scratch*	*they*	*year*
count	*give*	*man/male*	*sea*	*thick*	*yellow*
cut	*good*	*many*	*see*	*thin*	
	grass	*meat/flesh*	*seed*	*think*	
dance	*green*	*moon*	*seven*	*this*	
day	*guts*	*mother*	*sew*	*thou*	
die		*mountain*	*sharp*	*three*	
dig	*hair*	*mouth*	*shoot*	*throw*	
dirty	*hand*		*short*	*tie*	
dog	*he*	*name*	*sing*	*tongue*	
drink	*head*	*narrow*	*sister*	*tooth*	
dry	*hear*	*near*	*sit*	*tree*	

Even with this list, there are problems in applying it to some of the languages of Melanesia, Australia, and the South Pacific. Firstly, it contains words like *and* and *in*, which in some of these languages are not expressed as separate words, but as affixes of some kind. It contains the separate words *woman* and *wife*, even though in many languages both of these meanings are expressed by the same word. It contains words such as *freeze* and *ice* which are clearly not applicable in languages spoken in tropical areas. There are other words which *could* be included in a basic vocabulary for Pacific languages and which would not be suitable for other languages, for example: *canoe, bow and arrow, chicken, pig,* and so on. A basic vocabulary for Australian languages could, of course, include items such as *kangaroo* and *boomerang.*

Let us avoid the problem of exactly what should be considered basic vocabulary, and go on to see how we use a basic word list of this kind in a language in order to determine its relationship to another language. The first thing that you have to do is to examine each pair of words for the same meaning in the two languages, to see which ones are cognate and which ones are not. Ideally, whether a pair of words are cognate or not should be decided only after you have worked out the systematic sound correspondences between the two languages. If there are two forms which are phonetically similar but which show an exceptional sound correspondence, you should assume that there has been lexical copying, and the pair of words should be excluded from consideration. It is very important that you exclude copied (or borrowed) vocabulary when you are working out lexicostatistical figures, as these can make two languages appear to be more closely related to each other than they really are.

Let us now look at an actual problem. I will use the lexicostatistical method to try to subgroup the following three languages from Central Province in Papua New Guinea: Koita, Koiari, and Mountain Koiari. Rather than use a full 200-word list, I will make things simpler by using a shorter 25-word list and assume that it is representative of the fuller list:

	Koita	Koiari	Mountain Koiari	
1.	ɣata	ata	maraha	'man'
2.	maɣi	mavi	keate	'woman'
3.	moe	moe	mo	'child'
4.	ɣamika	vami	mo ese	'boy'
5.	mobora	mobora	koria	'husband'
6.	mabara	mabara	keate	'wife'
7.	mama	mama	mama	'father'
8.	neina	neina	neina	'mother'
9.	da	da	da	'I'
10.	a	a	a	'you (singular)'
11.	au	au	ahu	'he, she, it'
12.	omoto	kina	kina	'head'
13.	hana	homo	numu	'hair'
14.	uri	uri	uri	'nose'
15.	ihiko	ihiko	gorema	'ear'

16.	meina	neme	neme	'tongue'
17.	hata	auki	aura	'chin'
18.	ava	ava	aka	'mouth'
19.	dehi	gadiva	inu	'back'
20.	vasa	vahi	geina	'leg'
21.	vani	vani	fani	'sun'
22.	vanumo	koro	didi	'star'
23.	gousa	yuva	goe	'cloud'
24.	veni	veni	feni	'rain'
25.	nono	hihi	heburu	'wind'

The first thing that you have to do is distinguish cognate forms from forms that are not cognate. One way in which you can do this is mark how many *cognate sets* there are to express each meaning. For instance, in the word for 'man' (1), there are two cognate sets, as Koita and Koiari have forms that are clearly cognate (i.e. **vata** and **ata** respectively), whereas Mountain Koiari has **maraha**. You can therefore label the first set as belong to Set A, and the second as belong to Set B:

	Koita	Koiari	Mountain Koiari	
1.	A	A	B	'man'

On the other hand, the word for 'chin' (17) is quite different in all three languages, so we would need to recognise three different cognate sets:

	Koita	Koiari	Mountain Koiari	
17.	A	B	C	'chin'

Finally, the word for 'sun' (21) is clearly cognate in all three languages, so you would need to recognise only a single cognate set:

	Koita	Koiari	Mountain Koiari	
21.	A	A	A	'sun'

I will now set out the cognate sets for each of these three languages on the basis of the information that I have just given you:

	Koita	Koiari	Mountain Koiari	
1.	A	A	B	'man'
2.	A	A	B	'woman'
3.	A	A	A	'child'
4.	A	A	B	'boy'
5.	A	A	B	'husband'
6.	A	A	B	'wife'
7.	A	A	A	'father'

8.	A	A	A	'mother'
9.	A	A	A	'I'
10.	A	A	A	'you (singular)'
11.	A	A	A	'he, she, it'
12.	A	B	B	'head'
13.	A	B	C	'hair'
14.	A	A	A	'nose'
15.	A	A	B	'ear'
16.	A	B	B	'tongue'
17.	A	B	C	'chin'
18.	A	A	B	'mouth'
19.	A	B	C	'back'
20.	A	B	C	'leg'
21.	A	A	A	'sun'
22.	A	B	C	'star'
23.	A	B	C	'cloud'
24.	A	A	A	'rain'
25.	A	B	C	'wind'

Now you need to work out the degree to which each pair of languages among the three represented above shares cognates. Firstly, examine the pair Koita and Koiari. If you count the number of pairs in these two languages which are marked as cognate (i.e which are both marked A) and those which are marked as non-cognate (i.e. in which one is marked A and the other is marked B), you will find that there are 16 forms which are shared between the two languages, and 9 which are not. From this, you can say that 16/25 of the core vocabulary of these two languages is cognate. If you do this for the remaining pairs of languages from the three languages that we are considering, you will end up with three fractions, which can be set out in the following way:

Koita
$^{16}/_{25}$ Koiari
$^{9}/_{25}$ $^{12}/_{25}$ Mountain Koiari

You should now convert these figures to percentages:

Koita
64%   Koiari
36%   48%   Mountain Koiari

Now that you have the cognate percentage figures, you need to know how to interpret them. Clearly, Koita and Koiari are more closely related to each other than either is to Mountain Koiari. On the basis of these figures, you could therefore draw a family tree of the following kind:

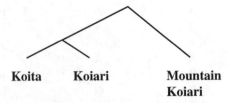

| Koita | Koiari | Mountain Koiari |

In terms of the degrees of relationship that I talked about earlier, these languages would all be contained within a single 'family', i.e. they share between 36 per cent and 81 per cent of their core vocabularies.

This was a rather simple example, because we considered only three languages. Although the same principles apply when we are considering cognate percentages for larger numbers of languages, the procedures for working out the degrees of relationship can become rather more complex. Let us take the following lexicostatistical figures for 10 hypothetical languages and interpret the data according to these same principles:

```
A
91%  B
88   86%  C
68   62   64%  D
67   65   66   63%  E
55   51   56   53   55%  F
57   53   54   57   56   89%  G
23   27   36   31   32   30   29%  H
25   28   33   29   27   34   22   88%  I
31   22   30   27   28   26   28   86   89%  J
```

Where do you start from in a more complicated case like this? The first step is to try to find out which languages in the data are *most* closely related to each other. To do this, you should look for figures that are significantly higher than any other figures in the table, which is an indication that these particular pairs of languages are relatively closely related to each other. On this table, therefore, the sets of figures that are set in bold type are noticeable in this respect:

```
A
91%  B
88   86%  C
68   62   64%  D
67   65   66   63%  E
55   51   56   53   55%  F
57   53   54   57   56   89%  G
23   27   36   31   32   30   29%  H
25   28   33   29   27   34   22   88%  I
31   22   30   27   28   26   28   86   89%  J
```

Communities A, B, and C are clearly very closely related to each other. Communities F and G also belong together, and so do the three communities H, I, and J.

Now you need to find out what is the next level of relationship. To make this task easier, you can now treat the subgroups that you have just arrived at as single units for the purpose of interpretation. To do this, you should relabel the units so that it is clear to you that you are operating with units at a different level of subgrouping. You can use the following labels:

ABC	I
D	II
E	III
FG	IV
HIJ	V

Now work out the shared cognate percentages between these five different lower level units, in order to fill in the information on the table below:

```
I
     II
          III
               IV
                    V
```

Where the new label corresponds to a single language on the original table, you can simply transfer the old figures across to the appropriate places on the new table:

```
I
     II
63%  III
               IV
                    V
```

However, where the new labels correspond to a number of different communities on the original table, you will need to get the averages of the shared cognate figures in each block and enter them in the appropriate place in the new table. So, in comparing I and II, you will need to get the figures for the shared cognates of A with D, of B with D, and C with D and enter the average of those figures under the intersection of I and II. Since A and D have 68 per cent cognate sharing, B and D have 62 per cent, and C and D share 64 per cent of their cognates, the average level of cognate sharing between I and II works out at 65 per cent. So, you can now add one more figure to the table:

```
I
65%  II
      63%  III
            IV
                  V
```

If you do this methodically for every pair of groupings, you will end up with the following table:

```
I
65%  II
66   63%  III
54   55   55%  IV
28   29   29   27%  V
```

You should now treat this table in the same way as you treated the first table — simply look for the highest cognate figures as an indication of the next level of linguistic relationship. From these figures it seems that I, II, and III are more closely related to each other than to either IV or V, as the shared cognate percentages range above 60 per cent, whereas they are in the 20–60 per cent range for the other groups. For the next step, you should group together I, II and III in the same way and relabel them (this time as, say, X, Y, and Z) as follows:

```
I, II, III    X
IV            Y
V             Z
```

Once again, calculate the averages of the cognate figures, which will work out to be as follows:

```
X
55%  Y
29%  27%  Z
```

It is clear from this final table that X and Y are more closely related to each other than either is to Z.

The final step in the procedure is to gather all of these facts together and represent the conclusions on a family tree that will clearly indicate the degrees of relationship between the ten original speech communities. At the lowest level of relationship, you will discover that the following units belong together, while D and E are on their own:

```
A, B, C
F, G
H, I, J
```

At the next level of relationship, you find that D and E belong to the same group as A, B, and C, while the others are all on their own. At the next level, F and G could be related to the same subgroup as the subgroup consisting of A, B, C, D, and E, with H, I, and J being a separate subgroup of their own. This situation can be represented in a family tree diagram in the following way:

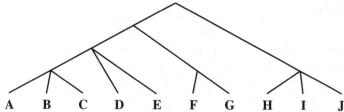

Having dealt in some detail with the claim that lexicostatistics enables us to work out degrees of relationship within a language family, I will now go on to discuss a second claim that lexicostatisticians sometimes make, though most linguists are now very cautious about this. If we accept the basic assumption that languages change their core vocabulary at a relatively constant rate, we should be able to work out not only the degree of relationship between two languages, but also the actual period of time that two languages have been separated from each other. Once the percentage of cognate forms has been worked out, we can use the following mathematical formula to work out the *time depth*, or the period of separation, of two languages:

$$t = \frac{\log C}{2 \log r}$$

In the formula above, t stands for the number of thousands of years that two languages have been separated, C stands for the percentage of cognates as worked out by comparing basic vocabularies, and r stands for the constant change factor mentioned earlier (the value in this formula is set at 0.805). The following table gives logarithms for numbers less than 1 for use in calculations of this type:

	.00	.01	.02	.03	.04	.05	.06	.07	.08	.09
.1	2.303	2.207	2.120	2.040	1.966	1.897	1.833	1.772	1.715	1.662
.2	1.609	1.561	1.514	1.470	1.427	1.386	1.347	1.309	1.273	1.238
.3	1.204	1.171	1.139	1.109	1.079	1.050	1.022	.994	.968	.942
.4	.916	.892	.868	.844	.821	.799	.777	.755	.734	.713
.5	.693	.673	.654	.635	.616	.598	.580	.562	.545	.528
.6	.511	.494	.478	.462	.446	.431	.416	.400	.386	.371
.7	.357	.342	.329	.315	.301	.288	.274	.261	.248	.236
.8	.223	.211	.198	.186	.174	.163	.151	.139	.128	.117
.9	.105	.094	.083	.073	.062	.051	.041	.030	.020	.010

So, going back to the earlier problem involving Koita, Koiari, and Mountain Koiari, if you wanted to know how long it has been since Koiari split off from Koita, you would take the cognate percentage of 64 per cent (the figure given on the table for these two languages) and convert it to a factor of one (0.64) and apply the formula:

$$t = \frac{\log.64}{2\log r}$$

$$t = \frac{\log.64}{2\log.805}$$

$$t = \frac{.446}{2 \times .217}$$

$$t = \frac{.446}{.434}$$

$$t = 1.028$$

This means that Koita and Koiari must have diverged 1.028 thousand years ago (i.e. 1028 years ago), which rounds off to about 1000 years. The Koiari migration from the mountains to the coast should therefore have taken place just before the French invaded the English in the famous Battle of Hastings in 1066.

This method of dating the divergence of languages is known as *glotto-chronology*. Following this methodology, it is possible to give approximate dates for the 'age' of the different degrees of relationships between languages. Thus:

Level of subgrouping	Years of separation
dialects of a language	less than 500 years
languages of a family	500 to 2500 years
families of a stock	2500 to 5000 years
stocks of a microphylum	5000 to 7500 years
microphyla of a mesophylum	7500 to 10000 years
mesophyla of a macrophylum	more than 10000 years

The following graph can be used to calculate roughly the time depth of any linguistic separation on the basis of the share cognate figures between two languages, if you want to avoid doing the calculations with logarithms that I have just shown you:

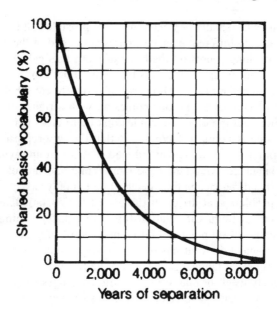

The techniques of lexicostatistics and glottochronology have not been without their critics. I have already hinted at a number of practical problems that are associated with these methods. Firstly there is the problem of deciding which words should be regarded as core vocabulary and which should not. Obviously, it may be possible for different sets of vocabulary to produce differing results.

Another difficulty involves the actual counting of forms that are cognate against those that are not cognate in basic vocabulary lists from two different languages. As I said earlier, ideally, copied vocabulary should be excluded from cognate counts, but to do this you need to know what the regular sound correspondences are between the two languages in order to exclude exceptional forms which are probably copied. However, since we are working with fairly short word lists, there may not be enough data to make generalisations about sound correspondences. Also, we are not likely to know much about the protolanguage if we are dealing with languages for which we have only limited amounts of data, and this will make it even more difficult to distinguish genuine cognates from copied vocabulary.

Lexicostatisticians in fact tend to rely heavily on what is often euphemistically called the *inspection method* of determining whether two forms are cognate or not in a pair of languages. What this amounts to is that you are more or less free to apply intelligent guesswork as to whether you think two forms are cognate or not. If two forms *look* cognate, then they can be given a 'yes' score, but if they are judged not to look cognate, then they are given a 'no' score.

Of course, two different linguists can take the same lists from two different languages, and since there is no objective way of determining what should be ticked 'yes' and what should be ticked 'no', it is possible that both will come up with significantly different cognate figures at the end of the exercise. For example, I have done counts on the basis of word lists calculated by other people and have ended up with figures between 10 per cent and 20 per cent higher or lower than their count. Of course, if two different scholars compare the same pair of languages and one comes up with a figure of 35 per cent cognate sharing, and the other concludes that there is 45 per cent cognate sharing, then one is going to have to say that the two represent different families within the same stock, while the other will end up saying that they are from two languages within the same family. In glottochronological terms, this could mean a difference in time-depth of up to 600 years.

A further problem that arises in the use of lexicostatistical figures to indicate degrees of linguistic relationship is that different linguists some times use different cut-off points for different levels of subgrouping, and there is not even agreement on what sets of terminology should be used to refer to different subgroups of languages. Compare the following two systems that have been widely used for classifying Pacific languages (in which the first system was the one that I gave you earlier in this section):

Level of subgrouping	Shared cognate percentage in core vocabulary
System A	
dialects of a language	81–100
languages of a family	36–81
families of a stock	12–36
stocks of a microphylum	4–12
microphyla of a mesophylum	1–4
mesophyla of a macrophylum	0–1
System B	
dialects of a language	81–100
languages of a sub-family	55–81
subfamilies of a family	28–55
families of a stock	13–28
stocks of a phylum	5–13

You can see from the lists above that the term *family* can actually be used by lexicostatisticians with two different meanings. While I have used the term in this textbook to refer to all languages descended from a protolanguage, according to System A above, a language family refers only to languages that share more than 36 per cent of their core vocabulary, while according to System B, languages in the same family must share more than 55 per cent of their core vocabularies. Other lexicostatisticians use terms that are not included in either of these lists to refer to particularly distant degrees of lexical relationships. Scholars investigating the interrelationships in the huge number of Austronesian languages, for example, sometimes also talk about *linkages* of languages as representing a particularly low level of subgrouping.

Another major problem in applying these figures is that they appear to be fairly arbitrary. The only figure that lexicostatisticians seem to be able to agree on reasonably consistently is that of about 81 per cent cognate similarity as representing the cut-off point between dialects and languages. It seems that as soon as speakers of two different speech traditions (and I use this term as a cover term to include both dialect and language as I do not want to make a distinction between the two at this point) have more than about a 20 per cent difference in their basic lexicons, then mutual intelligibility is lost. Beyond the language-dialect distinction, however, the choice of cognate percentage figures seems to have been based purely on whim, and has no sound scientific basis. So, we should seriously ask ourselves this question: how useful is this method of subgrouping if it has a scientific basis only at the very lowest level of subgrouping?

Apart from these practical problems, there are some more basic *theoretical* objections to these methods, which tend to destroy the validity of the underlying assumptions that I presented earlier. First, we need to question the validity of the assumption that there is a constant rate of lexical replacement in core vocabulary for all languages over time, and that this rate of re-placement is 19.5 per cent every 1000 years. This figure was arrived at by testing only 13 of the world's languages, and these were languages with long histories of writing, and 11 were Indo-European languages. However, differing cultural factors can affect the speed at which lexical replacement can take place. In Chapter 7, I described how lexical replacement can be accelerated in languages in which even basic vocabulary can become proscribed by taboo. The result of lexical replacement because of taboo is that even basic vocabulary, if given sufficient time, will be subject to replacement. If languages copy words from neighbouring languages in order to avoid a forbidden word, two languages which were originally very different from each other will end up sharing a high proportion of even their core vocabularies.

There is a second theoretical problem with lexicostatistics, and that involves the interpretation of the data. Given that change is random within the core vocabulary, it is logically possible for two languages to change the same 19.5 per cent of their core vocabulary every 1000 years and to retain the remaining 80.5 per cent intact over succeeding periods. It is also possible at the other extreme for two languages that in the beginning shared the same proportions of their core vocabulary to replace 19.5 per cent of their core vocabularies every 1000 years, yet for the 19.5 per cent to be different in each successive period. The result of this will be that two pairs of languages, while separated by the same period of time, might have dramatically different vocabulary retention figures depending on which items were actually replaced. Some languages will be accidentally conservative, while others will accidentally exhibit a high degree of change. Although the time depth would be the same, we would be forced to recognise two very different degrees of linguistic relationship.

For instance, after 2000 years, it can be expected that the range of core vocabulary retentions will be as low as 10 per cent in a few languages and as high as 80 per cent in a few others, while for most it will be around 64 per cent, as we would have predicted from the figures earlier. The languages that have retained 10 per cent and 80 per cent will *look* quite divergent, though they are in fact separated by the same time period as all of the others. We should not assume, therefore, that simply because two languages share a fairly low figure for cognate sharing, the degree of relationship is necessarily distant. This fact makes it impossible to be certain of the correctness of our interpretation of lexicostatistical data.

Finally, there are often practical difficulties in interpreting lexicostatistical data, for a wide variety of reasons, some of which have already been mentioned, and some of which may apply only in a particular situation. The data presented earlier as an illustration of a subgrouping technique was in fact highly idealised. It is not often that data from real languages produces a completely consistent picture without contradictions in interpretation. A more typical set of lexicostatistical data from a number of speech communities in the Milne Bay area of Papua New Guinea may look more like this:

```
Mwalakwasia
87%  Somwadina
82   86%  Biawa
72   71   82%  Sigasiga
74   73   76   78%  Lomitawa
64   62   84   69   80%  Sipupu
59   58   55   52   67   79%  Kelologea
62   59   71   66   79   86   78%  Meudana
74   72   76   65   74   76   70   71%  Kasikasi
74   74   80   67   72   62   55   66   76%  Guleguleu
```

In this set of data, there do not appear to be many clear discontinuities or breaks between one subgroup and another. The figures seem to merge gradually into each other, producing very little hope of drawing a family tree.

READING GUIDE QUESTIONS

1. What is a subgroup?
2. What is the difference between a shared retention and a shared innovation?
3. Why can similarities between languages that are due to shared retentions not to be used as evidence for subgrouping?

4. What is drift or parallel development? How does this affect the way we go about deciding on subgroups?
5. What sorts of innovations are the best kind of evidence for subgrouping?
6. What is lexicostatistics?
7. What basic assumptions underlie the method of determining linguistic relationships by lexicostatistics?
8. What is the inspection method of determining whether two forms are cognate or not?
9. What is the difference between core and peripheral vocabulary?
10. What is glottochronology?
11. What are some problems associated with lexicostatistics and glottochronology?

EXERCISES

1. Look at the Korafe, Notu, and Binandere forms in Data Set 7. On the basis of the reconstruction of the changes from the protolanguage that you worked out in the exercises at the end of Chapter 5, would you say that Notu belongs to the same subgroup as Korafe or Binandere? Why?
2. Look back at the reconstruction of the protolanguage for Aroma, Hula, and Sinaugoro that you did in the exercises for Chapter 5. What subgrouping hypothesis can you make for these three languages on the basis of shared innovations?
3. Look at the following forms in Proto Gazelle Peninsula (New Britain, Papua New Guinea). What is the subgrouping of the four speech communities that are represented? Give the justification for the answer that you propose. (Note that the superscript vowels represent phonetically reduced sounds that are nearly voiceless, and not stressable.)

Proto Gazelle	Pila-Pila	Nodup	Vatom	Lunga-Lunga	
*rat^u	rat	rat^u	rat	rat^u	'basket'
*vup^u	vup	vuvu	vup	vuv^u	'fishtrap'
*ram^u	ram	ram^u	ram	ram^u	'club'
*vasian^i	vaian	vaian^i	vaian	vasian^i	'sling'
*saman^i	aman	aman^i	aman	saman^i	'outrigger'
*pal^i	pal	pal^i	pal	pali	'house'
*liplip^i	liplip	livilivu	liplip	-	'fence'
*pem^u	pemu	pem^u	pem	pem^u	'axe'
*pisa	pia	pia	pia	pisa	'ground'
*tirip^u	tirip	tirivu	tirip	tiriv^u	'green coconut'
*kaban^i	kaban	kaban^i	kaban	kaban^i	'lime'
*up^u	up	uvu	-	uv^u	'yam'
*talisa	talia	talia	talia	talisa	'nut'
*papi	pap	pavu	pap	-	'dog'

*taŋis^i	taŋi	taŋi	taŋi	taŋis^i	'cry'
*iap^i	iap	iavu	iap	iav^i	'fire'
*mulisi	muli	muli	muli	mulis^i	'orange'
*beso	beo	beo	beo	beso	'bird'
*lisi	li	lia	li	lis^i	'nits'
*sikilik^i	ikilik	ikilik^i	ikilik	sikilik^i	'small'
*tas^i	ta	tai	ta	tas^i	'sea'

4. The following data comes from four languages spoken in the area of Cape York in northern Queensland in Australia. Examine the reconstructed protolanguage and the descendant forms, and suggest a subgrouping hypothesis on the basis of the shared innovations. There is one set of changes which is problematic for an otherwise strong subgrouping hypothesis. What original sound is involved?

Proto Cape York	Atampaya	Angkamuthi	Yadhaykenu	Wudhadhi	
*kaṯa	ɣaṯa	aṯa	aṯa	-	'rotten'
*kantu	ɣantu	antu	antu	antu	'canoe'
*puŋku	wuŋku	wuŋku	wuŋku	-	'knee'
*ɲaŋka	ɲaŋka	aŋka	aŋka	aŋka	'mouth'
*juku	juku	juku	juku	-	'tree'
*pinta	winta	winta	winta	inta	'arm'
*puɲa	wuɲa	wuɲa	wuɲa	uɲa	'sun'
*ṯipa	lipa	jipa	jipa	-	'liver'
*wapun	wapun	apun	apu	apun	'head'
*wujpu	wujpu	ujpu	ujpu	ujpu	'bad'
*ujpuɲ	ujpuɲ	ujpuɲ	ujpuɲ	ujpuj	'fly'
*ajpaɲ	ajpaɲ	ajpaɲ	ajpaɲ	ajpaj	'stone'
*ṯalan	lalan	jalan	jala	alan	'tongue'
*paṉṯal	waṉṯaw	waṉṯa:	waṉṯa:	-	'yam'
*ɹaṉṯal	ɹaṉṯaw	jaṉṯa:	jaṉṯa:	-	'road'
*pili	wili	wili	wili	-	'run'
*ɹuŋka	ɹuŋka	juŋka	juŋka	uŋka	'cry'
*ɹa	ɹa	ja	ja	-	'throw'
*ɹupal	ɹupaw	jupa:	jupa:	-	'white'
*ɹuṯu	ɹuṯu	juṯu	juṯu	uṯu	'dead'
*pilu	wilu	wilu	wilu	ilu	'hip'
*pupu	wupu	wupu	wupu	upu	'buttocks'
*ŋampu	ŋampu	ampu	ampu	ampu	'tooth'
*maji	maji	aji	aji	aji	'food'
*ŋukal	ŋukaw	uka:	uka:	ukal	'foot'
*miɲa	miɲa	iɲa	iɲa	iɲa	'meat'
*iwuɲ	-	-	iwuɲ	iwuj	'ear'
*ɹapan	ɹapan	japan	japa	-	'strong'

5. Look at the following data from six different languages and answer the questions below:
   (i) How many language families are represented in this data?
   (ii) What are your reasons for saying this?
   (iii) What factors can you suggest to account for the similarities between languages that you say do not belong to a single family?

A	B	C	D	E	F	
mwana	mwana	umwana	baceh	anak	bata	'child'
lia	dila	lila	girjeh	triak	ijak	'cry'
ɲwa	nua	nwa	nuʃidan	minum	inum	'drink'
moto	tija	umulio	ateʃ	api	apoj	'fire'
nne	ia	ne	cæhær	əmpat	ampat	'four'
kilima	mongo	ulupili	tel	bukit	bukid	'hill'
ceka	seva	seka	xændidan	tərtawa	tawa	'laugh'
mguu	kulu	ukuulu	saq	kaki	pa	'leg'
mdo	mokoba	umulomo	læb	bibir	bibig	'lip'
mtu	muntu	umuntu	mærd	oraŋ	tau	'man'
habari	nsangu	iceevo	xæbær	kabar	balita	'news'
moja	mosi	mo	jek	satu	isa	'one'
nabii	mbikudi	umusimicisi	næbij	nabi	propetas	'prophet'
mvua	mvula	imfula	baran	huʝan	ulan	'rain'
merikebu	maswa	ubwato	mærkæb	kapal	bapor	'ship'
dhambi	masumu	icakuvifja	zamb	dosa	kasilanan	'sin'
askari	kinwani	icita	æskær	askar	suldado	'soldier'
kidonda	mputa	icilonda	zæxm	sakit	sakit	'sick'
hutoba	maloɲi	isiwi	xutbæh	xutbah	salita	'speech'
hadhithi	ŋana	icisimicisjo	hædis	cerita	istoria	'story'
hekalu	kinlongo	itempuli	hæjkil	rumah	templo	'temple'
tatu	tatu	tatu	seh	tiga	tatlo	'three'
mti	nti	umuti	dæræxt	pohon	puno	'tree'
bili	zole	vili	do	dua	dalawa	'two'

6. Examine the following data from the Māori language of New Zealand and the now extinct Moriori language of the Chatham Islands. Do a count of the shared cognates between the two and estimate according to glottochronology when the two languages should have diverged.

Māori	Moriori	
pungarehu	*purungehu*	'ashes'
tuara	*tura*	'back'
kino	*wahike*	'bad'
kiri	*kiri*	'bark'
kopu	*takapu*	'belly'
rahi	*rahi*	'big'

manu	manu	'bird'
ngau	ngahu	'bite'
pango	pango	'black'
pupuhi	puhi	'blow'
iwi	imi	'bone'
u	u	'breast'
manawa	manawa	'breath'
tuakana	tukana	'brother'
tamaiti	timiti	'child'
ao	ao	'cloud'
matao	matao	'cold'
haeremai	haramai	'come'
tunu	tunu	'cook'
kani	motiha	'dance'
ao	ao	'day'
keri	keri	'dig'
paru	karupuru	'dirt'
inu	inu	'drink'
maroke	moroke	'dry'
puhuki	puhiku	'dull, blunt'
nehu	pawa	'dust'
taringa	tiringa	'ear'
fenua	fenua	'earth'
kai	kai	'eat'
hua	hu	'egg'
waru	tewaru	'eight'
kanohi	konehi	'eye'
hinga	hingi	'fall'
momona	ihara	'fat'
papa	papa	'father'
piki	piki	'feather'
ahi	ahi	'fire'
ika	ika	'fish'
rima	terima	'five'
pua	pua	'flower'
kohu	kohu	'fog'
waewae	wawae	'foot'
fa	tefa	'four'
hua	hua	'fruit'
pai	humaria	'good'
tarutaru	taru	'grass'
marama	marama	'moon'
faea	matehine	'mother'
maunga	maunga	'mountain'
waha	waha	'mouth'

ingoa	*ingoa*	'name'
kaki	*kaki*	'neck'
ihu	*purangaihu*	'nose'
tafito	*tafito*	'old'
tahi	*tehi*	'one'
tangata	*tangata*	'person'
takaro	*hokorereto*	'play'
tika	*tikane*	'right, correct'
paiaka	*purakautimu*	'root'
mataitai	*marurua*	'salt/salty'
onepu	*one*	'sand'
fitu	*tefitu*	'seven'
poto	*poto*	'short'
waiata	*karamiha*	'sing'
kiri	*kiri*	'skin'
moe	*moe*	'sleep'
auahi	*auahi*	'smoke'
maeneene	*maene*	'smooth'
huka	*haware*	'snow'
tao	*tuparipari*	'spear'
roromi	*romi*	'squeeze'
fetu	*fetu*	'star'
noho	*noho*	'stay'
pohatu	*pohatu*	'stone'
kaha	*kaha*	'strong'
momi	*momomi*	'suck'
ra	*ra*	'sun'
huku	*huku*	'swelling'
kau	*rewa*	'swim'
hiore	*hiore*	'tail'
ngahuru	*ngauru*	'ten'
matotoru	*matotoru*	'thick'
tupuhi	*meatae*	'thin'
toru	*toru*	'three'
arero	*warero*	'tongue'
niho	*niho*	'tooth'
rakau	*rakau*	'tree'
huri	*huri*	'turn'
rua	*teru*	'two'
ruaki	*ruaki*	'vomit'
hau	*hau*	'wind'
pakau	*pakau*	'wing'
wahine	*wahine*	'woman'
mahi	*mahi*	'work'
toke	*tunga*	'worm'

7. Examine the shared cognate figures below for a number of speech
    communities in central Vanuatu (which are located on the map below).
    Can you draw a family tree that shows the degrees of relationship here?

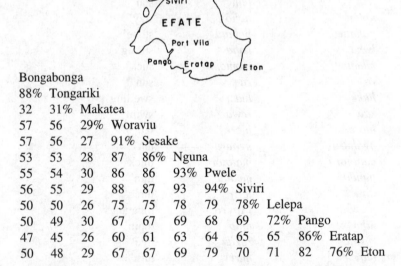

Bongabonga
88% Tongariki
32 31% Makatea
57 56 29% Woraviu
57 56 27 91% Sesake
53 53 28 87 86% Nguna
55 54 30 86 86 93% Pwele
56 55 29 88 87 93 94% Siviri
50 50 26 75 75 78 79 78% Lelepa
50 49 30 67 67 69 68 69 72% Pango
47 45 26 60 61 63 64 65 65 86% Eratap
50 48 29 67 67 69 79 70 71 82 76% Eton

8. The historical record shows that Tok Pisin in Papua New Guinea
    emerged as a separate language from English in the second half of the
    nineteenth century. A count of shared cognates in the basic vocabularies
    of Tok Pisin and English reveals that out of 200 items, the two languages
    have common sources for 146 items. On the basis of this evidence,
    approximately when should the two languages have diverged? What does
    the result say about the assumptions of glottochronology?

9. Refer to Data Set 10 and see if you can make any judgements about the subgrouping of Sepa, Manam, Kairiru, and Sera from lexicostatistical evidence.

10. You have seen that subgrouping depends on being able to distinguish shared innovations from shared retentions from the protolanguage. Features are reconstructed in the protolanguage partly on the basis of the extent of their distribution in the daughter languages, as you learned in Chapter 5. What methodological problem do we face here?

FURTHER READING

1. Theodora Bynon *Historical Linguistics*, Chapter 7 'Glottochronology (or lexicostatistics)', pp. 266–72.
2. Robert J. Jeffers and Ilse Lehiste *Principles and Methods for Historical Linguistics*, Chapter 8 'Lexicostatistics', pp. 133–37.
3. Winfred P. Lehmann *Historical Linguistics: An Introduction*, Chapter 7 'Study of Loss in Language: Lexicostatistics', pp. 107–14.
4. Sarah Gudschinsky 'The ABC's of Lexicostatistics (Glottochronology)' in Dell Hymes (ed.) *Language in Culture and Society*, pp. 612–23.

CHAPTER NINE

CAUSES OF LANGUAGE CHANGE

In Chapter 1, I discussed some of the common attitudes that people have towards language change. One of those attitudes was a sense of regret that languages should change at all, with people wondering why it should be that languages change in the first place. In this chapter I want to discuss some of the reasons that have been proposed for language change, ranging from the fanciful to the plausible.

9.1 ANATOMY AND ETHNIC CHARACTER

In the nineteenth century, some scholars attempted to find an anatomical explanation for language change, concentrating in particular on sound change. At that time, cultural differences were often assumed to be related to anatomical differences, and different ways of thinking and behaving were often said to reflect the superior or inferior intellects of different peoples. (Such views are of course now regarded as racist nonsense, and I am only mentioning them here in the interest of historical accuracy.) Following the same line of thinking, change in language, and especially sound change, was sometimes related to cultural differences between peoples.

For instance, there are two sets of sound changes in some of the Germanic languages of northern Europe. The so-called *First Sound Shift* took place in the entire area in which the Germanic languages were spoken, while the more far-reaching *Second Sound Shift* took place only in the southern area (where German itself was spoken). A famous linguist in the nineteenth century, Jakob Grimm, tried to explain this by saying:

It may be reckoned as evidence of the superior gentleness and moderation of the Gothic, Saxon, and Scandinavian tribes that they contented themselves with the first sound shift, whilst the wilder force of the southern Germans was impelled towards the second shift.

Such statements can easily become useful supports to politically sponsored racial beliefs, and indeed have been used in this way in the past, for instance in Nazi Germany.

Some sections of white South African society have also adopted similar kinds of explanations for changes that have taken place in the development of Afrikaans from earlier Dutch. Afrikaans and Dutch are very closely related languages, but to someone who knows Dutch, Afrikaans seems to involve a great deal of simplification and regularisation of some of the grammatical patterns of Dutch. It is not difficult to imagine that perhaps Afrikaans underwent this simplification as a result of language contact between the early Dutch settlers in South Africa and the other races who lived in the area at the same time. We do not know for sure under what circumstances Afrikaans developed its distinctive features in South Africa, but there are some Whites who have a vested interest in maintaining a more 'honourable' account of the origin of their language, rather than allowing it to be 'tainted' by input from household servants and people of other races. So, the far-reaching changes that took place in the phonology and grammar of the language were put down instead to the revolutionary spirit of the Dutch settlers in a new land, as evidenced by the following quote:

A conservative race living in a conservative environment does not as a rule indulge in great linguistic changes. The Dutch colonists of South Africa lived under very unconservative conditions. It was an entirely new kind of country, with new occupations and duties.

The environment that faced the British settlers in the same area was, of course, no different from that which faced the Dutch settlers, yet the British did not feel impelled towards the same radical changes in their language, so I have the strongest suspicion that the explanation for the changes that took place in the formation of Afrikaans will turn out to be other than purely environmental factors.

It has also been suggested that there were significant differences between the languages of 'civilised' people and those of 'uncivilised' people with respect to language change. There was once a commonly held view among European scholars that modern civilisation basically represented a corruption of a more pure and unspoilt form of human nature that was still to be found in the minds of what they came to call the 'noble savage'. We can obviously question the kinds of presuppositions that are involved here, but that is beside the point for the moment. What is to the point is the fact that scholars at the time also attempted to find some kind of relationship between the fundamental nature of 'primitive' languages as distinct from 'civilised' languages. It was claimed that 'primitive' languages contained more harsh, throaty sounds than 'civilised' languages. Just as civilisation was supposed to represent a degeneration of an original pure, natural state, so too was the supposed development of a preference for sounds produced further forward in the mouth. Such changes were equated with the laziness that characterised modern civilisation. The 'noble savage', it was argued, maintained language in its more pure, guttural state!

Historical linguists of this period also tended to look back with nostalgia to the grammatical structures of the protolanguage from which the modern Indo-European languages are derived. They admired the highly inflectional Proto Indo-European, which was said to represent a more 'pure' grammatical state, which had declined along with the development of civilisation in western Europe. Views such as these now warrant little further discussion. All that needs to be said is that it is quite impossible to relate any structural features of languages, whether they be phonetic features or grammatical features, to any differences in culture between two peoples. Such views represent pure racism.

The kinds of beliefs that I have been talking about are also compatible with an anatomical explanation for sound change. Some scholars in the past have said that because Africans have thicker lips than Europeans, they are incapable of producing certain kinds of sounds. The differences between Black and White English in America, for example, has in the past sometimes been put down to the physical inability of Blacks to speak English 'properly'! Again, there should be little need to criticise this kind of reasoning today, as all modern linguists operate on the basic assumption that language learning is purely a matter of exposure, and an individual's genetic make-up is completely irrelevant to the kind of language that he or she will eventually learn.

9.2 CLIMATE AND GEOGRAPHY

In addition to some of the more bizarre nineteenth century theories about language change that I have just discussed, there were some scholars who suggested that perhaps a harsh physical environment could produce harsh sounds in a language. What is meant by the 'harshness' of a sound of course is not usually very clearly explained, though from the examples that people give, it appears that phonetic harshness involves the presence of many 'guttural' sounds (i.e. glottal and uvular sounds) and the occurrence of many complex consonant clusters. The rugged terrain and harsh climate of the Caucasus Mountains in the former Soviet Union were sometimes said to have caused the languages of this region to develop such sounds.

It is not too difficult to prove that such views are nonsense. The Inuit of far northern Canada live in an environment that is as harsh as anywhere in the world, yet their phonetic system has been described by some scholars as 'agreeable'. (You should note that it is just as unacceptable, however, to describe the phonetic system as 'agreeable' as it is to say that it is 'harsh'. Both represent nothing but value judgements.) Similarly, the Australian Aborigines of Central Australia live in a harsh environment of a different kind, yet they have a sound system that has been called 'euphonic'. Evidently, what was meant by this was that these languages had relatively few consonant clusters, a fairly small number of phonemes, and relatively few 'guttural' sounds.

The languages of mountainous areas, it was sometimes argued, tended to change more rapidly than languages spoken closer to sea level, especially with regard to their consonants. Because of the higher altitude, it was suggested, there was greater effort involved in breathing, and this was supposed to make the consonants more susceptible to change. This argument can also be easily disproved. There are mountainous areas which have languages that have changed relatively little, and there are coastal people whose languages have undergone radical changes in their consonants.

9.3 SUBSTRATUM

The *substratum* theory of lingusitic change involves the idea that if people migrate into an area and their language is acquired by the original inhabitants of the area, then any changes in the language can be put down to the influence of the original language. (In Section 12.1 I discuss the question of how one language can influence another in its structure.)

It is well known that a person's first language will to some extent influence the way in which that person will speak a second language. We can all recognise foreign accents in our own language. It is quite easy to tell whether someone is a native speaker of English, or whether their first language is French, German, Chinese, or Samoan. While Black Americans today have English as their first language, it is often possible to point to features of the English spoken by Blacks which are not present in the English spoken by Whites. Some of these features of the English of Blacks, or *Black English Vernacular* as it is often termed, have been put down to the features of the original languages of the African slaves who were first transported to America hundreds of years ago. It may turn out that these features do not derive from African languages at all, but if, on the other hand, this argument turns out to be correct, then this would be an example of how substratum has influenced the direction that one variety of a language has taken.

The problem with the substratum explanation of language change is that it is sometimes used to explain changes in languages where the supposed substratum language (or languages) have ceased to exist. The influence of the substratum in such cases can be neither proved nor disproved. One example of sub-stratum influence that is often quoted involves the history of French. Before the time of the Roman Empire, what is now France was occupied by Celtic-speaking people (whose language was closely related to Welsh and Irish). France is now split into two major dialect areas, between the north and the south. Some scholars have suggested that this split corresponds to an earlier split in the original Celtic language, and that these differences were carried over into the Latin they spoke when they switched languages. While this is a perfectly plausible theory, since the original Celtic language no longer survives in France, it can neither be proved nor disproved.

In Melanesia too, the substratum theory has been used to explain some of the more unusual features of some of the Austronesian languages, as compared to the Austronesian languages that are found outside Melanesia. The argument goes like this: there were originally non-Austronesian populations throughout Papua New Guinea and the Solomon Islands, and when the Austronesian languages arrived, the original languages influenced the newly introduced languages in different ways before being replaced by the Austronesian languages. Once again, as these original languages no longer exist, it is hard to refute this theory. It is just as difficult, however, to prove it to be correct.

9.4 LOCAL IDENTIFICATION

The linguist Don Laycock once offered a different kind of explanation for why language change takes place, at least in some communities. In very small language communities, such as those found in Melanesia and in Aboriginal Australia, he suggested, languages may change simply to allow their speakers to distinguish things about their speech that are different from the speech of other people. People from linguistically very diverse areas, such as the Sepik in Papua New Guinea, have been reported as saying things like this:

It wouldn't be any good if we all spoke the same. We like to know where people come from.

Linguistic diversity in this kind of situation is therefore a mark of identification for a community.

For example, there are four communities that speak the Austronesian language called Sissano along the West Sepik coast. One of these communities originally spoke One, a non-Austronesian language, but their ancestors settled amongst Sissano speakers over a century ago and then acquired the Sissano language, which over time became their only language. However, they have retained some of the original One words in their Sissano. Laycock argues that in doing this, they are asserting their different history from the other Sissano-speaking communities.

When language is used as a tool for local identification in this way, it is conceivable that changes can be deliberate and planned. Of course it would be impossible to prove that the One people consciously decided to retain a handful of their own words when they switched to Sissano. I pointed out in Chapter 1 that it is possible for languages to be changed deliberately. There is one rather interesting case from an Australian language where people really *do* seem to have sat down and consciously done something to their language in order to create something special. In the Lardil society of northern Australia, there is a special speech style that is used in certain social situations instead of the ordinary, everyday kind of language. This special style is used only by men who have been fully initiated into the society. It is characterised by the use of words that are different from the ordinary style of speaking, though the grammar is the same in both styles. What is interesting about this case is that the words in this special style contain sounds that no other language in Australia contains, and which are completely absent from the ordinary style of speaking in this language. For instance, the word for 'vegetable food' in this special style can be represented phonetically as [m!i], where the symbol [m!] represents a sound very similar to the sound of a kiss. A fish is called [Li], where the [L] represents an ingressive lateral fricative. (This is essentially a slurp.) There is even one sound in this style that occurs in no other language in the world (at least, as far as we know). The sound is symbolised as [p'], and this represents the sound we make with our lips when we want to imitate somebody farting! The fact that these sounds are so unusual makes it look as if somebody has deliberately invented these words so that the initiated men could in a sense 'mystify' their speech, and clearly mark their special social status.

The urge for language to be used as a tool of identification can be particularly strong where the members of one ethnic group come to use the language of another ethnic group on a regular basis. What sometimes happens is that people will come up with their own distinctive vocabulary items and slang expressions as a way of signalling their distinct identity in what was originally a foreign language for them. Educated Papua New Guineans have learned English from their former Australian colonial 'overlords', yet nobody would mistake an ordinary Papua New Guinean speaking English for an Australian. Even the most fluent English-speaking Papua New Guineans for the most part do not *want* to sound like Australians. With this kind of attitude, people in Papua New Guinea have spontaneously come up with a number of colourful expressions which do not derive from Australian usage at all, such as the following:

That guy, he's really waterproof ia!
'That guy doesn't bathe very regularly.'

He's really service in greasing ladies.
'He's really good at chatting up women.'

Can I polish the floor at your place tonight?
'Can I stay overnight on a mattress (or mat) on your floor tonight?'

She sixtied down the road.
'She sped down the road.'

Invoking local identification as a causal factor in language change opens up the entire area of variability in the sociolinguistic literature and the associated non-linguistic conditioning factors. There is a vast array of variable facts about language that can be correlated to ethnic differences, or differences in gender or socio-economic class. In New Zealand, the fact that a working class Māori male in many respects speaks differently to a middle class European (or Pākehā) female is basically an example of the same kind of phenomenon. How would people react, for example, if an unemployed Māori school-leaver were to speak like a mayoress? He simply would not be speaking in the way that is appropriate to where he comes from. Similarly, if Her Worship were to suddenly adopt the street talk of such a young man, people would quickly wonder what she was trying to achieve.

9.5 FUNCTIONAL NEED

It is also true that some changes take place in language because a particular language *must* change in order to meet new demands that its speakers place upon it. As the functional needs of a language change (i.e. the range of situations in which a language is used becomes wider), some aspects of the language may be lost, while others may be added. These kinds of pressures do not generally affect the phonology, or even the grammar, but they can have drastic effects on the vocabulary. Words referring to cultural concepts that have become irrelevant may be lost, while new words may flood into a language to express important new concepts. In both Chapter 1 and Chapter 7, I described various aspects of lexical change arising from all sorts of different causes, so I will not go into this matter again at this point.

It should be pointed out, however, that while languages tend to develop lexical specialisations in areas that are of cultural importance, the mere existence of lexical specialisation should not, by itself, be taken as a sign that something is of particular cultural or environmental significance to people who use that word. For instance, I have recently heard the word *wedgie* on American TV programmes, which refers to the situation when one's underwear rides up uncomfortably between one's buttocks, as in *Excuse me, but I've got a wedgie*. As far as I know, this word is not part of either New Zealand or Australian English. I do not think that we should interpret this difference as meaning that American underwear manufacturers are inflicting a shoddy wedgie-prone product on the American people, or that Australasians are more tolerant than Americans of sartorial discomfort.

Some areas of lexical specialisation, then, develop for no particular reason, without any underlying cultural or environmental significance. When we compare the vocabulary of English with that of other languages, there are invariably areas of meaning in the other language that are encoded by single words for which we do not have single-word translation equivalents in English. For instance, in the Sye language of Vanuatu, we find words such as the following, though it would be difficult to find any particular cultural explanation for why they have words to express these meanings, while in English we don't:

elantvi	'complain unjustifiably that something is insufficient or not good enough'
livinlivin	'top of something that is teetering over an edge and is about to fall'
orvalei	'touch something that is unpleasantly soft or mushy'

There is even a whole book about meanings that it would be really handy to have words for in English. Douglas Adams and John Lloyd wrote the book *The Deeper Meaning of Liff: A Dictionary of Things that there aren't any Words for Yet*, in which they take place names and give them made-up meanings, such as the following:

Lostwithiel	'the deep peaceful sleep you finally fall into two minutes before the alarm goes off'
Nokomis	'one who dresses like an ethnic minority to which they do not belong'
Thrumster	'the irritating man next to you in a concert who thinks he's the conductor'

9.6 SIMPLIFICATION

Many of the sound changes that I described in Chapter 2 could be regarded as simplifying the production of sounds in one way or another. In dropping sounds, we are making words shorter, and therefore we need to exert less physical effort to produce them. The changes that come under the general heading of assimilation also clearly involve a change in the amount of effort that is needed to produce sounds as the degree of articulatory difference between sounds is reduced. Fusion, too, reduces the number of sounds in a word. One famous linguist, Otto Jespersen, made a great deal of the importance of simplicity as a factor in bringing about sound change:

> I am not afraid of hearing the objection that I ascribe too great a power to human laxness, indolence, inertia, shirking, easy-goingness, sluggishness, or whatever other beautiful synonyms have been invented for 'economy of effort' or 'following the line of least resistance'. The fact remains that there is such a tendency in all human beings, and by taking it into account in explaining changes of sound, we are doing nothing else than applying here the same principle.

Despite the obvious appeal of this argument as a major factor in explaining language change, there are also several problems associated with it. The first is that it is extremely difficult, perhaps even impossible, to define explicitly what we mean by 'simplicity' in language. Simplicity is clearly a relative term. What is simple for speakers of one language may well be difficult for speakers of another. Kuman speakers in the Simbu Province of Papua New Guinea fused the two sounds [gl] into a single velar lateral [ᵍl]. The principle of simplicity could be brought in as the causal factor, as this is an example of fusion. However, the velar lateral that results from this phonetic 'simplification' is a sound that speakers of all other languages find almost impossible to produce to the satisfaction of Kuman speakers.

Similarly, the interdental fricatives [ð] and [θ] developed in English out of the corresponding alveolar stops, presumably for reasons of 'simplicity'. Yet speakers of the many languages in the world that do not have these sounds find great difficulty in pronouncing them, and typically substitute a sound that they find simpler. A person from France will often substitute these sounds with [z] and [s] respectively (e.g. *zis sing* for 'this thing'); a Papua New Guinean will often substitute [d] and [t] (e.g. *dis ting*), while a Tongan will often substitute [v] and [f] (e.g. *vis fing*). And while English speakers have no trouble with [ð] and [θ], many find it difficult to produce the velar fricative [x], which German speakers have no trouble with.

A second problem is that if all sound changes were to be explained away as being the result of simplification, we cannot explain why many changes do *not* take place. If it is easier to say [ʌŋkaɪnd] than to say [ʌnkaɪnd] for 'unkind', why don't all languages change [nk] to [ŋk]? Why do only some languages undergo this kind of simplification, and why only at some times? As I said in Chapter 7, if language change were unidirectional we should all be speaking basically the same kind of language now.

A third problem is that some sound changes clearly do *not* involve simplification anyway. There is no way that the change called metathesis can be called simplification (though it does not make things any more complex either). Exactly the same sounds are found before and after the change, and all that has been altered is the actual order in which the sounds occur. And if phonetic fusion can be viewed as simplification, then surely phonetic unpacking must be just the opposite, as this creates two sounds from a single original sound.

Finally, you should also note that simplification in one part of a language may end up creating complexities elsewhere in the system. For instance, the change known as syncope (i.e. the dropping of medial vowels) can be viewed as simplification in that it reduces the number of actual sounds in a word, but syncope often results in the creation of consonant clusters in languages that did not have them. While a particular word may end up being 'simplified' as a result of syncope, the overall *phonotactic* structure of the language can be made much more complex. (By *phonotactics* I mean the statement of which phonemes can occur in what position in a word in a language, and which other phonemes can occur next to them.) How can we say that a change from a **CV** syllable structure to a **CCV** syllable structure involves simplification, when the insertion of an epenthetic vowel between consonants to avoid **CCV** sequences is also called simplification?

Simplification in the phonological system may also cause new complexities to arise outside the phonological system of a language. Some phonological changes, for example, can complicate things in the morphology.

In Chapter 2, I described the change by which final voiced stops in German underwent devoicing. This was viewed as an assimilatory change, as the voicing of the stops was taking on the lack of voicing in the following 'nothingness' of the end of the word. However, this simplification in the phonology of German has made the morphology of the language more complex. Examine the following data:

Singular			Plural			
*ta:g	→	ta:k	*ta:gə	→	ta:gə	'day'
*hund	→	hunt	*hundə	→	hundə	'dog'
*laut	→	laut	*lautə	→	lautə	'sound'
*bo:t	→	bo:t	*bo:tə	→	bo:tə	'boat'

In the earlier stage of German, the rule for the formation of the plural of these four nouns could be stated quite simply: add the suffix /-ə/. After word final stops were devoiced, the statement of this rule has become more complicated. Obviously the final stops were not devoiced in the plural, as there was a suffix at the end of the word that 'protected' them from the effect of this general change. So in modern German, the rule for the formation of the plural must be stated instead as follows:

(i)   With some words (e.g **laut, bo:t**), simply add the suffix /-ə/.
(ii) With other words (e.g. **ta:k, hunt**), add the suffix /-ə/ and at the same time change the final voiceless stop to the corresponding voiced sound.

The form of the singular noun does not indicate what the form of the plural will be. A student of German has to learn on a case-by-case basis what the plural will be. If you have learned the word /bo:t/ 'boat', there is no way of knowing just by looking at the word whether the plural will be /bo:tə/ or /bo:də/. So while the final devoicing rule can be viewed as simplication in the phonological system of the language, it has created complexities elsewhere.

Sound changes very often result in the creation of new grammatical patterns. Not all of these resulting grammatical changes, of course, involve new complexities in the resulting language. You saw earlier in this volume that grammatical changes can in some ways be viewed as operating in a kind of typological circle, in which there is a tendency for isolating languages to move towards the agglutinating type by phonologically reducing free forms to bound forms. Agglutinating languages then tend to move towards the inflectional type by phonologically reducing bound morphemes even further. And finally, the circle is completed when inflecting languages move towards the isolating type, once again by phonologically reducing inflections to nothing at all.

Not all grammatical changes can be explained as being the result of phonological simplification, however. Other grammatical changes occur for quite different reasons. Grammars tend to change so that any constructions which are unnecessarily unclear and complex become clearer and less complex. Speakers of languages try to make the structures of their languages neater and easier to learn. For instance, there are people who complain if they hear the following nouns in English used as singular nouns: *data*, *media*, and *criteria*. There are people who say the following is incorrect:

The mass media in New Caledonia often **expresses** *only the opinions of the French colonisers.*

These people would insist that only the following is 'correct':

The mass media in New Caledonia often **express** *only the opinions of the French colonisers.*

People who argue along these lines say that *media* is a plural noun, and that the corresponding singular is *medium*. Similarly, they point out that the singular of *data* is *datum*, and the singular of *criteria* is *criterion*.

Many people do not use these words as others say they should, however. The marking for plural on most nouns in English is a morpheme which has the allomorphs /-s/, /-z/ and /-əz/, as in the examples below:

parrot	parrots
cassowary	cassowaries
cuscus	cuscuses

The existence of the separate plural marking for a few nouns such as datum, medium, and criterion is in a sense a complication to the statement of the rule for the formation of plural nouns in English. What is happening is that some speakers of English are finding ways out of this difficulty. What they have done is reanalyse these irregular nouns as mass nouns rather than count nouns. Count nouns are those nouns in English that have separate plural forms, like those that we have been looking at. Mass nouns, however, do not have separate plural forms in English; they include nouns such as information, mail, and equipment. Thus, while the first of the sentences below is possible in English, the second is not:

This information is quite insufficient to make a decision.
**These informations are quite insufficient to make a decision.*

In the sentence that I gave earlier, where *media* takes a singular verb and does not have a separate plural form (i.e. nobody would say **medias*), you can see that this word is behaving in exactly the same way as *information* behaves. The original singular form *medium* is disappearing from the language as a way of referring to newspapers, radio, and television.

The second method that speakers of English are using as a way of avoiding this particular grammatical irregularity is to keep these nouns in the category of count nouns, but to form their plurals in the same way as all other nouns in the language. So some people might say:

What is the criteria that you used to come to that conclusion?
Those are not the only criterias that you can use to come to a conclusion.

9.7 STRUCTURAL PRESSURE

One explanation for sound change that has been put forward in recent years is
the concept of *structural pressure*. Linguists view languages as collections of
units at various levels, and the units relate to each other in very specific ways
at each level in the system. Languages, therefore, operate in terms of systems.
If a system becomes uneven, or if it has some kind of 'gap', then (so the
argument goes) a change is likely to take place as a way of filling that gap, so
as to produce a neat system. For instance, imagine that a language has a five
vowel system:

   i   u
   e   o
     a

Now suppose that the vowel /e/ underwent a change such that it was
unconditionally raised to /i/. This would result in the following system:

   i   u
     o
    a

This is an unbalanced system, as the language has a contrast between a front
and back vowel in the high vowels, but it has only a single mid vowel. There
are many languages in the world that have three vowel systems of the
following type, but relatively few that have four vowel systems such as that
which I set out above:

   i   u
    a

It would not be surprising to find that if a language had an unbalanced four-
vowel system, it would then shift /o/ to /u/ to match the change that had
produced the imbalance in the first place.

However, we cannot say that the pressure to fill gaps in systems like this is
an overwhelming force in language change. The most that we can say is that
languages that have gaps in their systems *tend* to fill them, but any attempt at
a general explanation of sound change that contains the word 'tend' is of little
value. Even a superficial examination of the world's languages reveals that
there are some which have gaps in their systems, and there do not always
seem to be changes taking place that would result in these gaps being

plugged. In the Motu language of Papua New Guinea, for example, there are voiced and voiceless stops at the bilabial, alveolar and velar points of articulation:

p   t   k
b   d   g

Motu also has nasals at the bilabial and alveolar points of articulation:

m   n

However, there is no velar nasal in Motu. Although there is clearly a structural gap in the phonological system of the language, there is no indication that there are any changes taking place in the language that would result in the creation of a new phoneme that would occupy this empty slot in the phoneme inventory. Quite the opposite, in fact — we know from a comparison between Motu and closely related languages that it acquired this gap relatively recently, by unconditionally losing all of its velar nasals.

9.8 SOCIAL UPHEAVAL

It certainly seems that, although language can be viewed as a system, there are forces lying in wait to destroy it, in addition to forces lying in wait to protect it. The fact that society needs that system to hold itself together is enough of a force to keep the system from falling apart in most instances. In the light of this comment, it is interesting to note that many linguists relate the spread of linguistic changes to periods of great social upheaval. The theory is that during periods of upheaval, there is less likely to be direct control of children by parents, so there would be less pressure of correction, thereby allowing innovations to go through uncorrected by the older generation. These innovations could then be passed on to the following generations, resulting in a change affecting the entire speech community.

The drastic phonological changes that took place in the history of Old Irish have been attributed by some to the introduction of Christianity into Ireland. The far-reaching changes that took place in the sound system of the Mbabaram language of far north Queensland in Australia (as illustrated in Data Set 1) have been put down to a shift in the people's location thousands of years ago from a lush coastal environment to a dry mountain-top environment, and the changes in lifestyle that this meant. The great grammatical and phonological changes that took place between Old English and Modern English have been explained by some as being due to the impact of the bubonic plague which killed millions of people in England, and of the Norman invasion of England in 1066. Thus, there were changes that were 'waiting to get out' in these languages, and they were unleashed by these drastic social disruptions.

There may be some truth in these suggestions, but we should not take this notion too far. While many social upheavals do greatly influence languages, this influence is usually concentrated in the lexicon, and phonological and grammatical changes do not necessarily reflect the extent of lexical changes. Christianity has been introduced into most of the same places in the Pacific in the last 200 years, yet these languages have not undergone the same kind of phonological change as Old Irish did. Not only this, but many of the same places in the Pacific underwent depopulation at the same time that was even more massive than in the time of the European plagues, as the Christian missionaries often unwittingly introduced diseases against which the people had no immunity — yet the languages did not generally undergo significant structural change. The explanation of the lack of correction of the child by its parents is a weak one. People nowadays regard correction in the home as being of little importance in the learning of a language by a child. It seems that much of a child's language-learning takes place in the child's peer group, rather than just from its parents.

READING GUIDE QUESTIONS

1. How do we know that language change is not caused by anatomical, cultural, or geographical factors?
2. What is the substratum theory of language change, and what are the weaknesses of this argument?
3. Can a language be deliberately changed by members of a speech community?
4. How valid is it to say that languages change because they have to change in order to meet new social needs?
5. To what extent is simplification a factor in causing language change to take place? What are some problems associated with this explanation of language change?
6. How might structural pressure cause a sound change to take place?

FURTHER READING

1. Jean Aitchison *Language Change: Progress or Decay?*, Chapter 7 'The Reason Why', pp. 111–28; Chapter 8 'Doing what Comes Naturally', pp. 129–43; Chapter 9 'Repairing the Patterns', pp. 144–55, Chapter 10 'The Mad Hatter's Tea Party', pp. 156–69.
2. Raimo Anttila *An Introduction to Historical and Comparative Linguistics*, chapter 9 'Why does Language Change: Social and Linguistic Factors', pp. 179–206.
3. Hans Henrich Hock *Principles of Historical Linguistics*, Chapter 8 'Sound Change: Structure and Function', pp. 148–66; Chapter 20 'Linguistic Change: Its Nature and Causes', pp. 627–62.

CHAPTER TEN

OBSERVING LANGUAGE CHANGE

10.1 THE TRADITIONAL VIEW

If you ask a speaker of any language the question: *Can you think of any changes that you can see taking place in your language now?*, you will be quite likely to get a positive answer. It seems that people are usually aware of some kinds of changes that are taking place in their language at any particular time. For instance, if you were to ask somebody what sorts of changes are taking place in English, you might get answers like this: *The word **whom** in sentences like **This is the person whom I saw yesterday** is being replaced with who.* If you were to ask speakers of Tok Pisin in Papua New Guinea what sorts of changes they were able to observe taking place in the language, they might comment on the fact that people are starting to say *moskito* instead of *natnat* for 'mosquito', and that some words are being shortened, with *mipela* 'us' becoming *mipla* and *bilong* 'of' becoming *blo*. A speaker of Bislama in Vanuatu might also comment in the same way that few people these days say *pigpig* for 'pig' — most people just say *pig*.

You saw in Chapter 1 that speakers of languages are often quite aware of changes that are taking place in their language, and that these changes tend to be regarded as 'corruptions' of the 'correct' or unchanged form of the language. I mentioned specifically that speakers of Pacific languages often regret the changes that they see taking place in their own languages, as words from English or other languages are replacing some of the original words in the languages.

Even though speakers of languages are often quite aware of changes that are taking place in their languages at a given time, it is rather surprising to find that for a long time linguists claimed that language change was something that could never be observed. Linguists claimed that all we could do was to study how a language behaved before a change and after a change, and to compare the two different stages of the language, but to study the change actually taking place was impossible. They argued that language change was so slow and so gradual that the differences between the different stages of language would end up being so far apart in time that we could not hope to be alive to see a change through from beginning to end, or even to see it having any significant effect on the language. One of the most important linguists of this century after Saussure was the American linguist Leonard Bloomfield, and he stated quite unambiguously in 1933 that:

The process of linguistic change has never been directly observed; ... such an observation, with our present facilities, is inconceivable.

Why did linguists say this, ignoring the obvious facts around them which ordinary speakers of any language can very clearly see?

As I mentioned in Chapter 1, Saussure is regarded as the originator of modern linguistics, and one of his major achievements was to divert attention away from the purely diachronic study of language to the synchronic study of language. In the following chapter, you will learn about the *neogrammarians*, who were nineteenth century scholars who claimed that they had established linguistics as a genuine empirical science. By this, they claimed to have developed linguistics as a field of study that was based on the observation of physical data, with generalisations that could be tested by referring back to a different (but comparable) set of data. The neogrammarians were able to point to earlier etymological studies and claim that there were never any scientific 'checks' on the conclusions that people made. This was because there was no distinction between systematic sound correspondences and sporadic sound correspondences. Only in the case of systematic sound correspondences can we claim to have made any scientifically valid generalisations.

However, Saussure reacted against the neogrammarians by claiming that *their* position was in fact basically unscientific. He said this because it was impossible to describe the changes in a language over a period of time without first of all describing the language at a particular point in time. To study scientific diachronic linguistics, we must first of all have two syn-chronic descriptions of the language taken at two different times, i.e. before and after the changes that we are studying. Saussure's *Course in General Linguistics* set out to describe the basic concepts that he felt were needed before it was possible sit down and write scientific synchronic descriptions of languages.

Saussure proposed a very rigid distinction between diachronic and synchronic descriptions, and expressed the point of view that historical information was totally irrelevant in a synchronic analysis of a language. By implication, we can assume also that Saussure would regard any guesses about the future changes a language might undergo as being quite irrelevant, and should not be included in a synchronic description of a language. In a synchronic description, all we should be interested in is describing the relations between the units in a system at a particular point in time.

This distinction between diachrony and synchrony can perhaps be compared to a movie film. A movie film is a sequence of still photographs, or frames. A description of an individual frame would be like a synchronic description of a language. But these individual frames, when they are viewed quickly one after the other, indicate movements like real life. A study of these movements would therefore be like a diachronic study of language; to carry out such a study, you would need to compare one of the frames with another further up or down the film strip.

So Saussure, and the linguists who followed him in the same tradition (including Bloomfield, as you have just seen), were in a sense blinded by their own theoretical approach. They failed to see language change in progress, even though everybody else could see it. Because they did not believe that language change could be seen, they did not even look for it! There are two different headings under which we can see language change in operation: *indeterminacy* in language, and *variability* in language. In the remainder of this chapter, I will cover both of these areas.

10.2 INDETERMINACY

To understand the concept of *indeterminacy* (or *fuzziness* as it is sometimes called), take a look at the following English sentences. Would you judge them to be grammatical or ungrammatical?

1. *James is chopping the firewood.*
2. *Daffodil must sells something at the market before she goings home.*
3. *The dogs don't try to keep off the grass.*
4. *Remy isn't wanting any money from me.*
5. *Who isn't that?*
6. *I saw a man coming from the bank get robbed.*
7. *Who did you come to the pictures without?*
8. *Jennifer said she will come yesterday.*
9. *I doesn't goes to church at Christmas.*

Some of these sentences are clearly grammatical. I am sure you could imagine an English-speaker actually saying sentences such as (1), (3), and (6). Some are also clearly ungrammatical, and people who speak English know they could not say things like (2), (8), and (9). But what about sentences (4), (5), and (7)? Are they grammatical or ungrammatical? They are clearly not as grammatical as (1), (3), and (6), but at the same time they are not completely ungrammatical like (2), (8), and (9). In fact, they seem to be neither one nor the other, or perhaps they are both at the same time. Thus, these sentences are *indeterminate*, i.e. neither clearly one nor the other.

There are many similar examples of indeterminacy in language. For instance, it is possible to derive many nouns from verbs in English by adding the suffix that we write as either *-tion* or *-ion*. So:

Verb	Noun
emancipate	emancipation
isolate	isolation
speculate	speculation
subject	subjection
connect	connection
delegate	delegation

We also have the noun *aggression* in English. If somebody were to say something like the following, we would feel that, while the sentence is not really all that good, we could still imagine that somebody might actually say it:

Saddam Hussein aggressed against Kuwait.

This sentence is also indeterminate, lying somewhere between grammatical and ungrammatical. The verb *to aggress* does not appear in the dictionary, but it is clearly not as bad as totally non-existent verbs such as *to teapot* and *to underneath*:

*This saucepan can teapot if we're desperate.
*The dog is underneathing the house.

(Note that the asterisk * marks the sentences as being ungrammatical in these cases.)

Because there are many examples like this in languages, linguists in the past have tended to deal only with those constructions that are clearly grammatical, distinguishing them from those that are clearly ungrammatical. Linguists who view judgements on grammaticality as either 'yes' or 'no' situations feel that the categories of language must be viewed as absolutely 'watertight'. But in fact categories in language are often very 'fuzzy'. Grammars are *not* watertight — they leak all over the place. Categories and rules are often very fuzzy or indeterminate in their application. By insisting that languages consist of a number of very strict and rigid 'either/or' types of rules, such linguists have ignored a lot of what is actually going on when people use their languages.

Indeterminate or semi-grammatical sentences are often evidence that grammatical change is in progress. Some people, for example, still object to the use of *access* as a verb, as in:

Remy accessed the internet.

arguing that this can only be used as a noun. While for some people it is no doubt true that *access* is only a noun, for other people it is also possible now to use it as a verb. My suspicion is that the people who use it as both a verb and a noun are going to win, and the variability that we see between English-speakers is evidence that change is now in progress.

The concept of linguistic indeterminacy also relates to the idea of the linguistic *system* as used by Saussure. He argued that in describing a language synchronically, we are listing the various units in the system of a language (i.e. phonemes, morphemes, words, phrases, clauses, and so on), and describing the ways in which these units interrelate (i.e. the grammatical rules for putting them together to make up larger units). In talking about describing *the* system of a particular language, Saussure is implying that for every language, there is one — and only one — linguistic system.

But here too, the theoretical assumption does not always fit neatly with what happens in individual languages. There is sometimes a need to recognise that within a single language, there might be more than one system in operation, even if these systems are partially interrelated in some way. Let us look at the phonology of the Motu language of Papua New Guinea as an example. If we look at the basic vocabulary of Motu, we will find that the language has five vowel phonemes: /i/, /e/, /a/, /o/ and /u/, as well as the following set of consonant phonemes:

p	t	k	k^w
b	d	g	g^w
m	n		
v		ɣ	h
	l		
	r		

Of these consonant phonemes, only /t/ has any major allophonic variation. You saw in Chapter 4 of this book that we can state the distribution of the allophones of this phoneme as follows:

/t/:
    [s] before front vowels

    [t] elsewhere

The labio-velar phonemes /k^w/ and /g^w/ are treated as unit phonemes in Motu for reasons of simplicity. If we treated them as sequences of sequences of two phonemes, i.e. velar stops followed by the phoneme /w/, then we complicate our description of the phonology in two ways:

(a) We have to introduce a separate phoneme /w/ which occurs only in this environment and in no other environment. This phoneme would be unlike all other phonemes in the language, which are restricted in their distribution.

(b) We would have to revise our statement of the phonotactics of the language to allow consonant clusters of just this type and no other type. Otherwise, syllables in Motu would be entirely of the type **CV** (i.e. a single consonant followed by vowel).

But if we include other words in the language which have been more recently introduced, we find forms such as the following:

tini	'tin'
maketi	'market'
su	'shoe'
traka	'truck'
hospitala	'hospital'

Those words violate some of the rules of Motu phonology that I have just described. The original neat complementary distribution between [t] and [s] has been destroyed, for one thing. And for another thing, the language now allows words containing consonant clusters in initial position (e.g. /tr-/) and in medial position (e.g. /-sp-/).

Linguists of Bloomfield's generation would probably have ignored these introduced words by saying that they were not really part of the language. They would probably include those introduced words that had been modified in some way in order to fit completely into the original sound pattern of Motu, so they would be happy to include words such as /makedi/ 'market', which some older people actually do use instead of /maketi/. This word avoids the disruption in the complementary distribution between [t] and [s] by substituting another sound which does not undergo the same kind of allophonic variation. Linguists of Bloomfield's generation would probably also be happy to include words like /gavamani/ in a dictionary of Motu as well, because the original consonant clusters of English have been totally eliminated. But, to ignore words such as /traka/ and /hospitala/ (or to describe only those words that fit 'the system') is to ignore the way that people actually use the language. Such a description, which recognises only a single phonemic system for the language, is clearly inadequate.

To describe Motu adequately, we need to recognise that there are *two* phonemic systems, one for original Motu words, where [t] and [s] are not phonemically distinct and where there are no consonant clusters, and another for introduced words, where [t] and [s] are phonemically distinct, and where some consonant clusters do occur. Speakers of the language are subconsciously aware of the existence of these two different systems, and could probably tell you which system a word belongs to if you asked them. There is variation between some forms (such as the variation that I have already mentioned between /maketi/ and /makedi/) which is evidence of competition between the two systems. Change is clearly under way in Motu, with the original single system being supplemented by a second partial system. Some introduced words are completely adapted to the original single system, while other words belong to the more recent subsystem. Finally, some words for some speakers belong in the original system, while for other speakers they belong in the introduced system.

More and more introduced words are coming to be assigned to the introduced system by all speakers, so we can assume that when the number of such words comes to be large enough, there is a possibility that the two systems will eventually be reanalysed as a single new system, and the original system will cease to operate. So, eventually we could expect [t] and [s] to come to be treated as completely separate phonemes in Motu (as you saw earlier in Section 4.3). Motu [t] and [s] are actually indeterminate in their status at the moment. In some ways we can say that they are allophones of one phoneme, while in other ways they seem to be phonemically distinct. This is therefore another example of how linguists in the past have ignored the fact that linguistic systems tend to be 'fuzzy'.

10.3 VARIABILITY

The other important concept that earlier linguists were blind to, and which stopped them from seeing changes in progress, was the concept of *variability*. Linguists traditionally believed that language was basically a yes-or-no kind of thing. While geographical varieties of languages (i.e. dialects) and social class varieties of language (i.e. sociolects) can to some extent be described as single systems of their own, which are independent of other systems, it is rather more difficult to deal with differences of style within the speech of a single individual in the same way. Probably all speakers of all languages alter their speech so that it matches the nature of the social situation they are in, even though they may not consciously be aware that they are doing it.

Linguists in the past found it difficult to describe these different styles of speech within a single fixed set of rules. For them, a rule either applied or it did not. The other possibility was that a rule could be completely optional, in which case it was entirely up to the speaker whether she or he would apply it or not in a given context. This led to the use of the phrase *free variation* in linguistics. Two variants that were said to be in free variation were supposed to be completely equivalent in all respects, and the choice of one over the other was supposed to be completely up to the individual.

Let us examine an example of a supposedly optional rule in the grammar of English. As you know, there is a rule in English which changes sentences such as the following:

Pipira chased the boys along the beach.

into sentences like this:

The boys were chased along the beach by Pipira.

Those two sentences express the same event, i.e. the same participants are involved in the same action, which takes place in the same location. Because of this equivalence between the two sentences, linguists in the past have argued that the choice of one form over the other to refer to this event is random. In grammatical terms, therefore, the passive rule is a completely optional rule in the grammar of English.

But the choice of a passive sentence over an active sentence is not completely random, if you look at the way that people actually use the two types of sentences. Compare the following two paragraphs, which differ only in that one contains active sentences, while the other contains the corresponding passive sentences:

I. *We expect children to learn to behave like adults by the time they are teenagers. We give them models of behaviour to follow, and we punish them when they do not follow them. When they do things the way we like them to, we reward them.*

II. *Children are expected to learn to behave like adults by the time they are teenagers. They are given models of behaviour to be followed, and they are punished when these are not followed. When things are done the way we like them to be done, they are rewarded.*

I think that you will probably agree that Paragraph I sounds more 'conversational', while Paragraph II sounds more 'literary', even though both are saying basically the same thing. If you examine the overall use of active and passive sentences in English, you will probably find that the active form is predominant in situations such as the following: in letters to friends, in private conversations with close relatives, in messages scribbled on the dust of somebody's car window, at home (if you speak English at home), or in a note pinned to a lecturer's door saying why you couldn't hand in your assignment on time. On the other hand, the passive is probably likely to be more frequently used in situations such as these: in letters applying for jobs, in formal speeches, in public notices, by a lecturer in front of a class, and in a student's essay for a course. The difference between these two sets of situations is that the first set is considered to be more casual or informal, while the second set is considered to be more formal. When speakers feel that the situation is casual, they tend to use more active sentences, but when the situation is more formal, they tend to use a greater number of passive constructions.

It is difficult to write these kinds of facts into a grammatical rule, so linguists in the past just tended to ignore these social considerations and simply described the passive rule as 'optional'. One of the most influential linguists of the past few decades, Noam Chomsky, expresses this view when he said that a grammar should describe an 'ideal speaker-hearer relationship', and it should ignore factors from outside language itself (such as the formality of a social situation). But language is not an 'ideal' system at all. It is in fact highly variable, and much of the variability is closely tied in with social considerations.

The importance of the concept of variability in language as an indication that language change is in progress was first described in detail by the American linguist William Labov. He studied the way people speak in the city of New York. He clearly documented the fact that there was no such thing as a single 'New York dialect', as different people there speak differently according to their own social class background, and also depending on the social context that they find themselves in while they are speaking. For instance, he found that some New Yorkers would say [kʰaː] for *car*, while others would say [kʰaɹ]. He did an extensive survey to find out which people used which form, and in what kinds of situations. He came up with the following results, according to the social background of the speaker:

	[ɹ] always present	[ɹ] sometimes present	[ɹ] never present
Working class	6%	12%	82%
Lower middle class	22%	37%	41%
Upper middle class	24%	46%	30%

These figures indicate that working class New Yorkers have no [ɹ] in such words in 82 per cent of cases, whereas upper middle class New Yorkers have no [ɹ] in only 30 per cent of cases. The lower middle class speakers lie somewhere in the middle linguistically, as they 'drop' their [ɹ] in 41 per cent of cases. Clearly, as we go higher up the socio-economic scale in New York City, we find that people use [ɹ] more and more.

But the story does not end there. Labov also found that the same person might use [kʰaː] sometimes, and [kʰaɹ] at other times. The choice between these two variants was not completely free, just as I showed you earlier that the choice between the active and the passive form of a sentence was not completely free. What Labov found was that all speakers, regardless of their social background, were likely to increase their use of [ɹ] in situations that they felt to be more formal. However, they were less insistent on the forms with [ɹ] when they felt that the situation was more casual, preferring instead to say [kʰaː]. Look at the following graph, which shows how people of the working class and the upper middle class increase their use of [ɹ] when the social situation increases in formality.

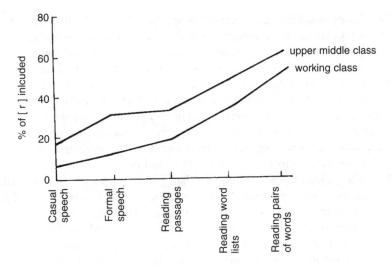

Something very interesting happens if we add in the figures for the lower middle class to the same graph:

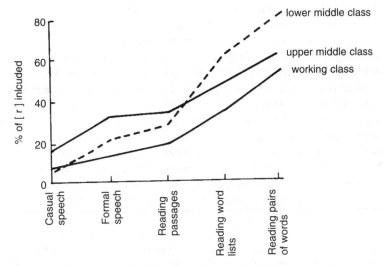

From this graph, you can see that when people from the lower middle class are using their most careful form of speech, they actually put in more [ɹ] sounds than the people who are above them socially. This might seem to represent some kind of contradiction to the earlier generalisation that I gave that the higher one's social class, the more likely it is that an individual will say [kʰaɹ] rather than [kʰaː].

What this apparent contradiction shows is that all speakers are aware that it is more socially acceptable to use the forms with [ɹ] than the forms without it. The more careful New Yorkers are being when they are speaking, the more likely it is that they will use the [ɹ] pronunciation. It is also clear that the higher classes in society are perceived as speaking 'better' English than the lower social classes. Even though the upper middle classes do not always pronounce their [ɹ]s, the lower classes feel that their speech sounds better than their own. People from the lower social classes in stratified societies commonly try to adopt the behaviour of their social superiors, and try to speak like them as well. There is social prestige not only in the clothes that we wear, the cars we drive, and who we mix with, but also in the way we speak.

Of all the social classes in a stratified society, it is usually people from the lower middle class who feel socially most insecure. The working class often regard themselves simply as working class, and do not expect to rise any higher. While they may not always like their place, at least they know what their place is. The upper middle class are already marked as being socially superior in so many ways — by their Porsches, their designer clothes, their yuppie addresses, their fresh pasta machines, their trendy technological devices, as well as the restaurants they dine in, and the people they mix with. But those in the lower middle class lie somewhere in between. They are not working class, and they are high enough in the social hierarchy that they can aspire to become upper middle class. They do not have all of the obvious trappings of their social superiors — the cars, the house, the household items, and so on — but one way in which they can increase their social status is by 'improving' the way they speak. So, when members of the lower middle class feel that they are being especially closely judged, they are more careful than anybody else about what they think is the 'correct' way to speak. This is why we get what is known as the *lower middle class crossover* on the graph that I have just shown you. This kind of crossover is quite common in studies of linguistic variation and it shows that there is a prestigious form that speakers are consciously trying to adopt. It is a kind of linguistic 'keeping up with the Joneses', and it is also an indication that linguistic change is in progress.

This kind of situation can lead the lower middle class into what is called *hypercorrection*. That is to say, people sometimes actually use a particular linguistic variable in a place where the higher classes would never use it, and where we would predict that it would never occur on purely historical grounds. For instance, in words like *father*, *Dakota*, and *data*, the lower middle class might pronounce these as if they were spelt *farther*, *Dakotar*, and *datar* respectively, when they are trying to impress other members of society. (In hypercorrecting in this way, they may impress the lower classes, but they are likely to make themselves look silly among their social superiors — although they will possibly not realise this.)

From all of these observations, it is clear that the English of New York City is in a state of change, and we are in a position to watch that change taking place. Back in the 1930s, the normal pronunciation of words like *car* in New York was without the [ɹ]. In old movies set in New York City, the characters hardly ever pronounced their [ɹ] sounds in such words. In many words, there is instead of [j] glide, such as in *thirty*, which was pronounced as [θəjti]. (This is where the stereotype arose that New Yorkers say *Toidy-Toid Street* instead of *Thirty-Third Street.*) In the 1950s and the 1960s, there was an increase in the number of [ɹ] sounds that people used, and this has led to the present situation in the 1990s. Presumably, after some time, the whole city will be pronouncing the [ɹ] all the time, and change in language will then have been completed. However, while we can see that the change is taking place, and we can see the direction in which the language is headed, there is no way that we can predict how long it will take for the change to work its way right through the language.

This discussion of the role of linguistic variability and social prestige in language very neatly explains how a language like English changes. English is the language of a large-scale society that is socially stratified. Moreover, this society is one in which upward mobility is possible, so people can aspire to reach greater social heights than the level in society that they were born into. However, not all societies are like this. Some societies may be stratified, but once an individual is born into a particular place in the society, there may be no hope of moving either up or down. The caste systems of many Indian societies are examples of such rigidly stratified societies, as also is the division of Tongan society into commoners, nobility, and royalty. Linguists need to do more research in order to find out what motivates the spread of linguistic changes in societies such as these.

Another kind of society we should consider is the small-scale society of areas like Melanesia and Aboriginal Australia. In these societies, people either know or are related to almost everybody else in the society. It is pointless to speak of upper middle class and working class in such societies, and high social status is something that is achieved by individuals who 'buy' their way up the scale by killing large numbers of pigs, or by demonstrating great generosity to other people in the form of presentations of goods and food. There are no privileged or underprivileged classes in these societies. Yet Melanesian languages change, just like any other language. Just as we can find synchronic evidence that change is taking place in English in New York city, we can also find synchronic evidence in the form of variability that change is taking place in the Lenakel language of the island of Tanna in Vanuatu. In this language, there is variability between the sounds [s] and [h] word finally. While there are minimal pairs word initially and medially to show that these two sounds are phonemically distinct, this distinction is being lost word finally, and we find variation between forms such as the following:

mis ~ mih	'die'
os ~ oh	'take'
pugas ~ pugah	'pig'

So, what factors are involved in the spread of changes in such societies? Western linguists do not yet know the answer. Perhaps what is needed is a well trained Melanesian linguist who really understands the dynamics of a Melanesian society as an insider. Until such a person carries out some detailed studies on the dynamics of language change in Melanesian societies, our understanding of language change will be incomplete. However, it appears likely that social networks function in such societies' norm-enforcement mechanisms, and that linguistic changes can be promoted or blocked by such networks.

10.4 THE SPREAD OF CHANGE AND LEXICAL DIFFUSION

In the preceding section, you saw how a linguistic change can spread from one small group of society so that it eventually affects the whole of society. You saw that in a socially stratified society in which there is social mobility, the force behind the spread of a change is that of social prestige.

When the neogrammarians (about whom you will learn more in the following chapter) were speaking of sound change, they claimed that these changes were conditioned by purely phonetic factors. They said that if a sound change applied in a particular phonetic environment in one word, then the same change also took place in all other phonetically comparable words at the same time. So, for instance, when final voiced stops were devoiced in German (a change that I have referred to a number of times already), the neogrammarians would argue that all final stops underwent this change simultaneously. Now that we are in a position to observe language change taking place, we can check on the accuracy of this assumption of the neogrammarians. In fact, we can show that this view of language change is quite misleading. Sound changes do not work like mechanical processes, in which every word submits to an overriding rule at the same time as all other words.

For instance, the variation in Lenakel between the sounds [h] and [s] (which I described at the end of the previous section) is not totally free. For one thing, some speakers are more likely than others to use the [h] pronunciations rather than the [s] pronunciations. For another thing, the variation is more likely to occur in some words than in others, and in yet other words there is no variability at all (at least not yet), and only [s] occurs. The less common words in the language tend not to exhibit the alternation between [s] and [h] at all, and we find only the [s] pronunciation. However, in words that are in more frequent daily use, the [h] pronunciation is more likely to be found. Although a change of [s] to [h] is clearly taking place in Lenakel, it is a change that is slowly creeping through the lexicon rather than affecting all words at once.

We can thus speak of *lexical diffusion* as being a major mechanism in language change, with sound changes beginning in a relatively small number of words, and later spreading to other words of the same basic phonological shape, with the change being completed only when it has worked through the entire lexicon. If you were to examine a language at any point from the time after a sound change has begun and before it has completely worked through the lexicon, you would probably find that it is impossible to predict which words will have undergone the change and which words will have so far remained unchanged. After a change has worked itself right through the lexicon it will look as though it affected all words of the same basic phonological shape.

Grammatical change may also spread through the lexicon in a similar sort of way as phonological change. I will now give an example of a language in which a grammatical change appears to be taking place, by which a plural suffix derived from the English *-(e)s* suffix is coming to be added to nouns in the Tok Pisin of some speakers of this variety of Melanesian Pidgin in Papua New Guinea. Until relatively recently, the difference between singular and plural nouns in Tok Pisin was marked by adding the plural marker *ol* before the noun phrase, as in the following examples:

man	'man'
ol man	'men'
liklik manggi	'small boy'
ol liklik manggi	'small boys'
traipela banana mau	'big ripe banana'
ol traipela banana mau	'big ripe bananas'
dispela haus	'this house'
ol dispela haus	'these houses'
dispela switpela popo	'this tasty papaya'
ol dispela switpela popo	'these tasty papayas'

There is a change that is beginning to spread in the language, by which a plural suffix derived from English *-(e)s* is coming to be used along with the older plural marker *ol*. The plural suffix that is coming to be used in Tok Pisin has the form *-s* after nouns ending in vowels or in consonants other than *-s*, while the allomorph *-is* is used after nouns ending in *-s*. This change is commonly observed in the speech of people who have been well educated in English, while less well-educated rural people tend to use only the preposed *ol* plural marker. The use of the suffix *-s/-is* is most widespread among university educated Papua New Guineans, and it is the speech of this small élite group that I will now examine.

It is interesting to note that some words seem to be more likely than others to add the new plural suffix *-s/-is*. The most likely words to take this suffix are words that we can call *nonce borrowings*, or words that are copied from English on an *ad hoc* basis, but which are not fully accepted as part of the ordinary lexicon of the language. These are the sorts of words that would probably not be understood or used by less educated speakers of the language, and they would certainly not appear in any standard dictionary of the language. So, for instance, university educated Papua New Guineans may use learned terminology such as the following with the English-derived plural suffix:

ol risos-is bilong yumi	'our resources'
ol politikal divlopmen-s bilong nau	'recent political developments'
ol staf-s bilong yunivesiti	'university staff'

Among the words that are accepted as genuine Tok Pisin words, there is not nearly as much use of the plural suffix *-s/-is* as there is in nouns that are copied from English on an *ad hoc* basis. However, it is possible to recognise a difference in behaviour between nouns that are of English origin and those that are derived from languages other than English. Nouns which have an English source can take the plural suffix *-s/-is*, whereas those that are not derived from English cannot take this suffix, for example:

ol de(-s)	'days'
ol hama(-s)	'hammers'
ol plaua(-s)	'flowers'
ol yia(-s)	'years'
*ol pekato/*ol pekato-s*	'sins' (from Latin)
*ol diwai/*ol diwai-s*	'trees' (from a local language)
*ol pikinini/*ol pikinini-s*	'children' (from Portuguese)
*ol kanaka/*ol kanaka-s*	'bumpkins' (from Hawaiian)

Even within the category of English-derived words, there are still some words which appear to be more likely than others to accept the new plural suffix *-s/-is*. Words that end in vowels are more free to behave in this way than those that end in consonants, and words that end in *-s* are the least likely of all to take the plural suffix. Thus:

*ol blanket/?*ol blanket-s*	'blankets'
*ol naip/?*ol naip-s*	'knives'
*ol tang/?*ol tang-s*	'tanks'
*ol pes/??*ol pes-is*	'faces'
*ol glas/??*ol glas-is*	'glasses'
*ol bisnis/??*ol bisnis-is*	'businesses'

What these examples show is that even a grammatical change can spread through a language gradually, diffusing through some parts of the lexicon before others. A new rule can apply to just a small part of the lexicon to begin with, and it can gradually extend to other parts of the vocabulary that belong to the same grammatical category.

In the case of the change that I have just described, it will of course be interesting to watch for any future developments. Perhaps the plural suffix will spread to more nouns in the language. Will the social prestige of the small élite who now use this suffix cause it to spread to lower socio-economic groups? Will the lower classes react against the tendency of the educated élite to exhibit their level of education in the way they speak Tok Pisin, preferring instead to maintain the original situation in which plurals were marked only by preposing *ol* before the noun phrase? If the change spreads further among the educated classes but not to the lower classes, could a genuinely *diglossic* situation result, in which two quite different varieties of the same language emerge, with each being used in a specific set of social contexts? Or will the educated élite succumb to the pressure of the majority of the population and simply abandon the plural suffix, with the language reverting to its original pattern? All of these different outcomes represent plausible possibilities, and there is no way that we can be certain of any particular outcome at the moment.

READING GUIDE QUESTIONS

1. Why did linguists traditionally regard language change as being unobservable?
2. What is indeterminacy in language and how is it involved in the observation of language change?
3. What is variability in language, and in what way can this be seen as evidence of language change in progress?
4. How did linguists in the past deal with indeterminacy and variability?
5. What does the lower middle class crossover refer to? What is the importance of this phenomenon?
6. What is hypercorrection? What does the existence of this kind of behaviour say about how changes spread in languages?
7. What is the basic error in the traditional view that sound changes operate with purely phonetic conditioning factors?
8. What is meant by lexical diffusion? How does this cause problems for the application of the comparative method?

EXERCISES

1. The vowel [ʌ] in English is normally reflected in Tok Pisin as [a], while the vowel [æ] corresponds to either [a] or [e], with some words having only [a], some alternating between either [a] or [e], and with 'learned' words nearly always having only [e], for example:

Tok Pisin

namba	'number'
bam	'bump'
san	'sun'
taŋ	'tank'
man	'man'
kabis	'cabbage'
blak/blek	'black'
fektori	'factory'
menesmen	'management'

Imagine a primary school educated person who speaks Tok Pisin and a little English talking to somebody with a university education in Tok Pisin. Although the less educated person knows that Tok Pisin has the expression **/graun malmalum/** (literally: 'soft ground') to refer to 'mud', she prefers to use the English word. But instead of pronouncing it in Tok Pisin **/mat/**, as you might predict, she pronounces it as **/met/**. What do you think is going on here?

2. In English, voiceless stops are generally aspirated, except after /s/ and before unstressed vowels, where they are unaspirated. The vowel /æ/ also tends to be phonetically quite long when there is a following voiced sound. Thus:

/stɒp/	[stɒpʰ]	'stop'
/stæmp/	[stæ:mpʰ]	'stamp'
/bæd/	[bæ:d]	'bad'
/ænd/	[æ:nd]	'and'
/hæpi/	[hæpi]	'happy'
/pɹɪti/	[pʰɹɪti]	'pretty'

In Papua New Guinea English, voiceless stops are generally unaspirated, and vowels are generally short (with many distinctions of phonemic length being lost, e.g. 'ship' and 'sheep' are both pronounced **[ʃip]**). Some Papua New Guinean speakers of English, especially educated women, tend to produce forms such as the following, which do not normally occur in either Papua New Guinea English or in native-speaker varieties of English (such as Australian English):

[stʰɒ:pʰ]	'stop'
[stʰæ:mpʰ]	'stamp'
[pʰɹi:tʰi]	'pretty'
[hæ:pʰi]	'happy'

What is going on here?

3. An Australian is likely to pronounce the word 'dance' as [dæns] and 'transport' as [trænspɒt] respectively. Imagine yourself to be an Australian speaking before a New Zealand audience that likes to ridicule people with recognisably Australian accents, and you find yourself saying [ʌndəstaːnd] for 'understand', instead of [ʌndəstænd], even though Australians and New Zealanders both say [ʌndəstænd]. Why might this happen?

FURTHER READING

1. William Labov *Sociolinguistic Patterns*.
2. Jean Aitchison *Language Change: Progress or Decay?*, Chapter 3 'Charting the Changes', pp. 47–60; Chapter 4 'Spreading the Word', pp. 63–76; Chapter 5 'Conflicting Loyalties', pp. 77–88; Chapter 6 'Catching On and Taking Off', pp. 89–107.

CHAPTER ELEVEN

PROBLEMS WITH TRADITIONAL ASSUMPTIONS

The comparative method that I discussed in the Chapter 5 was developed mainly in the 1800s, largely by German scholars. This method may seem very straightforward if you carefully apply it, following the steps that I set out in that chapter. However, it can sometimes be difficult to apply the method in particular situations. In this chapter, I will look at some of the problems that linguists have come across in applying the method. I will begin by looking at the historical development of the comparative method, and its refinement by the neogrammarians of last century, along with some of the difficulties in the method that they recognised from the very beginning. I will then go on to look at some of the more fundamental objections that modern linguists have raised to a strict application of the comparative method.

11.1 THE NEOGRAMMARIANS

The comparative method that I described in Chapter 5 was first developed in Europe, mainly by German scholars, and it was first applied to the languages of the Indo-European language family. This family includes all of the languages that were first recognised by Sir William Jones in 1786 as being descended from a common ancestor. It was perhaps natural that European scholars should investigate the history of their own languages first, as these were languages with a very long history of writing. This made it possible to start their reconstructions further back in time than they could have done with languages that were unwritten, or which had only recently been written. A long history of writing also made it posssible to check on the accuracy of reconstructions that had been made from the present.

After the period of European voyaging and exploration between the 1400s and the 1700s, scholars came into contact with a wide range of languages that were previously unknown in Europe. Word lists were compiled in 'exotic' languages for people to see the similarities and differences between them. Before the nineteenth century, a field of enquiry called *etymology* had become quite well established. This term is currently used to refer simply to the study of the history of words, though in earlier times the history of 'words' and the history of 'languages' were often confused.

Many of the early attempts at etymology would be regarded as childish by modern standards. One French scholar called Étienne Guichard in 1606 compiled a comparative word list in Hebrew, Chaldaic, Syrian, Greek, Latin, French, Italian, Spanish, German, Flemish, and English, in which he tried to show that all languages can be traced back to Hebrew! The kind of evidence that he presented to support his hypothesis was the existence of similarities between words such as Hebrew *dabar*, English *word* and Latin *verbum*. Some scholars who followed Guichard were more sceptical of these methods, and Voltaire, a famous French writer, described etymology as the science in which 'the vowels count for little and the consonants for nothing'. Unkind words, but true, at least as Guichard had applied it.

Sir William Jones's words in 1786 about Sanskrit and other Indo-European languages profoundly altered the perception of the nature of linguistic relationships among serious scholars. However, this did little to stop those less concerned with these more modern views from continuing in the path of earlier commentators — I hesitate now to use the word 'scholar' — in making random observations about similarities between languages as evidence of linguistic relationships. There were books published in the late 1800s which attempted to demonstrate the relationship between the languages of Vanuatu and those of the Middle East; this is a relationship that no modern linguist would take the slightest bit seriously, I should point out. Other scholars have taken random similarities in language and cultural artefacts as evidence that Hawaii was populated from Greenland; that parts of Polynesia were populated from South America; and that different peoples on earth were provided with aspects of their culture by beings from outer space. I wouldn't want to rule out these interpretations as impossible, but the linguistic evidence is certainly far from compelling, and modern linguists tend to assign these kinds of view to the lunatic fringe.

Sir William Jones also opened the eyes of European scholars to a whole new field of linguistic data by turning people's attention for the first time to Sanskrit and the languages of India, in addition to altering the perceptions that people had about the nature of language relationships. Jones emphasised that it was similarities in the *structure* of the Indo-European languages, rather than the individual similarities between words, that were important in determining language relationships. This observation led to a new intellectual climate in the study of language relationships, as scholars started looking instead for grammatical similarities between languages to determine whether or not they should be considered to be related. Lexical similarities, it was argued, were poor evidence of genetic relationship, as similarities between practically any word in any two languages can be established with enough effort.

Rasmus Rask in 1818 investigated the history of the Icelandic language on the basis of its grammatical similarities to other Germanic languages (such as Norwegian, German, and English), and largely ignored the lexicon. Rask also argued, however, that while individual lexical similarities were not good evidence of linguistic relationship, repeated occurrences of sound correspondences between words could not be due to chance, so these were good evidence of genetic relationship. By recognising only repeated occurrences of sound correspondences as valid evidence in the study of language, it was possible to exclude chance lexical similarities such as those noted above by Guichard for Hebrew, English, and Latin.

In 1822, Jakob Grimm described a series of sound correspondences that he had noted between Sanskrit, Greek, Latin, and the Germanic languages (which also include the now extinct Gothic language, as well as English). For instance, he noticed that very often, where Sanskrit, Greek, and Latin had a /p/, the Germanic languages had an /f/; where Sanskrit, Greek, and Latin had a /b/, the Germanic languages had a /p/; and finally, where Sanskrit had a /bh/,[1] the Germanic languages had a /b/ — for example:

Sanskrit	Greek	Latin	Gothic	English	
pa:da	pous	pes	fotus	foot	
-	turbe:	turba	θaurp	thorp	('Thorp' is an old word in English for 'village', but now it only occurs in place names, such as Mablethorpe, Scunthorpe, etc.)
bhra:ta:	-	-	-	brother	

(You should note that we are considering only the sounds written in bold type at this point. The remaining sounds have far less obvious correspondences than these, so perhaps you can appreciate the advantage in having learned to apply the comparative method using the much more straightforward correspondences that are to be found in the Polynesian languages!) The full set of sound correspondences that Grimm noted are set out below, along with the reconstructed protophonemes:

Proto Indo-European	Sanskrit	Greek	Latin	Germanic
*p	p	p	p	f
*t	t	t	t	θ

---

[1] The sounds that are represented by the digraphs bh, dh, gh in Sanskrit and by ph, th, kh in Greek are voiced and voiceless aspirated stops respectively.

*k	c	k	k	x
*b	b	b	b	p
*d	d	d	d	t
*g	ɟ	g	g	k
*bh	bh	ph	f	b
*dh	dh	th	f	d
*gh	ɟh	kh	h	g

Germanic voiceless fricatives correspond mostly to voiceless stops in the other languages, and Germanic voiceless stops correspond to voiced stops. Germanic voiced stops have a more complicated set of correspondences, as they correspond to voiced aspirated stops in Sanskrit and voiceless aspirated stops in Greek (with the Latin correspondences being somewhat less predictable in this case).

According to the methodology that I set out in Chapter 5, the forms in the left-hand column can be reconstructed for the language from which all of these languages were descended. That is, we reconstruct in the protolanguage the form that is most widely distributed in the daughter languages, and we reconstruct original forms that involve 'natural' rather than 'unnatural' changes. You can see that of the four descendant languages, Sanskrit is clearly the most conservative as it has undergone fewer changes in these consonants from the protolanguage (though there are plenty more changes in other aspects of the language!). The Germanic languages are clearly the ones that have changed the most since Proto Indo-European with respect to these consonants.

No scholar at the time thought to distinguish between sound correspondences that were without exception and those which appeared to be sporadic (i.e. which applied in some words but not in others). In fact, while the correspondences that Grimm noted were found to be true for very many words, there were at the same time many words in which the correspondences did not hold, and other correspondences were apparent instead. There were, for example, many voiceless stops in Sanskrit, Greek, and Latin that corresponded to voiceless stops in Germanic instead of voiceless fricatives:

Latin	Gothic	
spuo	**sp**eiwan	'spit'
e**st**	i**st**	'is'
nok**t**is	nax**t**s	'night'

The Gothic forms were not **/sfeiwan/**, /isθ/, and **/naxθs/** as we might expect if the correspondences noted by Grimm were to be completely general. However, it was soon realised that the correspondence of Sanskrit, Greek, and Latin voiceless stops to Germanic voiceless stops, and Sanskrit, Greek, and Latin voiceless stops to Germanic voiceless fricatives were in fact in complementary distribution.

In Chapter 5, you saw that when a conditioned sound change takes place in any of the daughter languages, the result is that the sound correspondence sets end up being in complementary distribution. So, once you have set out the full range of correspondence sets, you must check to see whether phonetically similar correspondence sets are in complementary or contrastive distribution. If it turns out that they are in complementary distribution, you need only reconstruct a single original phoneme that has undergone a conditioned sound change. The first of the two correspondences just mentioned was found only when Gothic had a preceding fricative, whereas the second correspondence was found when there was no preceding fricative. We can therefore reconstruct both correspondences as going back to a single voiceless stop series. This would make it necessary to reconstruct a conditioned sound change of the following form in the Germanic languages:

$$
\text{voiceless stop} \rightarrow
\begin{cases}
\text{voiceless} \ / \ \text{fricative} \underline{\qquad} \\
\text{stop} \\
\\
\text{voiceless} \ / \ \text{elsewhere} \\
\text{fricative}
\end{cases}
$$

More and more sound correspondences came to be recognised as being due to the influence of phonetic factors of some kind, such as the nature of the preceding or following sounds, the position of stress, or the position of the sound in the word (i.e. whether it occurred word initially, medially, or finally). By taking into account yet other phonetic factors, Herman Grassmann was able to account for a further set of consonant correspondences in these languages. Scholars had noted that some voiced stops in the Germanic languages corresponded to aspirated stops in Sanskrit and Greek (as covered by Grimm's statement, as you have just seen), but some voiced stops corresponded to unaspirated stops. Scholars were once again faced with a double set of correspondences.

Grassmann was able to show that these two sets of correspondences were also in complementary distribution, and that both Sanskrit and Greek had undergone conditioned sound changes. Note the following forms in these two languages:

Greek		Sanskrit	
do:so:	'I will give'	a-da:t	'he gave'
di-do:mi:	'I give'	da-da:mi	'I give'
the:so:	'I will put'	a-dha:t	'he put'
ti-the:mi:	'I put'	da-dha:mi	'I put'

The first pairs of forms in these two languages indicate that there is a regular morphological process of partial reduplication involving the initial syllable of the verb. This process derives the present stem of the root of these verbs, which are seen more clearly in the Greek future and Sanskrit past tenses. When a syllable containing an initial aspirated stop is reduplicated, the reduplicated syllable contains an unaspirated stop. In Chapter 2, this kind of change was described as dissimilation at a distance.

Grassmann related this kind of morphological alternation in these two languages to the unpredictable correspondence between Germanic voiced stops and Sanskrit and Greek unaspirated stops, as illustrated by the example below:

Sanskrit	Greek	Gothic	
bo:dha	pewtho	bewda	'bid'

According to Grimm's earlier generalisation about sound correspondences, where Germanic languages such as Gothic have /b/ we would have expected to find /bh/ in Sanskrit and /ph/ in Greek. Grassmann concluded that Sanskrit and Greek did in fact have these forms originally in words such as these but that the aspiration was subsequently lost under the influence of the aspiration of the stop in the following syllable. So, an earlier (and unrecorded) form of Sanskrit, for example, would have had /*bho:dha/, which would have corresponded regularly with Gothic /bewda/. However, with two adjacent syllables in Sanskrit containing aspirated stops, the first of these then lost its aspiration to become a plain stop. A parallel change was also suggested for Greek to explain the once apparently irregular correspondence for this language.

In 1875, Carl Verner was able to dispose of yet another set of apparently irregular forms according to Grimm's statement of sound correspondences in the Indo-European languages. If you compare Latin /pater/ with Gothic /fadar/, both meaning 'father', you will see that there is a correspondence here between Latin /t/ and Germanic /d/. However, you will remember from the statement of the corresondences that Grimm noted earlier that where Latin has /t/, we would normally have expected Germanic languages to have /θ/. Verner collected a full set of such irregular forms and showed that the correspondences of t = d and t = θ were in complementary distribution, with one correspondence showing up when the following vowel was stressed in Proto Indo-European, and the other correspondence showing up when the vowel was unstressed.

Grimm had stated earlier that:

> . . . the sound shifts succeed in the main but work out completely only in individual words, while others remain unchanged.

He stated this because of the large number of forms which did not fit his generalisations. However, with the discoveries of Grassmann, Verner, and others, most of these irregularities were eventually eliminated. Towards the end of the nineteenth century, scholars such as Brugmann and Leskien were stating that 'sound laws operate without exception'.

The sound correspondences that Grimm, Verner, and Grassmann had noted were restated as 'laws' to emphasise the fact that they could not be 'broken'. Newtonian physics gave Brugmann and Leskien a model of a closed system in which there could be no exceptions, just like the laws of gravity. Darwinian biology offered them a model of organisms developing according to un-bendable laws of nature (i.e. the survival of the fittest). This was the birth of the *neogrammarian* school, often also referred to as the *Junggrammatiker*, using a word taken from German.

The neogrammarians argued that these phonetic laws operated without exception in a language, and they argued further that the only conditioning factors that could determine the course of a sound change were phonetic factors. They claimed that it was impossible for semantic or grammatical factors to be involved in the conditioning of sound changes. Thus, for example, it would be impossible for a particular change to affect all words referring to trees, but not words referring to birds as well, and it would be impossible for a change to operate in nouns without affecting verbs at the same time. The only factors which could condition a sound change were phonetic factors such as the nature of the preceding and following sounds, the position of the sound in the word, and so on.

This was a very significant innovation in thinking for historical linguists. Once it was acknowledged that sound change was a regular process which operated without exceptions, it became possible for the study of etymology, or the study of the history of words (and therefore also of languages) to become *scientific* (i.e. rigorous and open to proof). Scholars now had a way of arguing scientifically against proposals such as those of Étienne Guichard who tried to relate all languages to Hebrew, as you saw earlier in this chapter. A sound correspondence or a similarity between two languages is of no value for reconstruction or for determining linguistic relationships unless it is *systematic* or *regular*.

In reconstructing the history of languages, you therefore need to make the important distinction between a *systematic* (or *regular*) sound correspondence and an *isolated* (or *sporadic*) correspondence. This is a distinction that I did not make in Chapter 5 when I was talking about the comparative method, but it is very important. Between steps 2 and 3 of the comparative method as I summarised it at the end of Chapter 5, therefore, we need to add a further step which says the following:

*Separate those correspondences which are systematic from those which are isolated (i.e. which occur in only one or two words) and **ignore** the isolated correspondences.*

Let us look at an example of what I mean by this. In addition to the forms that I gave in Chapter 5 for Tongan, Samoan, Rarotongan, and Hawaiian, let us also add the cognate forms below:

Tongan	Samoan	Rarotongan	Hawaiian	
fonua	fanua	ʔenua	honua	'land'

If we were to set out the sound correspondences that are involved in that cognate set, we would have an initial correspondence of **f** = **f** = **ʔ** = **h**, followed by a correspondence of **o** = **a** = **e** = **o**, then **n** = **n** = **n** = **n**, then **u** = **u** = **u** = **u**, and finally **a** = **a** = **a** = **a**. There is nothing new in the correspondences involving the initial consonants, nor the final segments /**-nua**/, but correspondence involving the vowels of the first syllable *is* different from any other correspondence that you saw in Chapter 5.

According to what I said in Chapter 5, you should assume that each set of correspondences that is not in complementary distribution with any other correspondence should be reconstructed as going back to a separate original phoneme. If we were to reconstruct this new correspondence as going back to a separate protophoneme, however, you would end up reconstructing a new phoneme which occurs in just this single word. Rather than complicate the statement of the phonemes of the original language, what you do is simply *ignore* such isolated correspondences, and reconstruct *only* on the basis of the evidence provided by systematic sound correspondences. You should therefore reconstruct the word for 'land' on the basis of regular correspondences only. There is not enough data in these four languages to allow you to decide whether the original vowel was /*e/, /*o/, or /*a/. The occurrence of reflexes of *o in both Tongan and Hawaiian might suggest that /***fonua**/ was the original form, with Samoan having undergone a sporadic shift of the vowel to /a/, and Rarotongan having upredictably shifted the vowel to /e/. Comparing these languages with non-Polynesian languages which also have cognates of this word, such as Fijian /**vanua**/, we might be tempted to reconstruct Proto Polynesian as having had /***fanua**/ instead. But whatever the reconstruction, we are simply going to have to accept that there have been some completely unpredictable changes in the vowels of some of these languages.

Another example to illustrate the same kind of problem involves the additional cogate set below:

Tongan	Samoan	Rarotongan	Hawaiian	
paaʔi	paʔi	paki	paʔi	'slap'

In this case, the medial correspondence of **aa** = **a** = **a** = **a** is not attested outside this cognate set, and the same is true of the correspondence of **ʔ** = **ʔ** = **k** = **ʔ**. The Samoan, Rarotongan and Hawaiian data is perfectly consistent with what you saw in Chapter 5, pointing to the original form having been /***paki**/. If the Tongan form were to behave as predicted, it should have been /**paki**/, but instead we find /**paaʔi**/. We must note that there has been an unpredictable change in Tongan of /*a/ to /aa/, and another unpredictable change of /*k/ to /ʔ/.

According to the Neogrammarian Hypothesis that sound change is without exception, there *must* be some kind of explanation for irregularities such as this. What neogrammarians said was that instead of being irregular, such correspondences must involve some other factors. It could simply be a matter of 'undiscovered regularity' — there may in fact be a regular phonetic conditioning factor which nobody has yet been clever enough to uncover. In this case, the explanation is perhaps that the Tongan form /paaʔi/ has been incorrectly identified as cognate with the forms in the other languages. Despite the similarity in the phonological shape and the meaning, it could be that this word is in fact derived from the quite separate (and not cognate) root /paa/, and that the final syllable is a suffix /-ʔi/, which is added to many transitive verbs in Tongan.

The neogrammarians did find some ways of accounting for some irregular sound correspondences as well, and it is to these that I will turn my attention in the following sections.

11.2 ANALOGY

The term *analogy* is used in a non-technical sense to mean that we find similarities between things that are not ordinarily regarded as being similar. In presenting an argument, we often 'draw an analogy' as a way of illustrating a new concept, by taking a concept that we know our audience is familiar with and showing how it is similar to the new concept that we are talking about. For example, if you were trying to explain the unfamiliar concept of complementary distribution of the allophones of a phoneme to a beginning student of linguistics, you could use an analogy to help get your point across. You might say that complementary distribution can be compared to the relationship between formal and non-formal education. Formal education is carried out only in certain contexts and by certain people (i.e. by qualified teachers in approved schools). Non-formal education also takes place in particular sets of contexts, but different ones, and is generally carried out by different people as well (i.e. out of school; by our parents, community leaders, agricultural extension officers, village leaders in Pacific villages, and so on). Similarly, you could say that certain allophones of phonemes may occur only in certain phonetic contexts, and other allophones in other contexts. Although there is nothing else in common between phonemes and education, we can use the similarity that does exist to illustrate this particular difficult concept.

Analogies can be represented by using a formula of the following type:

A:B::C:D

This formula is to be read as follows:

A is to **B** as **C** is to **D**

Alternatively, it can be read as follows:

*The relationship between **A** and **B** is the same as the relationship between **C** and **D**.*

Using this formula, we can represent the analogy that I just drew between phonemes and education as follows:

formal education: non-formal education:: one allophone: another allophone

This can be read as follows:

The relationship between formal and non-formal education is the same as the relationship between two allophones of the same phoneme.

Analogy was frequently invoked by the neogrammarians as a way of accounting for problematic sound correspondences in the languages that they were studying. I will now discuss analogical change in language under a number of headings.

(a) Analogical change by meaning

Analogy is a very powerful force in language change, and this fact was recognised by the neogrammarians. Speakers of a language often perceive a partial similarity between two forms on the basis of their meaning alone, even when there is no similarity in their actual forms. Speakers of languages sometimes even change the shape of a word to become more like that of another word to which it is related only by meaning. To do this is to change the phonetic shape of a word by analogy, and we can express this using the following formula:

$meaning_a$: $meaning_b$:: $form_a$: $form_b$

Given that the relationship between form and meaning in language is by and large arbitrary (as Saussure noted towards the beginning of this century), we would not ordinarily expect that two related meanings would be expressed by related forms. However, similarities in meaning sometimes *do* cause words to change their shape so that they end up being phonologically closer to each other than they would have been if they had been subject to all of the regular sound changes. Let us examine the history of the words for 'four' and 'five' in Latin:

		Latin	
*kwetwo:res	→	kwattwor	'four'
*penkwe	→	kwinkwe	'five'

If /*penkwe/ had changed according to the regular rules in Latin, it should have ended up as /pinkwe/ rather than as /kwinkwe/. Why, then, did /*p/ irregularly change to become /*kw/ in this single word in Latin? The answer is that on the basis of the similarity in meaning of the two words (i.e. both refer to numbers one after the other), this similarity is also extended to the shape of the words as well as their meaning. Speakers of Latin at some point in time changed one of these two forms so that it became a little more like the other. So, on the analogy of /*kw-/ initially in the word for 'four', /*p-/ shifted irregularly to /kw-/ in the word for 'five'.

Presumably, of course, the analogy could have gone the other way, with the word for 'four' shifting unpredictably to become more like the word for 'five'. If that had happened, presumably the word for 'four' would have ended up being /pattwor/ instead of /kwattwor/ (and the modern French word for 'four' would presumably have been something like *patre* instead of *quatre*!). In fact, in Germanic languages, this is exactly what happened. That is why the English words 'four' and 'five' both have initial /f-/. If the English word 'four' had not been influenced by the initial consonant of the next numeral, our word for 'four' today would have been written *whour*!

As a further illustration of the point that analogy operates unpredictably, let us turn our attention to the words *deux* 'two', *trois* 'three' and *quatre* 'four' in some non-standard varieties of modern French. When the word *quatre* appears before a noun that is pronounced with an initial vowel, some speakers of French now add a final /-z/ to the word *quatre*, making it *quatres*, on the analogy of the /-z/ at the end of the words *deux* and *trois*. So, compare the following examples:

	Standard French	Non-Standard French	
deux articles	dœz aʁtikl	dœz aʁtikl	'two articles'
trois articles	tʁwaz aʁtikl	tʁwaz aʁtikl	'three articles'
quatre articles	katʁ aʁtikl	katz aʁtikl	'four articles'

(b) Analogical change by form

Analogy need not take just meaning as the basis for comparing two forms, as in the examples that we have just looked at. Analogical change can also operate when there is a perception of partial similarities between two *forms* without any consideration of meaning. For instance, earlier in the history of English there was a word *ewt* which referred to a creature that looks like a small lizard. In modern English, this word has become *newt*, having unpredictably added an initial /n-/. It was not a regular change in English for /n-/ to be added to words that have initial vowels, so we need to find an explanation for this particular irregularity.

Once again, we can invoke analogy as the explanation. In English, we also have words like *name* which have always had an initial /n-/, and words like *apple*, which have always had an initial vowel. The indefinite article in English varies in shape between *a* and *an*, with *a* occurring when the following noun begins with a consonant, and *an* occurring when there is a vowel at the beginning of the noun. So, compare the following:

a name

an apple

The old word *ewt* began with a vowel, so according to this rule, the indefinite article should have taken the form *an* rather than *a*, i.e. *an ewt*. However, in saying *an ewt*, earlier speakers of English evidently stopped breaking up the words between *an* and *ewt* as they started to associate this phrase with phrases like *a name*, rather than with other phrases such as *an apple*. So, by analogy of one form with another, *an ewt* became *a newt*.

(c) Folk etymology

Another kind of analogy that we often find is referred to as *folk etymology* or *popular etymology*. Etymology, as you have already seen, is the study of the history of words. When we speak of *folk* or *popular* etymology, we mean that people who speak a language often make their own guesses about what the history of a word is on the basis of partial similarities to some other words (and in doing this they obviously have no interest in what the professional etymologist might have to say about the history of the word!). Speakers of the language may then actually change the word so that its pronunciation comes more into line with what they think is the origin of the word.

Folk etymology tends to take place in words that are relatively long and in some sense felt to be 'unusual' by speakers of the language. Speakers may then take part of this word, or all of it, and change it so that it looks more like a word that they already know. For instance, the word 'crayfish' in English was originally copied from an older French word *crévisse* (and it had nothing to do with fish at all). Ordinarily, such a word would probably have been copied into English as something like *creviss*. Although this word was a single morpheme in French, English speakers apparently felt that it was long or unusual enough in its sound that it must 'really' be two morphemes. They noted a partial similarity in meaning between French *crévisse* and English 'fish', as both are edible creatures that live in water, and they also noticed the partial similarity in shape between French *-visse* and English 'fish'. So, these earlier speakers of English changed the word to become 'crayfish' because they felt that was what the word should have been according to their own view of where it came from. Professional linguists, of course, would say that the word 'fish' originally had nothing to do with this word!

Folk etymology can be seen to be taking place when speakers make certain mistakes in pronunciation. A person who says *ashfelt* instead of *asphalt* is operating under this influence. Presumably they see the greyish-black colour of the asphalt (which is referred to as bitumen, tar, tar-seal, or tar macadam in other varieties of English) and equate it with the greyish-black ash from a fire, as well as the black colour of felt cloth, and rename it accordingly. A person who refers to *watercress* as *water grass* is doing the same thing, and so is somebody who says *sparrow grass* instead of *asparagus*.

(d) Hypercorrection

In Chapter 10, you saw how variability is involved as a factor in causing the spread of language change, and one of the concepts that you came across there was *hypercorrection*. Hypercorrection refers to the situation when a word may have two possible pronunciations, one of which is regarded as *prestigious* (i.e. looked up to, or having positive social value), while the other is *stigmatised* (i.e. looked down on, or having negative social value). In many varieties of English, for example, there are two different ways of pronouncing the word 'dance', i.e. /dæns/ and /dɑːns/. Of these, the second generally has higher social value than the first, and if you want to show people how educated you are, or you want to indicate that you are not from the working class, you might use the more 'posh' /dɑːns/ pronunciation. However, if somebody substitutes a variable sound in a word or in an environment where it is not appropriate, then that person is engaging in hypercorrection, or 'over-correcting'. For instance, if someone were to accidentally say /ʌndəstɑːnd/ instead of /ʌndəstænd/, this could be the reason.

Another example comes from Bahasa Malaysia. In the standard variety of this language there are words containing the phoneme /r/, and there are also words borrowed from Arabic that contain the voiced velar fricative /ɣ/. In the area of Malaysia known as Perak, there is a variety of the language that is known locally as Celaka Perak, which translates as 'the Perak misfortune'. You will no doubt guess from its name that people think that this dialect sounds 'funny', and that it is a stigmatised dialect. One of the features of Celaka Perak is that it merges the distinction between /r/ and /ɣ/, and all words containing these sounds are pronounced in Celaka Perak with the velar fricative. The result is that we find the following regular correspondences between standard Bayasa Malaysia and Celaka Perak:

Standard Bahasa Malaysia	Celaka Perak	
ratus	ɣatuih	'hundred'
ribu	ɣibu	'thousand'
buruk	buɣuk	'rotten'
loɣat	loɣat	'accent'

When somebody from Perak is trying to speak the standard language, one thing that they have to remember to do is to substitute /r/ for /ɣ/ in order to avoid sounding like Perak bumpkins. Mostly people can do this without making mistakes, but as there are only very few words containing /ɣ/ in the standard dialect, it is not too difficult to find people hypercorrecting in those few cases where there is *supposed* to be a velar fricative. So, if somebody from Perak pronounces /lorat/ 'accent' instead of /loɣat/, they are producing an irregular sound correspondence (at least in their own speech) as a result of hypercorrection.

11.3 CONVERGENT LEXICAL DEVELOPMENT

When words undergo *convergent development* you will also find that sounds do not have reflexes that you would have predicted from the earlier forms. What happens when two words converge in this way is that words which are largely similar in form (but not identical) and which have very closely related meanings may end up combining their shapes and their meanings to produce a single word that incorporates features of the two original words. If somebody combines the words *dough* and *cash* into the previously non-existent word *dosh*, you can say that in the speech of this person there has been convergent development of these two lexical items. Another example of this kind of change is in Bislama (in Vanuatu) where the English words 'rough' and 'rob (him)' end up as /**ravem**/, and not /**rafem**/ and /**robem**/ as we might have expected. The mixed word /**ravem**/ covers a wide range of meanings derived from the meanings of the two original words, i.e. 'rob, be rough to, do in a rough way, cheat, exploit'.

A similar development can be found when one language copies words from another language. What generally happens is that a language copies a single word from another language. However, there are cases when words in two different languages, which are partly similar in form and which are either the same or very similar in meaning, are copied at the same time into a third language. When such words are copied, they may take on a form and a meaning that have elements from both of the source languages. For instance, in New Zealand the English word *kit* (which also occurs in the compound *kit-bag*) seems to have taken on the meaning of the formally similar Māori word *kete* 'basket', and now Pākehā New Zealanders refer to traditional Māori baskets in English also as *kits*.

11.4 SPELLING PRONUNCIATION

Another factor that can interfere with the normal course of a sound change in literate societies is *spelling pronunciation*. Not all languages have spelling systems that accurately reflect their pronunciations, and English is a good example of such a language. We are all aware of the different pronunciations of *gh* in words like *rough*, *bough*, and *aghast*. It is possible for people to pronounce a word according to its spelling rather than pronouncing it as we would expect from its history. For instance, in English /***sj**/ sequences have regularly become /ʃ/ by a process of phonological fusion, as shown by words such as the following:

		English	
*sjuə	→	ʃuə	'sure'
*sjʊgə	→	ʃʊgə	'sugar'

Earlier, words like *suit, consume, sue,* and so on were also (as we would have expected) pronounced with /ʃ/. However, most of us now pronounce these with /s/ because of the influence of the spelling system. This has therefore produced an irregular set of reflexes in English of earlier /*sj/ sequences.

Another example of the same kind of development can be found in the Bislama language of Vanuatu. By the normal changes of the language, we would have expected the English word *country* to have ended up in Bislama as /**kantri**/, and this is indeed the shape of the word that we find in the closely related dialect of Melanesian Pidgin that is spoken in Papua New Guinea (i.e. Tok Pisin). However, many people in Vanuatu now pronounce the word instead as /**kauntri**/. This appears to be because people are pronouncing the word on the basis of their knowledge of how the word is spelt in English (even though its spelling in English does not reflect its actual pronunciation).

11.5 LEXICAL COPYING

Most books on linguistics refer to *borrowing* when one language incorporates a word from one language and adapts it to fit the phonological structure of another language. In this book I follow the preference of the linguist William Thurston in speaking instead of lexical *copying*, as this more accurately reflects what happens.

Some linguists may find this practice a little contrived, preferring to continue to use the traditional term *borrowing*. Certainly, the notion of lexical copying should not be taken too far, or we would be forced to refer to *copyright languages* instead of *source languages*, which is not my intention.

Lexical copying is another factor that can cause sound correspondences between two languages to show up as irregular or unpredictable. It is possible for a language to copy a cognate form from another language which has undergone different sound changes to its own words. If a sufficiently large number of words have been copied into a language, it sometimes becomes difficult to establish what the correct sound correspondences should be. Another result of lexical copying is that sometimes a single word in a protolanguage may appear to have two reflexes, both of which clearly derive from the same original form.

In English, for example, the regular reflex of /*sk/ is /ʃ/, but alongside words such as *ship* and *shirt* (which correctly reflect the original pronunciation) we also find words such as *skiff* and *skirt* which are derived from the same sources. It might be tempting to say that /*sk/ sporadically became /sk/ in English, while generally being reflected as /ʃ/. However, /*sk/ did in fact regularly become /ʃ/, and the /sk/ forms were reintroduced at a later date in words from Danish (which had not undergone the same change as English had by that stage). If you were trying to reconstruct the history of English phonology by applying the comparative method, you would therefore need to exclude *skirt* and *skiff* when you drew up your list of sound correspondences. You should not let the fact that there is a **sk** = **sk** correspondence between English and Danish force you to reconstruct an additional contrast in the protolanguage, as it is only the **sk** = ∫ correspondence that goes directly back to a phoneme in the protolanguage.

Sometimes when there are several different sets of sound correspondences in a number of related languages, some of these correspondences may be the result of lexical copying, rather than being directly inherited forms. While repeated (rather than sporadic) correspondences are normally taken to point to separate original forms, as you saw in Chapter 5 (as long as they cannot be shown to be in complementary distribution with other correspondences), it is possible for large scale lexical copying at different points in history to show up as separate sound correspondences. One famous case involves the Rotuman language of Fiji. Rotuman is spoken on the island of Rotuma in what is politically part of Fiji, yet it is closely related to the Polynesian languages. In addition to words that are clearly derived directly from Proto Polynesian, there are separate sets of sound correspondences between Rotuman and other Polynesian languages which suggest that there have been two waves of other Polynesian words that have been copied on a large scale into the vocabulary of Rotuman since it diverged from its sister languages.

When words are copied from languages which are unrelated, or only distantly related, this causes very few problems in recognition, as there will normally be sufficient difference in shape between the kinds of words found in both languages to make their source obvious. However, it can become very difficult to distinguish copied forms from directly inherited forms when words from one dialect are copied into another closely related dialect (as often happens in some of the smaller languages of Melanesia, for example), as these are generally very similar to each other. Look at the following examples from the Sinaugoro and Motu languages of Central Province in Papua New Guinea:

Sinaugoro	Motu	
ɣita	ita	'see'
ɣutu	utu	'lice'
ɣate	ase	'liver'
ɣulita	urita	'octopus'
tuliɣa	turia	'bone'
ɣatoi	ɣatoi	'egg'
leɣi	rei	'long grass'

From this set of cognates, there are two sound correspondences involving the velar fricative in Sinaugoro. Firstly, there is a correspondence of Sinaugoro /ɣ/ to Motu /ø/, and secondly there is a correspondence of Sinaugoro /ɣ/ to Motu /ɣ/. Clearly, however, you should be suspicious of the ɣ = ɣ correspondence, as there is only one example in the data. If you had more data, you would be in a better position to judge whether there is a single example of this correspondence, or whether there are more words in these two languages that correspond in the same way. If it turns out that this is in fact a sporadic correspondence in these two languages, its irregularity could easily be explained by saying that Motu copied the Sinaugoro word /ɤatoi/ for 'egg' instead of keeping its own original word /atoi/, which no longer exists in the language. However, there is no way of deciding just by looking at the Motu word /ɤatoi/, as it looks like a perfectly ordinary Motu word.

When dealing with copied vocabulary, things can get very complicated indeed when you come to carry out the reconstruction of linguistic history. Some languages have relatively little vocabulary that is of foreign origin, while other languages have incorporated huge numbers of words from other languages. Sometimes there has been so much vocabulary entering a language from outside sources that linguists are genuinely confused about what family the language belongs to. For instance, the Maisin language of Oro Province in Papua New Guinea has been variously described by linguists as being Austronesian with considerable non-Austronesian influence, non-Austronesian with considerable Austronesian influence, and finally as a truly mixed language. The confusion has arisen because whatever conclusion we come to, we must recognise that there has been massive copying of vocabulary from some outside source.

11.6 NON-PHONETIC CONDITIONING

Another criticism that has been made of the Neogrammarian Hypothesis in more recent decades relates to the structuralist belief in the 'strict separation of levels'. Structuralist linguists in the 1930s to the 1950s held that, when we analyse the phonological system of a language, the only facts that we should concern ourselves with are purely phonetic facts. Consideration from other levels of language such as grammar and semantics should be carefully excluded when we come to working out the phonemes of a language. This view of phonology in which there is a strict separation of levels in linguistic analysis is often referred to as *autonomous phonemics*, because phonemics is supposed to be completely autonomous, or independent of all kinds of facts except facts from the same 'level' of analysis. In insisting on this rigid dichotomy between different levels of analysis, the structuralists were little different from the neogrammarians, who also insisted that only phonetic conditioning factors could be involved in the statement of sound changes.

In more recent years, some linguists have questioned, and even denied, the need for the strict separation of levels that earlier linguists insisted upon. If we allow reference to grammatical facts, for instance, we are able to state the distribution of the allophones of phonemes in a much more straightforward manner, as this allows us to use terms like *morpheme boundary* or *word boundary*. As these are grammatical rather than phonetic concepts, structuralist phonemicists were of course unable to use terms such as these.

Although modern linguistics has now developed far beyond these methods and beliefs, it is still often argued that phonological changes over time should only be stated in terms of purely phonological conditioning factors, and that sound changes are never conditioned by grammatical or semantic factors. It is indeed difficult to imagine a sound change that operates in a language only in words referring to the names of trees, or which only applies to verbs involving motion away from the speaker, so we probably can say that sound changes cannot be conditioned by semantic features. However, it seems that some languages do, in fact, provide evidence that at least some sound changes apply only in certain *word classes* (or *parts of speech*) and not in others. Such a sound change clearly involves grammatical rather than purely phonological conditioning.

Paamese is an example of a language that has undergone a grammatically conditioned sound change. There is a correspondence of southern Paamese /l/ to northern Paamese /i/, /l/ or zero. The southern varieties directly reflect the original forms in Proto Paamese with respect to this particular feature, with the northern varieties having undergone the following fairly complex set of conditioned changes:

$$
l \rightarrow
\begin{cases}
\emptyset\,/ & \begin{cases} \#\ \underline{\quad}\ \text{non-high V} \\ \text{non-high V}\ \underline{\quad}\ e \\ e\ \underline{\quad}\ \text{non-high V} \end{cases} \\[2em]
l\,/ & \begin{cases} \underline{\quad\quad}\ \text{high V} \\ \text{high V}\ \underline{\quad\quad} \end{cases} \\[1.5em]
i\,/ & \text{elsewhere}
\end{cases}
$$

This rule states the following:

(a) The lateral /*l/ is lost word-initially before the non-high vowels /*e/, /*a/, and /*o/, and word-medially between /*e/ and any of these non-high vowels, for example:

		Northern Paamese	
*leiai	$\rightarrow$	eiai	'bush'
*alete	$\rightarrow$	aet	'flat area'
*gela	$\rightarrow$	kea	'(s)he crawled'
*melau	$\rightarrow$	meau	'megapode'

(b) The lateral was retained unchanged when it was preceded or followed by a high vowel (i.e. /*i/ or /*u/) in any position of the word, for example:

		Northern Paamese	
*asilati	$\rightarrow$	asilat	'worm'
*haulue	$\rightarrow$	houlu	'many'

*gilela	→	kilea	'(s)he knew'
*teilaɲi	→	teilaŋ	'sky'
*ahilu	→	ahil	'hair'
*tahule	→	tahul	'wave'

(c) In all other situations, /*l/ changed to /i/, for example:

		Northern Paamese	
*la:la	→	a:ia	'kind of bird'
*malou	→	maiou	'kava'
*meta:lo	→	meta:io	'European'
*to:lau	→	to:iau	'northeast wind'
*amalo	→	amai	'reef'
*avolo	→	avoi	'mushroom'

The interesting point is that none of the examples of word initial changes to /*l/ that I have just given involves a verb. Verbs, it seems, are completely immune in Paamese to any changes involving initial /*l/, though the same sound changes according to the regular rules in verbs in any other position in the word (as the examples above also show). Just so you can see that word-initial laterals in verbs are retained intact, examine the following changes:

		Northern Paamese	
*leheie	→	lehei	'(s)he pulled it'
*loho	→	loh	'(s)he ran'
*la:po	→	la:po	'(s)he fell'

If these forms had obeyed the rule that I have just presented, we would have predicted /**ehei**/, /**oh**/ and /**a:po**/ respectively. This is therefore a clear example of a sound change that does not involve purely phonological conditioning factors, but also involves grammatical conditioning.

11.7 THE WAVE MODEL AND LEXICAL DIFFUSION

The Neogrammarian Hypothesis upon which the comparative method rests has never been free from attack. Even when it was being formulated in its most rigid form in the 1870s by Brugmann and Leskien, there were people who claimed that their position was overstated. One of the points on which the neogrammarians were criticised related to their view of how languages diverge. In Chapter 8, I discussed the notion of *subgroups* of languages within larger families of related languages. This model of language change suggests that languages undergo sudden splits into two (or more) quite different daughter languages, and that once these splits have taken place there is no longer any contact between the new languages. Each new language, it is assumed, then continues completely on its own, undergoing its own completely individual sets of changes.

However, many scholars have pointed out that this model of language change is nothing but an unrealistic, highly idealised picture of how languages actually do change. It has been pointed out that languages seldom split suddenly. Generally what happens is that a language develops two closely related dialects which only very gradually diverge into separate languages. While these languages are slowly becoming more and more different, there is usually some degree of contact between the two speech communities, often with some kind of mutual influence between the two dialects. Even when the two dialects finally end up as distinct languages (i.e. when speakers have to learn the other speech variety as a separate system in order to be able to understand it), there is often mutual influence.

The neogrammarian model would also suggest that there are quite discrete or separate areas of linguistic uniformity within language or dialect areas. In reality, this is hardly ever the case. Languages are, in fact, heterogeneous and there are often no distinct boundaries between languages or dialects at all. A detailed study of any language area (even very small ones) will generally reveal the existence of a number of *dialects*, or local varieties of the language. However, the dialect boundaries are also often very indistinct, and it is often impossible to say where one dialect begins and the other ends.

I will now look at a particular example to show you what I mean. On the island of Paama in Vanuatu, the people speak a single language, the Paamese language, of which there are about 4000 speakers. The island itself is quite small, being only about 10 kilometres from north to south, and 4 kilometres from east to west. There are 20 villages on the island. Even within this speech community, which is tiny by world standards, there is dialect variation. Speakers of the language themselves recognise two dialects, a northern and a southern variety. These two dialects differ in the following respects:

(a) Sequences of /ei/ and /ou/ in the north correspond to /ai/ and /au/ respectively in the south, for example:

Northern Paamese	Southern Paamese	
eim	aim	'house'
keil	kail	'they'
oul	aul	'maggot'
moul	maul	'alive'

(b) The south often has /l/ where the north has /i/ or zero (as determined by the rule that I presented earlier), for example:

Northern Paamese	Southern Paamese	
amai	amal	'reef'
a:i	a:l	'stinging tree'

| tahe | tahel | 'wave' |
| mea | mela | 'get up' |

(c) The south has initial /g/ and /d/ where the north has initial /k/ and /r/, for example:

Northern Paamese	Southern Paamese	
raho	daho	'(s)he is fat'
rei	dai	'(s)he chopped it'
kea	gela	'(s)he crawled'
keih	gaih	'(s)he is strong'

(d) The north often has /a/ when the following syllable contains an /a/ whereas the south has /e/ in the first syllable and /a/ in the second syllable, for example:

Northern Paamese	Southern Paamese	
atau	letau	'woman'
namatil	nematil	'I slept'

(e) The south has /m/ and /v/ when the north has the labio-velars /mʷ/ and /vʷ/, for example:

Northern Paamese	Southern Paamese	
mʷail	mail	'left-hand side'
mʷeatin	meatin	'man'
vʷe:k	ve:k	'my sleeping place'
vʷakora	vakora	'coconut shell'

In addition to these phonological differences between the two dialects, Paamese speakers are also able to point to numerous lexical and morphological differences between the northern and southern varieties of the language (though I will not give examples of these as they are irrelevant to the point I want to talk about).

However, the picture is not nearly as simple as this. While the extreme north and the extreme south of this small island *do* differ in the ways that I have shown, it is in fact *impossible* to draw a single line that marks the boundary between the two dialects. To continue the discussion, I need to introduce the term *isogloss*. An isogloss is a line that is drawn on a map that marks two areas that differ in one particular linguistic feature. On the following map of Paama, each dot represents a single village. It is possible to draw isoglosses for each of these linguistic features. You will find that, while the northern and southern ends of the island have the features that I have indicated, the villages in the centre of the island share features from both the north and the south. So, for example, the isogloss dividing the features listed under (a), (c), and (e) above and the isogloss dividing the features listed under (b) and (d) are located as shown in the following map.

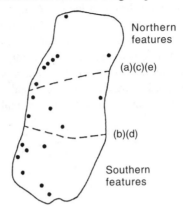

There is therefore clearly no single boundary that can be drawn between the northern and southern dialects of Paamese, as the isoglosses do not run together. This has been a very simple example because the island is so small and the number of linguistic features that I have given to illustrate the two dialects is also fairly small.

In a larger language, the situation can become much more complicated. In a language such as German, for example, there is a huge number of isoglosses criss-crossing the German-speaking area. While many of these do bunch together (to form an *isogloss bundle*), there are many other isoglosses that cross the bundle, and there are individual isoglosses that move away from the bundle in a direction all of their own, perhaps to rejoin the bundle at a later point, or perhaps to end up in a completely different part of the German-speaking area. The following map shows the Rhenish fan of isoglosses in the Dutch-German speaking area, which divides areas with fricative and stop pronunciations in words like *machen* 'make', *ich* 'I', *Dorf* 'village', and *das* 'the'.

Returning to the relatively simply example of Paamese, it turns out that even this discussion has been oversimplified, and that the real situation is more complicated. Even though I have set out a number of phonological correspondences between northern and southern Paamese, some words behave individually depending on whether they follow the stated correspondence or not. For instance, the correspondences between southern bilabial consonants and the northern labiovelar consonants (represented by /mʷ/ and /vʷ/) are grossly oversimplified. The reality of the situation is better shown by breaking these larger areas into much smaller areas, as set out in the following map.

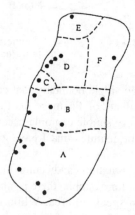

These areas are characterised by the following facts:

Area A:　There are no words containing labio-velar sounds, and all words contain plain labials.

Area B:　There are some words containing /mʷ/ but none with /vʷ/. Only a few words are consistently pronounced with the labiovelar nasal, including the following: /mʷeatin/ 'man', /mʷeahos/ 'male'.

Area C:　There are some words containing /mʷ/ and a few words with /vʷ /. These words include those listed for Area B, and also the following: /amʷe/ 'married man', /ti:mʷe/ 'friend', /vʷe:k/ 'my sleeping place'.

Area D:　There are some more words with /mʷ/ and several more with /vʷ/, including the following: /mʷeas/ 'dust', /romʷeite/ 'top', /umʷe:n/ 'work', /vʷeave/ 'cottonwood/, and /vʷaila/ 'footprints'.

Area E:　More words contain each of these two sounds rather than plain labials: /mʷail/ 'left-hand side', /vʷalia/ 'spider', /vʷeihat/ 'coastal rocks', /vʷaiteh/ 'door'.

Area F:　Yet more words contain labio-velars rather than plain labials: /mʷai/ 'he straightened it', /vʷakora/ 'coconut shell', /avʷe/ 'bell'.

The simple isoglosses that I drew earlier to separate the areas that *have* labio-velars from the areas that *do not* represent a gross oversimplification.

You can see that the labio-velars are more prevalent in Area F, and decreasingly prevalent until we get to Area A where there are no labio-velars at all. Which words will have labiovelars in any particular area seems to be quite unpredictable. Each word, in fact, seems to have its own behaviour. If the comparative method were strictly applied to this data, the facts that I have just described would need to be represented by recognising six 'dialects' in Paamese, with the following lexical correspondences between them:

A	B	C	D	E	F
meatin	m^{w}eatin	m^{w}eatin	m^{w}eatin	m^{w}eatin	m^{w}eatin
ame	ame	am^{w}e	am^{w}e	am^{w}e	am^{w}e
meas	meas	meas	m^{w}eas	m^{w}eas	m^{w}eas
mail	mail	mail	mail	m^{w}ail	m^{w}ail
mai	mai	mai	mai	mai	m^{w}ai

On the basis of the earlier statement that there was a northern dialect with labio-velars corresponding to a southern dialect with plain labials contrasting with correspondences between both dialects involving plain labials, we would probably want to reconstruct for Proto Paamese a contrast between labio-velars and plain labials. However, if we were strictly to apply the comparative method as I described it in Chapter 5 to the data that I have just set out, we would be forced to reconstruct six separate nasal protophonemes as there are six different sets of correspondences involving the nasals /m/ and /m^w/.

This brings us to the point where I should mention the French dialectologist Gilliéron. A *dialectologist* is a linguist whose speciality is the distribution of dialect features in a language. Gilliéron was a nineteenth century scholar who opposed the view of the neogrammarians, who were his contemporaries, when he made the famous statement that 'every word has its own history'. What he meant was that sound changes are not rigidly determined by purely phonetic factors, as the neogrammarians had so forthrightly stated. Instead, he said that only some words undergo a particular change, while others do not. Which words undergo a particular change can, in fact, be quite arbitrary, as you have just seen with the Paamese example. Gilliéron's view is totally incompatible with a strict application of the comparative method.

Gilliéron's view of linguistic change is consistent with what is referred to today as the *wave model*, and it contrasts sharply with the *family tree model* of change upon with the comparative method rests. The wave model implies that instead of sharp linguistic splits, changes take place like waves spreading outward from the place where a stone is dropped into water, travelling different distances with different stones, and crossing with waves caused by other stones.

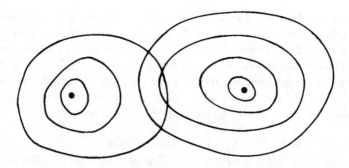

Despite the success of the comparative method in reconstructing a large number of different protolanguages, the wave model of linguistic change has gained respectability in modern linguistics through recent work on *lexical diffusion*. This refers to the fact that sound changes do not operate simultaneously on every word in a language which meets the conditions for the application of a particular change. For example, if a language undergoes the devoicing of word final voiced stops, what will often happen is that final voiced stops in just *some* words will lose their voicing first, and this change will then gradually spread throughout the lexicon to other words that are of basically the same phonological shape. That is exactly what seems to be happening in Paamese. The original distinction between /m^w/ and /m/ is being lost, with /m/ coming to replace the labio-velar in the south. However, the change is only gradually moving through the lexicon, having affected all words in the far south, and just some words in villages further north. Over time, we can predict that increasing numbers of words in the central villages will undergo this change such that eventually the dialects of these villages will ressemble those of the far south.

11.8 DIALECT CHAINS AND NON-DISCRETE SUBGROUPS

In the previous section I indicated that dialects cannot usually be separated by single lines of a map, and that what you will find instead is that different linguistic features need to be mapped individually by means of isoglosses. While isoglosses do tend to bunch together in bundles, individual isoglosses frequently stray, making it impossible in many situations to draw a family tree diagram showing dialect relationships.

In situations where isoglosses do not bundle together closely, a different kind of case can arise, which again demonstrates a fundamental weakness of the comparative method. With dialect differences such as these, it is possible for there to be no clearly recognisable boundaries at all between one dialect and another, with dialects only gradually merging into each other.

You will note in the map of isoglosses in the previous section that the entire German and Dutch language areas were included on a single map. The reason for this is that it is not possible to draw a single line on a map that separates the two languages. The Dutch-German political border represents a language boundary only in the sense that people on each side of this line have mutually unintelligible standard varieties. However, the local dialects of Dutch and German that are spoken on either side of the political border are little different from each other and people can readily understand each other.

What I am talking about in the case of Dutch and German is a *dialect chain* situation. Here, immediately neighbouring dialects exhibit only slight differences from each other, but as geographical distance between dialects increases, so too does the extent of difference between dialects. Eventually the point will be reached in a dialect chain where two different varieties will be mutually unintelligible, even though all of the neighbouring dialects in between are mutually intelligible.

Even the languages spoken by relatively few people in Aboriginal Australia and in Melanesia commonly exhibit dialect chain features. There is an area on the border between Queensland and New South Wales where cognate counts in the basic vocabulary of a number of neighbouring speech communities are relatively high and where the two varieties are mutually intelligible. However, when we compare the basic vocabularies of the speech communities at the extreme ends of this chain, the cognate percentage drops to a level at which mutual intelligibility is not conceivable.

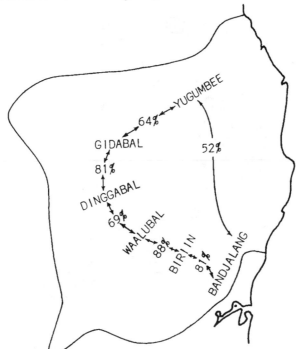

All of these speech communities are sharply differentiated from languages spoken outside the clearly definable area that is marked on the map, and cognate sharing between areas on either side of this boundary is very low. Because there is mutual intelligibility between neighbouring speech communities within this bloc, as well as a sharp contrast with speech communities that clearly do not belong to the bloc, some linguists have proposed the term *family-like language* to refer to such situations.

The same principle that is involved in the phenomenon of dialect chains can extend to more distant levels of relationship as well. A lexicostatistical comparison of the languages of central and northern Vanuatu has revealed that sometimes a particular language, or a number of languages, may satisfy the criteria for membership in more than one subgroup at a time. That is, not only can we have dialect chains, but perhaps even *language chains* as well. The lines around the areas in the following map of part of Vanuatu indicate which languages appear to belong together in lexicostatistically determined subgroups, and you will see that some of the areas overlap. This means that the languages in those areas appear to belong to two different subgroups at once.

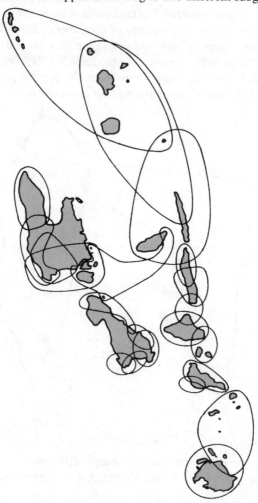

Of course, we should not place too much reliance on lexicostatistics as a method of determining subgroups, as I pointed out in Chapter 8. It may be that if we were to take into account the phonological and grammatical histories of these languages, the problem of languages that appear to belong to more than one subgroup at once might resolve itself. However, in the next chapter I discuss the fact that not only vocabulary diffuses from one language to another, but also structural features. This means that the problem of non-discrete subgroups may well be one that historical linguistics will have to learn to deal with.

READING GUIDE QUESTIONS

1. What is the basic difference between the study of etymology before the neogrammarians and in the present day?
2. What was the importance of Sir William Jones's statement in 1786 for the study of the history of languages?
3. What important contribution did Jakob Grimm make to the study of the history of languages?
4. What was the importance of Verner's and Grassmann's discoveries in the history of the Germanic languages?
5. What was the Neogrammarian Hypothesis? How did the neogrammarian view of language change differ from that proposed by Grimm?
6. How does the existence of sporadic sound correspondences affect the way that we apply the comparative method?
7. What is analogical sound change? How can it affect the way we apply the comparative method?
8. In what way can semantic or grammatical factors influence the direction of a sound change?
9. What is folk etymology?
10. What is spelling pronunciation?
11. What is meant by lexical copying? How can this cause sound correspondences between languages to become unpredictable?
12. How does the wave model of linguistic change differ from the family tree model?
13. What is lexical diffusion and how does this affect the application of the comparative method?
14. What is an isogloss? What is significant about the fact that isoglosses do not always coincide (and sometimes cross over each other)?
15. What is autonomous phonemics and what impact does the acceptance of this point of view have on the way that linguists view language change?
16. What is a dialect chain?
17. What is meant by non-discrete subgroups, and why is this a problem for the application of the comparative method?

EXERCISES

1. Papua New Guineans using English as a second language occasionally make errors such as the following in their speech:

Standard English	Papua New Guinea English
hibiscus	*hibiscuit*
pandanus	*panda nuts*
lingua franca	*lingo franco*

   (Another example of the same thing, but involving only a spelling change rather than a change in pronunciation, is the change from *surname* to *sir name*.) What factor is responsible for these unpredictable phonetic changes in the English of those people who might say these things?
2. People for whom English is their first language normally pronounce the word 'gibberish' as /dʒɪbəɹɪʃ/ and 'gesture' as /dʒɛstʃə/. What factors might be responsible for the very common pronunciation of these two words by Papua New Guineans as /gɪbəɹɪʃ/ and /gɛstʃə/ respectively?
3. The English word *ambassador*, when copied into Tok Pisin, would normally have become /embesada/. Some speakers actually say /embesirep/ instead. Can you say why?

FURTHER READING

1. John Samuel Kenyon 'Spelling Pronunciation', in Anderson and Stageberg (eds) *Introductory Readings in Language*, pp. 248–54.
2. Eugene Nida 'Analogical Change', in Anderson and Stageberg (eds) *Introductory Readings in Language*, pp. 86–92.
3. Leonard Bloomfield *Language*, Chapter 23 'Analogic Change', pp. 404–24.
4. Theodora Bynon *Historical Linguistics*, Chapter 4 'The Neogrammarian Postulates and Dialect Geography', pp. 173–97.
5. Otto Jespersen *Language: Its Nature, Development and Origin*, Chapters 1 to 4 'History of Linguistic Science', pp. 19–102.
6. Hans Henrich Hock *Principles of Historical Linguistics*, Chapter 15 'Linguistic Contact: Dialectology', pp. 426–71.

CHAPTER TWELVE

LANGUAGE CONTACT

There are many bilingual and multilingual societies in the world. Canada is officially bilingual, with both English and French functioning at the national level. Switzerland is officially quadrilingual, functioning in German, French, Italian, and Romansh. Other nations are more complex in their linguistic make-up, such as the former Soviet Union, India, or Indonesia, where there are hundreds of separate languages spoken. The most complex nations in the world in terms of their linguistic composition are the small Melanesian countries. Papua New Guinea boasts over 800 distinct languages, spoken by a population slightly larger than that of New Zealand (i.e. about three and a half million people). Nearby Vanuatu has only a hundred or so languages, but its population is much smaller, with the total number of people scarcely reaching 140,000!

However, just because a society is multilingual or bilingual does not necessarily mean that there is a great deal of language contact, as we can speak of language contact only when there are significant numbers of individual members of the society who are bilingual or multilingual. While Belgium recognises both Flemish and French as official languages, there is relatively little language contact as 85 per cent of the population is mono-lingual in either Flemish or French, and does not speak the language of the other group.

For genuine language contact to occur, there must be significant numbers of people who operate in two (or more) languages. But in world terms, monolingualism is relatively rare. This may come as a surprise to some people, especially to people from Western industrialised societies. There is a standard joke among migrants to Australia that goes like this:

Q. What is a person who speaks three languages?
A. Trilingual.
Q. What is a person who speaks two languages?
A. Bilingual.

255

Q. What is a person who speaks one language?
A. Australian.

People from Vanuatu generally speak two, three, four, and sometimes even more languages fluently, and they often find it incomprehensible that the average Anglo-Celtic Australian or Pākehā New Zealander speaks only English. In this chapter, I will explore some of the linguistic consequences of language contact in societies such as those of Melanesia and elsewhere where multilingualism is a fact of everyday life.

Up to now in this volume, I have frequently referred in passing to the results of language contact, though this has almost always involved discussion of language change that has involved lexical change as a result of new words being copied into the lexicon from other languages. In this chapter, however, I will be looking not so much at how languages can influence each other lexically, but at how the whole phonological or grammatical system of a language can be influenced by that of another language.

12.1 CONVERGENCE

When you hear somebody speaking and their first language is not English, it is generally very easy to recognise that he or she is not a native speaker of English. There are usually a number of tell-tale signs that indicate not only that the person is not a native speaker of English, but also what that person's first language actually is. By this I mean that it is often possible to recognise from the way somebody speaks English whether he or she is a speaker of French, German, Italian, Chinese, Japanese, Russian, or whatever other language. Typically, people carry over features from their first language into another language that they learn later in life, and we hear this at the phonological level as a *foreign accent*, and at the grammatical level as *learner errors*. However, it is not just among people who are learning a second language that one language can influence another. Even among people who can be considered to be fluently bilingual — that is, people who have been speaking two languages regularly and fluently from early childhood — we find that features of one language can cross over into the way that person uses the other language. The influence of one of the linguistic systems of an individual on the other linguistic system of that individual is referred to in general as *interference*.

Interference can occur in the phonological system of a language, in its semantics, or in its grammar. Phonological interference simply means the carrying over of the phonological features of one language into the other as an accent of some kind. This might involve the incorrect transfer of the distribution of the allophones of a particular phoneme into the other language in such a way that the phonological system of that language is violated. For example, the English of a Japanese-English bilingual who says *rots of ruck* instead of *lots of luck* has been influenced by interference from the fact that in Japanese there is no phonemic contrast between /l/ and /r/ as there is in English.

To illustrate grammatical interference, examine the sentence below which contains a relative clause. Sentences such as these are often produced by school children in Vanuatu who are learning English:

This is the book which I read it yesterday.

To a native speaker of English, this sentence contains an obvious error, namely the use of the pronoun *it* after the verb *read* in the relative clause. English grammar contains a general rule which deletes any reference to noun phrases in a relative clause that have already been mentioned in the sentence. Since the book has already been mentioned, there is no need — according to the rules of English grammar — to refer to it again, which is why we just say this:

This is the book which I read yesterday.

However, relative clauses in the first languages of children in Vanuatu schools typically require that the noun phrase be mentioned again in sentences such as these by means of some kind of a pronominal copy after the verb. To illustrate this kind of construction, I will give an example from one of these languages, i.e. Paamese:

Tu:s keke na-les-i naŋaneh keiek.
book which I-read-it yesterday this
'This is the book which I read yesterday.'

In the example above, you can see that in Paamese it is necessary to include an object pronoun referring to the book after the verb (in the form of the pronominal suffix /-i/). A speaker of Paamese who fails to delete the pronoun in sentences such as these in English is engaging in grammatical interference from his or her first language.

Semantic interference can also be referred to as *semantic copying*, as *loan translation*, or as *calquing*. A *calque* (or a *semantic copy* or a *loan translation*) is when we do not copy a lexical item as such from one language into another, but when just the meanings are transferred from one language to the other, while at the same time we use the corresponding forms of the original language. The term *hot dog* as a name for a kind of fast food originated in English, but in French in Québec the same thing is referred to as a *chien chaud*. *Chien*, of course, is the French word for 'dog' and *chaud* is the word for 'hot'. Thus, we can say that *chien chaud* is a calque based on English 'hot dog'.

If somebody from Vanuatu were to say the following, this would also be a calque on that person's first language:

He sat there and just listened to his kava.

Since kava is a drink, in English it is not something that we can 'listen' to. However, the verb that means 'listen to' in Vanuatu languages is also used to refer to the quiet contemplation of the rather delightful effect that a few servings of kava has on the system, and people from Vanuatu speaking English sometimes form a calque on the basis of their first language to produce sentences such as the one that I have just given.

As I said at the beginning of this chapter, I do not plan to enter into a great deal of discussion about lexical interference (or lexical copying, or borrowing) between languages, as this has been covered elsewhere in this volume (most notably in Sections 1.3, 7.4, and 8.2). However, I would like to mention at this point that, while the introduction of lexical items from one language into another does not necessarily affect the structure of the language that is receiving the new material, it is also possible that introduced lexical items can affect the phonology and the grammatical system of a language. In Chapter 4, I showed how words originating from English which have been introduced into the Motu language of Papua New Guinea now show signs of disrupting the previous complementary distribution between [t] and [s] and are in fact causing a phonemic split to take place in the modern language. It is also possible for completely new sounds to be introduced into a language via words copied from other languages. Bahasa Indonesia originally had no voiced velar fricative at all, either as a separate phoneme or as an allophone of some other phoneme. However, with the introduction of large numbers of words of Arabic origin into the everyday vocabulary of the language, we can now show evidence of phonemic contrast between /g/ and /ɣ/ in this language.

It is also possible for words from other languages to introduce new grammatical patterns into a language. To a very minor extent this has happened in English, as some words of foreign origin have kept their original plurals, e.g.

	Singular	Plural
Greek	*phenomenon*	*phenomena*
	criterion	*criteria*
Latin	*datum*	*data*
	index	*indices*
	cactus	*cacti*
Italian	*lingua franca*	*lingue franche*
Hebrew	*kibbutz*	*kibbutzim*

It is very rare for bound morphemes to be incorporated into the general grammar of another language, so it is unlikely that any of these patterns for the formation of plurals will spread beyond the words that originally introduced the patterns in the first place. In fact, most nouns of foreign origin are quickly adapted to the rules of the language anyway. So, the plural of *atlas* in English is now *atlases*, and not *atlantes* as we might have expected on the basis of the morphological behaviour of the word in its original Greek.

While the example that I just gave involved the influence of one language on another in the area of morphology, it is possible for lexical copying to influence higher levels of grammar as well. In Paamese, all verbs are required to carry prefixes which indicate the pronominal category of the subject, as well as a variety of tense and mood categories. So, from the root /loh/ 'run' (which cannot occur without any prefixes), we can derive the following inflected forms (among many others):

naloh	'I ran'
niloh	'I will run'
koloh	'you ran'
kiloh	'you will run'
aloh	'they ran'

However, verbs such as /sta:t/ 'start', /ra:u/ 'argue' (from 'row') and /ri:t/ 'read' that are borrowed from English are not permitted to carry any prefixes, and so a new grammatical construction evolved just to handle these new forms. There is a verb of the form /vi:/ in Paamese which functions as a copula in sentences such as the following:

Inau na-vi: meahos.
I   I-am man
'I am a man.'

The only kinds of words that could originally follow the verb /vi:/ in Paamese were nouns in equational sentences such as the above. However, in the modern language, verbs introduced from English have also been incorporated into the same grammatical construction, and the prefixes which would ordinarily have been attached directly to the verb root are now attached instead after the preceding copula, as in the following examples:

navi: sta:t	'I started'
kovi: ra:u	'you argued'
avi: ri:t	'they read'

You should note that in these examples, while a new pattern in Paamese grammar has emerged as a result of new words coming into the language, this pattern has not come from English. It is in fact a brand new pattern that has emerged out of the existing structural resources of Paamese as a way of coping with introduced vocabulary that speakers somehow felt did not 'fit' the language properly.

It is absolutely clear that languages can influence each other lexically (and, through lexical introductions, also to some extent grammatically), and it is just as clear that a speaker's first language can influence the way he or she speaks another language at all levels of language (i.e. in the phonology, the grammar, and the semantic system). However, there has been considerable debate in recent years on the question of whether one language as a whole can really influence another language as a whole (as against individual speakers of the language).

There is a significant body of literature on the subject of linguistic *diffusion* and *convergence*, which is based on the assumption that languages can and do influence each other. The term *diffusion* is used to refer to the spread of a particular linguistic feature from one language to another (or, indeed, to several other languages). One example of diffusion that is often referred to is the spread of the uvular [ʁ] in the languages of Europe. This is the kind of sound that you are taught to produce when you are learning to pronounce French words such as *rare* 'rare', *rire* 'laugh', and so on. Originally, these words were pronounced in French with an alveolar pronunciation, just as we find in Italian today. However, it appears that in the 1600s, speakers of French in Paris began to pronounce their *r* sounds as uvulars rather than as alveolar sounds. This change then spread to other language areas in Europe, and people in Copenhagen (in Denmark) were apparently doing the same thing in Danish by about 1780. The uvular pronunciation of *r* is now common in French, German, and Danish, and it is also used in some areas where Dutch, Norwegian, and Swedish are spoken. The following map suggests that the spread of the uvular *r* has hopped from city to city, and that it has then radiated out from the cities to the surrounding rural areas.

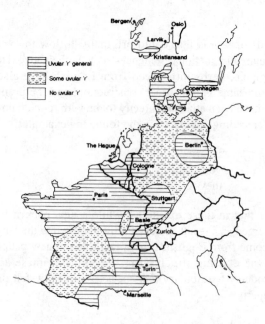

Albanian, Bulgarian, Romanian, and Greek, all spoken in the Balkans area of Europe, are only fairly distantly related to each other within the Indo-European language family. However, these languages share certain grammatical features that do not appear to be derived from their respective protolanguages. One of these features is the use of a special complex sentence construction instead of the infinitive construction to express meanings such as 'I want to leave'. All of these languages express this meaning instead by a construction that translates literally as something like 'I want that I should leave'. The following examples show that while the words that are used to express this meaning are quite different in these four distantly related languages, the grammatical construction is basically the same:

Albanian	*Due*	*te*	*shkue.*
Bulgarian	*Iskam*	*da*	*otida.*
Romanian	*Veau*	*sa*	*plec.*
Greek	*Thelo*	*na*	*pao.*
	I-want	that	I-should-leave
	'I want to leave.'		

This similarity between these four languages is not something that we would have predicted from Proto Indo-European, and the suggestion is that these four languages have *converged*, or come to resemble each other structurally as a result of a long period of linguistic contact and mutual interference.

Languages which have come to resemble each other as a result of linguistic convergence in this way are said to belong to *linguistic areas*, and the features that have diffused among the languages that belong to such an area are called *areal features*. Thus, in the case of the languages that I have just described, we could refer to the Balkans as a linguistic area (or sometimes as a *Sprachbund*, to use a word of German origin), and the special construction that I illustrated above would be called an *areal feature*. Linguistic areas can be recognised in a number of different parts of the world. Chinese, Thai, and Vietnamese all belong to a linguistic area, as all have developed phonemic tone distinctions. The Indo-European and the Dravidian languages of the Indian subcontinent have developed widespread retroflex consonants, which set them apart as a linguistic area, and a number of Bantu languages and Kalahari languages in southern Africa also constitute a linguistic area which is characterised by the presence of rather unusual click consonants.

A linguistic area can be characterised by shared phonological features, as well as grammatical features, as illustrated by the example given above of the construction in the Balkans linguistic area. In Section 7.2, I referred to the possibility that **SOV** word order has diffused from some non-Austronesian languages in Central Province in Papua New Guinea to the Austronesian languages, resulting in a linguistic area characterised by **SOV** syntax. Some scholars who have described both the Austronesian and the non-Austronesian languages of parts of the West New Britain province of Papua New Guinea have argued that syntactic convergence among these languages has been even more thorough than this, involving quite a number of different syntactic constructions. For many sentences, it seems that speakers of a number of different Austronesian and non-Austronesian languages in this area map their own words onto grammatical constructions that are almost identical. In fact, the same constructions are also found in Tok Pisin, even though this language is lexically derived mostly from English:

Non-Austronesian
| Anêm | Ezim | o-mên | da-kîn |

Austronesian
Mouk	Eliep	max	na-nas
Aria	Bile	me	ne-nenes
Tourai	Bile	me	na-nes
Lamogai	Bile	me	ne-nes
Lusi	Vua	i-nama	na-sono
Kove	Vua	i-nama	na-sono
Kabana	Bua	i-nam	na-sono
Kilenge	Vua	i-mai	na-sono
Amara	Eilep	i-me	a-nas

| Tok Pisin | Buai | i kam | mi kaikai |
| | betel nut | it-come | I-chew |

'Hand me some betel nut to chew.'

The diffusion of grammatical features in this way has caused some linguists to question further the validity and basic assumptions of the whole comparative method. Some languages appear to have undergone so much diffusion in the lexicon and the grammar that it can be difficult to decide which protolanguage they are derived from. According to the comparative method as I have described it in this volume, it is possible for a language to be derived from only a single protolanguage, yet some linguists have found it necessary to speak of *mixed languages*, which seem to derive from two different protolanguages at once.

Linguists tend to be thankful that such cases appear to be fairly rare. However, where such languages exist, they often produce much heated discussion as different scholars come down in support of undeniable membership in one language family or another, and yet others argue that such either/or conclusions do not accurately reflect the genuinely indeterminate nature of the language. One example of such a situation involves the languages of the Reef-Santa Cruz islands in the Solomon Islands of Melanesia, where there has been debate as to whether these are basically Austronesian languages that have been heavily influenced by non-Austronesian languages, or whether they are non-Austronesian languages that have been heavily influenced by Austronesian languages.

Despite the fact that areal studies of languages frequently refer to linguistic convergence, and scholars often speak of the 'borrowing' of features at all levels of language, there are some linguists who are reluctant to accept the possibility of syntactic copying between languages. While accepting the obvious fact that lexical copying occurs, as well as the possibility that individual words can bring certain morphological characteristics with them into another language, some linguists argue that grammatical patterns as such cannot be copied, or if they are, that this happens only in the rarest of circumstances. Facts which are often quoted as evidence of syntactic copying, these scholars argue, often turn out to have quite different explanations.

For instance, it is fairly frequently stated that Québec French is changing not only lexically, but also syntactically, in the direction of the dominant English language, and this tendency is widely condemned by purist Québécois. In English it is possible to end a sentence with a preposition (despite the claims of the prescriptive grammarians among us), as in the following:

That's the girl I go out with.

French differs from English in that it is not possible to end a sentence with the corresponding preposition *avec* 'with', and in order to express the same meaning, the sentence must be organised differently, as indicated below:

C'est la fille avec qui je sors.
that-is the girl with who I go-out
'That's the girl with whom I go out.'

In the French that is spoken in Québec, however, sentences of the following type, which closely parallel the English construction, are frequently heard:

C'est la fille que je sors avec.
that-is the girl that I go-out with
'That's the girl I go out with.'

Despite the close structural similarity between the English and the French patterns in those examples, we cannot assume that, merely because there are structural similarities between the two languages, one is necessarily derived from the other. Historical research reveals that there is in fact written evidence of the stranding of *avec* without a following pronoun in French going back about 600 years (which was well before French and English came into contact in Québec!). The same pattern is apparently still preserved in some French dialects in France that have not been in contact with English, and even in some other Romance languages, which suggests that the pattern goes back even further in time. Another point to consider is that, while we can strand any preposition in English without a following pronoun, this is possible in French only with the longer prepositions. With very short prepositions such as *à* 'to', this construction never occurs. So, note that the following is not possible in French:

*C'est la fille que j'ai   parlé à.
    that-is the girl that I-past speak to
'That's the girl I spoke to.'

12.2 LANGUAGE GENESIS — PIDGINS AND CREOLES

According to the model of language change that I have presented in this volume, every language is derived as a result of gradual change from a single language that was spoken in the past. However, there is one category of languages that appears to have evolved under rather special circumstances — the languages that are known as *pidgin* languages and *creole* languages. When speakers of several different languages come into contact in a situation where there is an urgent need to communicate and there is little social opportunity to learn whatever happens to be the dominant language, and where no other language predominates in terms of numbers of speakers, what often happens is that a pidgin language develops. The pidgin that forms has a vocabulary that derives largely from the dominant language, but the vocabulary is very much reduced in size. The grammar of a pidgin language is radically different from that of the dominant language, and typically involves much greater regularity than the grammar of the dominant language, as well as less redundancy. A pidgin language also tends to have only free morphemes with very few bound morphemes. In addition to these purely linguistic features, a pidgin language is generally used only as a second language by all of its speakers.

Pidgin languages have evolved frequently and in many different parts of the world when the contact circumstances have been ripe for their formation. When Melanesian labourers were taken by English-speaking Europeans from what are now Vanuatu, Solomon Islands, and Papua New Guinea in the nineteenth century to work on sugarcane plantations in Queensland and Samoa, the circumstances for the formation of a pidgin based on English vocabulary were ideal. There were speakers of large numbers of different languages working together under European overseers. Very rapidly a new language came into existence.

This language is still spoken in slightly different forms in Papua New Guinea (where it is known as Tok Pisin), Solomon Islands (where it is known as Pijin), and Vanuatu (where it is known as Bislama). Although between 80 and 90 per cent of the vocabulary is derived from English, there is also a sizeable proportion of words that come from a variety of different local languages. Some words of German origin have also found their way into Tok Pisin, while a significant number of words of French origin are found in Bislama. A fluent speaker of Melanesian Pidgin (which is how we can refer generically to these three dialects) cannot be understood by someone who speaks only English, and Melanesians who speak their variety of Pidgin cannot understand speakers of English unless they learn it in school. By all criteria, therefore, Melanesian Pidgin is a new and distinct language with its own phonology, grammar, and lexicon.

As an illustration of what a pidgin language is like, I will refer to Tok Pisin. As I have already indicated, the vocabulary of this language is largely of English origin, in this case about 80 per cent, though the words have been phonologically restructured to fit Melanesian sound systems, for example:

dok	'dog'
aus	'house'
rot	'road'
ren	'rain'
trausis	'trousers'

Of the remaining 20 per cent of the lexicon, most comes from the languages of the New Britain and New Ireland people who were the original labourers on the Samoan plantations. So, we find words such as the following:

kakaruk	'chicken'
kiau	'egg'
buai	'betel nut'
kunai	'long grass'
kulau	'drinking coconut'

The small number of remaining words in Tok Pisin do not come from English or from local languages, but from a variety of other sources. Such words include the following:

rausim	'take out'	From German *heraus* 'get out'.
beten	'pray'	From German *beten* 'pray'.
pater	'priest'	From Latin *pater* 'father'.
binataŋ	'insect'	From Malay *binatang* 'animal'.
pikinini	'child'	From Portuguese *pequenho* 'small'.
kanaka	'bumpkin'	From Hawaiian *kanaka* 'man'.
kaikai	'eat'	From Māori (or other Polynesian) *kai* 'eat'.

The vocabulary of Tok Pisin is also clearly 'reduced' with respect to that of English as well as that of Melanesian languages. This language lacks the vocabulary that we have in English to discuss many concepts in law, science, and technology, and it also lacks much of the vocabulary that is present in

Melanesian languages to name different parts of the natural environment, especially some of the rarer flora and fauna, as well as cultural practices.

Grammatically, if you compare Tok Pisin with English, you will find that Tok Pisin is much simpler in its structure, in that it is much more regular. For example, while English has many unpredictable past tense forms for verbs, Tok Pisin verbs are the same in all their forms. So, while in English we have to learn the past tense forms of the following verbs separately, verbs in Tok Pisin exist in only a single invariant form:

Present	Past
bring	*brought*
ring	*rang*
string	*strung*
ping	*pinged*

Differences in tense and aspect, which are sometimes marked in English by suffixes to the verb, are marked in Tok Pisin by independent grammatical words, for example:

Em   i   toktok.
(s)he predicate talk
'(S)he talks.'

Em   i   bin   toktok.
(s)he predicate past   talk
'(S)he talked.'

Tok Pisin grammar also differs from that of English in that it has far less redundancy built into its grammatical system. For example, in English, plural marking is expressed in a variety of different ways in a sentence, often in more than one way at once. For instance, it can be marked in the following ways:

(i)   by a separate form of the noun, i.e. *dog* vs. *dogs*, *child* vs. *children*, *man* vs. *men*, *woman* vs. *women*.
(ii) by a difference in the form of a preceding demonstrative, i.e. *this* vs. *these*, *that* vs. *those*.
(ii) by a separate form of the verb, i.e. *am* vs. *are*, *is* vs. *are*, *does* vs. *do*.

So, in the sentence below, the idea of plural is expressed in three separate places, as shown by the contrasting singular form:

Those women are singing.
This woman is singing.

In Tok Pisin, however, the idea of plural is expressed only once in the sentence, and even then it is optional. We can say the following to refer to one woman or to many women:

Dispela   meri   i   singsing i   stap.
this/these woman/women   predicate sing   predicate continuous
'This/these woman/women is/are singing.'

If you specifically want to mark the fact that there is more than one woman involved, you can use the plural marker *ol* at the front of the noun phrase, but you will note that none of the other words in the sentence are marked in any way:

Ol   dispela meri   i   singsing i   stap.
plural these   women predicate   sing   predicate continuous
'These women are singing.'

Pidgin languages can be formed in any situation where the contact circumstances are right. There are pidgin languages in which the lexicon is derived predominantly from Spanish, French, Portuguese, and Dutch in various parts of the world. It is not necessary that the lexicon of a pidgin should be derived only from European languages, as there also cases where pidgins have been formed out of non-European languages. In the Pacific, for instance, we find Hiri Motu which is widely spoken in Papua today, and this language is based on the vocabulary of the vernacular Motu language of the Port Moresby area. When outside labourers were introduced into Fiji, the resultant pidgin was not based on the vocabulary of English, but that of Fijian.

I mentioned at the beginning of this section that pidgin and creole languages tend to avoid bound morphemes, but the Tok Pisin examples do not illustrate this very well because English is a language that has relatively few prefixes and suffixes, at least when compared with many other languages of the world. In order to illustrate this point, and also to illustrate what a pidgin that is derived from a non-Indo-European language looks like, I will now give some examples from Hiri Motu and compare these with the vernacular Motu from which it is lexically derived. Some of the differences between these two languages involve the following points:

(a) Objects to verbs in vernacular Motu are expressed as suffixes to the verb, and these have the following shapes:

	Singular		Plural
First	-gu	inclusive	-da
		exclusive	-mai
Second	-mu		-mui
Third	-(i)a		-dia

In pidgin Motu (or Hiri Motu), objects are expressed by full form pronouns that have the same form as the subject pronouns. The grammatical difference between subject and object is shown by the position of the form in the sentence. The full form pronouns are the same in both vernacular and pidgin Motu, i.e.

	Singular		Plural
First	lau	inclusive	ita
		exclusive	ai
Second	oi		umui
Third	ia		idia

(b) Subjects to verbs are marked in vernacular Motu as prefixes to the verb, and the forms of these prefixes are as follows:

	Singular		Plural
First	na-	inclusive	ta-
		exclusive	a-
Second	o-		o-
Third	e-		e-

In pidgin Motu, subjects are expressed by placing the full pronoun in the subject position of the sentence and there is no further subject marking on the verb.

(c) To make a verb negative in vernacular Motu, there is a different set of subject markers from those that are used in the affirmative, as given above. The negative prefixes are as follows:

	Singular		Plural
First	asina-	inclusive	asita-
		exclusive	asia-
Second	to-		asio-
Third	se-		asie-

In pidgin Motu, negation is marked by placing the free form /lasi/ after the verb phrase. The word /lasi/ also occurs in vernacular Motu, where it is a word meaning 'no'.

The following examples are presented to show the difference between vernacular Motu and pidgin Motu. The two languages are not mutually intelligible, even though most of the words that occur in pidgin Motu are derived directly from roots that are used in vernacular Motu:

Vernacular Motu	Pidgin Motu
Ia e-ita-mu.	Oi ia itaia.
(s)he (s)he-see-you	you (s)he see
'(S)he saw you.'	(S)he saw you.'
Asi-na-rakatani-mu.	Oi lau rakatania lasi.
not-I-leave-you	you I leave not
'I didn't leave you.'	I didn't leave you.'

It is possible for a pidgin language eventually to replace the original vernaculars that in a sense 'spawned' it. This did not happen in the case of Melanesians who worked in Queensland and Samoa, as they generally just went to work overseas for three years and then returned home to their families who had stayed behind. However, if significant numbers of women are also brought on to the plantations and people are prevented by slavery from ever returning home, it is inevitable that the men and women from different language groups will marry and have children with whom there will be little option but to speak in the pidgin. This is what happened in the Caribbean among African slaves. While the multitude of African languages initially resulted in the slaves developing a pidgin based on English vocabulary, the following generations of slaves grew up speaking only the pidgin, and the original African languages ceased to be passed on at all. When a pidgin language replaces the original vernaculars that caused it to evolve in this way, we say that the pidgin has become a *creole*. Thus, to this day there are many creole languages in the Caribbean which evolved out of pidgins that were originally spoken on the slave plantations. In the South Pacific, pidgins have become creoles in some parts of northern Australia as the pidgins used by Aborigines have come to replace the original vernaculars.

Linguists have drawn a distinction in the past between pidgins and creoles because they have argued that there are structural differences between the two. Being only a contact language, a pidgin has generally been seen as a very basic sort of language indeed, with the smallest possible lexicon, as well as a very rudimentary grammar. However, once a pidgin becomes the mother tongue of a community, it is generally assumed that it undergoes rapid lexical and structural expansion in order to meet the normal needs of a community of native speakers.

The study of pidgin and creole languages has only relatively recently moved into mainstream linguistics. Pidgin languages have traditionally been regarded as poor imitations of 'real' languages, with no structure of their own. For instance, the governor of the colony of Papua in the early twentieth century called the Melanesian Pidgin of the time a 'most atrocious form of speech'. The typical view in the past was that a pidgin was nothing more than broken English, and many people still mistakenly refer to the language in this way, even though it has its own grammar, and is not mutually intelligible with English. The result of prejudices such as these has been that most linguists did not take pidgins and creoles as being worthy of serious study until the last few decades.

However, the tables have now turned, and pidgins and creoles are now seen by many as being central to an understanding of how languages change. So keen have some linguists been to see exactly how a pidgin originates that there was recently a proposal to produce a pidgin artificially and observe its formation. The idea was that a number of people who spoke quite different languages would be brought together in one place and 'fed' a number of basic words that they could use to communicate with other participants in the experiment. The researchers would then remain in the background for a period of months to see what kinds of grammatical patterns emerged when these words were put together to express meanings. The fact that this project was officially proposed is an indication of how serious some linguists were in searching for answers on the question of the origin of pidgins and creoles.[1]

Pidgin and creole languages have aroused this kind of interest because linguists are keen to find out how these languages acquire their structures. You may have noticed that up to this point I have spoken about pidgins and creoles having a predominantly English (or French, or Spanish, or Motu) vocabulary, yet they are still mutually unintelligible with the languages from which their vocabularies are derived. This suggests that pidgins and creoles are structurally very different from their *lexifier* languages (i.e. the languages from which their vocabularies are derived), and this is a point that I think you will appreciate from the examples of Tok Pisin structure that I presented earlier in this section (as well as in earlier chapters of this volume).

Many linguists have been struck by the fact that pidgin and creole languages often show strong parallels in their structure with their *substrate* languages rather than their *superstrate* languages. The term *superstrate* (or *superordinate language*) is used to refer to the dominant language in the contact situations in which a pidgin or creole language develops. In the case of Tok Pisin, for example, English is clearly the superstrate language. The *substrate*, on the other hand, refers to the vernaculars of the people who actually develop a pidgin or creole. In the case of Tok Pisin, the substrate languages would be the various vernaculars of the New Britain and New Ireland labourers who were originally taken to work in Samoa and Queensland in the nineteenth century. While the grammar of Tok Pisin is clearly different from that of English, it seems that when we examine many of the points of difference between English and Tok Pisin, we can find structural parallels with the substrate languages. For instance, the form *i* that occurs in the examples above as a 'predicate marker' corresponds roughly in shape and in function to a morpheme *i* that is found in Tolai (and many other of the substrate languages), for example:

Tolai
To   Pipira i   vana.
article Pipira predicate go
'Pipira is going.'

---

[1] The proposers of this project intended to use Papua New Guineans who spoke only their vernaculars and to throw them together in a situation that they could not have been expected to see the relevance of or fully understand. Although the possible advances to scientific knowledge from this project were great, it was justifiably refused permission by authorities in Papua New Guinea for its exploitative and inhumane aspects.

Tok Pisin
Pipira i   go.
Pipira   predicate   go
'Pipira is going.'

The existence of two separate forms of the first person non-singular pronoun in Melanesian vernaculars is also parallelled in the structure of the Melanesian Pidgin pronoun system but not in that of English. In Tok Pisin, there are two separate pronouns corresponding to the single form 'we' in English. Firstly, there is *yumi* which means 'we' when you are including the person you are speaking to (i.e. the so-called inclusive pronoun). Secondly, there is the form *mipela* which means 'we' when you are excluding the person you are speaking to (i.e. the so-called exclusive pronoun). This distinction is widespread in the substrate languages for Melanesian Pidgin, but English grammar does not make the distinction (and sometimes English-speakers even find it hard to use the pronouns *yumi* and *mipela* correctly).

The existence of such structural parallels between pidgins and creoles and their substrate languages has led many scholars to argue that pidgins and creoles are mixed languages in the sense that they derive their lexicons from the superstrate, while their grammars come predominantly from the substrate. If this interpretation is correct, then pidgin and creole languages differ dramatically in their genesis from other languages as they have multiple ancestors rather than a single ancestor. According to such a view, it would be impossible to classify Tok Pisin either as an Austronesian language or as an Indo-European language as it contains significant elements from both language families. (You will remember that I referred to the possible existence of mixed languages also in Section 12.1.)

You will also remember from the preceding section that some scholars today do not accept that languages can easily influence each other structurally. Linguists who hold this point of view sometimes extend this even to pidgin and creole languages, arguing that the existence of parallels in structure between pidgins and creoles and their substrate languages is not necessarily evidence that a pidgin has been structurally influenced by the substrate and they argue that other factors may also be involved. For instance, it could be equally argued that the 'predicate marker' *i* that I described earlier in Tok Pisin does not derive from the substrate at all, but that it derives from the English pronoun 'he' which may have been repeated after the subject noun phrase. Thus, *Pipira i go* 'Pipira is going' is not necessarily derived from the Tolai construction, but from a pre-pidgin 'broken English' sentence of the form *Pipira he goes* (and sentences of this type do sometimes occur when people are learning English as a second language).

Scholars who deny any significant impact of substrate structural patterns in the development of a pidgin or a creole language tend to point instead to what they see as the remarkable structural similarities between pidgin and creole languages that have radically different histories and even different lexical source languages. For instance, if you compare the grammatical structure of a simple intransitive sentence in Tok Pisin with the corresponding sentence in Haitian Creole spoken in the Caribbean (which has French as its lexifier language), you find that there are remarkable similarities between the two. Compare the following two sentences in these two languages:

Tok Pisin   *Em   no   bin   save.*
Haitian Creole   *Li   pa   te   konɛ̃.*
                 (s)he   not   past   know
                 '(S)he did not know.'

You can see that, although the words in these two languages are quite different in their shape, reflecting their different origins, the order in which the words occur is exactly the same.

This becomes even more significant if we compare the corresponding sentences in their respective lexifier languages. In English, the structure of the sentence *(S)he did not know* involves the following facts:

(a) The first element is the subject pronoun.

(b) The second element is the verb *do* which is put there to carry the tense marking. In this case, the tense is past, so the verb appears in the form *did*.

(c) The third element is the negative marker *not* (which optionally appears reduced in form to the suffix -*n't*).

(d) The fourth element is the verb *know* which occurs in the infinitive form, i.e. it does not take any suffixes for tense as this is already in the form *did*.

The corresponding French phrase *Il/elle ne connaissait pas*, however, has the following quite different structure:

(a) The first element is again a subject pronoun, of the form *il* 'he' or *elle* 'she'.

(b) The second element is the form *ne*, which marks the verb as being negative.

(c) The third element is the verb root *connaiss-* 'know'.

(d) Attached to this verb is the suffix -*ait* which marks the verb as being in the past tense, as well as agreeing with the subject *il/elle*.

(e) The final element is the form *pas* which, in conjunction with *ne* before the verb, also marks the negative.

Thus, the structures of the English and French sentences can be summarised as follows:

English   SUBJECT   DO+TENSE   NEGATIVE   VERB
French   SUBJECT   NEGATIVE   VERB+TENSE   NEGATIVE

The question that we need to ask ourselves now is this: if the structures of English and French are so different, how is it that the structures of the two pidgin and creole languages that are derived from them are so similar? Both Tok Pisin and Haitian Creole share the following basic structure in these sentences:

SUBJECT   NEGATIVE   TENSE   VERB

The two pidgin languages are closer in structure to each other than either is to French or to English. Clearly, this cannot be because of the influence of the superstrate languages, as English and French are quite different from each other. We cannot put this down to similarities in the substrate languages either, as these are the languages of New Britain and New Ireland in the case of Tok Pisin, and West African languages in the case of Haitian Creole, and these languages are quite different from each other.

One explanation that has been proposed in the past to explain facts such as these was that speakers of all languages are born with some kind of basic idea about how to simplify their language in situations where it is necessary, typically in language contact situations. This means that we all have some kind of ready-made instructions in our heads that tell us how to simplify our languages and to speak a kind of basic, understandable language where all we have to learn is the vocabulary. The reason why Tok Pisin and Haitian Creole exhibit such similarities is that people in both places share this basic set of instructions about how to simplify language.

Despite the existence of similarities such as this between Tok Pisin and Haitian Creole, it has become apparent that pidgin languages exhibit many differences as well as similarities. The apparently remarkable similarity between these two languages that you have just seen may in fact not be as significant as it appears. If we accept that both English and French structures are going to have their bound forms eliminated as well as grammatical redundancy reduced, it is almost certain that we will end up with four morphemes in whatever pidgin emerges in order to express this meaning. Given that the basic word order in both English, French, and the two sets of substrate languages is **SVO**, it is again predictable that the subject pronoun would end up coming before the verb. The verb in both English and French is the final element in the verb phrase in these clauses, so again it should not be a great surprise to find the other morphemes marking negation and tense occurring before it. The only real surprise is the relative ordering of the negative and tense marker in Tok Pisin and Haitian Creole, but with just this single similarity, we could suggest that this is due to mere chance.

Attempts to find shared structural characteristics among *all* pidgins and creoles have failed to reveal anything that is absolutely consistent for every case, and attention has since turned specifically to creoles. Pidgins, it is now felt, are less likely to show up any kinds of features common to all languages, because pidgins are by definition nobody's mother tongue. This means that there is always the possibility that substrate patterns could interfere with patterns derived from features that might be common to all languages. If parallel features develop among creoles, however, presumably this cannot be due to substrate interference as the speakers of such languages do not know any other languages. The prediction is that as a pidgin becomes a creole, it will expand structurally (as well as lexically). We should therefore be able to examine the structures of creoles in order to find out how it is that languages world-wide undergo creolisation. However, initial studies of the process of creolisation produced disappointing results. It has turned out, in comparisons between people who speak Tok Pisin as a second language and the increasing number who are growing up speaking it as their first language, that there are very few real differences in how the two groups speak the language.

The terms *pidgin* and *creole* are actually quite difficult to apply to particular situations when they are defined as they are in this section (even though these are the definitions that are given in almost all standard textbooks on the subject). As I have just indicated, in Papua New Guinea today, Tok Pisin is spoken as a second (or third, or fourth) language by the majority of the population, but a sizeable minority of urban Papua New Guineans, typically those whose parents come from different parts of the country and who speak different vernaculars, are now growing up speaking Tok Pisin as their first language. Do we say that Tok Pisin is a pidgin, or a creole, or a pidgin that is becoming a creole? The fact that there are no major differences in the speech of those who speak it as a 'pidgin' and those who speak it as a 'creole' makes the distinction seem almost pointless.

Some linguists have avoided this problem by redefining what a creole is. For them, the term *creole* should be used only to refer to a contact language which has developed over a very short period of time and which has developed out of a pidgin language that had not yet had time to acquire a stable structure. This would exclude Tok Pisin, for example, because it has had a stable structure for several generations. Linguists who adopt this revised definition find the study of these sorts of situations more interesting, because if the pidgin has not yet acquired a stable structure, *and* if the members of the following generation grow up with only this unstable pidgin as their input, any stable rules that develop in different creolising situations presumably reflect features of the human linguistic capabilities that we are all born with. What we are talking about here is the *Language Bioprogram Hypothesis* which has been formulated during the last decade and a half by scholars such as Derek Bickerton. According to this hypothesis, there are certain grammatical features that are predestined to emerge in the kinds of creolising situations that I am referring to.

Of course this is just a hypothesis at this stage, and the issue is currently being hotly debated among scholars, with some taking the view that creole languages ultimately derive much of their structure from their substrate languages, and other scholars supporting Bickerton's view that some kind of genetic structural predisposition is involved. The matter is nowhere near resolved, but one thing that has happened is that pidgin and creole languages have shifted from the periphery of linguistics to a central issue in historical linguistics.

12.3 ESOTEROGENY AND EXOTEROGENY

Quite apart from any individual scholar's position on the issue of substrate versus bioprogram, there is still the burning issue of how pidgins and creoles should be handled in a family tree model of language change. Pidginisation is generally regarded as a somewhat exceptional case in the evolution of languages. 'Normal' languages can be said to be descended from another language which is clearly recognisable as its ancestor. French, for example, is descended from Latin, and Samoan is descended from Proto Polynesian. But where do pidgin languages fit into the comparative method? Melanesian Pidgin does not have an ancestor in the same sense in which French has Latin as its ancestor. In 1840, Melanesian Pidgin did not exist, but by the 1860s, it was widely spoken in some parts of Melanesia, and had already spread to other areas where Melanesians had been taken as labourers, such as parts of Queensland in Australia.

What language is Melanesian Pidgin descended from? The family tree model breaks down when it comes to pidgin languages, because in a sense they spring out of nowhere! In an effort to force pidgin languages into the family tree model, some linguists might be tempted to classify Melanesian Pidgin as a Germanic language, and to place it in a subgroup along with English (as a kind of daughter language of English). Certainly the lexicon of Melanesian Pidgin is largely derived from English, but it is much harder to say that its grammar is derived from English grammar. Although there are many features of the grammar of Melanesian Pidgin which seem to derive from Austronesian languages, few linguists would go so far as to draw a family tree of the Austronesian languages with Melanesian Pidgin as one of the branches. After all, there are no systematic sound correspondences between Melanesian Pidgin and other Austronesian languages, as its lexicon is largely derived from English.

So pidgin languages tend to be either ignored, or placed in the 'too hard' basket by traditional comparative linguists. However, what happens when a language undergoes pidginisation is in some ways little different from what happens when 'normal' languages undergo ordinary linguistic change. There is nothing unusual about the kinds of sound changes that take place between a pidgin language and its lexical source language.

Many of the grammatical changes that take place in the development of a pidgin or creole language are also similar to the kinds of grammatical changes that take place in more 'normal' kinds of languages, and there are some linguists who do not see pidginisation as representing a special case in the study of language change at all. Rather than being problematic and peripheral to historical linguists, some would prefer to see pidginisation as being central to the study of language change. They would also argue that it is necessary to dismantle the family tree model that finds pidgin languages so difficult to incorporate. Many of the changes that took place when modern English evolved out of Old English after the Norman invasion in 1066 directly parallel the kinds of grammatical changes that take place when a pidgin language is formed. If you compare the grammar of modern Dutch and modern Afrikaans, it is tempting to describe Afrikaans as pidginised Dutch, as its grammar is certainly simplified and more regular than that of Dutch. In fact, perhaps all languages involve some kind of structural 'pidginisation' as they change!

Of course, the process of pidginisation cannot account for *all* language change. If this were true, then the vast majority of the world's languages would be creoles, which means that all languages should be structurally simple. However, while languages such as English and Afrikaans have undergone considerable simplication, there are other Indo-European languages, such as Lithuanian, which have retained their grammatical complexity. Speakers of modern Icelandic find it relatively easy to read thousand-year-old Norse sagas, which their close relatives the Norwegians can no longer read unless they learn Old Norse as a foreign language. This means that in addition to processes akin to pidginisation, there are other languages that change in the opposite way, building additional complexity into their languages.

The linguist William Thurston introduces a distinction between esoteric and exoteric languages as a way of explaining this difference. An *esoteric* language is one that is used primarily for intra-group communication, and which sets a group off from surrounding groups. Such languages tend to become increasingly complex as they are transmitted from generation to generation as they are subject to a number of functional pressures. Phonological efficiency is developed at the expense of morphological transparency, which means that there is likely to be a greater number of portmanteau morphemes, and a greater amount of allomorphic variation. Such languages typically develop suppletive morphological marking, and the lexicon makes an increasingly fine set of semantic distinctions. Originally optionally marked categories become grammaticalised. Outsiders typically find an esoteric language difficult to learn, which means that it functions even more efficiently as a marker of identity.

An *exoteric* language, on the other hand, is one that is also used for inter-group communication. Given the kinds of circumstances in which such languages are used, there will be many people for whom intelligibility rather than grammaticality is the primary concern. Such languages tend to develop in ways that make them easier to learn. Changes in exoteric languages are therefore likely to be in the opposite direction to those that are characteristic of developments in esoteric languages.

In introductory linguistics courses, linguists — sometimes even myself — often make the point to students that 'all languages are of equal complexity'. We do that for a purpose, as there is a temptation for people from technologically advanced cultures to think that languages such as English or Chinese might be more sophisticated than languages such as those of the Australian Aborigines. It is for this reason that Edward Sapir said in 1921 that:

We know of no people that is not possessed of a fully developed language. The lowliest South African Bushman speaks in the forms of a rich symbolic system that is in essence perfectly comparable to the speech of the cultivated Frenchman.

While all languages are amazingly complex, languages are in fact not all *equally* complex. Perhaps we linguists would be better in touch with reality if we were to say instead: the level of complexity of languages is in no way related to the level of technological complexity of the culture of their speakers.

Of course, if we are going to allow that languages can differ in their degrees of complexity, we need to offer some kind of absolute definition of what constitutes linguistic simplicity, as vague feelings are not going to be enough to go by. We also have to avoid the possibility that a particular pattern in Polish may be relatively complex for me as, say, an English-speaker, though a speaker of Russian may find it quite unchallenging, simply because the two languages are structurally similar to begin with. According to William Thurston, a language that approximates to the following characteristics can be described as simple:

(a)   There is an approximation to a one-to-one correspondence between form and meaning.
(b)   There is little stylistic or sociolinguistic variation.
(c)   There are relatively few grammatically marked distinctions.
(d)   There are relatively few bound morphemes, and these morphemes exhibit little allomorphic variation or suppletion.
(e)   Grammatical constructions would approximate towards one function per pattern, and the patterns would apply regularly, i.e. without special exceptions.
(f)   At the level of the lexicon, there would be few opaque idioms.

Whether a language is simple or complex is obviously relative rather than absolute. This means that it is possible to place languages on a continuum between two extremes. Comparing closely related German, Dutch and Afrikaans, for example, it is clear that in most respects these languages are structurally very similar, except that the Dutch inflectional system is simpler than that of German, while that of Afrikaans is simpler than that of Dutch. In this case, then, we clearly have a cline of structural simplicity: German → Dutch → Afrikaans.

The evolution of new languages can therefore be said to involve two different kinds of processes: exoterogeny and esoterogeny. *Exoterogeny* results in the development of a new exoteric language. In the most extreme example of this kind of process, words are simply taken from another language and mapped in the simplest possible way onto the phonological, syntactic and semantic patterns of the language that the community already speaks. *Esoterogeny*, on the other hand, involves the development of a new esoteric language, in which diversification proceeds in the direction of greater complexity.

Given that there is a continuum between a simpler and more complex language, the distinction between exoterogeny and esoterogeny is obviously also relative rather than absolute. A relatively simple exoteric language may develop, and if this language then comes to be emblematic of a single community, it may develop a new set of exoteric features. Some languages may only be called on relatively infrequently for use as intergroup languages, so the need for an easy language may be less urgent than in another situation where there is frequent use made of a language as a lingua franca. In such circumstances, we could expect that esoterogeny will proceed to differing extents.

The view that languages may be subject to pressures to move towards exoteric or esoteric types offers many historical linguists much to think about, and it certainly offers some serious challenges to those who insist on a rigid application of the family tree model of linguistic diversification. The family tree model does not cope well with notions such as 'mixed languages'. This kind of model, however, accepts that language mixing is a real phenomenon.

It is likely that the distinction between esoterogeny and exoterogeny will be ignored by some. It will be actively disputed by others, who will continue to push languages such as Tok Pisin into the 'too hard' basket. Others may be more open to accepting these kinds of views, though there are possibly still some questions that remain to be resolved.

While the correspondence between local emblematicity and esoterogeny on the one hand and use as a lingua franca and exoterogeny on the other is appealing, and many examples can be presented to make the correspondence appear convincing, we probably have some way to go before we can say that we have explained all instances of linguistic diversification according to this model. For instance, while it may be possible to invoke such explanations in the exogenetic development of Afrikaans out of Dutch — given what we know of the multilingual situation of the early Dutch settlers in South Africa — it would be much more difficult to account for the apparently exogenetic development of Dutch out of an earlier pattern that was more like that which we find in German.

And as soon as somebody puts up a boldly stated and very general theory, there will always be apparent counterexamples appearing in the literature. On the island of Erromango in Vanuatu, for example, there were originally several distinct — though closely related — languages, possibly as many as six. Around the time of first colonial contact — or possibly even before this — in the mid-1800s, one of these languages, known as Sye, came to be adopted as a general lingua franca, while the other languages became 'vernacularised', i.e. they came to function solely as intra-group languages. Given this scenario, we would expect that Sye should be the grammatically simplest of these languages, while the other languages should show signs of structural complexity. In fact, the reverse seems to be the case, with Sye being one of the more complex Oceanic languages, while the more restricted Ura language has undergone considerable morphological simplication in its patterns for expressing possession, as well as the ways in which it marks verbal objects.

12.4 LANGUAGE DEATH

In Chapter 1 I referred to the fact that a language can die. Language death is something that is almost always associated with language contact. The only situation in which a language may die without language contact taking place is in the comparatively rare situation in which an entire speech community is wiped out by a massive calamity such as a volcanic eruption, a military slaughter, or an epidemic. Such things have unfortunately happened in the past. Oral tradition in central Vanuatu tells of the once large island of Kuwae which was shattered by a volcanic cataclysm into the much smaller present-day islands of Tongoa and the Shepherd Islands. This massive eruption must have killed large numbers of people. Oral tradition records that, although a small number of people from Kuwae survived this holocaust, when the new, smaller islands were resettled by people from the nearby larger island of Efate, they brought with them their own language, which explains why the people from these islands speak a dialect of the Efate language to this day. Presumably the original language of Kuwae disappeared with the death of the last survivors of the eruption. The history of Aboriginal Australia is full of accounts of the extermination of whole communities of Aboriginal people by European settlers, often by the most inhuman methods such as the deliberate introduction of smallpox, or by vicious shooting sprees. Again, unknown numbers of languages disappeared from the record with the disappearance of their speakers.

Tragic as such circumstances are, they are of primary interest to scholars of history rather than linguistics. Language death typically occurs in much less catastrophic circumstances, and arises as a result of language contact over an extended period of time. When speakers of two languages come into contact and speakers of one of the two languages have power over speakers of the other language, either by force of social prestige or by demographic dominance, it is possible for speakers of the socially weaker language to abandon their language in favour of the dominant language. This has taken place in many parts of the world in the past, and is probably accelerating today as languages like English and French become increasingly dominant world-wide through the power of education, government, and the mass media.

Many Australian languages have disappeared, not because their speakers were exterminated, but because the generations of the past either chose to or were forced to speak to their children in English. Only about 1 per cent of Hawaiians today speak Hawaiian, the remainder having shifted to English, and Māori in New Zealand has shown signs of going the same way, with only about 10 per cent of Māori people today speaking the ancestral language. The languages in some parts of Papua New Guinea (especially in the Sepik) are under pressure, not from English, but from Tok Pisin. In Europe also, minority languages are under pressure from larger languages. Irish, Scots Gaelic, and Welsh are all under pressure from English; Friesian is under pressure from Dutch; and Breton is under pressure from French.

A description of the social circumstances surrounding the death of a language belongs in a volume on sociolinguistics, so in this book I will concentrate not on what causes a language to die, but on what happens to the language itself as it dies. Before I can do this, however, *some* discussion of what causes a language to die is necessary. To do this, I will outline what has happened in the history of Māori in New Zealand. From the time of the original settlement of Aotearoa (known to the outside world as New Zealand) about 1000 years ago, the Māori had uncontested control over their territory, and their language functioned as part of their flourishing culture. In the beginning of the nineteenth century, European settlers began arriving, initially in small numbers, and from the second half of the nineteenth century, in an increasing flood. The Māori lost much of their land to the settlers and quickly came under the military control of the settlers, and later also under their political and economic control. However, the Māori remained a largely rural rather than an urban people, living together in communities, and their language continued to flourish, even though their children learned English at school.

A major social change occurred after the Second World War as many Māori began moving from the rural areas to the cities and towns in order to get jobs. Without a fluent command of English, it was difficult to get jobs, and parents saw it as benefiting their children if they refused to speak to them in Māori and insisted on only English in the home. The next generation that grew up in towns therefore tended to learn only a little Māori (possibly from their grandparents who spoke little English), or none at all. Of course, the children of this generation who are today's teenagers and young adults have also grown up speaking nothing but English. It is probably not completely accurate to say that the Māori language began to die; rather, it began to commit suicide. The result is that today, about 90 per cent of Māori speak only the language of their original conquerors.[2]

In communities where it is recognised that a language is in a precarious situation, the remaining fluent speakers frequently comment on the fact that younger generations no longer speak the language 'properly'. Fluent speakers of Māori, for example, point to overwhelming lexical interference from the

---

[2] Many Māori see the possible loss of their language as a threat to their cultural identity and are taking steps to ensure that the language does not disappear. Older speakers of Māori are now being involved in special childcare centres and preschools known as *kōhanga reo* (literally: 'language nest') in which only Māori is used. Thousands of children are now growing up as fluent speakers of Māori.

dominant language, confusion of grammatical distinctions, and poor command of the stylistic repertoire. The same sorts of changes are found all over the world in situations where languages are showing signs of being replaced by other languages. Sometimes the older generations will attempt to correct the mistakes of younger *partial speakers* (i.e. those whose command of the language has suffered as a result of language shift taking place). This can, of course, cause partial speakers to become embarrassed and to avoid using the language with older people for fear of further correction. Rather than improving the chances of the language surviving, this may even make it less likely that it will survive, especially if it is a very small one as in the case of Australian Aboriginal languages.

One language that is recognised as being near to extinction is the Dyirbal language of the coast of northern Queensland in Australia. While the older people are recognised as being able to speak the language 'correctly', the younger generations have grown up either speaking no Dyirbal at all (using only English), or speaking a kind of Dyirbal that everybody recognises to be 'corrupted' in some way. At the simplest level, this involves the frequent use of words (and phrases) of English (or Pidgin) origin for which there are established Dyirbal words. Sometimes the younger people may have forgotten the original Dyirbal word, though in other cases they may use an English word even though they do know the corresponding word in Dyirbal.

The use of words of foreign origin is not necessarily a sign of imminent language death. If it were, then English with its huge number of borrowed words should be a prime example of a dying language. Instead, the enthusiasm with which English has accepted new vocabulary is generally taken as a sign of its extreme vitality. However, the speech of younger people in the Dyirbal community is also grammatically quite different from that of the older people. Younger speakers are reducing the morphological complexity of the language by eliminating some suffixes. The grammatical functions that were originally expressed by these suffixes are now often expressed by free forms that are derived from English, as in the following examples:

Old People's Dyirbal
Ban	ḍugumbil	ɲina-ɲu	jugu-ŋga.
feminine	woman	sit-nonfuture	log-on

Young People's Dyirbal
Ban	ḍugumbil	ɲina-ɲu	on jugu.
feminine	woman	sit-nonfuture	on log

'The woman sat on a log.'

Grammatical constructions that are very different from those of English are also particularly subject to change. The Dyirbal that is spoken by the older people has a very free word order, similar to what I described for Latin in

Section 7.1. This is possible because all noun phrases in Dyirbal are obligatorily marked by suffixes which indicate clearly which is the subject and which is the object. However, younger speakers tend to leave the ergative suffix off nouns that function as the subjects of transitive verbs, and distinguish the subject and object noun phrases by using a fixed **SVO** word order as in English. (See Section 7.1 again for more detailed discussion of ergativity.) Instead of using the ergative form **/buliman-du/** 'policeman (ergative)', a younger person might produce a sentence such as the following, with no suffix at all on the subject — which an older person would judge as ungrammatical:

> Buliman　　ŋanba-n　　　　ban　　　　buladi.
> policeman　ask-nonfuture　feminine　two
> 'The policeman asked those two (women).'

As the language comes under increasing pressure from English, we can expect that there will be greater influence of English vocabulary and structural patterns on the language. Some speakers are already producing sentences that are basically English even though they still contain fragments of Dyirbal, such as the following:

> They bin gunimariɲu but they never bin find-im.
> 'They looked for him but they didn't find him.'

The Dyirbal verb **/gunimariɲu/** 'look for' occurs in a sentence with an English subject, and with the past tense marker **/bin/** that derives from the earlier Aboriginal Pidgin. The object suffix **/-im/** on the verb *find* also derives from the pidgin.

The question of just what happens to the grammar as a language dies has begun to arouse considerable interest among scholars of language change. In one sense what has happened to the vocabulary and the grammar of Dyirbal is quite unexceptional. The incorporation of vocabulary from one language into another is, as we have seen, a perfectly normal aspect of language change. The kinds of grammatical changes that are taking place are also not radically different in nature from the kinds of changes that take place in situations of ordinary language change. In Chapter 7, I indicated that inflecting and agglutinating languages often evolve into isolating languages, and that morphological irregularities in languages tend to be eliminated by the process of analogy. Just as an accusative language can, over time, acquire an ergative structure, so the shift of Dyirbal from an ergative structure to an accusative structure marked by word order rather than by case suffixes is again perfectly within the bounds of normal language change.

What is exceptional in the case of Dyirbal is that the changes are happening on such a massive scale and in such a short period of time. These structural changes have all taken place within the space of 25 years. English began to undergo very similar sorts of changes from around the time of contact after the Viking and Norman invasions, but it took several centuries for this to happen. Another difference between the kinds of changes that are taking place with Dyirbal and those which happened in the history of English is that in Dyirbal, a change that results in the loss of some aspect of the grammar (such as the loss of the locative suffix /-ŋga/ in one of the examples above) has not been compensated for by a corresponding development somewhere else in the language. What has happened is that speakers have simply taken over the corresponding English form to express this function, i.e. the preposition *on*.

This has led some scholars to suggest that what happens when a language dies is somehow similar to what happens when a pidgin language comes into existence, except that events take place in the opposite order. Just as a pidgin in the early stages of its formation involves grammatical reduction and both structural and lexical variability, so too does a dying language. A pidgin also has a reduced stylistic repertoire compared to a 'normal' language, and we find the same thing with a language that is dying. Others have pointed instead to parallels in reverse between language death and creolisation. Just as a pidgin that undergoes creolisation is said to expand structurally, lexically, and stylistically, a dying language experiences structural, lexical, and stylistic reduction.

Although it need only take a break in transmission between a single generation for a language to be doomed, it is possible for features of an old language to be maintained over a relatively long period. In Section 9.4 I talked about how languages can sometimes change to allow a local group to mark its separate identity in some way. Although the examples that I gave there came from a Papua New Guinea context, this is not something that is restricted just to these languages. Very often when an ethnic group switches from one language to another, people develop ways of marking their ethnicity through their new language. There is a variety of English in America that is typically associated with Blacks as against Whites. Māori in New Zealand can often be distinguished from Pākehā by the way they speak English. Books about the history of Tasmanian Aborigines point out that the last fully-descended Tasmanian died in 1876, and her language died with her, yet some of the 4000 or so people in Tasmania today who are of Aboriginal descent (and who proudly identify themselves as Tasmanian Aborigines) still use the occasional word of Aboriginal origin in their speech. We can expect that while Dyirbal is doomed as a distinct language, the succeeding generations of people who belong to this community will continue to sprinkle their English with individual words of Dyirbal origin, even though there will be little or no evidence of Dyirbal grammatical structures.

READING GUIDE QUESTIONS

1. What is interference as distinct from diffusion?
2. What is calquing?
3. Can phonemes be copied from one language to another?
4. How can morphemes from one language enter another?
5. What is the difference between convergence and diffusion?
6. What is a linguistic area?
7. To what extent is syntactic copying possible?
8. What are the characteristics of a pidgin?
9. What is a creole?
10. What is the difference between a superordinate and a substrate language?
11. What is the Language Bioprogam Hypothesis?
12. What is meant by language death?
13. What parallels are there between pidginisation and creolisation on the one hand and language death on the other?

EXERCISES

1. Examine the data below from two different languages, one of which is vernacular Fijian and the other the pidginised form of Fijian that emerged on plantations in Fiji during the last century:

Language A	Language B	
na noqu vale	na vale koyau	'my house'
na nomu veiniu	na veiniu koiko	'your plantation'
na nona koro	na koro kokoya	'his/her village'
na nodra vale	na vale koratou	'their house'
na nodratou veiniu	na veiniu koratou	'their (three) plantation'
na nodrau koro	na koro koratou	'their (two) village'
na nomudrau bilo	na bilo kemudou	'your (two) cup'
na nomuni vale	na vale kemudou	'your (many) house'
na nomudou veiniu	na veiniu kemudou	'your (three) plantation'
na noda vosa	na vosa keitou	'our (many inclusive) language'
na neimami vosa	na vosa keitou	'our (many exclusive) language'
na meirau wai	na wai keitou	'our (two exclusive) water'
na meitou bia	na bia keitou	'our (three exclusive) beer'
na meimami bia	na bia keitou	'our (many exclusive) beer'
na medaru bia	na bia keitou	'our (two inclusive) beer'
na medatou wisiki	na wisiki keitou	'our (three inclusive) whisky'
na meda wisiki	na wisiki keitou	'our (many inclusive) whisky'

na tamaqu	na tamana koyau	'my father'
na tamamu	na tamana koiko	'your father'
na tamana	na tamana kokoya	'his/her father'
na ligada	na ligana keitou	'our (many inclusive) hands'
na ligadra	na ligana koratou	'their hands'

(Note that in the Fijian orthography that is used in these examples, the symbol *q* is used to represent a prenasalised voiced velar stop, which is phonetically [ŋg].)

(a) Which of these two languages is vernacular Fijian and which is the pidgin form of Fijian? What are the structural features which enable you to say this?

(b) Give the equivalents of the following phrases in both vernacular Fijian and pidgin Fijian:

your hand
your (two) father
your (many) father
his/her water
their (two) whisky
their (three) beer
our (many exclusive) house
their language
our (many inclusive) plantation
my cup

(c) Consider the following additional forms in Language A:

na tinamu	'your mother'
na tinana	'his/her mother'

On the basis of this information, give the following in both vernacular Fijian and pidgin Fijian:

our (many inclusive) mother
their mother
your (two) mother
your (many) mother
our (three exclusive) mother

2. Examine the following forms in Haitian Creole and in French:

French	Haitian Creole	
je suis malade	*m malad*	'I am sick'
ils sont malades	*yo malad*	'they (masculine) are sick'

elles sont malades	*yo malad*	'they (feminine) are sick'
j'étais malade	*m te malad*	'I was sick'
ils étaient malades	*yo te malad*	'they were sick'
nous achèterons	*n ap achte*	'we will buy'
je vais	*m ale*	'I am going'
vous irez	*u ap ale*	'you (plural) will go'
tu iras	*u ap ale*	'you (singular) will go'
il a couru	*li te kuri*	'he has run'
il est bon	*li bien*	'he is good'
elle va	*li ale*	'she is going'
je suis allé	*me te ale*	'I have gone'
il a acheté	*li te achte*	'he has bought'

(a) What are the features of Haitian Creole by which we can recognise that it has undergone the process of pidginisation?

(b) How would you express the following in French?

yo ap malad
m achte
n te kuri
yo te bien
u ap ale

3. Compare the following forms from Bandjalang language of northern New South Wales (in Australia) as it was spoken by people who learned the language in the early twentieth century and people who learned to speak it in the late nineteenth century. In what way are the changes that have taken place similar to the changes involved in the formation of pidgins and creoles?

Older People's Bandjalang	Later Generation Bandjalang	
gala gibirga:	gala gibirga:	'mahogany tree'
ga:ɲu gibi:ŋbilga:	ga:ɲu gibirga:	'mahogany trees'
gala bunawga:	gala bunawga:	'bloodwood tree'
ga:ɲu buna:ŋbilga:	ga:ɲu bunawga:	'bloodwood trees'
gala barbamga:	gala barbamga:	'spotted gum tree'
ga:ɲu barba:ŋbilga:	ga:ɲu barbamga:	'spotted gum trees'
gala buɖe:ga	gala buɖe:ga	'Moreton Bay fig tree'
ga:ɲu buɖe:ŋbilga:	ga:ɲu buɖe:ga	'Moreton Bay fig trees'
gala bilaŋga:	gala bilaŋga:	'oak tree'
ga:ɲu bila:ŋbiɲga:	ga:ɲu bilaŋga:	'oak trees'
gala ŋarulga:	gala ŋarulga:	'box tree'
ga:ɲu ŋaru:ŋbiɲga:	ga:ɲu ŋarulga:	'box trees'
gala jigam	gala jigam	'piece of meat'

ga:ɲu jigambil	ga:ɲu jigam	'pieces of meat'
gala wura:ŋ	gala wura:ŋ	'leaf'
ga:ɲu wura:ŋbil	ga:ɲu wura:ŋ	'leaves'
gala ḍinaŋ	gala ḍinaŋ	'foot'
ga:ɲu ḍinaŋbil	ga:ɲu ḍinaŋ	'feet'
gala deberdebe:r	gala deberdebe:r	'plover'
ga:ɲu deberdebe:rgan	ga:ɲu deberdebe:r	'plovers'
gala bagawaŋ	gala bagawaŋ	'leatherhead bird'
ga:ɲu bagawaŋgan	ga:ɲu bagawaŋ	'leatherhead birds'
gala muḍumḍar	gala muḍumḍar	'son'
ga:ɲu muḍumgir	ga:ɲu muḍumḍar	'sons'
gala baniḍar	gala baniḍar	'father'
ga:ɲu banigir	ga:ɲu baniḍar	'fathers'
gala balun	gala balun	'river'
ga:ɲu balungali	ga:ɲu balun	'rivers'
gala bagul	gala bagul	'canoe'
ga:ɲu bagulgali	ga:ɲu bagul	'canoes'
gala daba:j	gala daba:j	'dog'
ga:ɲu daba:jgali	ga:ɲu daba:j	'dogs'
gala muru	gala muru	'nose'
ga:ɲu murugali	ga:ɲu muru	'noses'
gala dubaj	gala dubaj	'woman'
ga:ɲu dubaymir	ga:ɲu dubay	'women'
gala wagaɲ	gala wagaɲ	'catfish'
ga:ɲu wagaɲmir	ga:ɲu wagaɲ	'catfishes'
gala bajgal	gala bajgal	'man'
ga:ɲu bajgalbajga:l	ga:ɲu bajgal	'men'
gala dugun	gala dugun	'mountain'
ga:ɲu dugundugu:n	ga:ɲu dugun	'mountains'
gala bargan	gala bargan	'boomerang'
ga:ɲu bargan	ga:ɲu bargan	'boomerangs'
gala mundu	gala mundu	'stomach'
ga:ɲu mundu	ga:ɲu mundu	'stomachs'
gala jamba:	gala jamba:	'carpet snake'
ga:ɲu jamba:	ga:ɲu jamba:	'carpet snakes'
gala ŋa:wun	gala ŋa:wun	'wood duck'
ga:ɲu ŋa:wun	ga:ɲu ŋa:wun	'wood ducks'

FURTHER READING

1. Robert J. Jeffers and Ilse Lehiste *Principles and Methods for Historical Linguistics,* Chapter 9 'Language Contact and Linguistic Change', pp. 138–59.
2. Theodora Bynon *Historical Linguistics,* Chapter 6 'Contact between Languages', pp. 216–61.
3. René Appel and Pieter Muysken *Language Contact and Bilingualism.*
4. Sarah Grey Thomason and Terrence Kaufman *Language Contact, Creolization, and Genetic Linguistics.*
5. Derek Bickerton *Roots of Language.*
6. Peter Mühlhäusler *Pidgin and Creole Linguistics.*
7. Suzanne Romaine *Pidgin and Creole Languages.*
8. Annette Schmidt *Young People's Dyirbal: An Example of Language Death in Australia.*
9. Hans Henrich Hock *Principles of Historical Linguistics,* Chapter 16 'Linguistic Contact: Koinés, convergence, pidgins, creoles, language death', pp. 472–531.
10. William R. Thurston *Processes of Change in the Languages of North-western New Britain,* Chapter 3 'Glotto-ontongeny', pp. 35–67.

CHAPTER THIRTEEN

CULTURAL RECONSTRUCTION

Different people who practise historical linguistics may have their own particular reasons for their interest in this field. Some may enjoy the intellectual challenge of applying a difficult technique to 'dig' into the past and find out about things that we could not know about otherwise. Some may be looking for 'universal' features of language and how languages change, in an effort to determine what it is that makes us uniquely 'human' (assuming, in fact, that we are radically different from other animals). And others may study historical linguistics in an effort to use the information it can provide to tell us something about the non-linguistic history of the people who speak the language. In this, the final chapter, I will indicate just what sorts of information historical linguistics *can* tell us about the non-linguistic history of a society, and how reliable this information is.

13.1 ARCHAEOLOGY

Once we start considering the question of cultural reconstruction, there are various ways by which we can tackle this problem. Archaeologists attempt to reconstruct cultures on the basis of the material remains left by people of the past. They uncover material that has been buried by natural processes of soil movement and they can use a variety of scientific methods to provide actual dates for the existence of particular cultural features and changes in cultures in the past, as long as some kind of material remains of these cultures have been retained into the present.

For instance, archaeologists are able to tell us that there have been people living in the land that is now Australia and Papua New Guinea for at least as long as there have been people living in what is now Europe. They can tell us with a fair degree of certainty that people were living 40,000 years ago on what was then a single huge land mass. There are human burials that were uncovered originally by erosion in one part of Australia that have been dated as very ancient, and in the Huon Gulf of Papua New Guinea, stone axe heads that are very similar to stone axe heads found in Australia and other parts of Southeast Asia have recently been uncovered in soil layers that are well over 40,000 years old. However, there are now suggestions coming out that this period is too short, and archaeologists are expecting to find evidence that there has been human occupation in this area for 60,000 years or more.

Archaeologists are able to tell us something of ancient trade routes. In the Pacific, goods such as valuable shells, clay pots, and obsidian (a kind of natural glass of volcanic origin) were traded over huge distances for long periods of time. They can often suggest who were the economically dominant partners in these trading networks. Archaeologists can also tell us something about population movements and other kinds of cultural contacts between people. For instance, they can tell us that the Australian Aborigines did not have dogs until about 4000 or 5000 years ago. By the time that the first Europeans set foot in Australia in the 1600s and 1700s, the dog was well established throughout Australia (except in Tasmania). Presumably, the dog was introduced to the mainland of Australia as a result of some cultural contact, either in the form of trading visits, or in the form of a migration by some outside group into Australia, or maybe even by people who were blown off course and were stranded there. Who these people were we do not know, but we can say with some certainty that once the Australian Aborigines arrived in their new home many thousands of years ago, they were not competely cut off from changes and developments that took place in other parts of the world.

Another major archaeological development that took place in the Pacific area was the spread of the first pottery in the island Pacific. This originated in the area known as the New Guinea Islands, i.e. New Britain, New Ireland, and Manus. This pottery then spread out into the Solomon Islands, Vanuatu, New Caledonia, and then on to Fiji, Tonga, and Samoa, between about 3000 and 3500 years ago. The development of this pottery style was also accompanied by new styles in the production of artefacts, as well as the spread of new animals. The culture of the people who were responsible for these cultural innovations is known as the *Lapita culture*, a name which is derived from the name of the place where their distinctive kind of pottery was first discovered in New Caledonia. There is also evidence to suggest that the Lapita people took domesticated pigs, dogs, and chickens with them wherever they travelled. If these people were raising pigs, archaeologists argue, this probably means that they were also agricultural, as it is necessary to feed pigs on sweet potato or taro if they are kept in pens rather than being allowed to forage in the wild. (Observant readers may be asking themselves if there was perhaps not some kind of direct or indirect contact between Australian Aborigines and the ancestors in southeast Asia of the Lapita people, which could account for the introduction of dogs into Australia. This is an interesting question to which we don't have any kind of firm answer.)

Although there is much that archaeologists can tell us, there are many other things that they cannot. They cannot tell us about a people's oral literature, for instance, nor can they tell us much about a people's kinship system. And although archaeologists can often tell us that there have been cultural contacts between one group and another in the past, they cannot always say exactly who the two groups were. And obviously, an archaeologist cannot tell us what language was spoken in the past by a group of people. If you want to know what language was spoken by the Lapita people, you will need to come to a linguist for ideas.

13.2 ORAL HISTORY

Another way by which we can attempt to reconstruct a culture is to look at a people's oral history. Eyewitness accounts of events are often passed on from one generation to another. In particular, oral histories are important for recording *genealogies* (or extended family histories). For instance, oral historians are sometimes able to tell us the approximate time that a particular village was established, with time being measured by counting generations back from the present. Sometimes oral tradition will record where the people of that village originally lived, who was their leader at the time they moved, and why the move actually took place.

Many other facts can be recorded in oral history, but there are often problems in interpreting oral history. Some stories that are passed on from generation to generation are just *myths* (or *legends*) that reflect the religious and social system of a community, and provide the basis for its religious and social organisation. Oral tradition of this type is of little interest to the oral historian, because these stories are based more on faith than on fact. For instance, the oral historian would not be particularly interested in the story of the origins of the coconut in parts of Melanesia that I talked about in Chapter 1.

Other stories, however, are based on actual historical events. The problem that we often face in dealing with stories such as these is that, although they are based on real events, the account of the event may have become distorted over time. For instance, it is possible that two different groups of people may pass on differing accounts of the same event, especially if there is an element of conflict between the two peoples involved. Although the stories may be recognisable as being about the same event, they may differ in their details, or sometimes even in their basic elements. Oral historians can therefore only accept evidence on which all tellers of a story agree, or evidence which appears independently in a number of different versions of a story. Because of these problems of a people's own account of its history, oral historians do not usually accept their evidence as valid if it goes back further than a few hundred years into the past. Clearly, this is not a very long time in comparison to some of the population movements and cultural developments that I describe in this chapter and elsewhere in this volume.

One very interesting example that we can look at is a story of a 'Time of Darkness' that is told in many societies in the Madang and Morobe provinces of Papua New Guinea, as well as in all of the Highlands provinces. Although these stories differ in detail according to where the story is told, or who the particular story-teller is, there is still a remarkable degree of agreement in the stories as they are told over this whole area. The story, in its basic form, goes something like this:

The people heard a loud noise [or sometimes felt an earthquake, or both], and felt that something awful was going to happen. Black clouds started to build up and they eventually blocked out the sun. Very quickly, the whole place was in darkness like the darkest night. People went into their homes to hide, and they heard something falling from the sky on to their roofs. When they looked out, they saw that it was raining ash. The darkness lasted for three or four days. When the sun reappeared, people found that the whole countryside was covered, and many food gardens had been destroyed, and many houses had collapsed.

This story sounds as though it is describing quite a disaster. However, while people from the Enga Province in the Highlands who tell the story believe that the Time of Darkness was a terrible thing, they also believe that it was the beginning of better times afterwards. After this tragedy, the sweet potato grew better in the gardens, and people had more wealth (in the form of pigs) for exchange. Many cultural developments were said to have followed directly from the Time of Darkness.

What this story sounds like is a description of a distant volcanic eruption, even down to the details about the long-term benefits mentioned in the Enga version of the story. This is presumably compatible with the enriching of the soil from fertile volcanic ash. This interpretation of the story can in fact be checked out according to modern scientific methods. There are deposits of volcanic ash in a layer at least 2.5 centimetres thick in the area indicated on the map below. The areas where stories about the Time of Darkness are reported are also marked on this map.

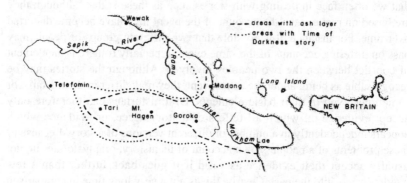

These two areas coincide very closely, so presumably the story and the layer of volcanic ash *are* connected historically. Geologists are able to locate the source of the ash as the volcano on Long Island (which is also marked on the map), and they suggest that there was probably a major eruption from this volcano sometime between 1640 and 1820.

The people who tell the Time of Darkness story claim very definitely that the story is 'historical' rather than 'legendary', and the date that we can arrive at for the event is somewhere between 1820 and 1860, based on a count of generations from the present. The version of the scientist and the version of the oral historian are quite clearly compatible therefore. Even the actual dates overlap, suggesting that perhaps the eruption took place closer to 1820 than any of the other possible dates.

But many much older historical events can also be recorded in oral history. In the central islands of Vanuatu, there were stories of a man named Roimata who sailed to these islands from afar and ended the local wars by setting himself up as a paramount chief over all of the islands. There are many miraculous happenings in which Roimata is said to have been involved which modern scientists would find hard to explain, but there other parts of the stories about this man that are much more open to scientific verification. The stories report that when Roimata died, his body was taken to a small island off the northern shore of the large island of Efate, where he was buried in full ceremonial regalia. At the same time that he was buried, representatives of the areas over which he held power were buried alive along with him, the men being anaesthetised with strong doses of kava, while the women were buried next to their husbands without the benefit of kava. The archaeologist José Garanger confirmed in the late 1960s that there was a large amount of truth in these stories when he excavated on the island of Eretoka. There he found the grave of a man on his own with pigs' tusks and other traditional decorations, and his grave was surrounded by the graves of numerous couples where the men were lying peacefully, and their wives beside them lay contorted in agony, as if having been buried alive.

The date of this burial was determined to have been around 700 years ago. This archaeological evidence can also be tied in with the linguistic evidence. In Vanuatu today, spoken among the 100 or so Melanesian languages are three languages which are more closely related to the Polynesian languages some thousands of kilometres to the east. Two of these three Polynesian languages are spoken in the central islands of Vanuatu within the area where Roimata is said to have held power. We can speculate, therefore, that Roimata was in fact an immigrant to Vanuatu from somewhere in Polynesia. Perhaps by his forceful personality, or perhaps by military dominance, he managed to establish hegemony in his new homeland. He even managed to pass his language on to at least some of the local people, although once he died, presumably the original languages made something of a comeback. Even so, the languages of Emae island and the villages of Ifira and Mele may well represent direct offshoots of Roimata's original language that was first spoken in Vanuatu 700 years ago. (The third of the Polynesian languages to which I just referred is spoken to the south, on the islands of Futuna and Aniwa.)

There are many other examples of oral tradition being confirmed by archaeological evidence, and for which we can also find supporting linguistic evidence. When Europeans first came to settle in New Zealand in the first half of the nineteenth century, they discovered that Māori oral traditions referred to large flightless birds which they called /**moa**/. These birds might have remained the stuff of myth and fantasy, as have dragons and unicorns,[1] except that from the 1860s onwards the bodies of birds with huge bones, and sometimes even feathers and mummified flesh, began to come to light. It rapidly emerged that these bones came from birds that looked a lot like emus or ostriches, but were much bigger, some being at least twice the height of a human from head to foot. This meant that the /**moa**/ was not mythical at all, but a real bird.

When the Māori first arrived in New Zealand (or Aotearoa, as it is referred to in the Māori language), they found a number of different species of this bird, and they developed a culture based in part on /**moa**/-hunting. We know that the Māori used to hunt the /**moa**/ because archaeologists have discovered charred /**moa**/ bones in fireplaces where food was cooked, and artefacts made of /**moa**/ bone. However, within a few hundred years, it seems, the /**moa**/ had been hunted to extinction, and all that was left was the name as it was recorded in oral tradition. The word /**moa**/ is found in most of the other Polynesian languages, though in these languages it means 'chicken'. Presumably when the first Māori arrived in Aotearoa and they came across these birds, they quickly abandoned their tiny chickens and took advantage of the much more plentiful amounts of meat that the /**moa**/ could provide, and in doing so transferred the name of their earlier source of protein to these newly discovered game-birds. (Another possible explanation for the lack of chickens in Aotearoa is that the Māori had not brought chickens with them in the first place — or perhaps they did, but they drowned or were eaten on the long journey there!)

Other fascinating questions to examine are the stories told by the Māori about their origins. Māori oral traditions tell of canoe voyages from the distant land of Hawaiki, many many generations ago. The stories record the names of particular canoes which came ashore at different locations along the coastline of the new land that they called Aotearoa, and modern Māori groups speak of their descent from one or another of these founding /**waka**/, or canoes. The name *Hawaiki* has the same origin as the name of the biggest island in Hawaii, which is phonemically /**hawai?i**/, as well as the name of the largest Samoan island, /**savai?i**/. Many of the people whose names are recorded as having travelled on these first canoes are then said to have engaged in heroic voyages of discovery in Aotearoa itself, resulting in the

---

[1] But some have suggested that the European tradition of the unicorn derives from early accounts of the rhinoceros, when few Europeans had actually travelled to Africa.

formation of many of the rivers, lakes, mountains, and volcanoes that are found in New Zealand today.

Australian archaeologists tell us that when the first Aboriginal people arrived on the continent, they came across what is referred to today as *megafauna*, or huge relatives of modern-day kangaroos and other marsupials. These became extinct thousands of years ago, but many fossil remains of these animals have been unearthed. The reason for the extinction of these animals is not clear, but it could be that they died out as a result of climate changes or hunting by humans, or a combination of these factors. Australian Aboriginal oral traditions do not describe animals that we can identify as now extinct megafauna, but one wonders whether the mythical bunyip or the rainbow serpent correspond to any animal that would be recognised by scientists. Some Australian Aboriginal groups from northern Queensland also have stories of people 'walking' from coastal islands to the mainland. This might seem to be pure legend now, but it may be that these stories date from a time when, geologists tell us, sea levels were much lower than they are today, and the islands were actually connected to the mainland by land.

13.3 COMPARATIVE CULTURE

You have seen that, by comparing a number of languages that share certain similarities, it is possible to reconstruct a protolanguage as the ancestor of these languages. If we regard culture as involving a system of interrelated facts in the same way as a language is a system of interrelated facts, then it should logically be just as possible to reconstruct protocultures in the same way as we reconstruct protolanguages.

Obviously any method of cultural reconstruction based on a method of *comparative culture* like this would not produce results with the same degree of likelihood as we have been able to produce for phonological reconstruction of languages, as our approach would have to involve the less well refined methods that we have for grammatical or semantic reconstruction. In fact, the actual units of a cultural system and the precise nature of the relationships between these units are probably going to be even more difficult to define than the interrelationships of units in grammar and semantics. (Anthropologists have long been envious of the techniques that linguists have developed for scientifically describing language, and have attempted to imitate these for describing culture.) The range of 'possible' changes in culture is probably even harder to define than the range of possible changes in grammar and semantics, which again makes cultural reconstruction harder. So, while cultural reconstruction by means of an adaptation of the comparative method is presumably possible, any conclusions that we reach in this way must be regarded as shaky.

Let us now look at an example of what I mean by comparative culture, to see how we might use the evidence of a variety of cultures to reconstruct an earlier cultural system. In Samoa, we find that there is an institution called the /fono/, which is a kind of meeting house. Most /fono/ are oval in structure, with a series of posts in the ground and around the actual building. The **fono** has 'members' who come from certain groups in society, and membership in these groups is passed on from father to son. The members select from among their number the person they regard as the most capable to represent them in the **fono**. Such a person is called a /matai/, and he sits inside the **fono** during the meetings, while the people he represents sit outside. In the meetings in the **fono**, all decisions are arrived at by consensus. In Kiribati, communities have a large rectangular meeting house called the /maneaba/. In each community there are various groups who have rights to sit in the /maneaba/, while others sit underneath the building during meetings. Decisions are arrived at by consensus. The similarities between the Samoan /fono/ and the Kiribati /maneaba/ are so great that we would almost certainly want to say that these are two cognate systems, and that they derive from the same source.

Let us now go to yet another society, this time that of the island of Malakula in Vanuatu. In this society, each community has a large rectangular building (which in Bislama is known as /nakamal/, but which has different names in each of the local languages). The /nakamal/ is partitioned off into areas that are regarded as progressively more sacred as one goes towards the back. Men can only go inside as far as the 'grade' to which they have been initiated, and initiation into the highest grade requires enormous payments of pigs and other traditional forms of wealth. Outside there is a series of carved images that are placed in memory of dead people and to which spirits of the dead return for certain ceremonies.

This system from Vanuatu, while it is apparently quite different from the systems of Samoa and Kiribati on the surface, still shares some basic features with these other systems. There is still a central meeting house to which there are restrictions of various kinds on access. Decisions are reached by consensus in each case. There are also representatives outside the meeting house — in one case living, in the other case dead. It is therefore not too difficult to imagine all of these features as having been present in the protoculture from which all of these different cultures have evolved. The problem, of course, is in deciding exactly what kind of protoculture we should reconstruct. It seems reasonable to reconstruct some kind of central meeting house with some kind of restricted access — but should we reconstruct it as oval (as in the case of Samoa), or as rectangular (as in Kiribati and Vanuatu)? Perhaps all we can say is that it was probably longer than it was wide. And was access restricted by birthright (as in Samoa), or by wealth (as in Vanuatu)? From the data that we have looked at, it is probably not possible to make a decision on this particular point.

Another question we could ask is: who were the representatives outside the meeting house? Again, there are various possibilities. Firstly, they may have been people who were not eligible to enter because they lacked the wealth (or perhaps because they were not 'born into' the meeting house). Perhaps they were people who were not eligible to enter because they were dead (and whose presence was indicated by carved posts instead). Again, on the evidence that is available we are not really in a position to come to a conclusion on this point.

Cultural reconstruction, difficult as it obviously is, is still a relatively simple matter in places like Polynesia. This is because the populations are located on small islands that are separated by large expanses of ocean, which means that day-to-day contacts were not possible between groups which might influence each other in unpredictable ways. (But there is plenty of archaeological evidence to indicate that different Polynesian peoples *were* in contact with each other, even over these huge distances.) Polynesian cultures also developed independently, because when Polynesian people settled on an island, there were never any other people living there. Cultural reconstruction in the Melanesian islands however (and in the rest of the world, for that matter) is much more complex, because we have to remember that in many cases there were original populations (who may in some cases have left no distinct modern trace). There were also opportunities for continual day-to-day contact between people of different cultural backgrounds over many thousands of years. Under these conditions, it is possible for cultural innovations to have spread in a criss-cross pattern over huge areas, thereby completely eliminating traces of the original cultures that we would need in order to apply any method of comparative cultural reconstruction successfully.

13.4 HISTORICAL LINGUISTICS

I have now discussed archaeology, oral history, and comparative culture as methods of reconstructing the cultural history of a society. These different methods all provide information that partly overlaps and is partly specific to each method. Archaeology and comparative culture can take us a long way back into the past. Only archaeology can give us reasonably accurate dates for cultural features, and only comparative culture can tell us anything about the non-material culture of a society. Oral history can tell us something about the history of a society, but it cannot take us very far back in time when it comes to detailed information.

The final technique of cultural reconstruction that we have at our disposal is *historical linguistics*. Historical linguistics can allow us to go back quite a few thousand years in time. This area of study can provide us with a number of different kinds of information about the history of a society, and this information can then be compared with the information that is provided by archaeology, oral history, and comparative culture as a double check. The kinds of things that historical linguists can tell us are described below.

(a) Relative sequence of population splits

Take a situation such as the following, where there is a language family with four members, subgrouped as shown:

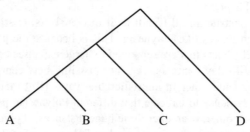

Here we have a number of languages that are all descended from a common ancestor. Languages **A**, **B**, and **C** all belong to a single subgroup, while Language **D** belongs to a different subgroup of its own within the same family. The languages **A**, **B**, and **C** further subgroup such that **A** and **B** are more closely related to each other than either is to **C**. This subgrouping is, of course, arrived at by considering the shared linguistic innovations or changes that have taken place from the protolanguage.

A situation like this will tell us that, at one stage in the history of these languages, there was a single language (Proto **ABCD**) which must have been spoken in a single community. This community then split, perhaps by migration, perhaps by a simple lack of contact between two areas without any migration taking place. The result of this split was that in one area, Language **D** emerged, while in the remaining area, the ancestor to languages **A**, **B**, and **C** was spoken. Next, Language **C** hived off from the protolanguage to modern **A** and **B**, and the final split was that which saw **A** and **B** become separate languages.

A subgrouping pattern of this kind would be compatible only with non-linguistic evidence which suggests that speakers of Language **D** split off relatively early from speakers of languages **A**, **B**, and **C**. Similarly, we would hope that non-linguistic evidence would be compatible with the fact that **C** then split off from **A** and **B**, and that the last split is also the most recent to have taken place, as suggested by non-linguistic evidence. For instance, if we look at the languages of Polynesia and of island Melanesia, we can draw a very simple subgrouping diagram:

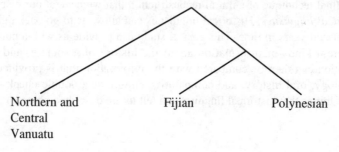

Northern and
Central
Vanuatu   Fijian   Polynesian

From this we can assume that all of the modern Polynesian languages go back to a common ancestor, and that this protolanguage split off from an earlier language that was ancestral to Proto Polynesian and Fijian. Furthermore, we can assume that this split took place *after* the ancestor of Fijian and the Polynesian languages split off from the language that was also ancestral to the languages of northern Vanuatu.

If we are talking about language splits, we are presumably also talking about splits in the populations of the speakers of those languages. In the case of Polynesia and island Melanesia, where the languages involved are spoken on small, isolated islands, we must also consider the relative age of migrations of entire peoples. I am speaking here of the *relative* age of population splits, and not the *absolute* age. That is, on the basis of linguistic evidence we can only say that the Fijian-Polynesian split took place later than the split from northern and central Vanuatu. We cannot say *when* these splits actually took place. The technique of glottochronology that we looked at in Chapter 8 is one way in which some linguists attempt to provide actual dates for population splits, though there are few who would take this seriously now as an accurate indication.

You should also note that, simply from an examination of a family tree, there is no way that we can tell which group moved away and which group remained in the original location (or, indeed, if both groups moved away in different directions). From the family tree above, for example, we cannot say for sure whether the Fijians migrated out of Polynesia, or whether the Polynesians migrated out of Fiji (or whether both groups migrated out of northern or central Vanuatu). It is only by referring to non-linguistic evidence that we can draw such conclusions. In the case of the Oceanic languages, archaeological evidence points to northern and central Vanuatu having been occupied considerably earlier than the islands of Polynesia, so it is probable that the Proto Polynesians originated as a result of a migration out of Fiji.

(b) The nature of cultural contact

Often, when we are able to isolate copied words from directly inherited (i.e. indigenous) words, we can tell something about the nature of the cultural contact that took place at the time the lexical copying took place. Compare the following words in English, for example:

law	justice
freedom	liberty
kingship	royalty

The words on the left are native English words, while those on the right are words copied from French after the invasion of England by the French-speaking Normans in 1066. While the pairs of words are very similar in meaning, most people would probably agree that the issues described by the words to the right are more worth dying for than those described by words on the left. A banner reading *Justice and Liberty* is a more effective call to revolution than one that reads *Law and Freedom*. This fact suggests that when these words were copied from French into English, something was regarded as somehow 'better' simply because it had a French name rather than an English name. That the French language had social prestige over English at the time is indicated by the following statement made by an Englishman in the English of the time:

Vor bote a man conne Frenss, me telth of him lute.

This translates into modern English as follows:

Unless a man knows French, one thinks little of him.

Another example of this kind comes from the American Indian language called Navajo. The Navajo word for 'corn' is **/na:da:ʔ/**. Non-linguistic evidence tells us that the Navajo have only fairly recently acquired a knowledge of corn, and that they learned about it from their neighbours, the Pueblo Indians, who speak a different language. Historically, we can reconstruct this Navajo word back to a compound, which literally meant 'enemy-food'. This suggests that when the Navajo and the Pueblo first came into contact with each other, the Navajo considered the Pueblo Indians to be enemies.

Finally, if we compared the vocabulary of modern Melanesian Pidgin with that of English, we would be able to reconstruct something of the nature of the social contacts that took place between Melanesians and Europeans when the language was in its formative years in the nineteenth century. A European is referred to as *masta* (from English 'master'), while Melanesians were referred to as *boi* (from English 'boy'). A Melanesian was a *boi* even if he happened to be married with five children of his own. A European on the other hand was a *masta* even if he was not yet old enough to shave (though he would then be called a *pikinini masta* 'European boy'). Any Melanesian who managed to make it in the work situation and become an overseer could never be called a *masta* himself — the best he could hope for was to be called a *bosboi* (from 'boss boy').[2] The development of these terms clearly indicates that the Europeans held power over the Melanesians when these words were originally incorporated into Melanesian Pidgin.

(c) Sequences of cultural contact with respect to population splits

It is sometimes possible to tell if certain cultural contacts took place before or after a population split took place. Let us look at the example of the introduction of the sweet potato into the Pacific.

---

[2] Speakers of modern varieties of Melanesian Pidgin have over the past few decades become increasingly aware of the English sources of these words, and these kinds of distinctions are becoming rare. Many people now use purely descriptive labels to refer to people, which do not assign particular status to either race. So, *masta* becomes *waitman*, *boi* becomes *blakman*, and the word *masta* has become a neutral term meaning 'boss', whether European or Melanesian.

We know from botanical evidence that the sweet potato was introduced into the whole Oceanic area relatively recently, and that it certainly was not one of the crops that the Proto Oceanic people brought with them when they settled the Pacific (such as bananas, breadfruit, or yams). Although sweet potato now seems to be very well entrenched in the cultures of Papua New Guinea, it did not arrive there until around the sixteenth century, and it probably came from eastern Indonesia. The sweet potato is not indigenous to Indonesia either; it was introduced to those islands by the Portuguese who first learned about it in South America in the fifteenth and sixteenth centuries. The sweet potato that seems so much at home in Polynesia today is also a recent arrival, though it was probably introduced directly from South America and spread from east to west.

It is also possible to argue on the basis of linguistic evidence that the sweet potato is a relative newcomer to Pacific diets. The word for 'sweet potato' throughout much of Polynesia is /**kumala**/, or something very similar. This word is possibly a direct copy of the word for 'sweet potato' in the Quechua language of Peru, where it is known as /**kumar**/. The same word is also found in many island Melanesian languages, including Fijian and some of the languages of Vanuatu and Solomon Islands (where it was almost certainly introduced in the nineteenth century). Normally, words in the island Melanesian languages have undergone a large number of phonological changes that often make Proto Oceanic words difficult to recognise. For instance, in the Paamese language of Vanuatu, original /***k**/ is regularly lost, for example:

		Paamese	
*a kai	→	a:i	'tree'
*a ika	→	ai	'fish'
*kapika	→	ahi	'Malay apple'
*masakit	→	mesai	'sick'
*penako	→	hena	'steal'
*a tansik	→	atas	'sea'

If there were a word of the shape /***kumala**/ in Proto Oceanic, by the regular changes in the history of Paamese this should have ended up in Paamese as /**umal**/. In fact, Paamese has /**kumala**/, which preserves both the /**k**/ and the final vowel. This therefore suggests that Paamese acquired the word /**kumala**/ (and presumably also the thing it referred to) *after* all of the other phonological changes had taken place in the language.

(d) The content of a culture
Given the fact that a language bears a very close relationship to the culture of the people who speak it, we can also tell something about the nature of the culture of a people simply by looking at the language that they speak. This applies as much to a language that is in use today as to a reconstructed protolanguage.

A major aspect of the relationship that holds between a language and the culture of its speakers is the fact that there is always lexical richness in areas of cultural importance, and there is a corresponding lack of lexical development in areas that are of little importance culturally. Speakers of Polynesian languages typically have a number of different names for different kinds of bananas and sweet potato, and taro. Of course, we would expect that the Inuit language of Canada would not have any words at all for any of these things, since its speakers live in a place where it is more appropriate to develop lexical specialisation for talking about snow.

When we apply this basic principle to a reconstructed protolanguage as a way of determining the content of a protoculture, we are using what is called the *Wörter und Sachen* technique of cultural reconstruction. *Wörter* is a German word meaning 'words', while *Sachen* means 'things', and the name of the technique itself translates as 'words and things'. Basically, the argument goes, if we can reconstruct a word for something in a protolanguage, then we can assume that the thing it refers to was probably of cultural importance in the life of its speakers, or that it was environmentally salient.

A considerable amount of research has already been carried out on reconstructing the vocabulary of the Proto Austronesian language that is the ancestor of all of the Austronesian languages spoken throughout the Pacific, as well as much of Southeast Asia. The reconstructed vocabulary for this language includes items expressing meanings such as the following:

'taro'
'yam'
'banana'
'sugarcane'
'sago'
'breadfruit'
'orange'
'pandanus'
'betel nut'
'coconut'
'casuarina tree'
'fallow land'
'cultivate'
'food garden'
'to weed'
'shoot, sucker of plant'

'wild pig'
'(of pig) root up ground'
'domestic pig'

'canoe'
'sail'
'sea travel'
'paddle'
'steer'
'bail out (water)'
'fish hook'
'derris poison (for killing fish)'
'high tide'
'giant clam'
'seaweed'
'conch shell'
'fish scale'
'octopus'

'clay pot'
'shoot'
'broom'
'needle'
'bow'

Applying this technique, the overall picture that emerges of the Proto Austronesian speaking society can be paraphrased as follows from the words of the Austronesian scholar Robert Blust:

they were settled people, occupied villages which contained some kind of public building and dwelling units, raised on posts (and thus entered by ladders), with thatched gabled roofs, internal fireplaces, and a number of storage shelves and wooden headrests. They possessed domesticated pigs, fowls and dogs. They hunted, wove, potted, used needle and thread, tattooed themselves, chewed betel nut and drank some kind of intoxicating drink . . . They had a well developed maritime technology, but also cultivated root crops, as well as rice and millet. They hunted heads, and used the bow and bamboo stakes in their hunting.

There is one further interesting point. For Proto Austronesian, there are two reconstructed words for 'pig':

| *babui | 'wild pig' |
| *beɣek | 'domesticated pig' |

Archaeological evidence indicates that there were originally no pigs in Melanesia and Polynesia. Also, the Oceanic languages only have a re-constructible word for 'tame pig', but none for 'wild pig'. This fits in nicely with the archaeological evidence, as we can conclude that it was Austronesian-speaking people who first introduced pigs into Melanesia and Polynesia. The only way to get to both of these areas from Southeast Asia is

by sea, so it is logical that Proto Oceanic would only have had a word for
'tame pig'. We would hardly expect people to have risked taking wild pigs
with them in their ocean-going canoes, as wild pigs can be quite dangerous.
Any wild pigs that we find in Melanesia and Polynesia today would therefore
have to be the descendants of these original tame pigs that had escaped over
the years and gone feral. Another interesting point is that in many of the non-
Austronesian languages of Papua New Guinea, the word for 'pig' seems to
have been copied from forms derived from /*beʁek/. This would be consistent with what I have just said, as there would have been no pigs at all in
areas occupied by speakers of non-Austronesian languages until they were
introduced by the first speakers of Austronesian languages.

(e) The homeland of a people
In addition to giving us some ideas about the content of a protoculture, the
Wörter und Sachen technique can also tell us something about the homeland
of a language family. (Note that the original homeland of a language family is
sometimes referred to in the literature by the German word *Urheimat*, from
Heimat 'homeland', corresponding to the term *Ursprache* meaning 'protolanguage', from *Sprache* 'language'.)

From the Proto Austronesian vocabulary that we have just examined, it is
obvious that the ancestral people must have lived on an island, or on the
mainland very close to the sea. They clearly lived in a tropical rather than a
temperate or cold environment. They lived in an area that had crocodiles, as
there is a reconstructible word /*buqaja/ 'crocodile'. This fact alone rules out
anywhere in Polynesia and many parts of island Melanesia as the Proto
Austronesian homeland, as these areas do not have native crocodiles. Using
all of the linguistic data that we have, we can reconstruct for these people a
homeland around Taiwan or southern China. We do know that around 10,000
years ago, the Chinese people pushed southward, presumably eventually
pushing out the ancestors of the modern Austronesian speakers, who then
spread to the Philippines and Indonesia, and eventually to the Pacific area.

We can sometimes use the *Wörter und Sachen* technique to make some
guesses about the actual routes followed by people in reaching their present
locations. There is, for example, a word for 'owl' everywhere in Polynesia
(except those areas that do not have owls). The word that we can reconstruct
for this meaning in Proto Polynesian is /*lulu/. In Hawaii, there are owls, but
the word that is used to refer to them is not a reflex of /*lulu/, but is a quite
different form altogether: /pueo/. From this, scholars have argued that Hawaii
might have been settled from an area where there are no native owls. One
such area is the Marquesas Islands, near Tahiti. On arriving in their new
home, the ancestors of the modern Hawaiians would have come across owls
again, but these birds would have by then been new to them so they would
have needed to find a new name.

Biologists have argued that certain species of mosquitoes were spread to
Polynesia by human settlement. In fact, in eastern Polynesia (Hawaii, Tahiti,

and the Marquesas), the first Europeans in the area hardly noticed any mosquitoes at all. In these areas, the original word for mosquito, /*ŋamuk/, had taken on the new meaning of 'sandfly', which is a smaller insect, but with an extremely itchy bite. In Hawaiian, the mosquito is now known by a different word altogether: /makika/ (which is possibly copied from English), and in Māori it is referred to as /waeroa/, which literally means 'long legs'. These facts suggest that when the Polynesians first arrived in Aotearoa and Hawaii, there were no mosquitoes there at all (or that they had come from a place where there were no mosquitoes). The original name that people knew came to refer instead to another small insect that also had a bite which caused itching, i.e. the sandfly. When the mosquito finally made its way into these islands (perhaps only with the arrival of the first Europeans), the people had to find a new name to refer to it, either by copying the word from English, or by creating a new compound from words that already existed in the language.

There are numerous examples of the same kind which indicate clearly that the Māori settled the much cooler island of Aotearoa from a more tropical location. We can probably reconstruct the Proto Polynesians as being drinkers of kava, and the word in their language for the plant was /*kava/. The early Polynesians had probably developed a set of fairly elaborate ceremonies associated with the drinking of kava, in contrast to those Melanesian societies further to the west where kava has probably always been drunk in a more recreational and a much less ritualised way. We can be reasonably certain both that the Māori came from a tropical area and that kava ceremonies were part of Polynesian culture when they left a thousand years ago because of the existence of reflexes of the original word /*kava/ in Māori. The kava plant only grows in tropical climates and will not grow in New Zealand. When the Māori first arrived in Aotearoa just under a thousand years ago, they certainly brought with them a knowledge of this tropical plant and the ritual with which it was associated. The name of the plant was retained, but it came to apply to another plant found in New Zealand that looked similar to the original kava plant, but it was reduplicated to indicate that the first settlers recognised the fact that it was not exactly the same plant. So in Māori today we have the /kawakawa/ plant. That kava drinking was associated with ritual when the Māori arrived is indicated by the fact that the regular reflex of /*kava/ in Māori is /kawa/, but this word has come to refer instead to the sprig of any tree that is used ceremonially, as well as ceremonial protocol in general.

There is another way of reconstructing the homeland of a protolanguage and that involves the *Age-Area Hypothesis*. This hypothesis says that the area that has the greatest diversity in terms of the number of first-order subgroups is likely to be the location of the original homeland. In saying this, we are assuming the lowest number of population movements in order to account for the geographical distribution of the subgroups (and remember that in historical linguistics we always choose the simplest and most reasonable solution to a problem rather than a more complex one, unless there are very good reasons for preferring the more complex answer). Let us take an example. Imagine that we have a language family that is divided up into a number of subgroups which are located geographically as follows:

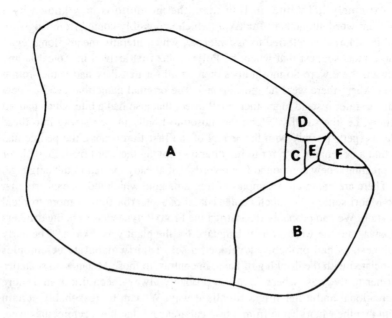

By the Age-Area Hypothesis, the original homeland is likely to have been the area in which the subgroups **BCDEF** meet. This would require that we set up only one major population shift from the original area, that of the subgroup **A** which moved to the west. On the other hand, if we were to suggest that the area covered by **A** were to represent the original homeland, then we would need to argue for *separate* movements for the populations of **B, C, D, E,** and **F** to get to their present locations in the east.

In Melanesia and the Pacific, the greatest area of subgrouping diversity in Austronesian languages is to be found in Melanesia rather than in Polynesia or Micronesia, and in Melanesia the greatest area of diversity is to be found in Papua New Guinea. This therefore suggests that the original homeland of the Oceanic languages lies somewhere in Papua New Guinea, and certainly not in Solomon Islands, Vanuatu, New Caledonia, Fiji, Micronesia, or Polynesia.

Turning our attention now to the non-Austronesian languages of New Guinea, if we were ever able to demonstrate that these are all descended from a common ancestor (which nobody has so far been able to prove), then the most likely area of the original settlement would have been either the Sepik or the Bird's Head area of Irian Jaya, as the map below indicates that these are the areas that have the greatest numbers of distinct 'phyla'.

Sometimes we find that languages or language families are splintered, or *discontiguous*; that is, they are spoken in areas that do not join, and are

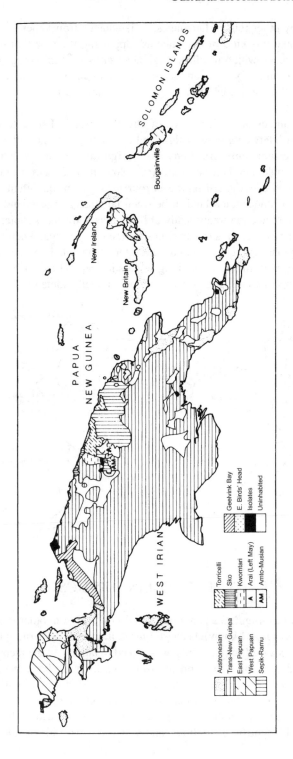

separated by other related languages, or languages from other families. We can often take this kind of evidence as supporting the idea that migrations have taken place which result in originally contiguous groupings becoming separated. Ordinarily, we can assume that languages, or entire language families, will occupy contiguous areas unless they are forced apart by some other factors.

The languages of the Tufi area of Oro Province in Papua New Guinea represent an interesting case of this kind of situation. In the following map, you can see that there are many discontiguous languages. The Maisin language is spoken in three separate areas, Notu in three areas, Korafe in two, Ubir in two, and Arifama-Miniafa in four. Apart from this, there are fairly large areas of unoccupied land in between languages. The inland Orokaiva people had a reputation traditionally of being a very warlike people, and quite possibly what happened is that they pushed their earlier inland neighbours out of their original neighbourhood into the safer uninhabited coastal areas, with the resulting very mixed-up looking linguistic map. The distribution of the languages in this area suggests that this was originally some kind of 'refugee' area.

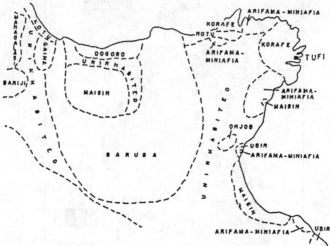

13.5 PALAEOLINGUISTICS

The term *palaeolinguistics* is not one that you will find in other textbooks of linguistics (as far as I know), because I made it up as I was writing this book. I created it because I felt that there was a need to talk about the reconstruction of the far distant past, beyond the time to which we have been able to reconstruct by means of the comparative method (but which non-linguistic sciences such as archaeology can still tell us something about). The word derives, of course, from the prefix *palaeo-*, which is attached to the names of a number of scientific disciplines, and which means 'old' or 'ancient', for example, palaeobiology, palaeoecology, palaeogeology, and palaeozoology.

Unfortunately, the comparative method of linguistic reconstruction does not allow us to go back in time nearly as far as other sciences. It is difficult to put dates to linguistic changes for which we do not have written records (though in Chapter 8 I did discuss glottochronology as one way of attempting to put actual dates on linguistic developments). It is probable that proto-languages such as Proto Indo-European and Proto Austronesian are not much more than 5000 years old, and certainly no older than 10,000 years old. The comparative method cannot take us further back in time for a very simple reason. Given that languages gradually lose vocabulary over time, when they have been separated for a very long period of time, they will have only a very small proportion of shared vocabulary. In order to set up systematic sound correspondences between languages, we need to have a reasonably large body of cognate items. When the corpus of shared items gets too small, we simply cannot recognise any systematic sound correspondences at all, and without systematic sound correspondences the comparative method becomes completely unworkable.

Archaeologists tell us that the modern variety of *Homo sapiens* (or modern humankind) is probably at least 100,000 years old. We do not know when human beings first acquired the capacity for language, but when humanity made its first major ocean crossing between Southeast Asia and what was then the continent of Sahul (which now consists of the islands of New Guinea, Australia, and Tasmania) at least 40,000 years ago (and possibly considerably more), the general assumption seems to be that those people were equipped with fully developed linguistic systems.

There are all sorts of interesting questions about language that we would like to have answers for. Did Proto Human ever exist as a single language? If so, what was it like? Who spoke it? And where did it develop? Or did *Homo sapiens* independently develop the capacity for language in a number of different locations? If so, how many original languages were spoken at the dawn of humanity? Fascinating questions indeed, but so far not questions that we can satisfactorily answer. The limiting factor here is simply that after 100,000 years, any similarities that there might once have been between languages have been obliterated by such a long period of separation and constant linguistic evolution.

It is not just the fact that the languages themselves have been changing, either. In order to reconstruct a protolanguage, we need to have information on *all* of the daughter languages. If crucial features of the parent language were retained in a language for which we now have no records, then those features will be unreconstructible. Over the millennia, uncountable numbers of languages must have developed and then disappeared with no trace, for a variety of catastrophic reasons: warfare, famine, diseases, natural disasters, climate changes, losses of territory with changing sea levels. So Proto Human (if it ever existed) is unreconstructible not just because of limitations in the comparative method, but also unreconstructible *in principle*, because we can never assemble the data that we need in order to be able to carry out such a reconstruction. It has been recognised for a very long time that the reconstruction of Proto Human is a dead-end, and as early as 1886, the prestigious Linguistic Society of Paris decreed that it would not host discussions concerning the origin of language, as it considered this pointless.

If we wanted to say anything at all about the nature of the first human language (or languages), the only possible course available to us would be to tackle the question as part of the quest for *linguistic universals*. A major thrust in linguistics in the last few decades has been the search for features of language that are common to all human languages. If we can establish that certain features are indeed found in all human languages, this raises the possibility that perhaps some aspects of language are 'wired in' at birth as part of some kind of innate (as against learned) language capacity, and that we might even have inherited such genetic information all the way back from our ancestors who spoke Proto Human. Obviously, this is just a theoretical possibility at the moment, and even if linguists were able to present us with some of the features of Proto Human in this way, we would still be a long way from having reconstructed the language as such.

Even without attempting to go back as far as Proto Human, we face severe problems when we try to link established language families further back than we have already been able to reconstruct. We know that Australia, New Guinea, and Tasmania were all settled ultimately from the same direction (i.e. from Southeast Asia), but we are unable to find any provable relationships between the languages of Australia and the languages of New Guinea and Tasmania, which were separated only when the rising oceans cut off Torres Strait (between New Guinea and Australia) about 8000 years ago, and Bass Strait (between Tasmania and Australia) possibly 12,000 years ago. In fact, while the existence of Proto Australian as the ancestor of all Australian languages has been widely assumed, it has never been satisfactorily proved by a rigid application of the comparative method. It has also long been known that the non-Austronesian languages of New Guinea are extremely diverse, and fall into a significant number of completely unrelated language families. (Of course, the relationship of the Tasmanian languages will forever remain a mystery because the last fluent speaker of any of these languages died in 1876, and the information that was recorded on these languages before then was so poor that it will never be possible to do anything useful with it in terms of linguistic reconstruction.)

Attempts to relate the Australian languages to languages further afield have been equally unsuccessful. For a while, scholars thought that the Dravidian languages might prove to be a good place to look, but it turned out that the similarities between the two groups of languages were too superficial to prove anything. The languages are typologically similar, but there is no evidence of systematic sound correspondence between the two families. Another scholar formulated what has come to be referred to as the *Indo-Pacific Hypothesis*, which suggests that there is a large language family consisting of all of the non-Austronesian languages of Melanesia, Tasmania, and the Andaman Islands (in the Bay of Bengal). This has remained nothing more than a hypothesis, and until someone can point to the existence of regular sound correspondences in any proposed sets of cognates, it is likely to continue to be regarded by mainstream historical linguists as being extremely suspect, at best.

But if the 'Indo-Pacific' languages, or just the Australian languages, or just the languages of New Guinea, do turn out to be descended from common ancestors, these ancestor languages are possibly going to be just as unreconstructible as Proto Human, and for basically the same reasons that I have just given. It may be that we are talking about languages that go back more than 40,000 years in time. Between then and now, there have been great changes in sea level. Once, most of the ocean between Australia and New Guinea was probably occupied by people speaking an unknown number of languages, and when the sea levels rose over time, there must have been considerable realignment of occupation patterns and languages.

The archaeological evidence that I referred to in the first section of this chapter opens up a number of questions concerning the origin of the Australian languages. Are the modern Australian languages all descended from a single protolanguage that may have been spoken 40,000 (or even 60,000) years ago? Or are they descended from the language of the people who introduced the dog about 5000 years ago? Or are some of the languages descended from an older, original language, and others descended from a more recently introduced language? Until linguists are able to carry their reconstructions further back in time than we are able to do at the moment, these questions will have to remain unanswered.

The kinds of questions that I am addressing here are not restricted just to a discussion of the settlement of Melanesia, Australia, and Tasmania. Archaeologists tell us that the indigenous peoples of North and South America (now known by a variety of names, including Indians, American Indians, Native Americans, Amerindians, Eskimo, Inuit, Maya, Aztec, Inca, and so on) are all descended from people who migrated from Asia via a land bridge that once existed where Bering Strait is now found. These migrations have not been dated with certainty, but most of the evidence so far suggests that they took place thousands of years after the migration of people into Australia and Melanesia. If the indigenous American languages were to be related in a single language family, then we would expect that the evidence for this relationship might be easier to find than with the languages of Melanesia and Australia. Unfortunately, linguists using the comparative method have been unable to come up with any reliable evidence that these languages are all descended from a common ancestor. These languages can be related into a number of separate large families, but there is, so far, no convincing evidence of any relationship further back in time between these large families.

The difficulty in establishing distant relationships has prompted some linguists to try new methods. Some have claimed successes in demonstrating that the Native American languages *do* have a common linguistic source, and others have claimed to demonstrate that the Australian languages *are* related to the Dravidian languages of India (as well as the Uralic language family, which includes Finnish, Hungarian, Estonian, Lappish, and a number of languages spoken in the Russian Federation, such as Samoyed). One scholar has attempted to demonstrate that the Australian, Dravidian, and Uralic languages are all related, but he did not use a method that is recognisable to ordinary comparative linguists. What he did instead was make use of a statistical comparison of root structures in representative languages from each of the three language families (assuming, of course, that the Australian languages *are* related in a single family). I will outline the technique that was followed below.

The vocabularies of a single representative language from each family were compared: Warlpiri in the case of Australian, Tamil in the case of Dravidian, and Finnish in the case of Uralic. Rather than searching for regular sound correspondences, a comparison was made in the initial syllables of words expressing the same meanings. Statistical calculations were then done to see whether the similarities in initial syllables that could be observed were purely random similarities or whether there were similarities that could not be put down to pure chance. Similarities that are greater than chance must have some kind of explanation — the most obvious one being that the languages have a common ancestor. A statistical study of the initial syllables in this particular set of languages did in fact reach the conclusion that the similarities were more than could be expected on a random basis.

Linguists will still be reluctant to accept that these languages are related, and I too would advise caution in interpreting these results. Because the argument involves statistics, it must first be considered in detail by comparative linguists who also have a good knowledge of probability theory. As a non-statistician, there are several other questions that come to my mind. Do the same results show up if we compare not just the initial syllables between the languages, but the whole words? According to this method, words as diverse as Finnish /**pakku**/, Tamil /**pari**/, and Warlpiri /**paṭina**/, all meaning 'break', and Finnish /**kuras**/, Tamil /**kuṇil**/, and Warlpiri /**kuturu**/, all meaning 'club', are counted as cognate because of the identity in the initial syllables. However, we might be less willing to count these as cognate if we were to consider the entire roots. Another question to consider is whether or not we get the same results if we compare a different Australian language with different Dravidian and Uralic languages.

While many attempts at palaeolinguistic comparisons fall far short of scientific respectability, the writings of Johanna Nichols since the mid-1980s have attracted considerable interest among some linguists, as well as archaeologists and others interested in establishing relationships at much greater time-depths than is possible using the comparative method.

Nichols' approach is more akin to population science in that she does not aim to study the evolution of individual languages, or even closely related groups of languages. Rather, she aims to study the history of 'populations' of languages. By this, she means that she considers large groupings of languages together, dealing not with particular features of individual languages, but broader general features of language groupings. Thus, she considers, for example, the languages of Australia or Africa as a whole. She pays attention not to whether structural features are present or absent, but to what are the statistical frequencies and distributions of features are within these larger populations of languages.

Such linguistic markers are considered to be akin to biological markers in that they can be used to identify affinities between populations at considerable time-depths. She argues that if, in the languages of a continent (or some other large geographical area), a feature shows up with a high frequency, this distribution is not something that is due to recent diffusion. When several markers of this type are shared, this is taken as being indicative of historical affinity. Of course, such features must be known to be typologically unrelated. It would not be terribly meaningful, for example, to examine the distribution of **SOV** word order and postpositions as these two features tend to go hand in hand in historically unconnected languages.

She examined a sample of 174 languages, which she divided into three major areas: (i) the languages of Africa, the Middle East, northern Eurasia and South and Southeast Asia, (ii) the Australia, New Guinea and Oceania, and (iii) the Americas.

She included in her sample a significant range of the genetic variety that was to be found within each of these three geographical areas. The kinds of linguistic features that she compares include things such as: basic clause alignment (i.e. whether there is nominative-accusative or ergative-absolutive marking in the clause), the presence vs absence of an inclusive/exclusive distinction in pronouns, the level of morphological complexity, whether or not inalienable and inalienable possession are distinguished, and whether or not there are nominal classifiers.

The actual application and interpretation of Nichols' method is complex and it is unlikely to become the standard model by which individual historical linguists will attempt to study linguistic relationships. However, she does draw some quite dramatic conclusions out of the data that she analyses, and I will now summarise some of her ideas.

Regarding Australia and New Guinea, she claims to have found evidence for the distribution of a number of features in some areas that are common to these languages and the western languages of her Old World grouping, such as case-marking systems, the lack of noun classes, ergativity and lack of tonal systems. Another set of features — accusativity, the presence of noun classes, and the presence of tones — has a much narrower distribution in Australia and New Guinea. These features tend to recur in eastern Asia. Finally, she identifies features that are characteristic of the entire area of Australia and New Guinea, including relatively simple consonant inventories.

From this, she concludes that an early linguistic stratum occupied the entire continent of Sahul (which is how archaeologists refer to Australia and New Guinea together before they were separated in relatively recent times by rising sea levels). A second stratum resulted from a later linguistic colonisation of the area, which has its greatest concentration of residual features in the northwest, which presumably represented the point of entry.

Applying the same kind of thinking at a world level, Nichols argues for a three-stage spread of human language since its origin in Africa over 100,000 years ago. Features that derive from this period, it turns out, are not discernible in modern languages, so we can only make assumptions about this period on the basis of non-linguistic evidence. The second period of linguistic history involves a spread of languages from the Old World areas across Eurasia around the Pacific Rim and through to the Americas between about 60,000 and 30,000 years ago. This would have been the period in which the languages of Sahul arrived in what is now New Guinea and Australia. Finally, in the post-glacial period, we see the development of complex and large-scale societies and the emergence of political and economic power, which has resulted in an overall reduction in linguistic diversity.

13.6 THE RELIABILITY OF CULTURAL RECONSTRUCTION

Having looked in detail at the kind of information that historical linguistics can provide about cultural history, we should ask ourselves an additional question: how *reliable* is this information, and how well does this information tie in with information provided by archaeology, oral history, and comparative culture? In general terms, what historical linguistics can tell us about cultural history depends on how we subgroup languages in a particular family, and what we reconstruct in the vocabulary of a protolanguage. Our conclusions about cultural history can therefore only be as accurate as our subgrouping and our lexical reconstruction.

You have already seen that subgrouping is not always certain. In some cases there may be contradictory evidence when you are trying to set up subgroups, depending on what sorts of facts you choose to give more reliance to. For instance, some scholars have argued that the area of greatest subgrouping diversity within the Austronesian language family includes those Austronesian languages which are indigenous to Taiwan, off the coast of southern China. This fits in nicely with the proposition that I have mentioned elsewhere in this chapter that the linguistic evidence suggests this part of the world as the Austronesian homeland. However, linguists who make this particular subgrouping claim do so on the basis of shared grammatical and phonological innovations in the languages of Taiwan, but what we regard as a shared innovation or a shared retention depends on what we actually reconstruct in the protolanguage itself. If our grammatical or phonological reconstruction itself contains errors, then the subgroupings that are based on those reconstructions will also be wrong. Some linguists, for instance, have claimed that it is in the Melanesian area that we have the area of greatest diversity in the Austronesian family (though most of these arguments have rested on lexicostatistical evidence, which you have already seen is not necessarily reliable). If this were true, then we would be speaking of a Melanesian homeland for Proto Austronesian, rather than a homeland in southern China.

Also, if our reconstruction of the content of the vocabulary of a proto-language is inaccurate, then any statements that we make about the nature of the original culture and the original homeland may also be misleading. It is not difficult for our lexical reconstructions to be wrong, as the *Wörter und Sachen* technique that I described earlier is not completely infallible as a way of reconstructing the culture of a people in the past. While the comparative method produces fairly reliable reconstructions of the earlier forms of words, we cannot always guarantee that we have reconstructed the correct original meanings. We have already seen that semantic reconstruction cannot be carried out nearly as confidently as phonological reconstruction. For instance, the modern Algonquian languages of North America (mostly spoken in Canada) have words for 'whisky' that are compounds of 'fire' and 'water', as well as words for 'train' that are compounds of the words for 'iron' and 'horse'. By strictly applying the comparative method, it would be logically possible to reconstruct Proto Algonquian words for both 'whisky' and 'train' that are based on these roots. Of course, we know from historical evidence that speakers of Algonquian languages came into contact with whisky and trains only with the arrival of the Europeans in the last few hundred years. These examples clearly involve parallel lexical developments, and such developments in related languages are often especially difficult to distinguish from shared innovations.

Where this technique produces cultural reconstructions that seem plausible within the bounds of what archaeologists already know, there is likely to be little significant dispute about their reliability. However, given that parallel semantic shifts can (and do) take place, it is logically possible for the *Wörter und Sachen* technique to produce archaeologically improbable protocultures. For instance, the form /*tusi/ can be reliably reconstructed as a Proto Polynesian word, and the reflex of this in most of the modern Polynesian languages means either 'write' or 'book' (or both). If we were to assume that this represents the original meaning of /*tusi/ then we would need to reconstruct Proto Polynesian society as having been literate. At the time of European contact, however, none of these societies was literate, and there is no archaeological evidence of writing on any of the Lapita pottery (though people were decorating these pots with hand-drawn designs). We know from written records dating from the time of the early European missionaries that the modern reflexes of /*tusi/ only came to refer to writing and books after contact with European missionaries. The original meanings of these words were more likely to have been 'make a mark', or something of that nature.

Earlier in this chapter I mentioned the work of Robert Blust in applying the *Wörter und Sachen* technique in the reconstruction of Proto Austronesian culture. He also concluded that iron was known by these early peoples, yet there is no archaeological support for this kind of reconstruction this early in history. Archaeologists are fairly confident that metallurgy appeared suddenly in Southeast Asia only about 2200 years ago, which was well after the spread of the Austronesian languages had taken place. So, linguists probably have to be more careful in distinguishing between direct inheritance and parallel semantic shifts in very ancient forms.

READING GUIDE QUESTIONS

1. What is archaeology and what kinds of historical information can archaeologists provide?
2. How reliable is the historical evidence provided by oral tradition? What factors influence the reliability of this kind of data?
3. What is meant by the term comparative culture? What kinds of historical information can it provide?
4. How can historical linguists tell us something about the relative order in which population splits take place?
5. What can we tell about the nature of cultural contact between two societies from linguistic evidence?
6. How can we tell something about the relative timing of a borrowed cultural feature from linguistic evidence?
7. What is the *Wörter und Sachen* technique of cultural reconstruction?
8. What are the problems involved in applying the *Wörter und Sachen* technique?
9. How can we make guesses about a people's homeland and migration routes from the linguistic evidence?
10. What can historical linguistics tell us about the very ancient relationships between populations?
11. What is meant by linguistic universals and what is their importance?
12. Can the existence of Proto Human ever be demonstrated or disproven? Why?
13. What are the inherent weaknesses in cultural reconstruction?

EXERCISES

1. In the languages of northern and central Vanuatu, the words for 'kava' are derived from a form that can be reconstructed with the form /*maloku/. A word derived from the same original form appears in Fijian, with the meaning 'quiet, subdued' (which is how kava makes the drinker feel if it is sufficiently strong). The Polynesian languages have

words derived from the reconstructed form /*kava/ to refer to the same thing. In some Polynesian languages this word also means 'bitter' (which is what kava tastes like when it is drunk). The languages of southern Vanuatu are not closely related to the Polynesian languages, and they have undergone many far-reaching phonological changes which generally make forms that are cognate with Polynesian words almost unrecognisable at first glance. The word for 'kava' in the languages of southern Vanuatu are mostly something like /**nikava**/, in which the initial syllable represents an earlier noun marker that has been reanalysed as part of the root.

From all of this evidence, do you think that kava may have been discovered once, twice, or three times?

2. Examine the following map showing the distribution of Austronesian languages on the mainland of the island of New Guinea. Assume that these languages originated outside of New Guinea, and say which direction you think they might have come from. Give your reasons.

3. In southern New Ireland and northern New Britain in Papua New Guinea, the following languages are found:

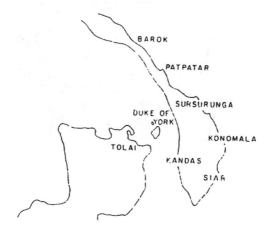

These are all related within a single subgroup, the internal subgrouping of which (as suggested by the lexicostatistical evidence) is as follows:

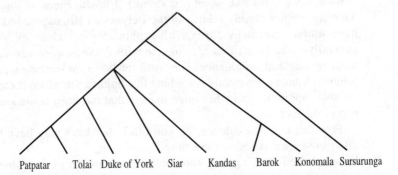

Patpatar   Tolai Duke of York   Siar   Kandas   Barok   Konomala Sursurunga

Can you suggest a possible pattern of migration that is consistent with this subgrouping, and with the fact that languages in the nearest related higher-level subgroup are spoken to the immediate north of Barok? Note also that the languages spoken to the south of Tolai are completely unrelated non-Austronesian languages.

4. The following words have been reconstructed for Proto Algonquian, the ancestor to the American Indian languages spoken in the areas shaded on the map below:

*weʃawe:minʃja   'American beech tree'
*name:kwa   'lake trout fish'
*a:çkikwa   'harbour seal'
*atehkwa   'woodland caribou'

The following maps show the area where each of these four species are native. On the basis of this evidence, where might you suggest that the Algonquian languages originated from?

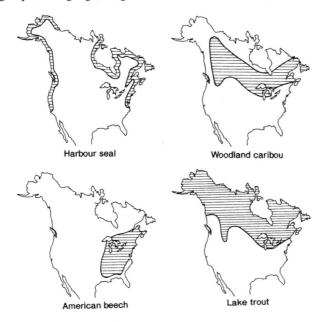

Harbour seal

Woodland caribou

American beech

Lake trout

5. In the past there have been theories that the Polynesians originated in South America and even from the islands off the coast of British Columbia. Most scholars regard such theories as belonging to the lunatic fringe. Why do you think they feel this so strongly?

6. Go back to Exercise 6 at the end of Chapter 8 in which you were asked to compare the Māori language and Moriori (the now extinct language of the Chatham Islands to the east of New Zealand). In the nineteenth century, some observers argued that the Moriori represented a pre-Māori Melanesian population. Do you think that this is likely? On the basis of the linguistic evidence, where do you think that the Moriori came from?

FURTHER READING

1. Theodora Bynon *Historical Linguistics,* Chapter 7 'Language and Prehistory', pp. 262–80.
2. Raimo Anttila *An Introduction to Historical and Comparative Linguistics*, Chapter 21 'Change and Reconstruction in Culture and Linguistics', pp. 377–88.
3. Morris Swadesh 'Linguistics as an instrument of prehistory' in Dell Hymes (ed.) *Language in Culture and Society*, pp. 575–84.
4. Donald Denoon and Roderic Lacey (eds) *Oral Tradition in Melanesia.*
5. Pamela Swadling *Papua New Guinea's Prehistory: An Introduction.*
6. Peter Bellwood *The Polynesians: The Prehistory of an Island People.*

7.   Brian M. Fagan *The Great Journey: The Peopling of Ancient America.*
8.   Alan Thorne and Robert Raymond *Man on the Rim: The Peopling of the Pacific.*
9.   Colin Renfrew *Archaeology and Language: The Puzzle of Indo-European Origins.*
10. Johanna Nichols *Linguistic Diversity in Space and Time.*

DATA SETS

The following sets of data are used in the exercises at the end of several chapters as an aid in acquiring different skills. Rather than repeat each set of data in each chapter, these Data Sets are attached as an appendix, and students are referred to the Data Sets by number in each particular question.

DATA SET 1 — PALAUAN (Micronesia)

*hataj	→	ʔað	'liver'
*lajaɣ	→	jarəs	'sail'
*ɹalan	→	rajl	'road'
*apuj	→	ŋaw	'fire'
*mata	→	mað	'eye'
*cinaɣ	→	sils	'light'
*cucu	→	tut	'breast'
*bulan	→	bujl	'moon'
*batu	→	bað	'stone'
*ikan	→	ŋikəl	'fish'
*huɹan	→	ʔull	'rain'
*laɲit	→	jaŋəð	'sky'
*buŋa	→	buŋ	'flower'
*pəɲu	→	wel	'turtle'
*dəŋəɣ	→	reŋəs	'hear'

DATA SET 2 — NGANYAYWANA
(New South Wales, Australia)

*ŋaːnaŋ	→	anaŋa	'who'
*wiːgan	→	igana	'snow'
*baːbaŋa	→	abaŋa	'father'
*miːgin	→	igina	'star'
*miːl	→	ila	'eye'
*gaːbulgaːn	→	abulgana	'shark'

321

*bargan	→	argana	'boomerang'
*winba	→	inba	'fire'
*buruluŋ	→	ruluŋa	'fly'
*wambuɲa	→	mbuɲa	'kangaroo'
*bagar	→	gara	'meat'
*ganaj	→	naja	'yam stick'
*dimin	→	mina	'nits'
*guruman	→	rumana	'boy'
*wigaj	→	gjaja	'food'
*gugaŋa	→	gwaŋa	'child'
*gubila	→	bwila	'possum'
*giɲinma	→	ɲirma	'scratch'

DATA SET 3 — MBABARAM
(North Queensland, Australia)

*wula	→	lo	'die'
*ŋali	→	li	'we'
*ɖawa	→	we	'mouth'
*guju	→	ju	'fish'
*guwa	→	wo	'west'
*ɖana	→	ne	'stand'
*bamba	→	mba	'belly'
*ŋaba	→	bo	'bathe'
*wuna	→	no	'lie down'
*ɖiba	→	be	'liver'
*gumbi	→	mbi	'penis'
*naga	→	ga	'east'
*ɲulu	→	lu	'he'
*gunda	→	ndo	'cut up'

DATA SET 4 — YIMAS AND KARAWARI
(East Sepik, Papua New Guinea)

		Yimas	Karawari	
*sikir	→	tikit	sikir	'chair'
*jakus	→	jakut	jakus	'string bag'
*samban	→	tamban	samban	'lover'
*panmari	→	panmaʎ	panmari	'male'
*sisin	→	tirin	sisin	'tooth'
*naniŋ	→	naniŋ	janiŋ	'fat'
*sambajm	→	tambajm	sambajm	'basket hanger'
*nawkwan	→	nawkwan	jawkwan	'chicken'

*nam	→	nam	jam	'house'
*sambɨn	→	tambɨn	sambɨn	'tail'
*sɨmun	→	tɨmun	sɨmun	'cane'
*pariapa	→	paʎapa	pariapa	'verandah'
*manbaw	→	manbaw	manbo	'death adder'
*tumbaw	→	tumbaw	tumbo	'crocodile'

DATA SET 5 — LAKALAI
(West New Britain, Papua New Guinea)

*kani	→	ali	'eat'
*ikan	→	ia	'fish'
*lima	→	lima	'hand'
*paʔa	→	vaha	'leg'
*ʔate	→	hate	'liver'
*kutu	→	utu	'lice'
*ʔunsan	→	hura	'rain'
*ʔanso	→	haro	'sun'
*lipon	→	livo	'tooth'
*danu	→	lalu	'water'
*taŋi	→	tali	'cry'
*tapine	→	tavile	'woman'

DATA SET 6 — SUENA AND ZIA
(Morobe Province, Papua New Guinea)

(This data has been slightly regularised.)

Suena	Zia	
ni	ni	'bird'
ɟo	jo	'mercy'
wo	wo	'meat, fish'
pu	pu	'pig'
wa	wã	'boat'
su	su	'soup'
wi	wi	'penis'
mu	mũ	'sap'
be	be	'mouth'
pigi	p̃igi	'lime'
me	mẽ	'shame'
ari	ari	'vagina'
goroba	gorobo	'cycad tree'
moka	moko	'inside'

wena	weno	'nose'
tuma	tumo	'back of neck'
duba	dubo	'throat'
ɟaɟo	jaɟo	'name'
ema	emo	'man'
me	me	'urine'

DATA SET 7 — KORAFE, NOTU AND BINANDERE
(Oro Province, Papua New Guinea)

Korafe	Notu	Binandere	
ɟoka	ɟo	do	'mercy'
ɟoʔka	ɟo	do	'inside'
ɟaʔka	ɟa	da	'betel nut'
ɟawo	ɟawo	dao	'name'
biɟo	biɟo	bido	'banana'
susu	susu-	tutu	'meaning'
toʔka	to	to	'hole'
-	tewo	teo	'bowl'
dubo	dubo	dubo	'throat'
dika	di	-	'tooth'

DATA SET 8 — PAAMESE (Vanuatu)

North	South	
eim	aim	'house'
amai	amal	'reef'
a:i	a:l	'stinging tree'
oul	aul	'maggot'
out	aut	'place'
he	hel	'step'
mea	mela	'get up'
takul	takul	'sago'
hae	hale	'outside'
keil	kail	'they'
teilaŋ	teilaŋ	'sky'
tahe	tahel	'wave'
moul	maul	'alive'
mavul	mavul	'broken'
houlu	haulu	'many'
ateli	ateli	'basket'

DATA SET 9 — MOTU
(Central Province, Papua New Guinea)

*tama	→	tama	'father'
*taŋi	→	tai	'cry'
*tari	→	tadi	'younger brother'
*ɣita	→	ita	'see'
*ɣate	→	ase	'liver'
*tina	→	sina	'mother'
*tiavu	→	siahu	'sweat'
*mate	→	mase	'die'
*ɣutu	→	utu	'louse'
*pune	→	pune	'bird'
*ðaŋi	→	lai	'wind'
*leŋi	→	rei	'long grass'
*bara	→	bada	'big'
*diba	→	diba	'right'
*geru	→	gedu	'nape of neck'
*garo	→	gado	'language'
*gʷada	→	gʷada	'spear'
*lata	→	rata	'milk'
*labia	→	rabia	'sago'
*maða	→	mala	'tongue'
*wabu	→	vabu	'widow'
*walo	→	varo	'vine'
*vui	→	hui	'hair'
*vavine	→	hahine	'woman'
*api	→	lahi	'fire'
*au	→	lau	'I'

DATA SET 10 — SEPA, MANAM, KAIRIRU AND SERA
(Coastal Sepik, Papua New Guinea)

Sepa	Manam	Kairiru	Sera	
tamota	tomoata	ramat	reisiouk	'man'
waine	aine	mwoin	tamein	'woman'
mata	mata	mata	tapuŋ	'eye'
giŋa	gaŋa	kwokala	suvətaŋ	'nose'
talŋo	kuŋi	tələŋa	tenerpiŋ	'ear'
lima	debu	kawi	ləvaŋ	'arm, hand'
lulu	ruru	sus	tuit	'breast'
dala	dara	sinai	tenei	'blood'
ŋamali	amari	waraŋ	rau	'sun'

kalewa	kalea	kaleo	bul	'moon'
wabubu	rodo	abwuŋ	puiŋ	'night'
ndanu	daŋ	rian	rain	'water'
makasi	makasi	nau	na	'sea'
pa:tu	patu	buŋ	ak	'stone'
ewa	ewa	luf	teiŋ	'fire'
kai	kai	kai	ai	'tree'
undu	udi	wur	bur	'banana'
keu	keu	wonau	biŋ	'dog'
manu	maŋ	mian	main	'bird'
mota	moata	vaniu	meni	'snake'
ika	ika	siasi	mwoiŋ	'fish'
ŋalambuti	laŋo	ləmwok	laŋ	'fly'
namu	naŋ	niam	nənei	'mosquito'
pela	pera	pial	nou	'house'
wawaraki	wauwau	bunbun	wuipul	'white'
mbotambo	zimzimi	silsir	neknek	'black'
ndisuau	tumura	marir	marir	'cold'
kani	kaŋ	an	ʔain	'eat'
sopu	mai	miai	ma	'come'
lako	lako	liak	pi	'go'
teke	teke	tai	pontenen	'one'
lua	rua	wulu	eltiŋ	'two'
toli	toli	tuol	eltiŋ pal	'three'
wati	wati	viat	eltiŋ eltiŋ	'four'
lima	lima	vələri	piŋgariʔ	'five'

DATA SET 11 — BURDUNA (Western Australia)

*pampura	→	papura	'blind'
*ṭuluŋku	→	ṭulutku	'crane'
*ŋaṭa	→	ŋaja	'I'
*kawuŋka	→	kawuka	'egg'
*kaṇtara	→	kaṭara	'root'
*papu	→	pawu	'father'
*ŋampu	→	ŋapu	'tree'
*waŋkan	→	watkan	'chest'
*kuṭara	→	kujara	'two'
*ṭuṇṭu	→	ṭuṭu	'narrow'
*muḷaŋkaɹa	→	muḷatkaɹa	'parrot type'
*ṭipa	→	ṭiwa	'dive'
*kumpu	→	kupu	'urine'
*puka	→	puwa	'bad'
*kuṇtal	→	kuṭal	'daughter'

*ŋaɳka	→	ŋaʈka	'beard'
*ʈuʈuŋkaji	→	ʈuɖukaji	'honey'
*paʈapuʈu	→	pajawuɖu	'dangerous'
*mukul	→	mu:l	'aunt'
*jimiɳʈa	→	jimiʈa	'scratch'
*kanpar	→	katpar	'spider's web'
*puŋkuʈi	→	pukuɖi	'kangaroo'
*paʈari	→	pajari	'fight'
*paʈa	→	paja	'drink'
*ŋuɳʈa	→	ŋuʈa	'lie'
*ʈukaɹa	→	ʈuwaɹa	'hiding'
*ɳuŋkun	→	ɳukun	'rotten'
*ʈa:paʈa	→	ʈa:waja	'wild plum'
*kakul	→	kawul	'testicles'
*parumpa	→	parupa	'wattle tree'
*piɳʈa	→	piʈa	'mud'
*waŋka	→	waka	'speak'
*miniɳʈa	→	miniʈa	'centipede'
*piɳkaʈi	→	piʈkaji	'dish'
*ʈiɳʈi	→	ʈiʈi	'clitoris'
*jukari	→	juwari	'stand'
*kankala	→	katkala	'wild potato'
*jakan	→	ja:n	'spouse'
*kuʈuɹu	→	kujuɹu	'word'
*ʈintiʈinti	· →	ʈitijiti	'willy wagtail'
*maɳʈa	→	maʈa	'arm'
*mintulu	→	mitulu	'fingernail'
*mika	→	miwa	'back'
*pukura	→	pu:ra	'devil'
*waɳʈa	→	waʈa	'give'
*ʈukuʈu	→	ʈu:ɖu	'smoke'
*maʈun	→	majun	'turtle'
*kukulaɹa	→	ku:laɹa	'dove'

DATA SET 12 — QUÉBEC FRENCH (Canada)

(Note that in these examples the symbol ɥ is used to represent a high, front unrounded glide.)

Standard French	Rural Québec French	
kanadjɛ̃	kanadzjɛ̃	'Canadian'
pəti	pətsi	'small'
baty	batsy	'beaten'
tɥe	tsɥe	'kill'

tyb	tsʏb	'tube'
tip	tsɪp	'guy'
tigʀ	tsɪg	'tiger'
diʀ	dzir	'say'
kʀokodil	krɔkɔdzɪl	'crocodile'
dyʀ	dzyr	'strong'
ɛ̃djɛ̃	ɛ̃dzjɛ̃	'Indian'
kɔ̃dɥiʀ	kɔ̃dzɥir	'drive'
avœgl	avœg	'blind'
pœpl	pœp	'people'
pʀɔpʀ	prɔp	'clean'
vinɛgʀ	vinɛg	'vinegar'
tabl	tab	'table'
filtʀ	fɪlt	'filter'
kɔ̃vɛ̃kʀ	kɔ̃vɛ̃k	'convince'
pakt	pak	'pact'
ãsãbl	ãsãm	'together'
sɛptãbʀ	sɛptãm	'September'
ɔ̃bʀ	ɔ̃m	'shade'
ʒœ̃gl	ʒœ̃ŋ	'jungle'
lãg	lãŋ	'tongue'
lãdmɛ̃	lãnmɛ̃	'the next day'
paʀskə	paskə	'because'
mɛʀkʀədi	mɛkrədzi	'Wednesday'
paʀl	pal	'speak'
tʀwa	twa	'three'

LANGUAGE INDEX

Below is a list of languages used as problems or to illustrate major points in the text. As stated at the beginning of the book, I have avoided quoting the sources of my information in the text to avoid creating a less readable and overly academic style. The list of languages below indicates the main sources of the information used. Sources without dates indicate personal communication or untitled and unpublished notes, while sources listed without names indicate my own field notes or general knowledge.

Greek	Bloomfield (1967)
Gumbaynggir	Eades (1979)
Hawaiian	William A. Foley
Hiri Motu	
Hula	Ross (1988)
Huli	Brian Cheetham
Icelandic	Cowan (1971)
Idam	Bailey (1975)
Ilokano	Bloomfield (1967)
Italian	Cowan (1971), Arlotto (1972)
Jajgir	Crowley (1979)
Juwaalijaaj	Austin, Williams, and Wurm (1980)
Kabana	Thurston (1987)
Kairiru	Laycock (1976)
Kara	Beaumont (1979)
Karawari	William A. Foley
Koiari	Tom Dutton
Koita	Tom Dutton
Korafe	Lynch (1977b), Farr and Larsen (1979)
Kuman	
Kwaio	Keesing (1975)
Lakalai	Johnson (1978)
Lardil	Dixon (1980)
Latin	Bloomfield (1967), Arlotto (1972)
Lenakel	Lynch (1977a)
Maisin	Lynch (1977b)
Manam	Laycock (1976)
Manga	Hooley (1971)
Māori	Williams (1985), William A. Foley
Mapos	Hooley (1971)
Marshallese	Lynch
Mbabaram	Dixon (1980)
Mekeo	Ross (1988)
Moriori	King (1989)
Motu	
Mountain Koiari	Tom Dutton
Mpakwithi	Crowley (1981)
Murut	D.J. Prentice
Ndao	Walker (1980)
Nganyaywana	Crowley (1976)
Notu	Lynch (1977b), Farr and Larsen (1979)
Old English	Arlotto (1972)
Orokaiva	Lynch (1977b)
Paamese	Crowley (1982)
Palauan	William A. Foley

REFERENCES

Aitchison, Jean 1981. *Language Change: Progress or Decay?* Fontana Paperbacks: Bungay (Suffolk).

Allan, Scott 1989. 'Review: Crowley, Terry. *An Introduction to Historical Linguistics*' in *Te Reo: Journal of the Linguistic Society of New Zealand* 32:95–9.

Anderson, Wallace L., and Norman C. Stageberg (eds) 1962. *Introductory Readings in Language.* Holt, Rinehart and Winston: New York.

Anttila, Raimo 1972. *An Introduction to Historical and Comparative Linguistics.* Macmillan: New York.

Appel, René and Pieter Muysken 1987. *Language Contact and Bilingualism.* Edward Arnold: London.

Arlotto, Anthony 1972. *Introduction to Historical Linguistics.* Houghton Mifflin: Boston.

Austin, Peter 1981. 'Proto-Kanyara and Proto-Mantharta historical phonology', in *Lingua* 54:295–333.

Austin, Peter, Corinne Williams, and Stephen Wurm 1980. 'The linguistic situation in north central New South Wales', in B. Rigsby and P. Sutton (eds) *Papers in Australian Linguistics No.13: Contributions to Australian Linguistics*, pp.167–80. Pacific Linguistics (Series A, No.59): Canberra.

Bailey, D.A. 1975. 'The phonology of the Abau language', in *Work Papers in Papua New Guinea Languages, Vol.9: Abau Language, Phonology and Grammar*, pp.5–58. Summer Institute of Linguistics: Ukarumpa (Papua New Guinea).

Beaumont, C.H. 1981. *The Tigak Language of New Ireland.* Pacific Linguistics (Series B, No.58): Canberra.

Bellwood, Peter 1987. *The Polynesians: The Prehistory of an Island People.* Thames and Hudson: London.

Bickerton, Derek 1981. *Roots of Language.* Karoma Publishers: Ann Arbor.

Biggs, Bruce G. 1972. 'Implications of linguistic subgrouping with special reference to Polynesia', in R.C. Green and M. Kelly (eds) *Studies in Oceanic Culture History, Vol.3*, pp. 143–60. Pacific Anthropological Records No.13. Bernice Pauahi Bishop Museum: Honolulu.

Bloomfield, Leonard 1967 (first published 1933). *Language.* Allen and Unwin: London.

Blust, Robert 1996. 'Review: Crowley, Terry. *An Introduction to Historical Linguistics*' in *Oceanic Linguistics* 35(2), pp.328–35.

Bolinger, Dwight 1968. *Aspects of Language.* Harcourt, Brace and World: New York.

Bruce, L. 1979. 'A Grammar of Alamblak (Papua New Guinea)'. Unpublished PhD dissertation, Australian National University (Canberra).

Burgers, M.P.O. 1968. *Teach Yourself Afrikaans.* David McKay: New York.

Bynon, Theodora 1979. *Historical Linguistics.* Cambridge Textbooks in Linguistics. Cambridge University Press: Cambridge.

Capell, A. 1973. *A New Fijian Dictionary.* Government Printer: Suva.

Clark, Ross 1979. 'Language', in Jesse D. Jennings (ed.) *The Prehistory of Polynesia*, pp.249–70. Harvard University Press: Cambridge.

Cowan, William 1971. *Workbook in Comparative Reconstruction.* Holt, Rinehart and Winston: New York.

Crowley, Terry 1976. 'Phonological change in New England', in R.M.W. Dixon (ed.) *Grammatical Categories in Australian Languages*, pp.19–50. Australian Institute of Aboriginal Studies: Canberra.

Crowley, Terry 1978. *The Middle Clarence Dialects of Bandjalang.* Australian Institute of Aboriginal Studies: Canberra.

Crowley, Terry 1979. 'Yaygir', in R.M.W. Dixon and Barry J. Blake (eds.) *Handbook of Australian Languages, Vol.2*, pp.146–94. Australian National University Press: Canberra.

Crowley, Terry 1981. 'The Mpakwithi dialect of Anguthimri', in R.M.W. Dixon and Barry J. Blake (eds) *Handbook of Australian Languages, Vol.1*, pp.363–84. Australian National University Press: Canberra.

Crowley, Terry 1982. *The Paamese Language of Vanuatu.* Pacific Linguistics (Series B, No.87): Canberra.

Crowley, Terry 1983. 'Uradhi', in R.M.W. Dixon and Barry J. Blake (eds) *Handbook of Australian Languages, Vol.3*, pp.306–428. Australian National University Press: Canberra.

Crowley, Terry 1995. *A New Bislama Dictionary.* Institute of Pacific Studies and Pacific Languages Unit (University of the South Pacific): Suva.

Crowley, Terry, John Lynch, Jeff Siegel and Julie Piau 1995. *The Design of Language: An Introduction to Descriptive Linguistics.* Longman Paul: Auckland.

Dempwolff, Otto 1934–38. *Vergleichende Lautlehre des Austronesischen Wortschatzes.* Zeitschrift für Eingeborenen-Sprachen, Beiheft No.15, 17, 19. Reimer: Berlin.

Denoon, Donald and Roderic Lacey (eds) 1981. *Oral Tradition in Melanesia.* The University of Papua New Guinea and the Institute of Papua New Guinea Studies: Port Moresby.

Dixon, R.M.W. 1972. *The Dyirbal Language of North Queensland.* Cambridge University Press: Cambridge.

Dixon, R.M.W. 1980. *The Languages of Australia.* Cambridge University Press: Cambridge.

Dixon, R.M.W. 1994. *Ergativity.* Cambridge University Press: Cambridge.

Eades, Diana 1979. 'Gumbaynggir', in R.M.W. Dixon and Barry J. Blake (eds) *Handbook of Australian Languages, Vol.1,* pp.244–361. Australian National University Press: Canberra.

Fagan, Brian M. 1987. *The Great Journey: The Peopling of Ancient America.* Thames and Hudson: London.

Farr, James and Robert Larsen 1979. 'A Selective word list in ten different Binandere languages', mimeo. Summer Institute of Linguistics (Ukarumpa).

Foley, William Auguste 1976. 'Comparative Syntax in Austronesian'. Unpublished PhD dissertation, University of California (Berkeley).

Grace, George W. 1969. 'A Proto-Oceanic finder list', in *Working Papers in Linguistics* 2:39–84 (March). University of Hawaii: Honolulu.

Groube, L.M. and John Lynch 1981. 'Lexicostatistical deviates', in John Lynch (ed.) *Readings in the Comparative Linguistics of Melanesia,* pp.273–81. Language Department (University of Papua New Guinea): Port Moresby.

Gudschinsky, Sarah 1964. 'The ABCs of Lexicostatistics (Glottochronology)', in Dell Hymes (ed.) *Language in Culture and Society: A Reader in Linguistics and Anthropology,* pp.612–23. Harper and Row: New York.

Haas, Mary R. 1969. *The Prehistory of Languages.* Mouton: The Hague.

Hock, Hans Henrich 1991. *Principles of Historical Linguistics.* Second revised and updated edition. Mouton de Gruyter: Berlin.

Holzknecht, Susanne 1989. *The Markham Languages of Papua New Guinea.* Pacific Linguistics (Series C, No.115): Canberra.

Hooley, Bruce A. 1971. 'Austronesian languages of the Morobe District, Papua New Guinea', in *Oceanic Linguistics* 19(2):79–151.

Jeffers, Robert J. and Ilse Lehiste 1980. *Principles and Methods for Historical Linguistics.* The MIT Press: Cambridge (Massachusetts) and London (England).

Jespersen, Otto 1922. *Language: Its Nature, Development and Origin.* Allen and Unwin: London.

Johnston, Ray 1978. 'Steps towards the phonology and grammar of Proto-Kimbe', mimeo. Summer Institute of Linguistics (Ukarumpa).

Joseph, Brian D. 1990. 'Book Notice: *An Introduction to Historical Linguistics*', in *Language* 66(3):633–4.

Jones, Alex I. 1989. 'Australian and the Mana languages', in *Oceanic Linguistics* 28(2), pp.181–96.

Keesing, R.M. 1975. *Kwaio Dictionary.* Pacific Linguistics (Series C, No.35): Canberra.

King, Michael 1989. *Moriori: A People Rediscovered.* Viking: Auckland.

Labov, William 1972. *Sociolinguistic Patterns.* University of Pennsylvania Press: Philadelphia.

Langacker, Ronald W. 1968. *Language and its Structure* (second edition). Harcourt, Brace and World: New York.

Lass, Roger 1975. 'Internal reconstruction and generative phonology', in *Transactions of the Philological Society*, pp.1–26.

Laycock, D.C. 1973. 'Sissano, Warapu and Melanesian Pidginisation', in *Oceanic Linguistics* 12:245–78.

Laycock, D.C. 1976. 'Austronesian languages: Sepik provinces', in S.A. Wurm (ed.) *New Guinea Area Languages and Language Studies, Vol.2: Austronesian Languages,* pp.399–418. Pacific Linguistics (Series C, No.39): Canberra.

Lehmann, Winfred P. 1962. *Historical Linguistics: An Introduction.* Holt, Rinehart and Winston: New York.

Lincoln, Peter Craig 1976. 'Describing Banoni'. Unpublished PhD dissertation, University of Hawaii (Honolulu).

Lynch, John 1977a. *Lenakel Dictionary.* Pacific Linguistics (Series C, No.55): Canberra.

Lynch, John 1977b. 'Notes on Maisin — an Austronesian language of the Northern Province of Papua New Guinea?', mimeo. University of Papua New Guinea (Port Moresby).

Lynch, John 1979. 'Changes in Tok Pisin Morphology', mimeo. University of Papua New Guinea (Port Moresby).

Lynch, John 1980. 'Proto-Central Papua phonology', mimeo. University of Papua New Guinea (Port Moresby).

Marsack, C.C. 1973. *Teach Yourself Samoan.* The English University Press: London.

Mühlhäusler, Peter 1986. *Pidgin and Creole Linguistics.* Basil Blackwell: Oxford.

Nichols, Johanna 1992. *Linguistic Diversity in Space and Time.* University of Chicago Press: Chicago

Parker, G.J. 1970. *Southeast Ambrym Dictionary.* Pacific Linguistics (Series C, No.17): Canberra.

Pawley, Andrew 1972. 'On the internal relationships of the Eastern Oceanic languages', in R.C. Green and M. Kelly (eds) *Studies in Oceanic Culture History, Vol.3,* pp. 1–142. Pacific Anthropological Records No.13. Bernice Pauahi Bishop Museum: Honolulu.

Pei, Mario 1966. *The Story of Language.* Allen and Unwin: London.

Pulgram, Ernst 1961. 'The nature and use of proto-languages', in *Lingua* 10:18–37.

Renfrew, Colin 1987. *Archaeology and Language: The Puzzle of Indo-European Origins.* Jonathan Cape: London.

Romaine, Suzanne 1988. *Pidgin and Creole Languages.* Longman: London.

Ross, Malcolm 1988. *Proto-Oceanic and the Austronesian Languages of Western Melanesia.* Pacific Linguistics (Series C, No.98): Canberra.

Sapir, Edward 1921. *Language: An Introduction to the Study of Speech* (first edition 1921). Harcourt, Brace and World: New York.

de Saussure, Ferdinand 1966. *Course in General Linguistics*. Translated by Wade Baskin. McGraw-Hill: New York.

Schmidt, Annette 1985a. 'Speech variation and social networks in dying Dyirbal', in Michael Clyne (ed.) *Australia, Meeting Place of Languages*, pp.127–50. Pacific Linguistics (Series C, No.92): Canberra.

Schmidt, Annette 1985b. *Young People's Dyirbal: An Example of Language Death in Australia*. Cambridge University Press: Cambridge.

Schütz, Albert J. 1985. *The Fijian Language*. University of Hawaii Press: Honolulu.

Shopen, Tim 1987. 'Research on the variable (ing) in Canberra, Australia', in *Journal of the Linguistic Society of Australia* 5:45–52.

Swadesh, Morris 1964. 'Linguistics as an instrument of prehistory', in Dell Hymes (ed.) *Language in Culture and Society: A Reader in Linguistics and Anthropology*, pp.575–84. Harper and Row: New York.

Swadling, Pamela 1981. *Papua New Guinea's Prehistory: An Introduction*. Gordon and Gotch (in association with the National Museum and Art Gallery): Port Moresby.

Thomason, Sarah Grey and Terrence Kaufman 1988. *Language Contact, Creolization, and Genetic Linguistics*. University of Berkeley: Los Angeles.

Thorne, Alan and Robert Raymond 1989. *Man on the Rim: The Peopling of the Pacific*. Angus and Robertson: North Ryde (New South Wales)

Thurston, William R. 1987. *Processes of Change in the Languages of North-western New Britain*. Pacific Linguistics (Series B, No.99): Canberra.

Todd, Loreto 1974. *Pidgins and Creoles*. Language and Society Series. Routledge and Kegan Paul: London.

Tryon, D.T. 1977. 'Non-discreteness and the problem of language subgrouping', in *Talanya* 4:57–63.

Walker, Alan Trevor 1980. 'Sawu: A language of Eastern Indonesia'. Unpublished PhD dissertation, Australian National University (Canberra).

Walker, Douglas C. 1984. *The Pronunciation of Canadian French*. University of Ottawa Press: Ottawa.

Williams, Herbert W. 1985. *A Dictionary of the Maori Language* (seventh edition). GP Books: Wellington.

Index